KU-733-979

The Horde

The Horde

HOW THE MONGOLS CHANGED THE WORLD

MARIE FAVEREAU

THE BELKNAP PRESS *of* HARVARD UNIVERSITY PRESS
Cambridge, Massachusetts
London, England
2021

Printed in the United States of America

Third printing

Library of Congress Cataloging-in-Publication Data

Names: Favereau, Marie, 1977– author.
Title: The Horde : how the Mongols changed the world / Marie Favereau.
Description: Cambridge, Massachusetts : The Belknap Press of Harvard University Press, 2021. | Includes bibliographical references and index.
Identifiers: LCCN 2020043301 | ISBN 9780674244214 (cloth)
Subjects: LCSH: Golden Horde—Civilization. | Golden Horde—History. | Civilization, Mongol. | Mongols—History.
Classification: LCC DS22.7 .F37 2021 | DDC 950/.2—dc23
LC record available at https://lccn.loc.gov/2020043301

Contents

Note on Transliteration

This book includes many terms originating in non-English languages. Most of these terms have numerous acceptable English spellings. I have attempted throughout to prioritize both accuracy and legibility.

Spellings of persons' names follow well-established English-language forms (e.g., William of Rubruck, Michael Palaiologos). The common spelling of Genghis Khan, however, is given here under its historically correct form of Chinggis Khan, a usage shared by most historians of the Mongol Empire. I use common Europeanized spellings of titles such as caliph and emir. Place names are also given in common anglicized forms when these are available (e.g., Caucasus, Herat). I sometimes reference current geographic terms (e.g., China, Europe) that may appear anachronistic in context; however, these terms are useful for orienting readers and hopefully won't offend specialists.

For the spelling of Mongolian terms and names, I largely follow the system employed by Christopher Atwood in *Encyclopedia of Mongolia and the Mongol Empire.* These spellings are based on the Uighur-Mongolian script, as pronounced in the Mongolian language of the relevant time period. In some cases, however, I use more common forms (e.g., Hülegü instead of Hüle'ü). And in some cases Mongolian terms are given in their Turkic and Russian forms (e.g., *tarkhan*, *yarlik*), in accordance with common usage in the sources and in scholarship.

Arabic words and names have been transliterated according to the system used in the *International Journal of Middle East Studies,* except that I omit the dot diacritic (e.g., I use h instead of ḥ). In most cases the transliteration of Persian and Turkic words follows the same simplified system. Russian has been transliterated according to the system of the Library of Congress, without diacritics. For Chinese names I have employed the pinyin system.

Introduction

A POWER OF A NEW KIND

The Horde was neither a conventional empire nor a dynastic state, even less a nation-state. It was a great nomadic regime born from the Mongol expansion of the thirteenth century, an equestrian regime that became so powerful it ruled virtually all of today's Russia, including western Siberia, for almost three centuries. The Horde was the most enduring regime of all those that descended from the Mongol conquerors. Yet, despite the rich evidence we possess about the Horde, it remains little understood. Far more has been written about the Ilkhanids, the Mongol rulers of the Middle East, and the Yuan, the dynasty inaugurated in China by descendants of Chinggis Khan. The fascinating tale of the Horde remains as though behind a veil.

This book reveals the Horde's story, which begins in the East Asian steppe where, in the early thirteenth century, Chinggis Khan united the nomads—Mongols and other steppe peoples—and began building the largest contiguous empire in the world. Chinggis gave four of his sons each his own *ulus,* his own people, and territory in which to establish themselves. Key to this history is the inheritance of Jochi, Chinggis's eldest and chief heir. Jochi was entrusted with the conquest of the steppe west of Mongolia, a vast region that reaches its ecological limits in Hungary. Jochi, however, slighted his father, and Chinggis stripped his priority to the throne. The consequences were profound. In the 1240s, after Jochi died, his sons, warriors, and their families moved to the temperate zone between the Volga-Ural region and the Black Sea where they established a new kind of Mongol administration, largely independent of the empire. The Jochid pioneers maintained Mongol practices but would never go back to Mongolia. In less than three decades, a few thousand people became hundreds of thousands, creating a sophisticated social organization able to sustain their own imperial formation. This multitude recognized itself as ulus Jochi and referred to their empire as Orda—the Horde.

The Horde was a flexible regime, able to adapt to internal changes and external pressures. The Horde was also wealthy and powerful enough to rule its neighbors and secure autonomy from the Mongol center. Jochid leaders recalibrated relations with the other descendants of Chinggis to maintain stability, and they kept control of the cities and trade routes between the Aral and Black seas, securing critical commercial avenues. Indeed, the Horde dominated Eurasian continental trade and, in the process, shaped the trajectories of Russia and Central Asia until the sixteenth century.

Historians know this mighty and influential regime as the Golden Horde or the Qipchaq Khanate, a reference to the Qipchaq people, prior inhabitants of the lands the Horde took over. These scholars increasingly have recognized the Horde's historical significance and yet rarely have attempted fully to explain it. This book seeks to examine the Horde on its own terms, to grasp how this regime emerged, developed over the centuries, adjusting and transforming while keeping its nomadic character. Importantly, we need to put native concepts, such as ulus, *sarai* (sedentary cities the nomads built, including a major one called simply Sarai), khan (ruler), and *beg* (nomadic leaders) front and center to explain the Horde from within.

This book not only captures the obscured social and political nature of the Horde, it also reconsiders the Horde's legacy—its impact on global history. In the second half of the thirteenth century, economic exchange intensified, integrating almost all of Eurasia. Today most historians have accepted the notion of a Mongol world empire, coalescing in one economic system the main subsystems of the Eurasian landmass, roughly divided into East Asia, the Islamic world, the Slavic world, and Europe.[1] Under Mongol domination, faraway regions of the globe came into contact more than superficially and, for at least a century spanning the mid-1200s to the mid-1300s, these regions were linked in a common network of exchange and production. For the first time, people and caravans could travel safely from Italy to China.

Historians used to call this unprecedented commercial boom Pax Mongolica, the Mongol Peace, in reference to the post-conquest stability of the Mongol dominions and the far-flung exchange that stability enabled. Yet, as recent scholarship notes, relations among the descendants of Chinggis Khan were not peaceful. Nor was there peace, exactly, between the Mongols and the peoples they conquered. The notion of peace here should be understood more clearly as conquered peoples' acceptance of Mongol domination. But we need not discard the concept just because the word "peace" is not entirely appropriate. Here I reexamine the Pax Mongolica as the Mongol exchange: a macro-historical phenomenon on par with such world-shaping phenomena as the Trans-Saharan trade or the Columbian exchange. Understood as the Mongol exchange, the global moment created by Chinggis Khan's successors comes into focus.[2]

The Mongol exchange is a monumental shift that facilitated the flourishing of art, the development of skilled crafts, and the progress of research in various areas such as botany, medicine, astronomy, measurement systems, and historiography. The increased production and circulation of manufactured objects, often driven by Mongol leaders themselves, is another major effect of this world phenomenon. Ceramics, manuscripts, textiles, music, poetry, weapons: the Mongols wanted everything to be produced and distributed inside their territories. The Mongols also imported goods and enacted policies to attract traders. The khans valued merchants, granting them lofty distinctions, legal privileges, and tax exemptions. Nomads invested in travel equipment, weaponry, and fashionable clothing, and they craved furs, leather, and imported luxury fabrics made of silk and cotton. The steppe had its understood social markers, some of which necessitated manufacture and trade: carrying expensive weapons indicated status; so did wearing jewels, belts, hats, fine robes, and leather boots. High-ranking women had a distinctive way of dressing and wore a conical headdress (*ku-ku*

Pottery figure of a Mongol man (China, fourteenth century). Mongol herders, male and female, wore a *deel,* a large overcoat made from cotton, silk, or wool. (Metropolitan Museum of Art, Purchase, Gift of Elizabeth V. Cockcroft, by exchange, 2008)

or *boqta*) as a widely recognized symbol of their status. The "Mongol fashion" made an impression on foreign travelers, who noted that many people, even Europeans, wanted to look like them.

In some senses, manufactured objects were luxuries for the nomads, yet the nomads were not frivolous. Luxuries were vital to the Mongol political economy. Long-distance exchange and circulation of manufactured goods were not essential to subsistence, yet they were the backbone of the social order. Mongol economics relied on the circulation of these goods, in particular their redistribution from the khan to the elites to the commoners, a system that simultaneously reinforced social rank, created bonds of dependence, and gave even the least in society a reason to feel invested in the success of the regime. Steppe nomads further understood circulation as a spiritual necessity. Sharing wealth mollified the spirits of the dead, the sky, and the earth.

Across Eurasia, the Mongols enjoyed clear hegemony over the circulation of goods from the mid-thirteenth until the mid-fourteenth

Illustration of a bowl with an image of a panther (Horde, fourteenth century). Big cats were symbols of rule; khans collected them for prestige and for hunting.

century, and while some of the Mongol regimes faltered in this period, the Horde continued to facilitate long-distance trade. The Mongols built dense economic connections from the Mediterranean to the Caspian Sea to China. This was due in part to their integrative policies: the Mongols welcomed new subjects into their societies, regardless of those subjects' origins, religions, and ways of life. Even freshly defeated enemies were brought into the fold. The Mongols shrewdly combined state power—over treaties, currency issuance, taxation, supervision of roads—with liberal exchange policies. Although tributes were a key source of revenue, the Mongols provided tax exemptions in order to encourage commerce. And the Mongols approached partnerships fluidly, making alliances on the basis of common interest rather ethnic or religious affiliation—although they exploited such affiliations as well. In the 1260s the Jochid elite even converted en masse to Islam in order to win powerful friends and trading partners in Muslim-ruled lands. Berke Khan, the Jochid leader at the time, did not lack true religious conviction, but nor were he and his top advisors blind to the realpolitik benefits of their decision and nor did they scorn non-Muslim partners.

The Jochid conversion solidified links between Mongol imperialism and Mamluk Egypt, one of many relationships that made the Mongol exchange a global phenomenon. The Jochids also established trading relationships with Russians, Germans, Genoese, Venetians, Byzantines, and Greeks, and their trade network at times could reach as far as Flanders. In truth, the Columbian exchange should be seen in part as a legacy of the Mongol exchange, as historians have established that Christopher Columbus was looking for a quicker, safer route to India, possibly after he had heard of Marco Polo's travels to the Mongol imperial center in the Far East.[3] The Mongol exchange, on this view, is not really a historical turning point from the medieval to the modern, although the Pax Mongolica tends to be perceived this way. Rather, the Mongol exchange transcends the separation between medieval and modern. The Mongol exchange bridges the gap between the ancient world's Silk Road and the modern world's Age of Exploration, transforming our historical perception of both.[4]

We must distinguish between the Mongol exchange and the Mongol Empire, as they are not the same thing. Certainly it is important to note their mutual influence: how they produced each other, how they interacted with each another, and how they finally parted ways, as the dynamics and effects of the Mongol exchange lasted long after the collapse of the empire. One of the remarkable dimensions of the interaction between empire and exchange is that the empire did not disrupt the exchange. The Mongols interfered with the economic organization of their subjects and projected their power farther than any other imperial formations of their time. Yet the Mongols understood that control over craft production, currency, traders, harvests, and crops had to be flexible and supple, and respectful of the practices and traditions of dominated peoples. Thus, for instance, when Mongols conquered new territories, they usually minted coins that were familiar to the locals and were easily accepted in existing circuits of exchange. Furthermore, the Mongols did not try to extract value from subjects no matter the cost to the subjects—that is, the Mongols did not enslave their subjects and work them to death, as much later colonial regimes in the Atlantic world did. Rather, the goal of Mongol imperial oversight and intervention was to motivate and empower subjects to produce and trade across the empire, thereby enriching their Mongol overlords. Why was there no clash between globalization and empire building during the height of Mongol domination? This is a phenomenon that needs explaining, and I believe the explanation lies in the unique imperial policies of the Mongols.

Over the past several decades, scholarship on the Mongols has developed tremendously. Thomas Allsen's work is especially important.[5] He was the first to demonstrate that the Mongol Empire must be understood as an integrative system beyond the regional divisions—the Chinese territory, the Middle Eastern territory, the Qipchaq steppe, and so on—that formed in the wake of Chinggis Khan. Drawing on Allsen's work, a new generation of historians has reinterpreted the history and legacy of the empire. Masterfully conducted by Michal Biran, Nicola Di Cosmo, Peter Jackson, Hodong Kim, Timothy May, David Morgan, and others, new research demonstrates that a holistic view is necessary to understanding the functioning of the Mongol Empire.[6] What happened in Qaraqorum, the Mongol imperial capital, resonated deeply in Sarai, the Jochid capital on the lower Volga River. (Readers should not be misled by terms such as "capital." These cities were built and favored by the khans, but the khans did not live in them except during annual festivals and on other special occasions. As I detail throughout the book, khans lived on the road, migrating with their people and herds.)

Scholars have begun to sweep away old stereotypes of marauding plunderers showing instead that the Mongol Empire was a complex political, social, and economic entity resembling a federation or a commonwealth. Our challenge now is to combine the bird's-eye view with a microhistory perspective of Mongol Eurasia. The idea of global microhistory is to connect the local and world registers, in order to deepen our understanding of both. The small scale, the voices of individual people and the scenes of their lives, provides details that inform worldwide history. The voices of individual people may be hard to track down, especially from early periods. But the task is not impossible, especially when the voices are those of the Horde—a well-documented case, if not one that has otherwise received comprehensive treatment.[7]

Holism has shown us that the Chinggisid empire was full of mutual influences, as its various portions shaped each other. But that does not mean the empire was a monolith. Its diversity emerges in microhistorical accounting. The empire fostered several enduring nomadic regimes led by the Jochids, Chagatayids, Ögödeids, and Toluids, named for four sons of Chinggis Khan. Each of these regimes deserves to be studied separately, in detail. This study focuses on the Jochid regime—the Horde—illuminating its particular implementations of and departures from Mongol styles of rule and examining the longstanding effects of Jochid policies on global history.

While scholars have recognized that nomads could create complex political structures, scholars also have yet to fully grasp the nomads' level of agency in the Mongol exchange, in particular the Horde's impact on Eurasian geopolitics. Large questions remain. In what ways did the Mongols, the Horde in particular, shape the world around it? How were the Horde and other Mongols shaped by their encounter with the outside world? How did Mongol rulers adapt their inherited traditions of governance without losing their nomadic and historically anchored identities?

The Horde transformed as the world around it changed. As such, the Horde was also a product of the Mongol exchange. This raises the question of the weight of the Horde's agency on the global system, especially on the so-called peripheries of northern Eurasia and Siberia.

Indeed, one of the most interesting aspects of the Mongol integrative system lies in the rise of northern Eurasia, specifically Russia. The political and economic development of the Russian principalities under the Horde's domination also enabled the Horde to grow out of the Mongol matrix. Russian vassalage was a relationship that influenced both partners—the Russians and the Jochids—decisively.

Much of the Jochid influence on Russia derived from the Horde's trade policies, which helped to create the largest integrated market in premodern history, a network that connected the circuits of the Baltic, the Volga, the Caspian Sea, and the Black Sea in a single operative system, which was itself linked to Central Asia, China, the Middle East, and Europe. Against the enduring stereotype of parasitical nomads, we find that the Horde generated wealth. Consummate generalists, nomadic leaders repurposed military logistics to enhance long-distance trade, drawing on the army's messenger system (the *yam*) to ship goods and commercial orders. And while the Horde and other Mongols were primarily herders, they also learned to manipulate their environment and exploit natural resources such as salt, medicinal herbs, and wood. They planted millet and organized extensive fish farming. They firmly controlled access to grasslands, trade routes, and marketplaces and enticed foreigners to trade near their headquarters. The Mongols also took advantage of the skills and capacities of those they conquered. Hordes expanded their commercial networks in part by taking over existing nexuses of craft and trade. The goal was not to pillage these locations—although the Mongols sometimes did pillage—but to encourage the inhabitants to continue the work at which they already excelled so that the Mongols could reap the rewards through taxation. Thus even if few Jochids settled in the subjugated port towns and salt-mining villages of the Black Sea region, the Horde benefited by taxing the merchants and producers plying their trades there. The result was dramatic, as the Horde filled in the gap between markets east and west, north and south, enabling a continental economic order.

The Horde's social, political, and economic systems were products of both continuity and change. All were in fact processes, malleable and subject to adjustment as circumstances dictated. Most basically, day-to-day life involved movement, as hordes rarely stayed long in one place. The nomads migrated across their territories, following seasonal changes to ensure their herds' access to pasture and their own access to suitable campsites. The seasons also dictated when the Mongols made war. Foreign policy, a critical dimension of Mongol-led globalization, was in constant flux. The Jochid khans were especially agile in their diplomacy, forming a complex web of multilateral relations driven by trade and shifting alliances. Mamluk Egypt, Byzantium, Poland-Lithuania, Muscovy, Venice, and Genoa were all involved in commercial exchanges with the Horde; all were at times its allies and at other times its enemies. What looks like political inconsistency was in fact calculated strategy. Even identity was a fluid process, as the Jochids turned to Islam while still embracing the law and spiritual sensibilities of the steppe—law and sensibilities that were themselves the products of generations of development.

The wonder is that the Horde managed to maintain a distinctive social and political order devoted to assimilation and globalization. How? How did it adopt others and adapt to them? How, as the central Mongol Empire collapsed in the second half of the thirteenth century, did the Horde keep alive a system of commercial exchange driven by Mongol methods of governance? Even the best-documented works on the Black Sea trade and the Horde have not properly answered these questions.

"Horde," when it was applied to the people of Jochi, was an old word for a new regime. The term itself has a long history that can be traced back to the time of the early Han in China (207 BCE–9 CE).[8] Most historians equate the Mongolian term *orda* with a khan's court and his main military headquarters. Wherever there was a khan or other nomadic leader—whether the great khan, the ruler of the Mongol Empire; the khan of the Horde or another ulus; or the chiefs heading each of the migratory masses in a given ulus or territory—there was a horde. To the Mongols themselves, "horde" had a wide and complex meaning. A horde was an army, a site of power, a people under a ruler, a huge camp. These meanings did not exclude one another; in concert, they captured the sense that the regime was coextensive with its mobile people. A horde did not have to be in one place in order to govern itself or sedentary subjects; hordes migrated, dispersed, and gathered anew, all while exercising control. Mongols embedded mobility into their strategies of rule, as I discuss in detail in chapter 3.

Much of the literature about the Horde—and other Mongol regimes—uses the word "khanate" to denote the imperial formations that emerged from the Mongol Empire. This term comes from the Persian *khānāt.* Struggling to understand the alien political institutions the Mongols created, Persian administrators coined "khanate," modeling it on their own "sultanate." Persians thus emphasized the position of the khan. But while the khan was a leading figure, each regime was a collective power. Jochi's ulus, Tolui's ulus, and all the other uluses were jointly ruled. They had a single overarching leader who also led his own horde, while other hordes within the ulus had their own administrators. Major decisions were made by the khan in consultation with advisors and elites, including the administrators of the hordes the khan did not oversee directly. And the ulus's wealth was shared among all its people, albeit unequally. Given the distributed nature of authority in Mongol society, terms such as "horde" and "ulus" are more useful in describing nomadic power formations than is "khanate." And many contemporaries writing about Mongol rule did use the term "horde" to name this changeable sort of empire built on mobility, expansion and assimilation, diplomacy, and trade. A power of a different kind required a different kind of name.

The term "horde" entered Persian, Arabic, Russian, and all European languages following the Mongol conquests, and it is widely used today to denote a large crowd of unruly or uncontrollable people. This usage is a distant echo of "horde" as it appears in medieval sources written by travelers, many of them religious men otherwise accustomed to sedentary lives. These observers saw the Mongol power as brutal yet socially constructive. Foreign witnesses admitted the difficulty they faced in grasping who the Mongol newcomers were and what they wanted, and often travelers were scared by what they encountered. From these medieval accounts, permeated by the awe and fear of their authors, we get the modern sense of a horde as a powerful and frightening mass.

When discussing the people of Jochi, I used the term they used for themselves—Horde, with a capital H. I also use the Mongolian appellation ulus Jochi. "Ulus" bears various meanings in the medieval sources, but mostly it refers to the peoples descended from and conquered by

Jochi, Chagatay, Ögödei, and Tolui, the four sons of Chinggis and his chief wife, Börte. In the course of his conquests, Chinggis came to rule many subjects, whom he bequeathed to his heirs. These peoples included warriors and their families, craftsmen, merchants, and farmers. They were nomads, including Mongols and other steppe dwellers, and sedentary peoples. All these people comprised an ulus. Although historians may translate "ulus" as "state" or "empire," according to contemporaries, an ulus was not primarily a territorial entity but instead bore the sense of a sovereign political community. Ulus Jochi, then, refers the descendants of Jochi together with all their subjects—whether nomadic subjects who fully assimilated, such as the Qipchaqs or Mongols of non-Jochid lineages, or sedentary subjects who maintained a separate ethnic identity, such as the Russians.

As such, ulus differs from horde. A horde is more precisely a nomadic regime or power. An ulus, by contrast, encompasses the people—both the sovereign and all his subjects. The historian and anthropologist Lhamsuren Munkh-Erdene points out that, in the thirteenth- and fourteenth-century sources, the meaning of ulus was close to that of the common Mongolian word for people, *irgen.* "The Medieval Mongol ulus was a category of government that was turned into a 'community of the realm' and as such it was assumed to be 'a natural, inherited community of tradition, custom, law and descent', a 'people' or irgen," he writes.[9]

The Horde was socially diverse and multiethnic, but its leadership came from a core of dominant steppe clans, most of them Mongol subgroups: Qonggirad, Kiyad, Qatay, Manghit, Saljut, Shirin, Barin, Arghun, and Qipchaqs. The heads of these groups bore the title of *beg.* As the Horde became increasingly oligarchic in the late thirteenth century, power devolved from the khan to the begs, the nomadic leaders who joined the khan in a governing council. The begs acknowledged the khan's primacy because he was a descendent of Chinggis Khan's eldest son, Jochi. But that status did not make a khan all-powerful. To be elevated on the felt rug—the procedure for enthronement—an aspirant had to associate himself with powerful begs. Similarly, to rule effectively, a khan needed the begs on his side. They supported him and, if he failed, deposed him. This was especially the case after the 1350s, during and following a period known as the *bulqaq*—anarchy. In the course of this period, several pretenders to the Jochid throne struggled to take and keep power. While they foundered, the locus of authority shifted definitively to the begs. They maintained the Horde's governing traditions, sought to elevate new khans who could rule in the image of Chinggis and his descendants, and pursued power for themselves.[10]

No single study has heretofore treated the Horde as a case of effective empire building, but historicizing this specific form of collective power is essential for understanding post-Chinggisid steppe societies and the nomads' role in Eurasian history. I hope that this book will serve as a model for grasping the impact of nomadic empires on world history—and that the book will help readers rethink the conventional view of empires as invariably sedentary powers. Historically, sedentary powers have indeed erected powerful empires, often dominating nomads in the process. But nomads have also established sovereignty over sedentary peoples. By capturing the notion of a moveable state, this book offers a new perspective on collective power and on the fascinating shapes it can take.[11]

If the Horde were projected on today's maps, it would stretch across a region occupied by Ukraine, Bulgaria, Moldavia, Azerbaijan, Georgia, Kazakhstan, Uzbekistan, Turkmenistan, and Russia, including Tatarstan and Crimea. The history of the Horde is therefore a shared legacy. That legacy does not belong exclusively to the national narratives of any of these nation-states, narratives centered on linguistic, ethnic, and religious communities that had very different experiences with the Horde and today invest those experiences with a range of meanings. As a result, the historiography of the Horde has tended to depend very much on the standpoint of the historian. Where nationalisms solidified in opposition to Mongol rule, historians have told one kind of story; where nationalisms presume continuity with the Mongol past, historians have told another kind of story.

In Russian nationalist scholarship, the Horde is an alien entity with disruptive effects on the formation of the Russian nation. In the Soviet Union, the Russian experience of vassalage to the Horde was distorted, marginalized, and often simply erased from textbooks. Historians and archaeologists were not allowed to use the terms "Horde" or "Golden Horde." Instead, the Mongol regime that conquered the medieval Russian principalities was called the "Tatar yoke."[12] But Tatars—a group often conflated with Mongols—and other Muslim peoples now living in the Russian Federation see the Horde's rule as a formative period in their history. Indeed, the Islamization of the Eurasian steppes, Crimea, and Eastern Europe is one of the Horde's most important legacies. Islam, as practiced in the Horde after the mid-thirteenth century, was a unifying force in Central Asia.[13]

The sweep of the Jochids across so many different peoples was enabled in part by their liberal style of rule. Like most empires, the Horde accommodated diverse religious communities. The toleration practiced by nomadic leaders reflected their respect for wide-ranging approaches to belief and superstition. Indeed, the Mongols readily adopted the spiritual practices of other steppe peoples before striking out into Eurasia with their eyes on conquest, so the idea that a single polity might accommodate multiple belief systems was not unfamiliar to them. Thus the Horde's steppe descendants could embrace Islam even as they continued to practice their old spiritual traditions, conquered peoples faced no obstacles in practicing their traditions, and religious dignitaries visiting the Horde enjoyed protected status whether they were Muslims, Jews, Armenian Christians, Catholics, Russian Orthodox, or Pagans. Toleration was a pragmatic option. As the Franciscan friar Iohanca put it in 1320, the Jochids "could not care less to what religion someone belongs as long as he performs the required services, pay tributes and taxes and satisfies his military obligations according to their laws." Toleration also served power aims. In addition to allowing free practice of diverse religions, the Jochids provided special financial and legal protections for Christian and Muslim clergy because the Horde's leaders knew that the support of religious elites would enhance Jochid legitimacy in the eyes of conquered peoples.

Some of the most significant beneficiaries of Jochid protections were Russian Orthodox clergy and institutions, which blossomed under Mongol rule. Russian scholars—whose work dominates historical writing about the Horde—have lately paid more attention to this process of development, moving beyond nationalist biases by asking questions that do not presuppose the oppressiveness of the supposed Tatar yoke. These scholars are reconciling Russia with the Islamic dimension of its past: their question is not how Russia survived the Horde, but how the Horde helped to create modern Russia.

English-language scholarship has been more likely to take for granted the Horde's contributions to Russia's development. In particular, the question of the Horde's legacy has often been linked to the rise of Muscovy, the Grand Duchy of Moscow.[14] The goal of this scholarship is to understand how the Horde influenced the institutions of Muscovite power and therefore of Moscow's successor, imperial Russia. Yet, as exciting as this discourse is, it leads to dead ends. Because this scholarship is based primarily on Russian sources, it is limited by the contents of those sources, which are in many ways rich but do not include much information on the Horde's administrative systems. I therefore turn to a range of other sources in order to show how the Horde functioned administratively and how it handled relations with its Russian vassals. When we take as our subject the Horde, rather than the Russians, the Mongol influence on the emergence of Moscow and the development of the Russian imperial state comes into sharper focus.

The Russian principalities experienced extraordinary economic vitality during their vassalage to the Horde. New cities were built—as many as forty in northeastern Russia during the fourteenth century. Artisanal production grew dramatically and trade developed rapidly, bringing Eurasian long-distance commerce to the Baltic sphere, the far north, and small towns such as Moscow itself, which burgeoned only after the Jochids bestowed favor on Moscow's leading family. But while scholars have acknowledged all this, they have struggled to properly explain it.[15] I argue that Russia's economic growth was a product of the Horde's political agenda. The Jochid khans prioritized fluidity in commercial markets and used their foreign policy to ensure the productivity of the fur and silver trades, which were essential to the development of Novgorod, one of the economic centers of the Russian principalities. When Russian princes and boyars objected to granting foreign traders access to their territory, the Jochids forced the Russians to relent, a move that proved extremely valuable to Russian development. At the same time, the Jochids granted Russian elites financial and legal protections that facilitated production in the orchards, fisheries, farms, and craft workshops those elites owned. The Jochid-dominated Eurasian trade network was a source of Russian wealth and therefore power.

If historians have so far failed to appreciate the influence of the Horde on the development of Russian power, they have also misunderstood the political relationship between the Horde and the Russians. Scholars have perceived the Russians as members of a "steppe frontier," at the periphery of Jochid power, whereas in fact Russians were deeply enmeshed in the nomadic state.[16] The Jochid khans considered the Russian principalities part of their dominion. The Horde took censuses of the people living in the principalities and taxed them. The Jochids did not impose direct rule over the Russians but did closely supervise the grand prince of Vladimir, the highest-ranking figure in the Russian principalities. The principalities benefited from the khans' military support, land grants, and tax exemptions. Protection for the Russian Orthodox clergy was a constant feature of Jochid politics. The clergy affirmed Jochid sovereignty and in return received lucrative financial benefits that contributed to the church's thriving. Marriages between Jochid princesses and Russian princes strengthened connections between the Horde's rulers and their vassals. The Jochids also rewrote the process of succession to the position of grand prince and eventually placed his throne in the hands of the Muscovites. The Jochids in many ways created Moscow's authority, fundamentally altering the course of Russian history.

This story begins in the East Asian steppe in the late twelfth century. The steppe was divided among the Mongols and other nomadic groups. Only the most prominent of the groups, such as the Tatars, Kereit, and Naiman, claimed collective names and were recorded in the Persian, Chinese, Russian, and other sources available to historians today. Steppe nomads were not all cut from the same cloth, but they did share a number of political, social, spiritual, and economic institutions. The first chapter provides a broad picture of the complex and dynamic relations among these nomadic groups.

Chapter 1 also traces Chinggis's rise to power in 1206 and the violent process whereby he and his followers unified the steppe nomads under the banner of the Mongols. I describe the Mongol conquests in Central Asia, a process that was completed in 1221, and uncover the causes of the Mongol expansion. I show that, contrary to the prevailing view, the Mongols did not seek the annihilation of sedentary civilizations. Rather,

Chinggis Khan and his sons' primary goal was the submission of other steppe nomads.

The second chapter opens with Chinggis's apportioning of the Mongol Empire among his sons. The inheritance structure on which Chinggis relied was in part his own invention and in part an adaptation of steppe redistribution systems that long predated him. This is a key theme of the book: Mongol rulers drew on deep traditions of social and political organization but modified these traditions as befit their circumstances. The Jochids were especially innovative, as reflected in their efforts to assert Mongol-style governance over Eastern Europe, where political life was nothing like that of the steppe. Chapter 2 shows how consequential Chinggis's modification of traditional practice was for the future development of the Horde.

The second chapter ends with the Jochid conquest of Hungary in the western margins of the Qipchaq steppe, which would become the new homeland of the Horde's leaders. By the time the Horde established its dominance in the Qipchaq steppe, Chinggis Khan had died. So had Jochi; his successors took on the key tasks of consolidating the Jochid regime. Apparently, before Jochi's death, he profoundly disappointed his father, resulting in Chinggis's rescinding Jochi's place as heir to the position of great khan—the Mongol throne. But the empire survived the tumult and remained expansive, integrating China, Iran, Russia, and Eastern Europe.

The middle part of the book examines the Horde as a new kind of empire. Chapter 3 explores how ulus Jochi organized itself politically and adapted to its natural and human environment. I explain how the ulus handled its first succession controversy, after Jochi's death. The result was a foundational agreement between two of Jochi's sons, Orda and Batu, and the creation of the two wings of ulus Jochi under their leadership: the White Horde (*ak orda*), under Batu's leadership, and the Blue Horde (*kök orda*) under Orda's. The Horde as a whole would be ruled by Batu, whose lineage retained the throne for more than a century. This is another example of tradition and innovation operating in concert. On the one hand, the Jochid lineage remained supreme: no one outside the lineage was considered a legitimate candidate for the office of khan. On the other hand, the traditional priority given to elders over juniors was upset, as Orda was Batu's senior. Much as Jochi, the eldest of Chinggis's sons, was demoted from his position of seniority, so too was Orda. The balance between seniors and juniors was always critical in Mongol societies; it contoured relations in the family and in the court of administration. It was also subject to revision as needed. By relinquishing his claim rather than fighting for the throne, Orda helped to inaugurate a time of peace within the Horde. This is another theme we will see repeatedly across the book: in the Mongol world, separation was a prophylactic against civil war. The steppe was vast, allowing plenty of space for rivals to part amicably and pursue their own ends with relative autonomy. Thus while the White Horde, under Batu, was the center of Jochid governance, Orda's Blue Horde could function largely on its own while cooperating with the White Horde for the good of the larger ulus Jochi.

Both wings of the Horde thrived in the mid-thirteenth century. The Horde harnessed new lands and sedentary subjects and fostered a dynamic market on the steppes. Contemporary travelers described an impressively organized nomadic society involving large numbers of people and massive encampments with city-like facilities. Observers marveled at the swiftness with which the members of the Horde packed and unpacked during their seasonal migration. These observers noted the nomads' facility in driving animals and fording rivers, their massive carts overflowing with goods, and the security of their communities. Although the Horde was dominated by nomads, Batu encouraged the development of settlements and cities to support sedentary subjects. His regime reflected the imperatives that had driven centuries of nomadic leaders: to enable movement of the herds and accrual of wealth so that riches could be redistributed in accordance with the social hierarchy of the community. Batu and other Jochid leaders pursued these goals using new means, as befit the ecology of their westerly empire and the needs and aptitudes of dominated peoples—another exercise in the flexibility of Mongol governance. Most important among these dominated peoples were the Russians, whose close relationship with the Horde began under Batu. Batu also asserted a great deal of political autonomy from the wider Mongol Empire, yet the Horde remained economically embroiled in the empire, receiving tax money collected by the other uluses while contributing portions of its own receipts in turn. Redistribution and circulation were foundational at every level of the Mongol community.

Chapter 4 begins with struggles for succession to the office of the great khan in the 1260s. The conflict led to a war among Chinggis Khan's descendants. Jochi's ulus broke off from the empire definitively and lost substantial financial resources as a result. Under the leadership of Berke Khan, the Horde had to find new means of economic security and political authority, forging a self-governing entity independent of the great khan and fending off pressure from other Mongols. In particular, the Horde was threatened by the ulus of Hülegü, Tolui's son. Hülegü sought to take over Middle Eastern lands that Chinggis had pledged to the Jochids, and Hülegü nearly strangled the Horde economically through a trade embargo. But the Horde persevered thanks to a complex new trade alliance involving Genoa, Mamluk Egypt, and Byzantium. Berke's public conversion to Islam helped bring the Mamluks into the Jochid fold, while asserting the Horde's independence from the Mongol center. The Jochids lost the war with Hülegü, who was able to consolidate a new Toluid-aligned ulus on the Horde's doorstep. The people of this ulus were known as the Ilkhanids, and at their height they ruled a vast but fractious empire from Syria to Pakistan. But, in a sense, the Jochids won their regime. They would have to tolerate adversaries on their southern border, yet the clash with Hülegü solidified the Jochids' autonomy from the larger empire. The Horde no longer paid allegiance to the great khan, and by the end of the 1260s, the Jochids had definitively recovered from the war. Through military force, taxation, and colonization, the Horde came to dominate the most lucrative trades of the Volga region: the fur, slave, and salt trades. And the Jochids' alliances marked the beginning of the Mongol exchange.

Chapter 5 explores the foundations and effects of the Mongol exchange. Under Möngke-Temür, Berke's successor, the Horde managed a tremendously lucrative network that assured the regime's power and stability and had transformative impact on European politics. Möngke-Temür's reign was a period of peace for the Horde, thanks in part to his shrewd power-balancing instincts. Although the Jochids had secured their independence, Möngke-Temür saw advantages in exerting his influence within the wider Mongol system. Möngke-Temür used his prestige and political acumen to mediate conflicts among the other Mongol uluses and capture the benefits of long-distance trade. In the late thirteenth century, the Jochids also asserted leadership over their western frontier, dominating portions of Moldavia and deepening their relations with Christian powers. The key figure in the far west was Nogay, an acolyte of Berke whose power continued to mount under Möngke-Temür. After Möngke-Temür died, Nogay attempted to assert himself as khan, but he lacked the pedigree to take office. The result was a painful and transformative civil war within the Horde. Most importantly, the succession crisis following Möngke-Temür's death incubated a new kind of power within the Horde: that of the begs, the nomadic chieftains. It would take several more decades, but eventually the begs would become, for all intents and purposes, the Jochid government.

The Jochids managed to restore order in their ruling houses after the civil war, and the early fourteenth century witnessed the pinnacle of the Mongol exchange. In chapter 6 I consider some of the key effects of Mongol-led globalization. Close to home, these effects included the flourishing of settlements and cities, as diverse peoples flocked to the Horde to trade there, labor in local workshops, and proselytize among the nomads. This process of "steppe urbanization" was encouraged by the Horde's leaders and by other nomadic elites, who financed the construction of stone churches and mosques, palaces, and sizable farms. The nomads also built complex irrigation and drainage systems for their cities, which flooded at times because of their proximity to rivers and inland seas. None of these settlements featured fortifications, towers, or outer walls. The nomads wanted their cities open because, as they said, "He who is afraid, let him build towers."[17]

In imperial and foreign affairs, Özbek Khan followed the example of Möngke-Temür by working closely with the Genoese, Venetians, Mamluks, and Byzantines. Özbek was fiercely competitive—his was no Mongol Peace. The Eurasian economic development that proceeded under his supervision was the consequence of high-stakes struggle among the Horde, the Ilkhanids, Byzantines, Italians, Germans, and Russians. Under Özbek the Horde took a more muscular and interventionist approach to Russian political affairs, placing the Muscovite princes on the throne of Vladimir, even though other Russian leaders had stronger claims to the office. Özbek also played a delicate game with the Ilkhanids, allying with or attacking them when either option suited him. In the late 1330s, the Ilkhanids suddenly fragmented, which furthered Jochid dominance of the Mongol exchange. Trade through the southern, Ilkhanid-dominated route withered and was diverted to northern routes through the Horde. But the eventual collapse of the Ilkhanids in the late 1350s was not entirely a good thing for the Jochids. The resulting power vacuum in the Ilkhanid territories would become a significant hazard to the Horde.

In the 1360s, the main lineage of Jochid khans stemming from Batu ended. Chapter 7 digs into the extinction of Batuid rule, which led to the bulqaq—anarchy. There were several sources of crisis at the time. One was the Black Death, a pandemic that became an economic catastrophe, shutting down trade and shriveling the Jochid cities. The abandonment of the cities was less a reflection of panic than strategic withdrawal, another longstanding Mongol tradition, practiced at the levels of empires, battles, and ordinary life. A second source of crisis was the faltering of the Yuan, the Mongol dynasty in China. The Yuan, too, practiced a strategic withdrawal in the face of a Han Chinese rebellion, with significant consequences for the Horde. But the bulqaq was above all a succession struggle, the causes of which are plain as day: Özbek and other late Batuid khans made a habit of purging their competitors, hollowing out their lineage. The fall of the Batuids created an opening for the begs. One in particular, Mamai, became *beglerbeg*—head of the begs—and ruled for almost twenty years in the late fourteenth century in association with multiple puppet khans from Jochi's lineage. All the while, assorted pretenders fought over the throne, and in time Mamai's power waned. In the 1380s his forces suffered important losses to the house of Moscow, signaling the weakening of the Jochid regime.

The final chapter covers the aftermath of the bulqaq and later history of the Horde. The solution to the Batuid collapse proved to be yet another innovation within the confines of Mongol-style governance. With the Batuids out of power and the Ordaids—the natural successors of the Batuids—unable to assert themselves, the time came for other Jochid lineages, descended from Jochi's other sons, to take over. The khan who revived the Jochids was Toqtamish, who descended from Jochi's son Toqa Temür. Toqtamish won the support of many of the wealthiest begs, deposed Mamai, and put the Horde on the road to renewed economic and political fortunes. Toqtamish possessed ambition; in Islamic sources, he is portrayed as a unifier who brought together the Blue and White hordes. In fact, the hordes had been unified in the past, but Toqtamish came to power after a period of deep distress and was celebrated accordingly. Toqtamish demonstrated the resilience of Chinggisid traditions in a world where they were slipping away, thanks to the fall of the Yuan and the Ilkhanids.

Toqtamish engaged in a widely misunderstood relationship with Temür, better known in the modern West as Tamerlane. Tamerlane was a powerful beg who rose to rule the ulus of Chagatay. Tamerlane is frequently depicted as lording over Toqtamish, but in fact the two were sometimes allies and sometimes rivals, and they were well-matched militarily. Tamerlane intended to take advantage of the power vacuum in the former Ilkhanid territories and rule them as well, a position from which he could threaten the Horde's trade networks as Hülegü had. Tamerlane helped Toqtamish take the Jochid throne, but then the two leaders turned against each other. They fought to a standstill, until another powerful beg came to Tamerlane's aid. That beg, Edigü, commanded a large army in the eastern regions of the Horde and resented Toqtamish for favoring the western begs over himself and his people, the Manghit. Edigü helped Tamerlane secure victories over Toqtamish, and eventually Edigü's forces ejected Toqtamish from power, a moment that has provoked further misunderstanding.

It is commonly said that the end of Toqtamish's rule was the end of the Horde. I argue differently: the end of Toqtamish's rule was a further evolution. Importantly, Toqtamish was still alive when he left the throne. His departure from power, then, dissociated the person of the khan from the office. This would be the final turn toward the begs. The khan previously had life tenure, for he ruled with the mandate of the deity *Tengri,* the Sky or the Heavens. Now rule was understood in more worldly terms. It belonged to whoever could earn the support of the begs, and when that support was lost, a new ruler took charge. After Toqtamish, the Horde split into regional powers. Yet these regimes continued to pay fealty to the Mongol ancestors—Chinggis, Jochi, Batu, Berke, Özbek, and others. The post-Toqtamish hordes maintained their strength well into the fifteenth century.

Nomadic regimes like the Horde had a great ability to reshape themselves. Their empires followed complex trajectories, not linear patterns of rise and fall. It is often said the Mongol Empire collapsed in the 1260s, during the first major crisis of succession to Chinggis's throne, a claim that seems quite ridiculous when historians account for the intricate relationships across the hordes that lasted for two centuries thereafter. When an empire breaks up into component parts, our instinct is to say that it is no more. When Mongol regimes broke apart, they showed their resilience. The new powers were born not of the destruction of Mongol politics but of the mobility and flexibility built into Mongol politics. The history of the Horde makes clear that Mongols knew well the power of a careful retreat. It was not necessary to struggle endlessly on behalf of a khan, a lineage, or some notion of an integrated territory. Mongol ways of life and rule were more expansive and more durable than any one regime.

Traditionally historians writing about the Horde have relied on written sources produced by subjugated sedentary populations. To understand the Horde more accurately and from within, this book draws on a wider variety of sources. Some come directly from the Mongols. These include imperial orders, diplomatic letters, and coins. As a commercial power focused on long-distance trade, the Horde invested much political capital in its coins, the designs of which offer deep insights into the motivations underlying official actions. Much can also be learned from commercial documents, trade manuals, merchants' narratives, and multilingual glossaries produced for medieval travelers. Alongside coins, these sources paint a vivid picture of a mercantile milieu in which tradesmen mixed with translators, clergy, foreign travelers, official weighers, and educated slaves.

Other valuable sources include the *qari söz,* "the old word"—steppe epics recorded in the sixteenth and seventeenth centuries, which incorporate histories of the Horde from its zenith.[18] I also look to a range of rich archaeological material excavated throughout Horde territories. The material remnants include dishes, tools, household items, garments, and objects used for official and ritual purposes, such as metal belts and mirrors. Mongol construction could be ephemeral—it often had to be, so that hordes could move seasonally—but archaeologists have uncovered burial sites, settlements, craft workshops, and places of spiritual importance showing that the Mongols also invested in permanent structures. Archaeological research has advanced considerably in just the last fifteen years, providing new resources for historians to draw on. Textual sources written in Arabic, Turkic, Russian, Old Italian, Latin, Persian, and other languages round out the archive, helping us understand what occurred during the three centuries when the Horde rose, expanded, and finally dissolved into the post-Jochid polities of West and Central Asia.

There is a persistent myth that a nomadic culture must be dominantly oral. This book belies the myth, drawing on the written products of an administratively complex empire, which synthesized practices drawn from the Uighurs, Chinese, and diverse Turkic groups in the Volga and Caspian regions, as well as old Mongol practices from the East Asian steppe. I make use of *yarliks,* variously translated as diplomas or imperial orders, produced by the Horde's chancellery. These were written statements of law, policy, or status. For instance, a yarlik might announce a person's position or confirm their ownership of land. Khans and begs also engaged in significant diplomatic correspondence by means of letters. A substantial number of yarliks and letters are preserved in Russian archives, and more can be found preserved in Venice, Genoa, Rome, Vienna, Simferopol, Warsaw, and Istanbul.

The records of relations between the Horde and the Mamluk Sultanate are especially revealing. The two powers had a high volume of exchanges; we can identify more than eighty diplomatic missions over the course of two centuries. The contents of the letters among khans, sultans, and their ambassadors are available through the Arabic sources, providing concrete information about political and military issues. A careful reading allows us to penetrate the formal conventions of the time and understand the practicalities of the alliance between the Horde and the sultanate.

Surprisingly, we know of no dynastic chronicles or official histories written for the khans of the Horde.[19] This is a significant departure from other Chinggisid courts, where khans commissioned a great deal of literature celebrating their own deeds. Juvaynī and Rashīd al-Dīn, to name only the most famous writer-secretaries, produced major histories for the great khan and the Ilkhanids. In the absence of official written narratives, histories of the Horde's rulers and begs circulated orally and were eventually put to paper in the sixteenth and seventeenth centuries. These sources are historiographically important, providing a perspective on the Jochid khans after their power had waned. The khans often appear weaker than their own contemporaries portrayed them, as unable to rule without the advice of the begs and the guidance of the Sufi shaykhs, who became folk heroes as the Horde embraced Islam.[20]

From all these sources, as well as secondary writings by scholars across the years, emerges a nuanced portrait of a Mongol regime very different from the one that endures in the popular imagination. In the chapters that follow, readers will encounter the beauties and complexities of nomadic life in the steppe. These pages are brimming with remarkable personalities and events. I detail the pains and triumphs of war, the fascinating details of medieval Eurasian societies, the skill and creativity with which nomads negotiated changing human and natural environments, and the sophisticated practices and theories of governance on which the Horde relied.

Throughout it all, three themes arise. First, nomads were expert administrators who did not need to rely on their sedentary subjects to forge an empire, because the nomads possessed governing institutions of their own—institutions that persisted in modified forms long after the Mongol Empire and the Horde dissipated. Second, though it is common to think of medieval peoples—and nomads especially—as bound by unchanging tradition, the Horde was a product of continuous evolution. The Horde was indeed steeped in the imperial traditions of the steppe nomads, but it adapted and departed from these traditions when faced with challenges that demanded novel solutions. What we must recognize is that change was not a repudiation of nomadic character; dynamism is inherent in mobile ways of life and rule. This points to an important conclusion: Mongol imperial successes came not in spite of nomadism but because of it.

The final theme binding the various strands of the book is that the Horde changed the world. Mongol rule transformed, and Mongol rule was itself transformative. In Eastern Europe, it was Jochid vassals who unified disparate Slavic peoples into their recognizable modern forms—Bulgarians and Romanians, for instance. Many peoples of Russia and Central Asia as we know them today still look to the Horde as their national taproot. The Horde's commercial network was, for centuries, the foundation of economic fortunes in the Mediterranean and the key avenue of transmission between Europe and Asia. The Horde introduced the vitality and ingenuity of nomads into the lives of sedentary peoples, with lasting consequences.

1

The Resilience of the Felt-Walled Tents

In summer 1219 Mongol armies were gathering in the Altai Mountains, near the source of the Irtysh River. By this time Chinggis Khan had been fighting for decades and he knew the upcoming Central Asian campaign would be one of his toughest. He had asked his four sons to join him, so that his people would see their ruling family was strong and united. Chinggis also sent for Master Qiu Chuji, the most respected Taoist leader of northern China. The seventy-one-year-old Qiu Chuji was highly influential, and his flock was growing as people looked to his guidance amid war and famine. Until this point Qiu Chuji had refused to work with the Mongols, just as he had refused to serve the Chinese emperors, but Chinggis hoped Qiu Chuji would change his mind. For Chinggis, Taoist support would be priceless, helping the Mongols pacify northern China while they were busy conquering Central Asia. But there was another reason, too, that Chinggis requested the master's presence. The khan was now in his late fifties, while the typical warrior barely reached his forties. Chinggis could no longer take each year for granted, and he hoped to learn from Qiu Chuji the secret of longevity.[1]

Qiu Chuji accepted the invitation because, in his words, "it was the will of Heaven." Perhaps he also thought he might gain something from a relationship with Chinggis. The old master set out westward, taking nearly two years to reach the Khan at his camp south of the Hindu-Kush Mountains, in the last days of April 1222. At their first meeting, the conqueror asked the monk, "Have you a medicine of immortality?" Qiu Chuji replied, "There are means for preserving life, but not medicines for immortality." Satisfied with Qiu Chuji's honesty, Chinggis gave him the appellation *shinsen,* the immortal, and ordered Qiu Chuji's tents pitched just east of his own. Such proximity was a marker of honor and trust. The Taoist master spent more than a year in Chinggis Khan's camp and in Samarkand, which the Mongols had taken in 1220. In several conversations, Qiu Chuji explained the doctrine of the Tao and advised Chinggis Khan to avoid cruelty and sensuality and warned him not to go hunting anymore.[2]

Qiu Chuji could not give Chinggis immortality, but the old monk did provide the backing the Mongols wanted. Chinggis sought conquest, not destruction; Qiu Chuji helped Chinggis secure the surrender of the northern Chinese and their acceptance of the Mongol order. An able administrator, Qiu Chuji knew the Mongols would provide better government to the region. Chinggis repaid the esteem, making Qiu Chuji his emissary: Qiu Chuji was granted supreme jurisdiction over the Taoists, and his followers were made *tarkhans* of the Mongols—honored persons exempted from military conscription and taxes. Qiu Chuji and his followers recited scriptures on Chinggis's behalf and prayed for his longevity. In 1224, on the way back to northern China, the monk stopped in Zhongdu, where he ordered his new headquarters built. That same year, he sent his followers throughout the region to take control of temples and summon the Buddhist and Taoist clergies to submit to the Mongol Empire.

Three years later, both Qiu Chuji and Chinggis Khan died. Firsthand accounts suggested that the conqueror had been wounded during a hunt and succumbed to his injuries. The Taoists, Buddhists, and others whom Chinggis had made tarkhans kept their special status under Mongol rule; in return, they would forever worship Chinggis Khan, his descendants, and their descendants.

We have too readily accepted the stereotype of supremely violent Mongols who conquered much of Eurasia with stunning ease. The unstoppable nomads featured in textbooks, films, and TV shows appeal

90°
100°
KIRGHIZ
TÜM
50°
OIRAT
KHANGAI
KE
NAIMAN
ALTAI MOUNTAINS
NAIMAN
TIEN SHAN
Takla Makan
N
UIGHURS
Forest
Steppe
40°
Imperial Heartland
NAIMAN Nomadic Power
UIGHURS Sedentary Power
0
100
90°
100°

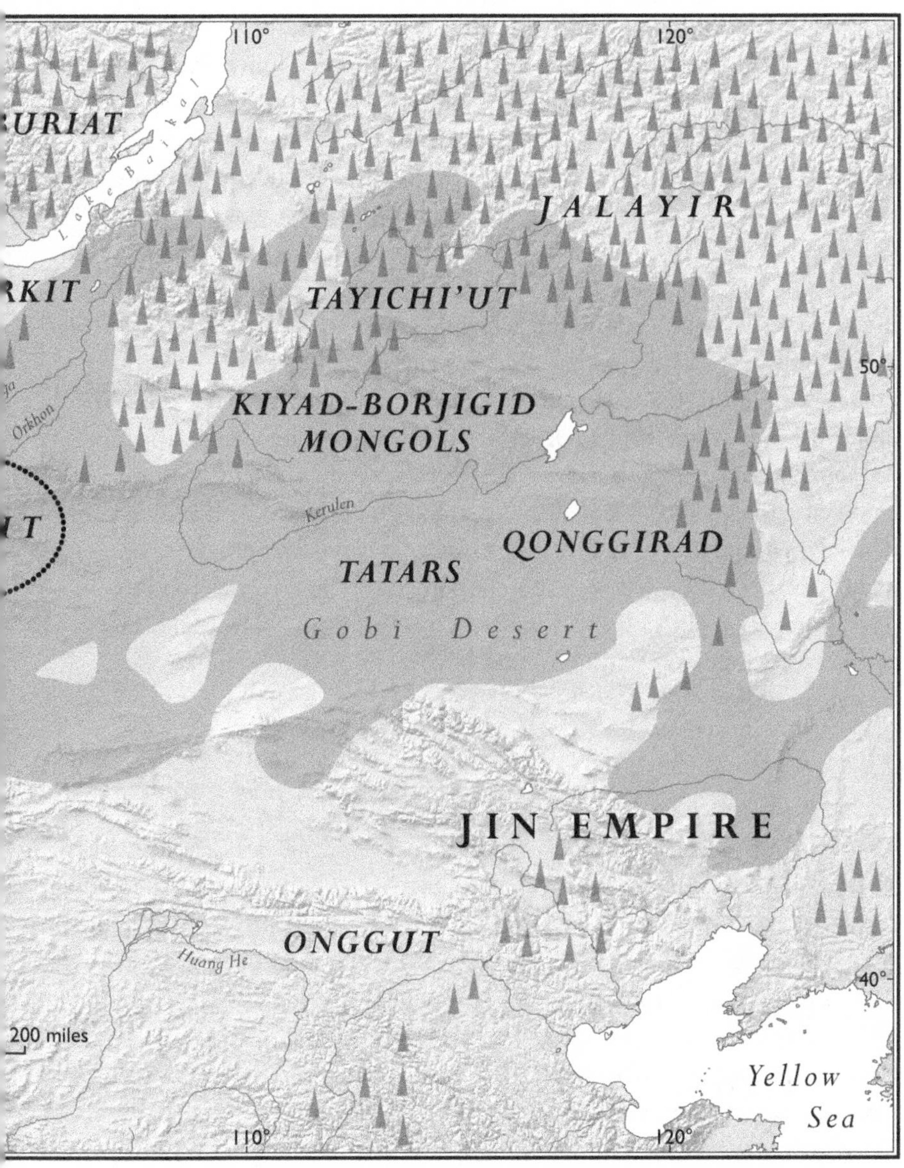

The twelfth-century East Asian steppe, showing locations of the major nomadic powers and the Orkhon Valley, the spiritual and political center of the steppe world and the region that would become the Mongol imperial heartland.

to us because they are both dramatic and reassuringly familiar. But this vision of an empire of the sword is false. It omits Qiu Chuji and all the others who respected the Mongols' political acumen. The vision of bloodthirsy marauders leaves no place for acknowledging Mongol state-building, rendering the regime of Chinggis and his descendents a historical anomaly: an empire lacking all ambition. To understand what Chinggis Khan really wanted and to make sense of how his Mongols came to dominate Eurasia, we need to move beyond such simplifications and retell the story from the Mongols' perspective. We need to tell a story not just of warfare but also of politics: agile diplomacy, economic cooptation, religious appeals, administrative development, migration, assimilation, and so on. The Mongols had a unique political economy based on long-distance trade, circulation rather than accumulation of goods, sharing across social strata, and systems of hierarchy derived from the deep well of steppe history. This system both affirmed and flowed from the cosmology that the nomads credited for their power. The Mongols sought to build durable regimes on the basis of their nomadic cosmology and traditions, and in this effort, they were remarkably successful.

Life in the Steppe

The steppe was a continent of diversities, geographically and culturally. The Felt-Walled Tents—a generic name the Mongols used to refer to themselves and fellow nomadic groups—were not all identical, but they shared a number of economic strategies and social institutions. Most centrally, the nomads shared a common political culture. Their world was a network of *oboqs,* groups whose members claimed a single, often legendary, ancestry. The members of a given oboq had a common surname and together worshiped their dead, but they did not necessarily live close to each other. Nor did an oboq necessarily claim unity; subgroups followed their own leaders. Unity within and among oboqs could, however, arise. To bolster their strength, oboqs coalesced into larger political communities under powerful leaders—khans and their supporters. When oboqs merged, they chose a new collective name for their group: a group that went to war together, made trade alliances, arranged political marriages, shared and celebrated their ancestors collectively, and meted out justice. The fortunes of this larger coalition depended on the khan's ability to maximize the number and loyalty of his following. In the twelfth century, the most prominent Felt-Walled Tents were Tatar, Merkit, Kereit, Naiman, and Mongol. Each protected its own territory.[3]

The vast majority of pastoral nomads followed no religious dogma, but they had a common spiritual framework based on venerating and controlling the spirits of the dead and appeasing the spirits of nature. Rituals included sacrifices of horses and sheep, which were fed to the life-size stone statues erected to ancestors. The living poured meat, fermented milk, and fat into the mouths of the statues, or smeared their stone faces with grease. Among all the steppe nomads, regardless of family or oboq, the concept of *Tengri* held a central cosmological position. Tengri was the sky. It was also God, and everything that stood out for its size. As the eleventh-century Muslim scholar Mahmūd al-Kāshgarī put it, "Tängri means God; the infidels"—that is, the nomads—"call heaven tängri and likewise everything that impresses them, e.g. a high mountain or a large tree. They worship such things and they call a wise man *tängrikän.*" Tengri was associated with *sülde,* the vital force that gave warriors majesty, male strength, and good fortune. Sülde, Tengri, the imminent presence of the dead, and the broader cosmology of which they were elements shaped social relations across the steppe, from the Tatars in the east to the Naiman in the west. It was the veneration of their common ancestors that bound oboq members together; exclusion from these collective rituals meant banishment from social life.[4]

Across nomadic communities of the steppe region, oboq members further identified themselves through their *uruq:* their personal male lineages. Yet all lineages were not created equal, so common herdsmen tried to associate themselves with more prestigious lineages through alliances. However, even if commoners became kin with nobility, their birth rank remained conspicuous. Steppe-dwellers were divided not only into nobles and commoners but also between longtime members of high-status uruqs and newcomers.[5]

The Mongol oboqs were divided between Niru'un and Dürlükin. The Niru'un comprised more than twenty oboqs that came from a single legendary ancestress, Alan Gho'a. She had three sons who were born when she was a widow; she claimed that they were the sons of heaven, destined to rule over the commoners. Bodonchar, the youngest, became the founder of Chinggis Khan's lineage, called the Kiyad-Borjigid. The Niru'un supplied the Mongol leadership class. Following a strict requirement that they marry outside their oboq, the Niru'un married among the fifteen or so oboqs of the Dürlükin. The Dürlükin were commoners, denied any official political role. But while they were politically dependent—they could not rule—they were economically independent. Described as *bo'ol,* free men, they gained materially from their allegiance to, and protection by, a strong leader. Highly mobile, bo'ol could also break their bonds of allegiance, leaving a chief as quickly as they had gathered to support him. This social and political flexibility created instability, but leaders could also sturn the bo'ol into a massive, if temporary, military force. One such leader, Qabul Khan, a descendant of Alan Gho'a through her son Bodonchar, managed to unify the Mongol oboqs in the mid-twelfth century. Soon after, however, the Tatars—allied with the Jin, who ruled northern China—killed Qabul Khan's successor and destroyed the unified Mongol army.[6]

One of the Mongol chiefs who had succeeded Qabul Khan was Yesügei Ba'atur, a Kiyad-Borjigid from the region of the Burqan-Qaldun Mountain, the source of the Onon, Tula, and Kerulen rivers. Possibly a grandson of Qabul Khan himself, Yesügei Ba'atur was the father of Chinggis Khan. Chinggis Khan was born with the name Temüjin, after a Tatar man captured by his father on the day of the birth, around the year 1160. For Temüjin, carrying the name of the defeated was an auspicious sign. In the steppe world, to vanquish one's enemies meant taking everything they had: warriors, women, children, goods, herds, names. The name of Temüjin signaled the strength of the boy's family and the success, at least for one day, of Yesügei Ba'atur's battle to reassert the old supremacy of Qabul Khan.

When Temüjin was a boy, the center of the steppe world was the Orkhon Valley, the old imperial site of the Türks. The valley was dominated by the Kereit. To the west, on the upper Irtysh River, lay Naiman territory. The Kereit and Naiman, not the Mongols, were masters of the steppe. The Kereit and Naiman elites spoke Turkic and had partially converted to Christianity under the influence of the Nestorian Church. In an effort to outdo each other, To'oril of the Kereit and Tayang Qan of the Naiman accumulated men, weapons, alliances, and prestige. Yesügei Ba'atur sided with the Kereit. Later Chinggis Khan would subdue the Kereit and the Naiman in the course of a protracted effort to defeat all challengers among the steppe peoples.[7]

But long before that, when Temüjin was around nine years old, his father was killed by Tatars. As Temüjin was too young to succeed his father, the Tayichi'ut took the Mongol leadership and threatened the boy's life. The Tayichi'ut were powerful Niru'un who had ruled the Mongols after Qabul Khan's death. Mongols who had been under Yesügei Ba'atur's authority abandoned their deceased leader's family to follow the Tayichi'ut, leaving Temüjin's mother and her children to fend for themselves. They were excluded from the collective sacrifices to the ancestors.[8] The swift fall of Temüjin's family demonstrated how rapidly allegiances among steppe societies could shift. Alliance might arise through *anda,* sworn brotherhood, or *kuda anda,* the bond of marriage, but these alliances were fluid. More durable was the duty of vengeance; blood feuds spanned generations. Temüjin built his reputation on his determination to avenge his father and to restore the Mongols to the stature they had commanded under Qabul Khan.[9]

The Rise of Temüjin

Because marriage was a source of alliance, the choice of a spouse was political. When powerful families were involved, the ramifications could be significant. Such was the case when Yesügei Ba'atur, shortly before his death, decided to marry young Temüjin to the daughter of a Qonggirad chief, a girl named Börte. Men—and boys—of the Mongol oboqs of the Onon Valley typically married Olqunu'ud women. This unusual alliance with the Qonggirad chief Dei Sechen would bring more prestige to Yesügei Ba'atur. The Qonggirad were Dürlükin, but they were among the wealthiest Mongol oboqs. Pledging Temüjin to Börte was bound to exacerbate tensions with the Merkit, who were Qonggirad allies by marriage. Competition between the Mongols and Merkit was already high, in part because Yesügei Ba'atur had captured his wife, Temüjin's mother, from her Merkit husband. In addition the Merkit were allied with the Naiman, while the Mongols allied with the Naiman's rivals, the Kereit. The new marriage alliance of the Mongols and the Qonggirad was a direct threat to the Merkit.

Temüjin's adolescence is poorly documented. We only know that he was imprisoned by the Tayichi'ut, escaped from them, and began to forge small-scale alliances. During these tough times, his courage, endurance, and prestigious ancestry gained him the support of a number of Mongol warriors. Around 1180, when Temüjin was about twenty years old, he had enough stature to claim Börte as his bride and brought her back to his camp. Soon after, however, the Merkit retaliated by raiding his camp and kidnapping Börte. But now Temüjin could call on allies. Supported by Jamuqa, his anda, and by To'oril, the Kereit leader and former ally of Yesügei Ba'atur, Temüjin responded by organizing a military campaign into Merkit territory. After the campaign, Temüjin negotiated for the release of Börte and was eventually able to retrieve her.[10]

Temüjin's political success against the Merkit earned him higher standing. He won further backing from the Kereit and the support of the Jin, with whom the Mongols had had diplomatic and trade relations at least since the time of Qabul Khan. Jin foreign policy was fundamentally to use one group of nomads against against another; the Jin had supported the Tatars against the Mongols and now they hoped to control the Tatars through the Mongols. In 1196, with powerful allies on his side, Temüjin went to war against the Tatars, longstanding rivals. It took six years to subjugate the Tatars, but no sooner had Temüjin defeated his enemy than he also needed to reject the allies who helped him to victory. The son of the Kereit leader To'oril began to fear Temüjin's rise. When Temüjin required a Kereit princess as a bride for his eldest son Jochi, it became clear that Temüjin hoped to usurp the Kereit throne. To prevent this, To'oril's son attacked the Mongols and defeated them on the battlefield. Temüjin swore to his warriors that he would strike back. In 1203 he turned against To'oril's army and soundly defeated the Kereit. Such was the world of ever-shifting steppe alliances.

Temüjin's goal was not to eliminate the Kereit but to incorporate their power into his own and succeed them. Temüjin seized To'oril's golden tent and tableware, both symbols of Kereit sovereignty, and distributed them among the Mongols as spoils of war. The appropriation of the Kereit's symbols and position signaled the scope of Temüjin's ambitions. For centuries before the Kereit made the Orkhon Valley their headquarters, it had been a land of kings. Early occupants had included the Xiongnu, leaders of a powerful nomadic empire from the second century BCE until the late first century CE. From the sixth to the eighth century CE, the valley had been the heartland of the Gök-Türks (Eastern Türks), before the Uighurs conquered it. After displacing the Kereit and claiming the Orkhon Valley, Temüjin could feel justified in declaring, "I have attained the high throne."

When Temüjin and the Mongols took over, the material legacy of the old powers was still strikingly visible. The *balbal,* stone statues the Türks had built by the hundreds, and the ruins of Uighur cities dotted the valley. The Mongols were impressed by the Gök-Türk monuments. On one of the great square monoliths, the new rulers could still read the advice of Bilge Kagan, one of the last Gök-Türk leaders:

> The place from which the tribes can be (best) controlled is the Ötükän mountains. Having stayed in this place, I came to an amicable agreement with the Chinese people. They give (us) gold, silver, and silk in abundance. The words of the Chinese people have always been sweet and the materials of the Chinese people have always been soft. . . . Having heard these words, you unwise people went close (to the Chinese) and were killed in great numbers. If you go towards those places, O Turkish people, you will die! If you stay in the land of Ötükän, and send caravans from there, you will have no trouble. If you stay at the Ötükän mountains, you will live forever dominating the tribes![11]

The political significance of the Orkhon Valley and surrounding Ötükän Mountains overlapped with, and indeed was inseparable from, the area's spiritual significance. The steppe peoples believed that those who controlled this space were blessed with sülde, the vital force that held peoples together and created empires. When the Mongols took over, they set about performing their own rituals. By appropriating the sacred site of the Xiongnu, Gök-Türks, Uighurs, and Kereit, the Mongols captured their sülde and harnessed it to fuel their expansion.

The Orkhon Valley was not only spiritually and strategically essential; it also held vast economic potential. The area was an amazingly rich grassland and a hub of the horse and cattle trade, with trade routes extending into China and across Central Asia. Given all that it provided, the valley was the perfect location from which to consolidate power. Temüjin established his main winter camp there and, to better solidify his control of the local population, he added another wife to his family—a Kereit princess. Her sisters married his eldest and youngest sons, Jochi and Tolui. Orkhon became a durable headquarters. Three decades after Orkhon's capture by Temüjin, his third son Ögödei would build a palace there and found Qaraqorum, the capital of the Mongol Empire. Temüjin and his descendants would go even further than Bilge Kagan, who was content to send merchants outward from his protected base. The Mongols would force their powerful neighbors to come to Orkhon, in the heart of the steppe, to trade on the Mongols' terms.[12]

But before that, Temüjin would need to bring those powerful neighbors to heel. Even as Temüjin was at war with the Kereit, a coalition of rivals was forming against him. In 1201 Tayang Qan, the Naiman chief, organized an alliance with the Merkit and Mongols opposing Temüjin. These forces threw their weight behind Jamuqa, formerly Temüjin's anda, and elected him khan. But Temüjin gathered elite warriors and, after some four years of combat, was victorious. The Naiman surrendered in 1204 and were soon followed in surrender by the Merkit. Jamuqa was executed. Like the Kereit, the vanquished Merkit warriors and their families were assimilated, and their leading women were married into Temüjin's family. Old enemies became Mongols.[13]

The Birth of the Mongol Ulus

In spring 1206, the Year of the Tiger, an assembly of the Felt-Walled Tents, known as a *quriltai,* gathered near the sources of the Onon River. The numerous assembly members included chiefs of the Tayichi'ut, Qonggirad, Kereit, Tatars, Merkit, Jadaran, Naiman, Jalayir, and Baya'ud, who were preparing to submit to Temüjin and embrace Mongol leadership. As they collected for the meeting, Temüjin's standard was hoisted. The standard was a pole with the tails of nine white-haired horses at the top, symbolizing the peace and unity of the Felt-Walled Tents under Mongol rule. The rituals involved in the ceremony were secret and were not officially recorded. According to Rashīd al-Dīn, a Persian historian of the Mongols writing in the early fourteenth century, the creator of Temüjin's enthronement ritual might have been Teb

Tengri, an influential shaman who also suggested Temüjin's new title. Temüjin was not proclaimed merely khan: he was *Chinggis* Khan, a term meaning "mighty," or possibly "universal," denoting Temüjin's extraordinary abilities as ruler of all. This was a clear break from recent political practices. Temüjin's challenger Jamuqa had borne a common Türk title, *Gür Khan,* and the former Kereit protector had had the appellation *Wang Khan,* a Chinese title granted by the Jin. Temüjin's status was meant to be higher than those of Jamuqa and others who had ruled over the disparate nomadic groups. Temüjin's indigenous title, unheard of in the history of the steppe empires, was a clear message that the Mongols were no one's subordinates. They were a unified power who understood themselves to occupy the top of the political hierarchy.[14]

The quriltai marked the birth of the Mongol *ulus,* a political community in which biological kinship and previous forms of belonging were subordinated to a loyalty that crossed family boundaries. The unifying creed involved acceptance of new rules, new hierarchy, and collective responsibility for the welfare of community members. The new Mongol regime borrowed from the Kereit and the Naiman, absorbing their institutions to create its own. Chinggis Khan molded his *keshig,* his imperial guard, on the Kereit guard and rewarded his faithful supporters by giving them positions in the keshig and missions to accomplish on behalf of the ulus. He also provided the Mongols with a literate secretariat and asked the Uighur scribe Tatar-Tong'a, who formerly worked for the Naiman's leader, to educate his sons and create the first Mongolian script, based on the Uighur script. The description of the rewards he bestowed upon his individual companions and the allocation of the imperial positions were later recorded in the *Secret History of the Mongols,* the earliest official history of the Mongol ulus in the Mongolian language.[15]

The new regime had two major aims. One was to establish the supremacy of the leader's family and his lineage. Under Chinggis Khan and his descendants, ruling status could only be inherited; Chinggis's descendents did not all rule, but only they had the opportunity to serve as sovereign. Thus the new social order would revolve around Chinggis Khan's father's line, the Kiyad-Borjigid, renamed the golden lineage. Members of other lineages became bo'ol, politically dependent upon the golden lineage. Attendance at the quriltai was equated with acceptance of this new status. In exchange for subordination, bo'ol received certain benefits, such as a right to a share of war booty. And bo'ol could still build successful carreers as high-ranking army officers and administrators. These advantages explain why several free groups such as the Jalayir and the Baya'ud willingly accepted the subordinate role.

The Kiyad-Borjigid had not always been considered the most prestigious Mongol line, but now all bo'ol had to accept that their own lineages were of lower status than the golden lineage. The supremacy of the golden lineage was rigidly enforced: although bo'ol could marry into the ruling family, Chinggis Khan and his descendents firmly imposed patrilineal inheritance rules to ensure that generations of relatives were barred from the throne. In the new regime, all became subordinate to Chinggis and his direct descendants, even his elder uncles and kinsmen from collateral branches—a clear break from the old order that was based on seniority. The regime still maintained the distinction between *aqa* and *ini,* elder and junior status, but only to the extent that this distinction did not interfere with the preeminence of the golden lineage.[16]

The second goal of the new regime was to integrate new members, expanding the workforce and the army. If the Mongols, like other steppe nomads, did not eliminate their defeated enemies, it was because they needed subjects to serve their economic and military power: absorption of defeated people was the engine of Mongol growth. This was a long-standing practice. After the Tatars were subjugated in 1202, Chinggis Khan announced a vicious regime of tamping down any potential threat from his new subjects. "We shall measure the Tatars against the linchpin of a cart, and kill them to the last one," he declared, referring to any who were taller than the linchpin, which effectively meant all the adult men. "The rest we shall enslave: some here, some there, dividing them among ourselves." In fact Chinggis Khan did not slaughter every adult man; later sources report that many Tatars were assimilated into the Mongol ulus, becoming part of the imperial elite. As promised, this did involve the division of most Tatar families, the better to ensure their integration as Mongols.[17]

New warriors—whether Tatar or others—were incorporated into the Mongol army by means of the *tümen,* the military structure. Long before the Mongols, the Xiongnu and the Türks had engineered the tümen, which involved a census of combat-capable men, conscription of those men, a system for dividing up military units, a table of officer ranks, and a structure for distributing spoils. The tümen was a decimal system; warriors were grouped into nested units of ten thousand, one thousand, one hundred, and ten men, like a set of Russian dolls placed one inside another. Chinggis Khan's new military units were composed of warriors who did not originally belong to the same clan, a deliberate choice to undermine possible solidarity and rebellion against the regime. All warriors were required to provide their own weapons, horses, and other military equipment. They did not live together but were expected to congregate for expeditions and to fight side by side. High command was entrusted to Chinggis Khan's closest followers, chosen for their loyalty, bravery, and experience in war.[18]

The Mongols' ability to absorb people was the great strength of their military organization. While defeated warriors were incorporated to strengthen the army, other subjugated peoples were distributed within the Mongol society at large, joining families and strengthening the society and economy. The relative ease with which steppe peoples integrated under Mongol rule reflects the similarity of nomads' lifestyles. All the groups that the Mongols incorporated were mobile and had developed similar strategies for surviving in the harsh environment they shared. What is more, while rejecting Mongol control was perilous, joining the society and furthering its expansion was profitable. Once the incorporated enemies and bo'ol proved their value, they received a share of war spoils. Indeed, having proven their loyalty, they could even restore—to an extent—their distinct oboq within the Mongol ulus. One of the highest rewards for a devoted follower was the right to bring together his scattered clan. Thus when Chinggis Khan's old comrade and official cook, a member of the Baya'ud, was appointed to the khan's keshig, the trusted aide said, "If I can choose a reward, my elder brother and younger brother, Baya'ut, are scattered about among all kinds of foreigners. If you are going to reward me, I should collect together my Baya'ut elder and younger brothers."[19]

The keshig itself was a key organ of the new regime, a superelite with thousands of members who shaped the first Mongol central government. More than just a guard unit, the keshig was also a tool for consolidating power, establishing loyalty, and carrying out foreign policy.

The keshig combined elite fighters, administrators, stewards of the ruling household, and diplomatic hostages—sons of allied foreign elites who were asked to serve the khan and his next of kin for a fixed period. The links the hostages secured between the Mongols and their neighbors were essential to the growth and stability of the empire; in time, foreign contacts would aid the regime's efforts to negotiate relations with surrounding sedentary powers—the Jin, Tangut, and Song in China and the Uighurs and Qara Khitai in Central Asia.

Meanwhile, Chinggis Khan's comrades-in-arms and close relatives received key positions in the keshig as night guards, day guards, official cooks, doorkeepers, stewards, grooms, and quiver-bearers—guards who were allowed to keep their bows in the presence of the khan. Beyond the khan's physical protection, the keshig supplied the mobile court and handled its logistics. Court administrators collaborated with other administrators beyond the keshig, such as tax collectors and the "great judges." The keshig not only preserved the lives of the khan and his clan but also served to personalize the state under the khan's leadership by equating the functioning of the court with the functioning of the household and equating loyalty to the regime with loyalty to the leader.[20]

Another dimension of the keshig's importance lay in its distinction from the golden lineage. By means of the keshig, Chinggis could welcome his most devoted and talented followers into his inner circle, even as they were excluded from the ruling family. For example, Sübötei, whom Chinggis Khan considered his most able commander, was a keshig member. Sübötei did not belong to the golden lineage, but his loyalty was unquestionable. His ancestors had allied with Chinggis's in the first half of the twelfth century, and his family followed Temüjin when Temüjin split from Jamuqa. By the time Sübötei was just thirty years old, he had almost fifteen years of combat experience and had personally fought at Temüjin's side. Chinggis granted Sübötei the official title of *ba'atur,* meaning brave, a title Chinggis's own father had held. For men such as Sübötei, who were so valuable to the regime yet could never hold supreme power, a high office in the keshig provided opportunity, prestige, and access to the political center that was otherwise unattainable.[21]

After 1206 the quriltai became the key governing institution of the Mongol ulus. Mongol political culture was now based on the concentration of power in the hands of members of the golden lineage, and governing would be a collegial process involving extended face-to-face negotiations with elites at these assemblies of the Felt-Walled Tents. This made for a mixed system, one in which the khan made decisions but great assemblies convened to show their support. While we do not know exactly what legal power the assembly exercised during the quriltai, we do know that major decisions were never made without their presence. The entire political elite, including women, was required to attend the quriltai to legitimize the khan's orders through demonstrations of consensus. By showing up, elites also demonstrated that they belonged in the leading stratum of society. Moreover, the quriltai was the occasion when the khan would distribute positions, rewards, punishments, and missions.[22]

By incorporating the keshig, the quriltai, the military, familial assimilation, and the complex and interwoven hierarchy of lineages and seniority relations, the regime created a social and political order that was simultaneously novel and traditional, flexible enough to provide opportunities to the non-ruling class and rigid enough to centralize power. By adopting the sites, symbols, rituals, and some governing structures of its predecessors, the regime established continuity that gave subjects a sense of familiarity: the ruling family had changed, but life could continue in a manner normal enough to enable assimilation. Meanwhile, pathways to social advancement encouraged bo'ol to back the regime. At the same time, these strong integrative mechanisms were combined with strict policing of lineage, preventing bo'ol from accessing the supreme office. Social assimilation and total political exclusion were two sides of the same coin.

This nimble structure certainly belies stereotypes of the Mongols as bloodthirsty raiders. Chinggis was not satisfied with defeating enemies; nor were his nomadic predecessors. The Mongols wanted not only victory but also legitimacy. They wanted not just to prove their military bona fides or settle blood feuds but also to govern. They wanted power for themselves but understood that achieving it required a delicate balance in which potential rebellions were suppressed using both incentives and punishments. The name of Chinggis Khan redounds in history not only because he was a great warrior and strategist who commanded loyalty from fellow warriors, but also because he instituted an enduring political order that reshaped the steppe world and, as we will see later, influenced governance and society far beyond the borders he and his successors established.

Yet, for all its success, the new regime fostered intense resentment. Many members of the Felt-Walled Tents did not easily accept their lower status or the destruction of their ancestral oboq. The painful process of unification under Mongol rule continued well beyond 1206, as subject populations rose up to challenge the domination of the golden lineage.

Crushing the Opposition

Chinggis Khan gave his son Jochi a domain in the westernmost part of the Mongols' empire, where he was to establish his ulus. But if Jochi was to prove a worthy successor to his father, expanding his domain and subjugating his neighbors on behalf of the Mongol Empire, he would have many challenges to overcome.

Jochi's ulus bordered the lands of the Hoi-yin Irgen, the Forest Peoples, in southern Siberia. These included the Merkit, who just a few years earlier had joined Tayang Qan's league in violent opposition to Te-

Illustration of a gold bracelet from the Horde (fourteenth century). The inscribed verse, in Persian, contains a common benediction: "May the creator of the world protect the owner of this [bracelet], wherever he may be."

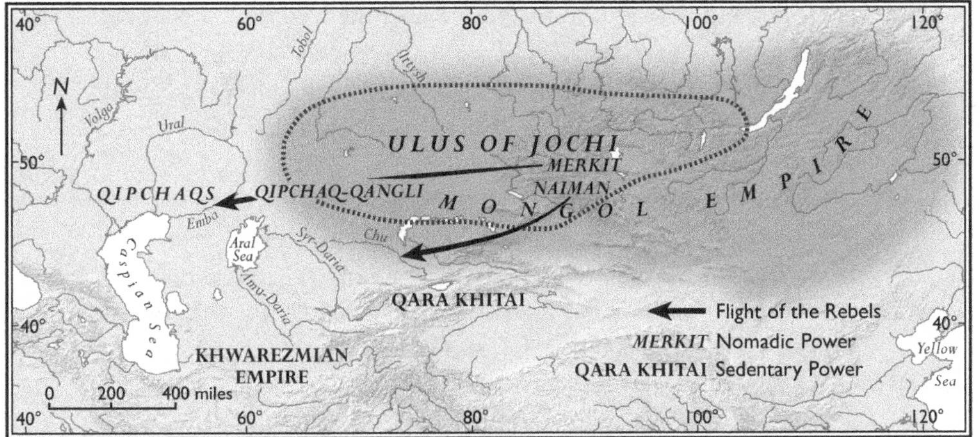

Path of the Merkit and Naiman rebels after their defeat by the Mongols.

müjin. In 1207–1208 Jochi began to subjugate the Forest Peoples, and Chinggis gave them to Jochi as subject peoples. At roughly the same time, the Merkit and Naiman reunited to rebel against Chinggis Khan and Jochi, gathering along the Irtysh River to attack the regime's positions. At a quriltai, subjects loyal to the khan debated what should be done with the rebels. That the Merkit and Naiman and the Mongols were old adversaries lent a dire cast to the situation. The rebels were not outsiders to be defeated and then assimilated; they had already had their chance to assimilate, and indeed had pledged to assimilate in 1206. Now they were reneging, proving to be blood enemies who would refuse to submit to the Mongols until they had nothing left to fight for. In response the Mongol regime decided it would extend no mercy to the rebel coalition. Jochi was tasked with leading the campaign against them.[23]

With the aid of the Oyirad, a group of Forest Peoples with longstanding ties to the steppe nomads, the Mongol forces rushed to the Irtysh River and fell on the rebels. Chinggis himself commanded forces and fought on the battlefield, as reported in the *Secret History*. In the course of open battle, the Merkit chief Toqto'a beki was killed by an arrow. The rebels then fled, most of them drowning as they desperately tried to cross the wide Irtysh. Once on the other side, the survivors split. The Naiman fled westward, seeking asylum in the lands of the Qara Khitai. The Merkit fled even farther west; they had no other choice, as the eastern and southern routes would lead them to the heart of the Mongol power, and to the north lay nothing but the depths of the Siberian plain. As Toqto'a beki had died in battle, his sons "could not bury him, nor could they take his body away." So they cut off his head and took it with them.[24]

The Mongols made their Merkit prisoners pay for the uprising by reducing them to slavery and dispersing their families. In a decree, Chinggis made clear that the Merkit had betrayed him: "I had said that they be kept together as one tribe, but these same people have now revolted," he noted. He thus ordered that the captives be parceled out and "distributed here and there down to the last one." Nor was Chinggis content to allow Naiman and Merkit fugitives to escape after they had been defeated: he ordered his riders to pursue them deep into Central Asia. The Felt-Walled Tents needed to learn not only that revolt would lead to total dissolution through forced assimilation of the offending bloodline but also that secession would be punished by death.[25]

The pursuit of the last rebels was a major military operation. The *Secret History* reports that Chinggis Khan selected from among his many generals four commanders to lead the hunt: "These four hounds [have] chisels for snouts and awls for tongues. With hearts of iron and whips for swords, eating the dew and riding the wind, they go. On killing days they eat the flesh of men. On fighting days they take men's flesh as their provisions. . . . You asked who these dogs are. They are Jebe and Qubilai, Jelme and Sübedei." Trained for special missions, the four commanders knew how to lead their men on long-distance raids. They could fight in open battle or bring down targets one by one. Sübötei was chosen to go after the Merkit and Jebe was put in charge of the Naiman hunt.[26]

The revenge operation against the Naiman and Merkit would have enormous, and perhaps unintended, geopolitical consequences. Chinggis Khan set out to settle a blood feud by defeating those who had provide disloyal. But in the process, he wound up upsetting the balance of power with the Mongols' western neighbors, the Qara Khitai and the Qipchaqs, as the Naiman fled into the Qara Khitai's protection and the Merkit into the Qipchaqs'.

The Mongols knew that Güchülüq, son of the last Naiman ruler, had found refuge at the Qara Khitai court after Chinggis had subdued the Naiman in 1204. The surviving Naiman rebels were sure to seek refuge with Güchülüq and his Qara Khitai protectors. Also known as the Western Liao Empire, the Qara Khitai ruled a huge swath of Central Asia and had old ties with the Naiman, who were their eastern neighbors. Güchülüq rapidly adopted Qara Khitai titles and ways of life and married into the family of the gür khan, gaining access to the inner circle of power.[27]

Gür Khan Zhilugu had his own reasons for hosting the Naiman chief. In contrast to Chinggis Khan, who implemented the tümen system, the Qara Khitai ruler relied on mercenary armies, which could abandon their patron and even shift into the service of the enemy if they were not paid in a timely manner. Seizing an opportunity, Güchülüq offered to gather his scattered people and place a contingent of hardened Naiman warriors at Zhilugu's service. This was much-needed support for the gür khan: he faced a potential Mongol threat and, as the Buddhist leader of largely Muslim subjects, a skeptical internal population given to rebellion. But the acceptance of Güchülüq proved to be a deal with the devil, as the Naiman chief sought power for himself. He attracted refugees fleeing the Mongols and even Zhilugu's mercenaries. By 1211 Güchülüq had amassed an army 8,000-strong. He ambushed his protector, deposed him, and kept him as captive. Zhilugu died two years later in Güchülüq's custody.[28]

Güchülüq wanted to be the new gür khan, but both the Qara Khitai elite and their subjects considered him an outsider. The sedentary Muslim population was especially unwilling to support Güchülüq. The problem was not just that Güchülüq wasn't Muslim—a nomad born into Nestorian Christianity, he had converted to Buddhism when he married into the Qara Khitai ruling family—the source of tension lay in Güchülüq's policies. In predominantly Muslim cities such as Kashgar, Almaliq, Khotan, and others, Güchülüq had allowed his troops to plunder and destroy harvests. He had also forced the Kashgarians to host and sustain his non-Muslim troops, which led to bloody frictions within the city. According to Muslim-authored sources, Güchülüq forced Muslims to wear Khitan clothes—which meant behaving like "idolaters," as the Persian historian Juvaynī put it—and prohibited them from expressing their faith in public.[29]

But while it is clear that Güchülüq mistreated some of his Muslim subjects, it is less clear that he systematically rejected their right to practice their faith. These allegations came from authors with an agenda of their own: writing after the Naiman had been deposed, they hoped to secure the favor of new leaders by celebrating them as liberators. Those leaders were Mongols. In 1218 Jebe's Mongol forces arrived and began clashing with Güchülüq's. As Jebe took over Qara Khitai towns, he promised the Muslims toleration and religious freedom—the usual characteristics of Mongol government. The reassuring Jebe won support from local Muslim authorities and Qara Khitai officials such as Isma'īl, the commissioner in the city of Kāsān. Isma'īl turned his support to the Mongols and led Jebe's troops to Kashgar, where Güchülüq had retreated. As the Mongols approached, Güchülüq fled southward. The Mongols pursued him for months, finally catching him in the Badakhshan Mountains of northeastern Afghanistan. Isma'īl struck the final blow, killing Güchülüq and chopping off his head. The commissioner-turned-Mongol-warrior hammered a pike into his trophy and paraded it along the streets of Kashgar, Yarkand, and Khotan. Muslim sources claim that the Mongols were welcomed in these cities, hailed as saviors. Yet Chinese sources report that the city dwellers only resigned themselves to Mongol power when they saw Güchülüq's head. One way or the other, the Qara Khitai dominions passed into Mongol hands, and the Naiman power ceased to exist.[30]

As for the Merkit, after the Irtysh River disaster, the survivors found their way to Uighur country. But, having already sided with Chinggis Khan, the Uighurs turned the Merkit away. The Merkit then migrated some three thousand miles westward, seeking refuge beyond Chinggis Khan's sphere of influence. They found hospitality in lands the Mongols had never entered, in the region between the Ural and Volga rivers. This region belonged to the Qangli, an eastern branch of the Qipchaqs.[31]

The Qipchaq peoples had come from the east. Initially, the various migrants had little in common except their flight: escaping the wars that swept over northern China when the Jin came to power, successive waves of Qipchaqs arrived on the banks of the Ural River in the twelfth century. Over the years, the contingents of wandering peoples coalesced in the immense steppe belt extending toward Hungary, where they created an intricate social and political community. They had no supreme ruler, but they did have seasoned warriors, trained in diplomacy and deeply enmeshed in the politics of their neighbors. Women of the Qipchaq elite often married Russian, Hungarian, Georgian, and Bulgarian princes. Men offered cavalry services to rulers spanning from Caucasian Georgia to India. Some historians have described the Qipchaqs as stateless, but it would be fairer to call them state-avoidant. The Qipchaqs escaped oppressive empires and their appetites for slaves, conscripts, and taxes. Possessing an army likely more numerous than Chinggis's—and equally skilled at mounted archery—the Qipchaqs were the lords of the western steppe.[32]

When the Merkit rebels came seeking refuge, they were welcomed by the Ölberli, the dominant clan of Qipchaq nomads in the Volga-Ural area. The Mongols soon learned what had happened and sent a messenger demanding that the Ölberli turn over the fugitives. But the Ölberli were not cowed. After all, this was probably their first encounter with the Mongols, so they had no reason to fear and no reason to submit. The Ölberli chief answered that he had offered the Merkit hospitality and would not go back on his word. For the Ölberli, the Merkit warriors were highly valued as auxiliary forces ready to serve, much as the rescued Naiman had been for the Qara Khitai.[33]

Chinggis Khan dispatched Sübötei, his most able and loyal commander, who had special carts with iron-shod wheels built to withstand the rocky terrain. Sübötei's archers converged with a vanguard commanded by the Mongol Toquchar, on the western border. The combined forces of Sübötei and Toquchar defeated the Merkit in battle at the Chem River, in the western part of present-day Kazakhstan, most likely in 1217 or 1218. As the high commander, Jochi dealt the final blow by ordering the slaughter of the eldest son of Toqto'a beki, the Merkit chief who had been killed years before at Irtysh. Some Merkit survived, but they would never again exist as a people.

Now the Ölberli Qipchaqs knew what the Mongols were capable of. Did they also know that, in the Mongol conception of foreign relations, the protectors of the rebels became enemies? The Mongols' feud with the Merkit would soon be extended to the Merkits' protectors: the Mongols would track the Qipchaqs with the goal of killing their leaders, an important episode I detail in chapter 2.[34] For now, though, let us turn back east, to China, where Chinggis Khan was prosecuting another war even as he was mopping up the last of the Merkit and Naiman rebels.

On to China

In 1209 Chinggis invaded the empire of the Tangut, also known as the Xi Xia, a Tibetan-Burmese people who ruled what is today northwestern China. The Tangut became Mongol targets for several reasons. First, they controlled the trade routes and networks of the so-called Silk Road, which the Mongols wanted to monopolize. Second, the Tangut had welcomed the son of the Kereit ruler Wang Khan when the Mongols removed him from the Orkhon Valley: protecting a Mongol enemy made them blood rivals. And finally, the Tangut were allied with the Jin, the Mongols' sometimes enemies, sometimes allies, and always rivals. Defeating the Tangut would deprive the Jin of a buffer between themselves and the Mongols and cut off Tangut aid in advance of a war.[35]

In April 1210, after almost a year of fighting, the Tangut gave in. They were not conquered, though, and were not absorbed into the Mongol ulus. They provided the Mongols with a huge tribute paid in woollen and satin textiles, camels, and falcons. The Tangut also agreed to end their relations with the Jin and to establish a military alliance with the Mongols. As it turned out, the Tangut would prove unreliable partners—indeed, a nightmare for the Mongols. The final defeat of the Tangut would take many years more and require the bloodiest campaign of Chinggis Khan's career, as I discuss in chapter 2.[36] In 1210–1211, though, what Chinggis needed were allies, not conquests, because the Jin, in China, were reemerging as a serious and immediate threat. They had regrouped after a war against the southern empire of the Song and a period of internal struggles. The new Jin ruler sent envoys to Chinggis Khan demanding tribute. The Jin were activating their traditional steppe policy: divide and rule. In particular, the Jin sought repeatedly to corrupt the nomads' alliances by bribing their partners, in hopes of destroying any unity that accrued among the Felt-Walled Tents under Chinggis Khan.

In 1211 Chinggis launched his first great onslaught on northern China. Jebe and Söbötei assisted him. Chinggis's sons also took part: Jochi, Chagatay, and Ögödei led the right wing. Another commander, Muqali, led the left wing. After the Mongols passed the fortified border, the Onggut, nomads dwelling on the Chinese frontier, rallied behind them. The Mongols came close to the Jin's capital, Zhongdu, near modern-day Beijing, but then left unexpectedly. In the fall of 1212, only a few months later, they returned. When the Jin offered peace, Chinggis promptly accepted in order to spare his troops having to besiege the capital. The Jin paid tribute in gold, silk, and horses, and offered Chinggis Khan a Jin princess for a wife. But soon the Mongols realized they had been tricked. The Jin had moved their seat of government from Zhongdu to Kaifeng, on the Yellow River. In May 1215 the Mongols stormed Zhongdu. It was the first time Chinggis Khan had attempted to lay siege to such a large and fortified city. After eight months—possibly longer, according to some sources—the Mongols won the decisive, bloody battle and captured the city.[37]

At the same time he was besieging Zhongdu, Chinggis Khan pushed other troops to the east, where the Jin had moved their capital. He also recruited Chinese defectors from the northeast, including generals, administrators, and siege engineers. The Khitan people in Manchuria also joined his ranks in large numbers. The Khitan resented the Jin, who had supplanted their forefathers, the once powerful Liao. (The Khitan were Liao descendents who had stayed in place after the defeat. Those who left for Central Asia built the Qara Khitai Empire.) In 1216 the worn-out Jin seemed close to surrender. Chinggis Khan entrusted his commander Muqali to stay and pacify the region, while the khan left for his homeland. His goal was to economically integrate China, Mongolia, and Central Asia, and he was well on his way.[38]

The City Became a Deserted Ruin

By the close of the 1220s, political life on the Central Asian steppe had changed dramatically. Uighurs, Qarluqs, and other local Turkic powers had rallied behind the Mongols. The Naiman, Merkit, and Qara Khitai had been destroyed. And there was clearly more to come: the Mongols were engaged in repeated operations beyond their ancestral lands and showed no signs of letting up. Leaders of neighboring territories were under extreme pressure either to preemptively submit to the Mongols or to cast their lot against Chinggis, his sons, and his generals.

Among those feeling the pressure was Muhammad, shah of the Khwarezmian Empire, whose territory to the west of the Mongols occupied portions of present-day Afghanistan, Iran, Uzbekistan, and Turkmenistan. Muhammad's capital, Urgench, was located in an oasis on the southern coastline of the Aral Sea. Shortly after Jochi and Sübötei's decisive victory over the Merkit, Muhammad made his decision. After a few years of relative peace with Chinggis Khan, backed by a trade agreement, Muhammad attacked in 1219. He launched the operation across his northern border, where his scout troops fell on a Mongol camp on the Quylï River. The camp belonged to Jochi's warriors, who were resting after the campaign against the Merkit and the Naiman. Muhammad's troops struck the camp while Jochi's men were away, killing or capturing women and children and taking large amounts of booty. The Mongol warriors returned, contained the attack, and then withdrew at nightfall. The Mongol warriors had no order from Chinggis Khan to battle; they were only a small contingent. Yet they had checked the Khwarezmian army.[39] Although the Mongols initially retreated, war with the Mongols would prove a disastrous error for Muhammad.

Why would Muhammad take on such a powerful enemy? Most basically, because he was no less ambitious than Chinggis Khan, and because he thought he would win. Muhammad was a fighting sultan who had for twenty years expanded his control over cities and lands at the expense of the Qara Khitai. Well before the Mongols had become involved with the Qara Khitai, Muhammad was already meddling in their affairs. Some reported that he made a deal with Güchülüq the Naiman to break the Qara Khitai gür khan, in hopes of appropriating Qara Khitai territories. And Muhammad's troops conquered the Qara Khitai cities of Bukhara and Samarkand in 1207–1210.

In Islamic sources, Muhammad looks less like a conqueror in his own right and more like a weakling who poked a Mongol hornet's nest. "The cause of these Tatars," the contemporary historian Ibn al-Athīr wrote, referring in fact to the Mongols, "only prospered because of a lack of a strong defender." Ibn al-Athīr accused Muhammad of having enfeebled his people by eliminating other princes and sultans, leaving himself the only one who could mobilize troops against the Mongols. The truth, however, was that Muhammad had built up a huge empire with a large army and a constellation of walled cities built to endure powerful attacks. The trouble was that, unlike the Mongols, Muhammad invested little in administration. His regime also lacked a proper system of communication; there was nothing like the Mongol *yam,* the messenger network that enabled centralized control of far-flung administrators, official traders, and armies. (I describe the yam in detail in chapter 3.) And while Muhammad technically commanded a large force, his soldiers were mercenaries. Both poor communication and the fighters' independence led to a lack of cohesion among Muhammad's Khwarezmian troops.[40]

Still, this army, or a version of it, had served Muhammad well. But when it came to the Mongols, he underestimated his foe. The Mongol army was smaller, but it was far more organized and capable, and it was especially well-placed to undermine Muhammad's defensive advantages: Mongol warriors were trained and equipped for mobility, whether on road or off, which proved essential when they had to cross rivers and penetrate mountains en route to Muhammad's strongholds. And, above all, the Mongols knew how to assault a fortified place. During the long and bloody contest with the Jin, they had mastered a range of siege techniques. Chinggis had recruited Chinese artillery corps equipped with stone catapults, which were more powerful and precise than the torsion siege engines and counterweight trebuchets known in Western Europe. The Mongols had also mastered the use of Chinese gunpowder for incendiary missiles and other explosives. After Zhongdu, even the massive mud-brick walls of Muhammad's fortresses failed to intimidate.[41]

There was a lot Muhammad could not have known about the Mongol military when he ordered the raid on Jochi's camp. But he probably should have known more than he did. His first mistake was to blithely ignore the Mongol forces mounting so nearby, as Güchülüq the Naiman was amassing his own troops in Qara Khitai territory. Muhammad and the people around him appreciated that the Mongols were able warriors, but he did not see them as a direct threat and believed he could resist them even if the Qara Khitai fell. Instead of focusing on the Mongols, Muhammad busied himself with what he thought were more urgent matters. He chose to take advantage of the Qara Khitai's internal weakness by pursuing the conquests of Bukhara and Samarkand. But while doing so satisfied Muhammad's expansionist interests, the conquests also put him on a collision course with the Mongols. With the Qara Khitai dismantled by the Khwarezmians from the west and the Mongols from

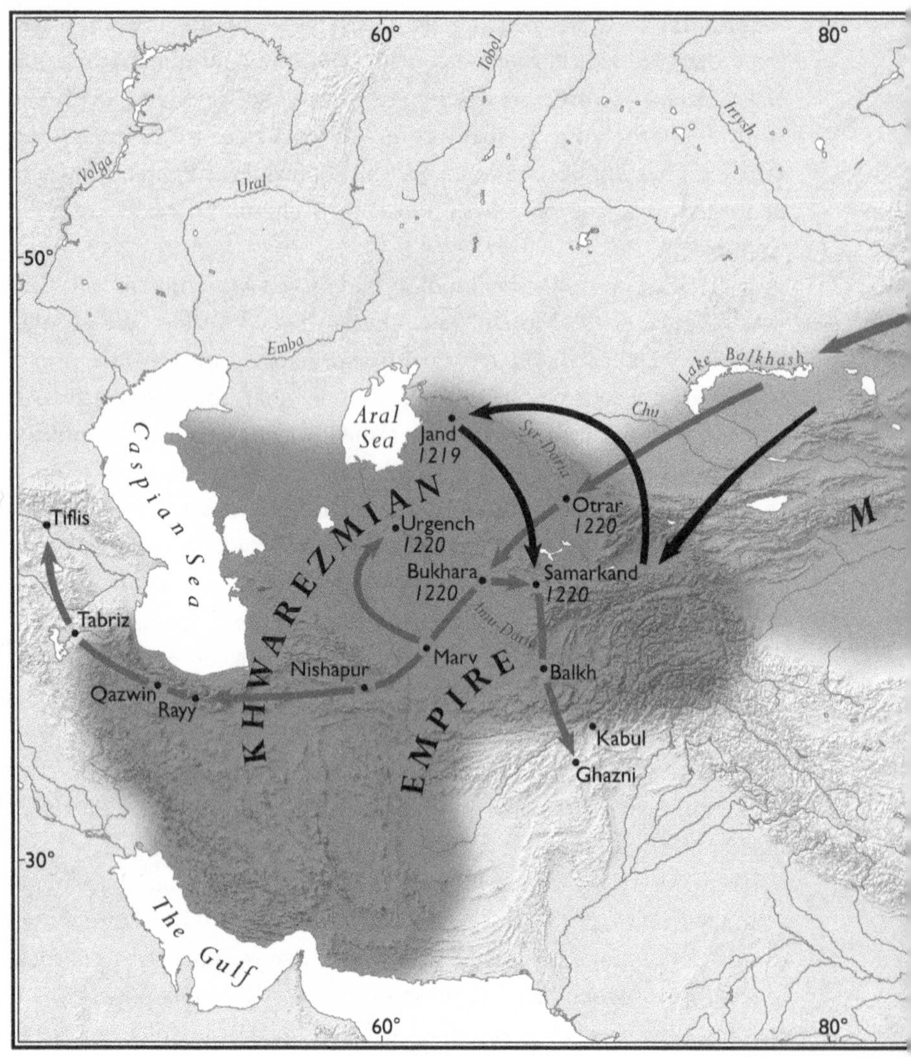
60°
80°
50°
30°
Volga
Ural
Tobol
Irtysh
Emba
Lake Balkhash
Chu
Aral Sea
Jand 1219
Syr-Darya
Caspian Sea
Otrar 1220
Tiflis
Urgench 1220
KHWAREZMIAN EMPIRE
M
Bukhara 1220
Samarkand 1220
Amu-Darya
Tabriz
Marv
Nishapur
Balkh
Qazwin
Rayy
Kabul
Ghazni
The Gulf

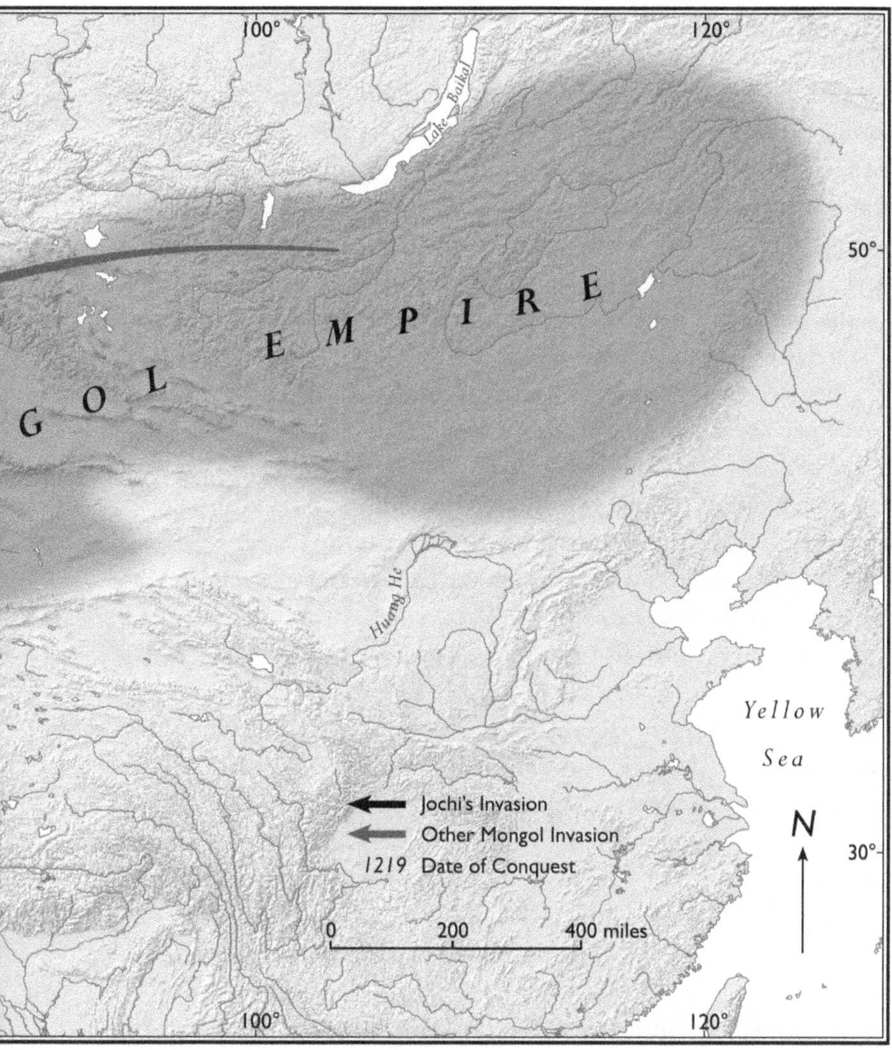

Conquest of the Khwarezmian Empire in Central Asia and Iran, showing routes of the Mongol invasion.

the east, Muhammad found himself sharing a border with Chinggis Khan.[42]

The conflict began in the context of trade. Bukhara and Samarkand, old centers of the Muslim intelligentsia, were also active commercial hubs, which attracted the attention of the Mongols. In 1218 Chinggis Khan sent a caravan of about 450 merchants carrying a vast quantity of gold, silver, silk, sables, skins, and other goods to Bukhara and Samarkand. But Muhammad's governor in Otrar, the city nearest to the Mongol territories, stopped the caravan en route. As soon as the news reached Chinggis Khan, around July–August 1219, he dispatched an envoy to inform Muhammad that the caravan was being prevented from reaching its destination, in spite of the trade agreement between the two empires. Muhammad responded by accusing the merchants of spying; he ordered them killed and had their goods sold for his own benefit in the marketplaces of Bukhara and Samarkand.[43] It was around that time that the Khwarezmian army launched its attack on Jochi's camp.

Muhammad controlled the routes beyond Otrar to Central Asia, Iran, and Iraq, which meant the Mongols, so invested economically and politically in commercial exchanges, were now cut off from essential trade partners. Chinggis understood Muhammad's obstruction of the Mongol traders as an act of war. And yet it would be unfair to suggest, as Muhammad's contemporary critics did, that Muhammad was merely being provocative. For one thing, the accusation of spying probably was not wrong. The *ortaq,* Chinggis Khan's licensed merchants, observered goings on and foreign courts and relayed what they learned back to the imperial center.

Of course, Muhammad had his own spies at work in Mongol camps, but even if the accusation of spying was a pretext to legitimize the economic isolation of the Mongols, there were nonetheless strategic reasons to push back against the Mongols, who were showing clear signs of aggression. Jochi had led several military missions on the fringes of Muhammad's empire, and the competition over the Qara Khitai lands enraged Muhammad and his entourage. By 1218 Muhammad had ample evidence of the Mongols' strength, based on the flow of Qara Khitai refugees into his territory. Indeed, Muhammad's armies were brimming with people fleeing the Mongols, simultaneously strengthening Muhammad's hand and inspiring concerns about what the Mongols were capable of. Qipchaq horsemen working for the Khwarezmians had also encountered the Mongols and could tell stories of their skill and bravery in combat.

Chinggis's response to the murder of his merchants was a classic example of Mongol psychological warfare. The Mongol custom was to engage in ritualized exchanges with their adversaries before battle. Their diplomacy was terrifying and perverse, often involving contradictory messages offering enemies a last chance to surrender—an effort to provoke their anger and push them to behave offensively. Once offended, the Mongols felt they had the right to fight and kill. In the case of the Khwarezmians, Chinggis's envoys carried a letter, saying, "You kill my men and my merchants and you take from them my property! Prepare for war, for I am coming against you with a host you cannot withstand." His anger provoked, Muhammad had the chief Mongol ambassador killed and humiliated the ambassador's companions by having their beards shaved. He sent the companions back to Chinggis Khan with the message, "I am coming to you, though you were at the end of the earth, to deliver punishment and to treat you as I treated your followers."[44]

At this point Muhammad and his councilors understood that the Mongols were a force to be reckoned with, but they believed they were well positioned to do battle. Yet their first failures emerged in the course of preparations, as the lack of cohesion within the Khwarezmian Empire and its forces came to the fore. Muhammad's advisors were at odds. One, the respected lawyer Shihāb al-Dīn al-Khīwaqī, urged that the provincial governors gather their scattered armies and the Muslim elite be requisitioned to provide troops and cash. The lawyer also advised that the shah's army move immediately, faster than the Mongols, and wait for them on the banks of the Syr-Daria River, confronting the Mongols at their first major obstacle. But Muhammad's emirs and court councilors had other plans. They thought that the Mongols would struggle to cross the big rivers and the narrow passes of the Tian Shan Mountains, which lay between the Mongols and Muhammad's army. Rather than rush troops to the river, Khwarezmian commanders allowed the Mongols to cross the Syr-Daria and advance inland. These commanders figured that they could ambush the Mongols, who presumably did not know the landscape, in the mountain passes.[45]

It is impossible to say whether the outcome of the war would have been different had the commanders followed Muhammad and his advisor, Shihāb al-Dīn al-Khīwaqī. But what is clear is that the Mongols knew what they were getting into as they penetrated the difficult topography of the region. What Muhammad did not appreciate was a distinctive feature of Mongol warfare: the systematic use of extreme advance troops. These horsemen carried light equipment and no heavy war engines. Their purpose was not to plunder or destroy fortifications and villages—though if they needed to attack a stronghold, they built siege weapons on the spot—but to pave the way for mass armies by scouting routes and gaining accurate information on the locals and the enemy. Sometimes they worked as an assassination unit, too. Jebe and Sübötei led the contingent, known as the Westward. Their first mission was to kill Muhammad.[46]

The Westward comprised anywhere from ten thousand to thirty thousand horsemen, according to various sources. Ibn al-Athīr reported that, while other Mongol armies were elsewhere, these scouts and fighters "travelled west of Khurasan" and "penetrated deep into our lands."[47] This reflected another distinguishing feature of Mongol warmaking. The Mongols were unparalleled masters of military coordination, able to deploy multiple large-scale operations simultaneously. Chinggis would dispatch several armies, each taking on different aspects of a larger strategy. Thus while Jebe and Sübötei were assigned to one force, Jochi could lead another. Jochi was ordered to penetrate the Tian Shan Mountains, seize control of the Khwarezm area, and then join his father's army at Samarkand.[48]

Meanwhile the Westward relied on local guides to find their own path. They learned that the Amu-Daria River had a crossing point at the Five Waters, near the mouth of the River Vakhsh, exactly at the present-day border between Afghanistan and Tajikistan. The Mongols easily crossed at the Five Waters, despite finding no boats there. The troops were proficient at river crossings, much as they were used to traversing mountainous terrain and attacking fortified cities. Ibn al-Athīr recounted how

> they made what resembled large troughs out of woods and covered them with cattle skins so that they would be impermeable

> to water. They placed their weapons and belongings in them and then urged their horses into the water and held on to their tails with those wooden troughs tied to their own bodies. Thus each horse dragged a man and each man dragged the trough that was full of his weapons and other things. All of them crossed over at one time and the first thing Khwārazm Shāh knew of them they were with him on the same ground.[49]

Once the Mongols had crossed the Amu-Daria, the Khwarezmians made no further attempts to stop their invasion. Muhammad realized that he could not defeat the Mongols in open battle and instead ordered his subjects and forces to hunker down. He withdrew to Khwarezm and Khorasan to gather more troops, and he instructed the people of Bukhara and Samarkand to barricade themselves and prepare for siege. But the few thousand mounted guards he left to defend the cities proved no match when the Mongol armies attacked in February and March 1220. The guards quickly abandoned their positions, the citizens surrendered, and Chinggis Khan forced the local merchants to return what they had stolen from his traders.[50]

Muhammad, constantly moving and hiding, dispatched troops to protect the other cities of the area—Otrar, Rayy, Qazwin, Marv, and Nishapur. But all eventually suffered the same fate as Bukhara and Samarkand. Every time a city put up real resistance, the Mongols destroyed their defenses, forcing the citizens to fill in moats and demolish battlements. Citizens were also ordered to provide lists of local elites, merchants, and craftsmen; elites and merchants were forced to give up all they possessed, while craftsmen were considered useful and therefore sent east. The Mongols kept women, children, and workers for themselves, scattering and apportioning the captives among their many camps. By 1221 all the cities except the capital, Urgench, had fallen. Urgench, which was located in the heart of what used to be Muhammad's empire, "was left standing in the middle like a tent with a broken rope," according to Juvaynī.[51]

In cases in which the Mongols did not empty the cities they conquered, they left behind a handful of men under the command of an official known as a *daṛughachi* or *basqaq*. The warriors forced the citizens to provide them food, cloth, money, and labor. In the cities of Hamadan

Khusrau Anushirvan Orders the Execution of Mazdak and his Followers, c. 1300, from an Ilkhanid version of the Persian *Book of Kings (Shahnama).* Mongols punished disloyalty by publicly executing rebel leaders. (Pictures from History / Bridgeman Images)

and Herat, the strategy proved disastrous, as the inhabitants soon killed the darughachi and the Mongols were forced to strike back. After the dust settled, the Mongols integrated surviving city dwellers into their armies and forced them to march as a massive infantry to impress their enemy.

This sort of display was an important Mongol tactic. Because Chinggis Khan's armies were often outnumbered, captives could make their numbers look bigger. The Mongols paraded these deceptively large forces in order to encourage their enemies to surrender without a fight. The Mongols also would put captives on display outside the walls of besieged cities and sometimes abuse the prisoners in plain sight, demoralizing the population awaiting its fate. Mongol armies also used captives as human shields, placing the captives between themselves and their enemies.

In addition to plundering people, the Mongols took property from their victims, albeit under strict military discipline. These were not looting throngs but rather warriors under orders and on a mission. They took only what they could carry and burned what they could not. These were not personal trophies or booties; the spoils were sent to the Mongol camps, where they were distributed according to the tümen. The camps themselves were well run, primarily by women who followed the warriors, managing herds and other supplies. They Mongol armies seemed to be wholly self-sufficient, which left a deep impression on outside observers. "The Tatars do not need a supply of provisions and foodstuffs," Ibn al-Athīr wrote, again conflating the Mongols with their erstwhile rivals, who were brought into the fold under Chinggis Khan. "Their sheep, cattle, horses, and other pack animals accompany them and they consume their flesh and nothing else. The animals they ride dig the earth with their hooves and eat the roots of plants, knowing nothing of barley. Thus, when they make a camp, they require nothing from without." Observers of the Central Asian campaign witnessed the full capability of the Mongols, from their strategic and tactical acumen to their frightening mobility, strict discipline, and adaptability to new environments and changing weather conditions.[52]

As early as 1220 Chinggis Khan took control of the region between the Syr-Daria and the Amu-Daria rivers, amounting to almost the entirety of contemporary Uzbekistan. But Muhammad remained at large. The Westward tracked him across northern Iran, all the way to the southern coast of the Caspian Sea. He abandoned his retinue, baggage train, and family. Protected by a small elite guard, he changed his identity and disappeared. Rumors swirled that he was hiding in a castle on an island in the Caspian. Merchants and other witnesses reported that they had seen him in the Iranian cities of Hamadan and Rayy. The many contradictory stories that circulated about Muhammad betrayed the simple fact that no one knew where he was or whether he was alive. This again spoke to the great weakness of his regime: the lack of a communication system. People were left in the dark as to what was happening, and false and puzzling information about their missing ruler prevented his remaining loyalists from organizing. Ibn al-Athīr recorded that "Khorasan and eastern Iraq have become 'a loose beast' with no defender and no sultan to protect them, while the enemy prowls the country, taking or leaving what he wishes."[53]

Reading Muhammad's contemporary critics, one has the impression that the war was easy on the Mongols, that they suffered little and easily overcame a grossly unprepared, disjointed, and poorly led Khwarezmian army. But the truth is more complex. The war lasted two long years, from 1219 to 1221, during which several cities and fortresses were taken with enormous effort and at great cost. The siege of the fortress of Mansurkuh took the Mongols ten months and the capital, Urgench, was besieged for at least four months. As Ibn al-Athīr reported of Urgench, "the city became a deserted ruin" by the time it fell into Mongol hands. Recent scholarship suggests that Chinggis considered the siege of Urgench a failure, as the Mongols were supposed to take the city, not destroy it. A large number of Mongol warriors died during the siege from naptha bombs and stone projectiles and in hand-to-hand combat. The Mongols themselves estimated that they lost more than the city did—and the city was devastated. The challenge of the siege was no doubt exacerbated by leadership squabbles, as Chinggis's sons did not all agree on strategy. Elsewhere, at Qazwin in 1220, inhabitants fiercely resisted the Mongols, taking countless Mongol warriors' lives and as many as 40,000 Qazwinians. The Mongols would not have needed to take so many captives as new warriors had they not suffered serious casualties themselves. And the war was hardly an unalloyed political victory for Chinggis. Jebe's victories gained him considerable wealth and prestige, which made him a threat to Chinggis. There is reason to believe that Chinggis sent Jebe after Muhammad in order to keep the general occupied, lest Jebe turn on his khan.[54]

That Chinggis emerged successful from his campaign against the Khwarezmians was due only in part to his own strength. He also benefited from Muhammad's political and military mistakes and the lack of support for Muhammad from other parts of the Islamic world. A persistent rumor in the Islamic sources mentions that the Abbasid caliph, based in Baghdad, wrote to the Qara Khitai contingents in Muhammad's armies, inciting them to abandon their sultan, even offering them money. The caliph's rivalry with Muhammad evidently prevailed over considerations of a possible alliance between the two Muslim leaders.[55]

The Mongols also failed to completely destroy their Khwarezmian enemy, as Muhammad's son Jalāl al-Dīn fled to India. The Mongols pursued him all the way to the outskirts of Lahore and then turned back. Jalāl al-Dīn settled in the Punjab, gathered forces, and turned the area of present-day Kabul into an armed borderland. It took the Mongols ten more years to annihilate Jalāl al-Dīn's resistance and bring the era of the sultans of Khwarezm to an end. Even then, Jalāl al-Dīn's loyal mounted guard, known as the Khwarezmiyya, fled to

Iraq, Syria, and Egypt and entered the service of the local Ayyubids as mercenaries and elite mamluks, ready to resume the fight against the Mongols.[56]

Perhaps most significantly, the Central Asian campaign drove—or revealed—deep fissures within the Mongol ruling family, resulting in the removal of Chinggis's favor from Jochi, his eldest son. Into the 1220s and throughout the Central Asian war, there had been no question that Jochi was Chinggis's chief heir: the next khan of all the Mongols, if he lived long enough to accept his father's throne. Indeed, the war should have solidified Jochi's position. In Khwarezm, while his brothers Chagatay and Ögödei conducted secondary operations, Jochi's army was independently carrying out the central mission. The mass army made a grueling trek down the Syr-Daria River, capturing town after town en route to the capital, Urgench. Jochi's forces defeated the towns, preventing them from reinforcing the capital, then captured Urgench itself. It was also Jochi who led the subjugation of the Forest Peoples and the destruction of the Merkit in western Kazakhstan. He was making good on the promise his father had made: all these lands were granted to Jochi before they had even been conquered. And now it was Jochi doing the conquering. Each military victory bolstered his legitimacy as ruler of Siberia and Central Asia—in the opinions of the locals and, crucially, of fellow Mongols.

Yet there were two critical missteps. First, though Jochi took Urgench, the city was almost entirely destroyed in battle. A center of trade, crafts, and the intelligentsia, Urgench was most useful intact. But Jochi failed in this respect. Second, what Jochi recovered from Urgench was shared only among himself and his brothers, as if the spoils were his to distribute. The sons left no *qubi,* no share, for their father. Chinggis was furious. He refused any audience with his sons until they begged his pardon, which they obtained only through the mediation of Muqali and other close companions of their father's. But while Chinggis forgave his sons, he diluted Jochi's claim to Khwarezm by granting his second son Chagatay a share of the region's tax receipts. This was the beginning of a new strategy for Chinggis's regime. Concerned that none of his sons would become so powerful as to unseat him, Chinggis began using his sons as checks against each other, implementing a system in which one of them might have possessions and rights in another's territories. And instead of a chief heir, Jochi was now an equal, subject to the same constraints as his brothers.[57]

By Spring 1222, when the Taoist monk Qiu Chuji arrived to visit Chinggis Khan, the Mongol leader was getting old, and his sons were jockeying for primacy. Chinggis appointed no heir; the question of his succession was to remain open, creating the conditions for a fierce competition after his death in 1227. And the alienation of Jochi would only increase, laying the foundations for the autonomy of his descendents—the Horde—in the decades to come.

2

Into the West

Jochi's missteps during the Central Asian campaign had cost him his place as Chinggis Khan's heir apparent, but that hardly meant Jochi was disinherited. He had lost his claim to the throne, yet he was still granted peoples and lands of his own, and lands into which his ulus had an exclusive right to expand. At the same time, he would have to share with his brothers some of the revenues of his territories, and they would have to share their revenues with him. This was a new system, the brainchild of Chinggis Khan, who was both a warrior and lawgiver. But if the law was new, it was not, strictly speaking, novel. The balance of power that Chinggis inscribed in his inheritance scheme reflected the deeply important role of sharing in Mongol political economy, a role that predates the khan's law.

Ostentatious generosity was an old governing practice among steppe peoples. Leaders dispensed their wealth, showing themselves to be a kind of father to the people, an unparalleled provider. Thus, during postwar quriltai, Chinggis publicly redistributed war booty, cattle, and captives. Sharing was an activity not only of the leader. Mongols of all social classes redistributed wealth throughout the course of their lives; sons and daughters did not wait for their parents to die to receive their share of the family fortune.

The three central institutions of redistribution were herd sharing, wedding gifts, and payouts after collective undertakings such as raids and seasonal mare milking. Herd sharing, which I discuss in more detail in the next chapter, saw lower-ranked Mongols lending their animals to more high-ranked ones, yet poorer herders could also milk animals belonging to the wealthy. During the milking season, herders brought fermented milk to the khan, who in turn distributed it to the people during the drinking festival. As we saw in the last chapter, war spoils were distributed from the top downward via the tümen system. As for wedding gifts, when their children married, wealthy herders shared their livestock and dependent people with the couple. A daughter brought to her marriage a significant *inju,* dowry, while a son received a share of his family's livestock. Distribution to sons was fairly equal, although the eldest and youngest were often favored. Once married, a couple lived in separate *ger,* felt tents, and if they had enough livestock and wealth might leave the family camp. The eldest son moved the farthest from his parents and often formed a separate camp. Only the youngest son, called *ochigin,* the hearth keeper, lived with his parents until they died. Then he inherited their remaining livestock.[1]

As these practices indicate, the sharing system had some egalitarian features; collective herds and downward redistribution of war booty brought a degree of material comfort to commoners. But sharing also reinforced hierarchy, as inheritance norms ensured the concentration and perpetuation of family wealth. These norms were flexible; a ruler or community could decide to elevate a junior figure over a senior one, thereby ensuring greater wealth or power to the junior even though, by tradition, seniority mattered among the steppe nomads. The hierarchy was therefore malleable, and with it the political system. Chinggis Khan took advantage of this flexibility when he demoted Jochi from his chief heir to a kind of first among equals, whose priority did not include succession to the great khanship.

Chinggis treated his chief wife's four sons as a wealthy herder would, but he had more than livestock to share. He had huge territories, thousands of human beings, and his own ruling position. By the 1220s the empire was colossal, including the former dominions of the Qara Khitai and the Khwarezmian Empire. In the course of twenty years, Chinggis

Khan had integrated the Felt-Walled Tents, including the stubborn Tayichi'ut, Tatar, Kereit, Naiman, and Merkit, and gained control of entire Mongolia. In 1207–1208 Jochi had brought under Mongol rule the Oyirad, Kirghiz, Buriat, Tümet, and the other small but enduring peoples of the Siberian forest. Between 1207 and 1212, the Onggut, Uighur, Qarluq, and Manchurian Khitan, all sedentary neighbors of the Mongols, had submitted of their own will. At roughly the same time, Chinggis Khan had successfully attacked western, northern, and eastern China, bringing to temporary allegiance the Tangut in 1211 and the Jin in 1215–1216. Korea had fallen in 1219. By the time he was ready to parcel out his wealth, Chinggis Khan dominated one-third of Eurasia.

Chinggis distributed the steppe among his sons. Chagatay received western Turkestan, Ögödei Jungharia and later central Mongolia, Tolui eastern Mongolia, and Jochi western Mongolia and the Siberian forests and later the western (Qipchaq) steppe. No member of Chinggis's family was expected to live in the more densely populated areas like northern China, Khorasan, and Khwarezm, where the lifestyle was more urbanized and largely sedentary. But high-ranking Mongols of the golden lineage did not need to live in these places in order to benefit from the wealth their residents produced. The imperial kin were assigned portions of the urbanized territories and received shares of the tax revenue generated there. The Mongol assignees operated a bit like absentee landlords, appointing secretaries and accountants—who might be natives of the territories—to represent their interests on the ground. The appointees took the census, verified accounts, and controlled payment delivery. Thus, in addition to Chinggis Khan's central secretariat, smaller local administrations developed to manage the assets of the Mongol beneficiaries.[2]

The favor bestowed on Jochi demonstrates that Chinggis considered him his eldest, even though Jochi was most likely not Chinggis's son by blood. Jochi was probably Börte's son by a Merkit chieftain, but Chinggis raised Jochi as his own. The official historiography of the Mongol Empire—revised after 1251 under the aegis of the descendants of Tolui, who competed with the Jochids for power—portrays Jochi as a bastard. Nevertheless, Jochi received one of the best territories, located farthest away from his native lands: "as far in that [northwest] direction as the hoof of Tartar horse had penetrated." This distance marked Jochi as the eldest, just as the eldest son of a typical herder would settle farthest from his parents. The allotment included the Syr-Daria Valley and the Volga-Ural region, the heart of the Qipchaq steppe through which the Volga River ran and irrigated the best pastures in northwestern Asia. Jochi also received the Irtysh basin and parts of Khwarezm and was guaranteed control over places and people yet to be conquered. Finally, Jochi was granted ancestral *nuntug*—a homeland to retire to and in which to bury his next of kin. Jochi's nuntug was in Merkit and Naiman territories in the region of the Irtysh River between southern Siberia and the Altai Mountains.[3]

Chinggis also apportioned his warriors. He gave each of his sons 4,000 Mongols—a significant number considering that his army counted probably no more than 150,000 Mongols, as distinct from conquered peoples. These inherited warriors enjoyed special status; they could not be transferred to other members of the imperial kin. In addition, these forces were commanded by men of real ability. Chinggis made it clear that he chose these commanders because they were wise and more experienced in warfare than his sons were. At least formally, the commanders were serving their masters—the four sons—of their own free will. These commanders became the nuclei of four new keshig, one for each of Chinggis's sons.[4]

The mounted archers at Jochi's service were organized in *minggan,* contingents of a thousand, headed by elite warriors of varied origins. His commanders were Mongols from the Tayichi'ut, Hushin, Kinggut, and Je'üriyet. The diversity of the troops was deliberate; old oboq divisions had to be broken. There was only one ruling family: Chinggis Khan's immediate kin and its golden lineage. There was only one ulus: the Mongols. Chinggis's policy was to turn people away from their origin and family and toward the ulus. His chief method was to create entirely new social units bound by military hierarchy. He was replacing blood kin with martial kin.

The core of Jochi's horde comprised a keshig of 4,000 seasoned Mongol warriors and their families. The rest of his horde was made of numerous servants, slaves, and foreign recruits. Forced conscription in conquered lands and the taking of thousands of war captives would soon multiply the original numbers by ten.[5]

Mongol archer on a horse, ink and gold on paper (early fifteenth century). Although the depiction is romanticized, the drawing captures distinctive features of Mongol warriors: the owl-feathered headdress, composite bow, pearl earrings, and ornamented harness. (bpk Bildagentur/Berlin Staatsbibliothek/Photo: Ellwardt/Art Resource, NY)

Our Land They Have Taken Away Today and Yours Will Be Taken Tomorrow

While the *yeke Mongghol ulus,* the Mongol Empire, quickly digested the large dominions of the Khwarezmian Empire, Sübötei, Chinggis' foremost commander, asked to be the one who would be sent back to the west—to the Qipchaq steppe. Chinese and Mongol sources report that Sübötei wanted to finish off the Qipchaqs once and for all. He could count on the support of Jebe and the men of the Westward, an elite unit and the most experienced of the Mongol armies. The Westward's plan was to force their way through the Caucasus Mountains and into

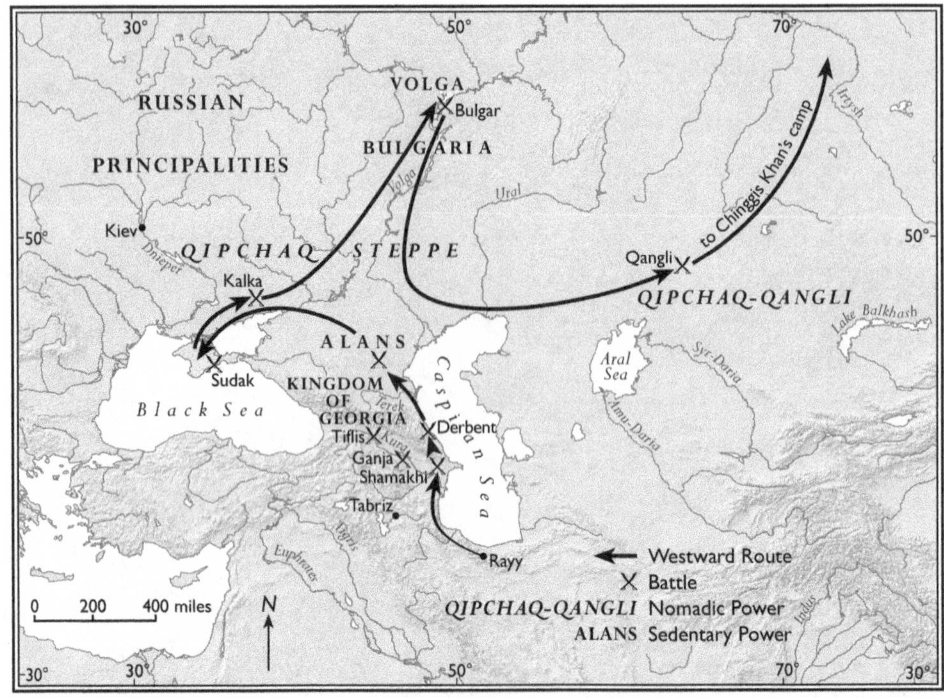

The 1221–1223 campaign of the Westward, from Iran to Russia through the Caucasus and back to Mongolia.

the Qipchaq steppe. Jochi and the mass army would then link up with the Westward at the Volga River. Their combined forces, 50,000 warriors or more, would subjugate the peoples of the Volga-Ural before turning back east.

In winter 1220–1221, the cold was intense and thick snow covered the grasslands. The Westward suffered in northwestern Iran. To endure the long winter, Jebe and Sübötei quickly moved their men to southern Azerbaijan. Along the way, they passed the city of Tabriz, where the ruler, Uzbek Ibn Pahlawan, helped the Mongols, providing them with horses, clothing, and cash. Tabriz, one of the future financial centers of the Mongol Empire, was left untouched, and the Westward carried on. They hoped to reach the Kura River and winter in the Mughan plain, between the lesser and the greater Caucasus ranges. A huge field of mud in the summer, Mughan promised green grass and mild temperatures during the cold season. The Westward crossed the Kura and settled in for winter. They had entered the Kingdom of Georgia.[6]

At that time, King George Lasha, the Georgian leader, was in full preparation for a crusade. Distracted by these ambitions, and confident in the capacity of his forces, he underestimated the urgency of the Mongol threat. Arguably that confidence was well-earned: since the foundational rule of Queen Tamar, George Lasha's mother, the Georgians had been the dominant power in the Caucasus, and they did have a powerful military. The contemporary Armenian historian Kirakos noted the great esteem in which Georgians held their cavalrymen, a robust army that excelled at shock combat. But Kirakos also reported that the Georgian peasants, rather like their king, did not appreciate the gravity of the situation. Indeed, they did not even recognize that their lands were being invaded. Instead, the Georgian people welcomed the Mongols. The Georgians believed the Mongols were Christians who "had with them a portable tent-church, as well as a miracle-working cross," which multiplied food supplies endlessly. We do not know how the Georgians came to believe as they did; possibly some Mongol warriors wore what appeared to be Christian crosses or carried standards depicting symbols that resembled crosses. Yet the Mongols had no interest in parleying with the Georgians; quite the opposite: the Mongols assaulted the fortified cities of Ganja and Tiflis and "put [the inhabitants] to the sword, one and all."[7]

King George eventually responded by partnering with his Muslim neighbors in Khilāt, Tabriz, and al-Jazīra. Together they decided to fight the invaders in spring. But the Westward did not wait for the seasons to change, as the Georgians had expected. Instead the Mongols allied with Kurds, Turkmen, and other locals who came to demolish the Georgians. By January 1221 Sübötei and Jebe had firm control over the Kingdom of Georgia. The Georgians no longer posed a threat, so the Mongols allowed the Georgian kingdom to survive in a diminished form. The Mongols' objective was to take what they needed from the area, especially horses, and they saw no advantage in killing more inhabitants and tearing down buildings.[8]

The next challenge facing the Mongols would be one of the most difficult of the campaign: the crossing of the Greater Caucasus. The Westward's commanders recognized that they would need dependable guides, appropriate equipment, more horses, and gifts with which to mollify the locals and thereby stave off conflicts that were not worth fighting. After all, the Mongols had a powerful enemy to take on—the Qipchaqs—and did not need trouble along the way to the battlefield. Instead of heading into the Greater Caucasus at once, the Mongols withdrew and regrouped. They turned back to Azerbaijan and sought the richest towns, where they demanded cloth, food, and cash and destroyed places where people refused or were not able to give them what they wanted. The Mongols would use these articles to fund their crossing of the Greater Caucasus. In winter 1221–1222, the Mongols were back in the Mughan plain, ready to resume their mission.

The Greater Caucasus are the highest peaks of Eastern Europe. Only one passage would allow a large army to cross from Mughan, but that route was protected by fortifications: Alexander's Gates, the legendary defenses built by Alexander the Great to keep his territory safe from the northern barbarians. The route followed the west coast of the Caspian Sea along a rocky strip of land until it passed Shirvan, the southern gate, and Derbent, the northern gate. To attack the gates from the south was nearly impossible. The Shirvan shah, the local ruler, was weak compared with the Georgians, but he controlled the gates, and whoever controlled the gates controlled the pass through the Greater Caucasus.[9]

Jebe and Sübötei probably understood that pressing their heavily armored men—reportedly up to 20,000 of them—and thousands of horses and camels into the pass would amount to suicide. Instead the Westward went looking for the Shirvan shah in Shamakhi, the local capital, which sat in the mountains. As earlier in Central Asia, the Westward left their carts and siege engines behind. Throughout the campaigns in the Caucasus, the Mongols kept a safe camp in Mughan with their baggage and surplus horses. A Georgian source reported that when the Mongols entered the mountains, they had only bows and horses with them—no armor, provisions, or swords. Their horses were unshod—remarkable, as they were traversing rocky terrain.[10]

In fortified Shamakhi, the Mongols used ladders to climb the walls and quell inhabitants' fierce resistance. Given their lean provisioning, the Mongols must have built the ladders en route. The Westward also "gathered together some [dead] camels, cattle, sheep and other animals and the corpses of some local victims and of others, threw them on top of one another until they made a sort of hill, which they climbed and so dominated the town." Some of the Mongols got stuck in the rotting bodies, and the hill of corpses and carcasses sank. However, the Mon-

Illustration of a Mongol iron helmet with half mask, eye slits, and nose guard (Horde, thirteenth or early fourteenth century). Helmets of this style were common among the military elite and were used in West Asia by Qipchaqs and Russians as well.

gols repeated their assaults until at last "the inhabitants lost heart, overcome by fatigue, tiredness and exhaustion." Much literature on Mongol combat describes easy battles with overmatched opponents, but this was decidedly a hard-fought victory. No sooner had the Mongols taken the city than they learned that the Shirvan shah had already left Shamakhi for Derbent.[11]

What came next was trickery. Jebe and Sübötei made known that they were ready to negotiate, and the Shirvan shah fell into their trap, sending a group of ten notables from Derbent. The Mongols killed one of the envoys in front of the others to scare them into submission. The Mongols then pressured the envoys to turn over their best horsemen, who would navigate the Westward through the narrow passes to avoid

Derbent. The Mongols must have learned that the fortress could be bypassed through the mountains. It took the troops at least two weeks to cut their way through the snow, "chiseling stone," and "filling up abysses" with anything they found, before they finally appeared behind the Derbent fortress wall from the north. This was a huge tactical advantage, for the inhabitants expected them to attack from the south. We still do not know how the Westward made it around the fortress, even with the help of local guides. Unprepared for the assault from the north, the locals quickly surrendered and offered the Mongols food and safe passage. At this point, Jebe and Sübötei probably called back their men, baggage, and horses from Mughan. The full complement could now safely penetrate the Greater Caucasus.[12]

On the north side of the range, the Alan, Lakz, and other Caucasian peoples were waiting. They had heard of the Mongols and knew what the Mongols had done to the Georgian kingdom. To fight back, they had gathered a contingent of Qipchaqs, who were excellent mounted archers. After testing the Qipchaqs on the battlefield and finding that they did not break, the Westward decided to negotiate directly with the Qipchaqs, cutting out the Caucasians and making a separate peace. Jebe and Sübötei's spokesmen explained to the Qipchaqs, "We and you are of one [stock]. These Alān are not the same as you that you should aid them, nor is their religion the same as yours. We will promise you that we will not trouble you and we will bring you whatever money and clothing you want, if you leave us to deal with them." The Qipchaqs agreed and departed. But they would not get much chance to enjoy their gifts. When the Westward turned against the Alan and the Lakz, they moved into the steppes between the Caspian Sea, the Don River, and the Black Sea, where many Qipchaqs resided. The Qipchaqs in the area had disbanded into many small camps and did not expect the sudden and intense Mongol attack. According to Ibn al-Athīr, Jebe and Sübötei "seized back many times more than they had provided."[13]

Qipchaq survivors took refuge in the northern lands of the Russians and in Crimea, where the Qipchaqs had their main trading post at the fortified harbor of Sudak. The Westward followed them and plundered the town. Its inhabitants sailed to the other side of the Black Sea to hide in the Seljuq Sultanate. By emptying Sudak of its merchants, destroying their businesses, and isolating the peninsula, the Mongols struck at the heart of the Qipchaq world. The Qipchaqs had no supreme leader to kill and no capital city to seize, but they did have a prosperous commercial nexus to crash. Sudak connected the Dnieper, Don, and Volga arteries to the Byzantine Empire, the Seljuq Sultanate, Bulgaria, and even the Syrian-Palestinian coast. It is no accident that travelers used to call the Black Sea the Sea of Sudak. The region was a commercial hub, with a mixed population of Greeks, Venetians, Armenians, Jews, and Turkmen engaged in agriculture and trade. Before the Mongol assault, the Qipchaqs controlled the Sudak markets, where merchants traded slaves and furs, and cash and textiles arrived in large quantities from Anatolia. The Mongols shut down the harbor and left, then set up camps in the ample pastures of the Qipchaq steppe.[14]

Seeking partners in the fight against the Mongols, Khan Köten, a Qipchaq chief, went to Kiev to negotiate with the *kniazia,* the Russian princes. Such alliances were not unheard of; being neighbors, Qipchaqs and Russians occasionally joined forces against common enemies. This time the Qipchaqs came in large numbers and brought gifts, "horses and camels, buffaloes and girls." The *Chronicle of Novgorod,* one of the earliest Old Russian histories, reports that the Qipchaqs also brought the kniazia a warning about the Mongols: "Our land they have taken away today; and yours will be taken tomorrow." Kniaz Mstislav Mstislavich of Galicia, Khan Köten's son-in-law, sided with Köten and summoned his Russian "brothers" to do the same. But the kniazia dithered and bickered. They had no clear leadership and constantly contested with one another. Ultimately they separated into two camps, southerners and northerners. Mstislav Romanovich, the kniaz of Kiev and the supreme ruler of the southern lands, sided with Mstislav Mstislavich and the Qipchaqs. They were joined by the princes of Chernigov, Smolensk, and Volhynia. The senior princes of the northern lands refused to join the alliance; they were engaged in other conflicts closer to their area. The kniaz of Vladimir-Suzdal, the dominant principality in the north, was levying troops against the Livonians. One source reports that the kniaz did send his nephew, the kniaz of Rostov, with troops, but they moved too late to rendezvous with the southern Russian forces.[15]

The meeting point for the Russian and Qipchaq armies was thirty miles south of Kiev. For months, men, horses, provisions, and weapons came by land convoys and riverboats. Food and military equipment were loaded on carts to follow the massive army as it moved slowly down the western bank of the Dnieper River. In May 1223 the Russians gathered with the Qipchaq archers. A high estimate holds there were around 80,000 men, but only 15,000 of them were well-equipped warriors. The Russian and Qipchaq cavalrymen wore similar armor: a mail hauberk with short sleeves designed for horse riders, a tall helmet, and a complete or partial iron facemask with nasals and holes for the eyes.[16]

Preparing for war, the Mongols sent their first delegation to the kniazia. The delegation was tasked with carrying out diplomacy in the Mongol style: offering peace, with the expectation that they would be turned down. As ever, the Mongols believed it was crucial to create a narrative in which the opponent was the aggressor and themselves the hurt party. They would not engage in a fight without first being scorned, for it was the enemy's offense that convinced the Mongols they had moral justification to use lethal violence. The Russian sources report that the Mongol envoys claimed they were interested in war only with the Qipchaqs and that the kniazia could still withdraw from a conflict that was not theirs. "We have not occupied your land, nor your towns, nor your villages, nor is it against you we have come," the envoys said, according to the *Chronicle of Novgorod.* "We have come sent by God against our serfs, and our horse-herds, the pagan Polovets men." (Polovets was a common Russian term for the Qipchaqs.) The Mongols asked the Russians to chase out the Qipchaqs and seize their goods. The kniazia answered by killing the Mongol ambassadors. Now the Mongols could declare war, having satisfied their moral code. They sent a second delegation. "Since you have listened to the Polovets men, and have killed all our envoys, and are coming against us, come then, but we have not touched you," the delegation announced. "Let God judge all."[17]

Soon after, around mid-May, Mstislav Mstislavich forded the Dnieper with a detachment of a thousand men, including Qipchaq warriors, and ran into a small Mongol outpost under what was likely Jebe's command. The outnumbered Mongol warriors had to flee into the steppe. To protect their commander, they hid him inside a Qipchaq burial mound. Yet he was caught by the enemy, and Mstislav allowed the Qipchaq warriors to execute him. If the commander was indeed Jebe, it was an inglorious end for a warrior of his stature. At this stage Russians and Qipchaqs were confident of imminent victory, but they would soon be thwarted, even without Jebe to defeat them.[18]

The decisive battle was fought on May 31, 1223. Sources do not say exactly where, but we know for certain that the Mongols chose a spot somewhere on the banks of the narrow Kalka River, north of the Azov Sea, and drove the kniazia there. The Mongols suddenly attacked while the Russian vanguard was crossing the river, precluding an organized defense.[19] The Russians suffered massive losses, including a number of *voivodes*—senior military officers—and princes. Among those lost was the kniaz of Kiev, whom the Mongols executed. The kniaz of Chernigov and his son died while retreating. The withdrawal was slow and painful, and the Kievans panicked. Rich families and merchants took their belongings on boats and abandoned their houses. Ibn al-Athīr writes that some of the refugees reached "the lands of Islam"—most likely a reference to the Seljuq Sulantate. The Qipchaqs retreated by the thousands "to the woods and the mountain tops, abandoning their lands." The *Chronicle of Novgorod* blames the Qipchaqs for the defeat, claiming that their advance cavalry withdrew too early and in great confusion and that the Qipchaqs turned against their Russian allies and killed them for their horses and clothes. In the immediate aftermath of the battle, the Mongols plundered villages all the way up to the Dnieper, where Qipchaq territory ended, before turning to the Volga and onward to the east.[20]

Near the Volga, the Mongols took an opportunity to conquer the Muslim Bulgars, who had a small but old and prosperous kingdom in the region of the modern Tatar city of Kazan. The Bulgars had heard about the Russian and Qipchaq defeat and prepared a new strategy to fight back. The Bulgars grasped that the Mongols excelled at sieges and open battles, so they refused to engage on these terms. Instead they ambushed the Mongols, constantly assaulting and harassing them, and prevented them from deploying their cavalry. Having already lost thousands of men, Sübötei's forces were quickly spent. They gave up and turned away down the east bank of the Volga River.[21] In fall 1223 or early 1224, the Westward headed back to Mongolia, a march of thousands of miles. Along the way, they merged with Jochi's mass army. Strengthened by these fresh forces, they crossed the Ural region, met with their "old friends" the Qangli, and killed their chief, the Ölberli khan.[22]

Popular histories, and global histories touching on the Mongols, often see the Westward's mission as an unqualified success. The Mongols covered more than 5,000 miles, apparently winning battle after battle, effortlessly. However, specialists paying close attention to the original sources have shown that the campaign was in fact frustrating and hard-fought. It lasted three and a half years, and the Mongols often met strong local resistance. They lost many men—according to Ibn al-Athīr, only 4,000 of the Westward survived. The Volga Bulgars not only repulsed them but also found a weakness in Mongol warfare—a weakness that other enemies would later exploit. And the Mongols gained only short-term surrenders; not a single defeated enemy agreed to pay tribute. The Westward severely disrupted the fragile economic and political balance of the Caucasus, Crimea, and southern Russia, but as soon as the warriors turned their backs, "the route[s] opened up and goods were exported as before," Ibn al-Athīr reports. In 1224 trade had already restarted and reconstruction commenced throughout the Georgian kingdom, the Qipchaq steppe, and the Russian villages that had been sites of combat.[23]

The Deaths of Jochi and Chinggis

When the returning army reached Mongolia, a great quriltai assembled and celebrated the success of Sübötei and his men. But Jochi was not there; he went instead to his camp on the Irtysh River. He was ordered to continue the pursuit of the Qipchaqs, yet he did not prepare any new campaigns. When his father asked him to come to Mongolia to explain his defiant attitude, Jochi said he did not feel well and begged to be excused. No one in Chinggis's entourage believed Jochi. Someone passing by his tents reported that he was, in fact, leisurely hunting during the time of the proposed meeting. Finally, in winter 1226–1227, Chinggis himself, accompanied by his other sons Chagatay and Ögödei, took off to summon Jochi. But Jochi died in February 1227, before his family reached him. He was less than forty years old. According to Rashīd al-Dīn, Chinggis "was sorely grief-stricken" when he heard the news of Jochi's death, all the more so as "the report" of Jochi's insubordination "was proven false and it was established that Jochi had been ill of the time and not on the hunting field." Crippled with guilt, Chinggis designated a new heir to the ulus of his eldest: Jochi's son Batu would take over.[24]

Chinggis followed Jochi into the afterlife. Chinggis's death came in the context of renewed war with longtime enemies. While the Westward was fighting in the Qipchaq steppe, the Mongols were also fighting in the east, against the Jin. The Tangut, reluctant allies of the Mongols since their 1210 pact, were supposed to send siege experts to aid the khan's army. But the Tangut reneged on their promise. In 1223 Muqali, the Mongol commander in the war with the Jin, died in battle, and the Tangut withdrew. In 1225 the Tangut even signed a separate peace with the Jin.

In autumn 1226 Chinggis Khan marshaled his armies to punish the Tangut. But he was struggling at the time from a bad wound—perhaps one he had suffered during a hunt two years earlier. His sons and commanders wanted a temporary withdrawal, arguing that the Tangut would wait. "They won't leave, carrying off their towns with pounded-earth walls," Chinggis's advisors told him. "They won't leave, abandoning their permanent camps." Yet Chinggis decided not to delay his revenge. He ordered his armies to fight and died while they were attacking the enemy. The Tangut surrendered, but the Mongols plundered, enslaved, and killed them with no mercy. It is not clear exactly how Chinggis's life ended, but the Mongols made the Tangut pay for the death of their khan.[25]

After Chinggis Khan died, large-scale military operations were suspended for nearly two years. In 1229, at the quriltai enthroning Ögödei as Chinggis's successor, the attendees agreed to carry out a new onslaught on the Qipchaq steppe. But for the time being, only scout troops set out. The mass army would follow after the end of the Jin campaign, which was still in full swing. The pacification of northern China did not evolve as expected, and the Jin posed a continuous threat. Sübötei himself was sent to fight. Chinggis Khan's youngest son, Tolui, died on the Jin front in 1232, before the Jin definitively succumbed two years later.[26]

The Qipchaq Guerrillas

The scouts Ögödei sent west after his 1229 enthronement learned that a new threat was rising among the Qipchaqs. His name was Bashman. A chieftain and member of the Ölberli elite, Bashman garnered the support of warriors and the wider public. From his territory along the Akhtuba River, an eastern branch of the lower Volga, he built a loose alliance with Alans, Russians, Bulgars, Bashkirs, and others committed to beating back the Mongols.

When the Mongol scouts arrived in the Volga region, Bashman and his supporters began to attack their positions. The Mongols failed to force the Qipchaqs to face them in open battle and therefore could not use their cavalrymen properly. Bashman was more mobile than the Mongols and he knew the terrain better. He also had mastered the techniques of guerrilla warfare that the Bulgars had successfully implemented some years earlier. According to the Persian historian Juvaynī, who provided one of the key sources on the Mongols,

> having no lair or hiding-place to serve as a base, [Bashman] betook himself every day and night to a different spot. And because of his dog-like nature he would strike wolf-like on every side and make off with something. Gradually his evil grew worse and he wrought greater mischief; and wherever the [Mongol] army sought him they could not find him, since he had departed elsewhere. Most of his refuges and hiding places were on the banks of the [Volga]. Here he would lie concealed in the forests, from which he would spring out like a jackal, seize hold of something, and hide himself once again.[27]

Bashman became a local hero and more people joined his forces. This alarmed the Mongols because Bashman's actions prevented any new operations in the west. The lower Volga was a crucial nexus on the route to Europe; the Mongols needed to secure direct land communication between Qaraqorum, their newly established seat of power, and the western steppe, and Bashman was in the way. What is more, under Bashman, the Qipchaqs were in a position to create mass unrest. Chinese sources report that the Mongols responded by putting massive forces into a new campaign to annihilate the "rebels" out of fear that "an uncontrollable fight might break out in the steppe." After a quriltai on the banks of the Onon River in 1235, the Mongols launched large-scale operations to control the Volga-Ural region and the basin of the Volga. They decided that their first targets would be Bashman and the Bulgars whom the Mongols had earlier failed to conquer. The next target would be the Russian principalities. The Mongols had kept their sights on the kniazia since the Westward mission. The Mongols knew the Russians could be dangerous, though nothing like the Qipchaqs, who had been reborn from their ashes.[28]

Sübötei, whose knowledge of the Volga region and whose expertise in Qipchaq warfare were indisputable, led the shock troops. He was probably the strategist behind the whole campaign, although he was not the high commander of the army. That job fell to Batu. Princes from the four branches of the golden lineage assisted him. By 1236 Sübötei had killed or enslaved Bashman's followers, wives, and children, but Bashman himself was still at large. He took refuge on an island in the Volga estuary and disappeared. Möngke, Batu's cousin, took charge of the search. His Mongols built 200 boats and scoured the river. The search party interrogated locals on both banks until they found an old woman left behind in a hastily abandoned camp. She gave up her chief's lair, and soon enough the Mongols had captured him. Once caught, Bashman asked Möngke to carry out his execution, but the Mongol refused. Instead, he entrusted the task to his brother Böchek as a reward, for Böchek had proven staunchly committed during the chase. Bashman was cut in half, which meant the Mongols were denying him the noble death they usually granted to enemies of high status. In the Mongol belief system, bones symbolized descent through the male line, so Mongol executions typically were carried out by strangulation or another method that left the victim's bones intact. To break bones, as Böchek did Bashman's, meant destroying an entire lineage.[29]

At roughly the same time Möngke and Böchek were hunting Bashman, Sübötei was focused on the Bulgars and other remaining unconquered groups of the lower Volga. He had a large force at his disposal, far larger than he had commanded in the Westward. Drawing on intelligence gathered during the Westward's last mission in the region, Sübötei marched against Biliar, Suwar, and Bulgar, the key settlements of the area. This time the inhabitants could not repulse the Mongols and offered to surrender. Some locals fled to the northern forests or to Russian cities and villages; those who stayed were soon forced to work and fight for the Mongols. In 1236 Sübötei stormed Saqsin and Summerkent, close to the Volga delta, and gained control of the Bashkirs' land, also known as Great Hungaria.[30]

Over the subsequent years, the Mongols brutally subjugated the Qipchaqs. Many were taken to Mongolia and reduced to bo'ol. The Qipchaq herders who stayed in the lower Volga were required to surrender to Mongol masters if they were to survive in what had once been their land. According to the *Secret History,* Sübötei created a special force of Qipchaqs, Merkit, Naiman, and Bulgars to watch over the peoples of the Volga. They shaped the first *tammachi* of the western territories. Tammachi were permanent or semi-permanent garrison troops who dealt with revolts, protected tax collectors, and sometimes collected taxes themselves. They were more than an army; they established a preliminary administrative and coercive structure that paved the way for long-term occupation. Just as the keshig was the key institution for of governance, the tammachi was the key institution of settlement.[31]

Diverse fates awaited the Qipchaqs who escaped Mongol domination. Several hundred Qipchaq families left the lower Volga, crossed the Black Sea, and resettled in Central Europe, where they were welcomed by Hungarians and European Bulgars. The rulers of these groups had old ties with the Qipchaq elite. However, most Qipchaq refugees ended up in captivity and served as domestic slaves in Europe or as mamluks in the Ayyubid armies. Alans, Bashkirs, and Volga Bulgars had similar experiences. After nearly two decades of warfare, the Qipchaq steppes and the Volga-Ural region had fallen into Mongol hands. Only the Russians remained in resistance.[32]

Into the Russian Lands, the Snow, and the Mud

Batu amassed the army south of Ryazan principality, near the modern Russian city of Voronezh. From there, the Mongols launched exploratory and raiding expeditions. It was the cold season; in the Russian lands warfare was on hold and the kniazia were not prepared to face Batu's onslaught. According to Friar Julian, a Hungarian of the Dominican Order who encountered the Mongols in his eastward travels, the Mongols "waited for ground, rivers, and marshes to freeze" and then attacked.[33] In December 1237, the submission of the Russians began with the conquest of the fortified city of Ryazan. Its inhabitants had refused the Mongols' demand for a tithe: one-tenth of everything, including people. The next target—the neighboring city of Vladimir, the capital of Vladimir-Suzdal and seat of the grand prince—was in Batu's sight.

The Mongols had combined their forces and refined their war plans. Alongside Sübötei, who developed strategy, important members of the golden lineage were involved. Among them were Batu's brothers Orda, Berke, and Shiban and his uncles Güyük and Möngke. Their wives, children, and household servants took part in the campaign. They had thousands of horses and camels, as well as huge siege engines built for the occasion.[34] The Mongols targeted not places but rulers such as Grand Prince Iurii Vsevolodovich, who was the most powerful kniaz of northeastern Rus. He did not repeat the mistake the Russians had made fifteen years earlier. He did not mock the Mongol envoys when they came with their "submit-or-die" letter, and he did not gather massive forces to beat the Mongols in a single open battle, as the Russians had tried at the Kalka River. Instead the grand prince tried to negotiate. But other kniazia, and members of his family, wanted to resist.

In the same winter, a fight erupted near Kolomna, another fortress in Ryazan principality. Mongols and Russians had run into each other on the border between Ryazan and Vladimir-Suzdal. It appears a Mongol contingent chasing Russian troops from Ryazan fell on reinforcements sent from Vladimir and the small town of Moscow. The Mongols were led by Kölgen, the fifth son of Chinggis Khan. The Kolomna clash was blindly violent. Neither side showed mercy. Many senior people were killed, including the voivode of Vladimir, the son of the kniaz of Ryazan, and Kölgen. The battle was not only one of the bloodiest of the 1230s campaign against the Russians, but it also determined the fate of that campaign. The lack of a coordinated Russian defense in the northeast precipitated the loss of the military elite of Vladimir-Suzdal, which devastated Russian leadership for the remainder of the war. The death of Kölgen may also explain why the Mongols stormed the entire area afterward, as they considered the shedding of Chinggis Khan's blood a sacrilege that required revenge. In January 1238 the Mongols took control of Kolomna and Moscow, which they burnt before besieging Vladimir in early February.

It took just a few days to capture Vladimir, but Grand Prince Iurii Vsevolodovich escaped to the woods near the Oka River. In early March 1238, the Mongols took him by surprise, apparently bypassing

Lithograph inspired by medieval Russian miniatures showing Batu's conquest of the Russian principalities. (Private Collection © SZ Photo / Bridgeman Images)

his guard posts and attacking where the Russians least expected it. The Mongols decapitated the grand prince, a practice they had used before: the sight of a ruler's head terrorized his people and accelerated their submission. A decapitated head was also proof of death in a world where false rumors, about the dead and the living, were common.[35]

After Vladimir came more cities, including Rostov, Jaroslavl, and Tver. All fell into Mongol hands.[36] The Mongols campaigned in the north over two successive winters. After defeating the leadership in the northeast, they moved on to the northwest. They gained some ground, but local resistance and muddy terrain forced them to pull back and abandon their plans for Novgorod, which they left untouched. In several places the inhabitants burned their own lands and villages to stop the enemy. Starvation spread in the whole area. This contributed to the determination of the Mongols to move southward in the direction of the Dnieper River, where Kiev lay.

In winter 1240–1241, it was the Kievan prince's turn to abandon his subjects rather than face the Mongol onslaught. After receiving Möngke's envoys, and perhaps ordering their murder, he fled to Hungary with his family and boyars—the aristocracy of old Rus. No leader stood up to organize the defense of Kiev nor southern Rus in general. A source reports that the Mongol armies made an impressively loud arrival in Kiev, such that one could hear nothing above the roar of their horses, camels, and carts. In November or December 1240, the Mongols captured the city in a few days and left it half destroyed. From there they captured the westernmost principalities, including Galicia, whose kniaz had already left for Hungary. In December the Mongols stormed the harbor of Sudak again.[37]

Modern historians estimate that no more than 50,000 warriors attacked the Rus. On the other side, Vladimir-Suzdal, the biggest principality, had around one million inhabitants and a force of a hundred thousand warriors. The Mongols knew they were outnumbered, but the Russians did not take advantage of their numerical superiority because the Russians thought it was themselves who lacked numbers. Their poor intelligence led them to believe there were hundreds of thousands of Mongols. What is more, the Mongols knew where to find the Russians—they had counted the Russian towns and villages, evaluating the size of each—but the Russians never grasped where the Mongols hid and how they moved.[38]

In the principalities of Ryazan, Vladimir-Suzdal, Kiev, Volhynia, and Galicia, the Mongols followed a similar strategy. They attacked the villages, lesser cities, and small fortifications before besieging the local capital. Once they had destroyed the outlying places that helped to supply the capital, the city could not hold out for long. Meanwhile the Mongols helped themselves to the food, fodder, and labor they prevented from reaching the capital. After they drained a region of its main resources, they moved on to their next target.[39]

The Mongol season of warfare was the opposite of the Russian. Russian local armies consisted mainly of peasant conscripts, who were available to fight in spring and early summer. It was most unusual to conduct warfare in fall and winter because in September and October, peasants scattered for harvesting and other field and farm work, and they often stayed indoors during the coldest months. No Russians expected to do combat at this time of the year. The Mongols, by contrast, retreated to the steppe in late spring and summer for the milking season and went to war during the cold season. This explains why Mongols always had the initiative over the Russians and other peoples of the Volga region. The Mongols successfully imposed on the Russians a seasonality that destroyed their agricultural system.[40]

The Russians presented intermittent but harsh resistance. For example, the inhabitants of Kozelsk, a small town on a hill near the Zhizdra River, were able temporarily to resist the Mongols by exploiting the terrain: the ground around the town was soaked from river runoff, the swamps, and melting snow. The Mongols could not bring siege engines close to the city walls, which gave the Kozelsk inhabitants an opportunity to destroy the Mongol catapults. Some 4,000 Mongols were killed. After the Mongols finally captured Kozelsk, they were not able to find their dead in the rubble and the mud. Thus did the Mongols learn to call Kozelsk "the evil city." In four years of fighting in the lower Volga and the north, Batu lost several commanders and thousands of warriors beyond those killed at Kozelsk. But the Russians had no coordination and too many serious leadership problems to stop the larger Mongol war machine.[41]

During the Russian campaign, the Mongols gained control of some twenty cities. They did not destroy all these cities. Rostov, for example, was spared after its inhabitants accepted peace terms. Kiev, on the other hand, rejected an identical offer and was sacked. No city held out longer than Kozelsk, which lasted seven weeks or so against the siege. But most Russian towns resisted for no more than a few days. The Mongols were experts in siege warfare and had accumulated even more experi-

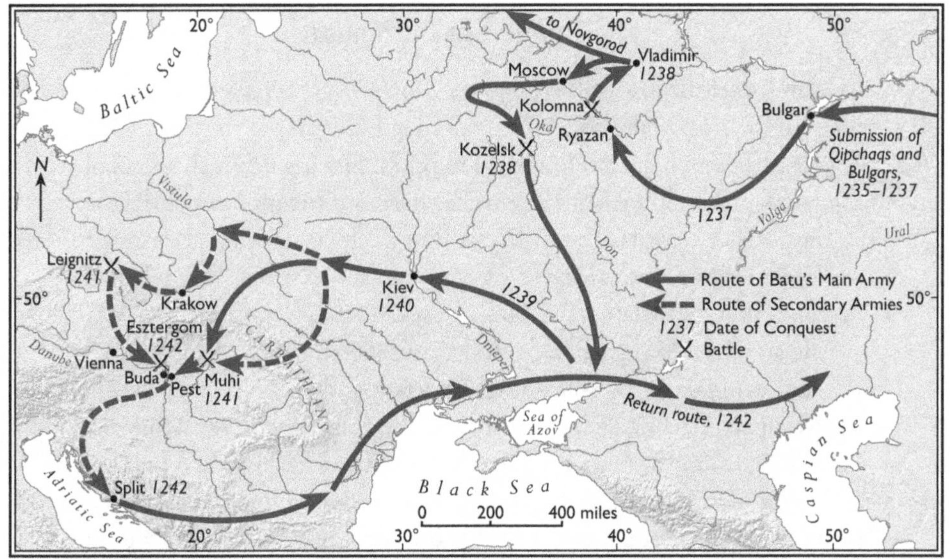

Batu's campaigns against the Qipchaqs, Russians, Bulgars, and Hungarians, 1235–1242.

ence throughout their recent operations against the Jin. They had taken military engineers with them, most importantly Xili Gambu, a Tangut general who seconded Batu. The Russians appeared helpless when faced with siege engines they had never seen before. Adapting Chinese technology, the Mongols built catapults twenty-six feet high and weighing five tons. Such a machine could throw a stone heavier than 132 pounds up to 164 yards. For a commander like Sübötei, who had conquered more than thirty stone and brick fortresses in China, Central Asia, and Iran, the wooden and earthen walls of Russian cities presented no real challenge.[42]

What *was* challenging for the Mongols was the terrain. Muddy and swampy grounds limited their operations to the coldest months and restricted their range of activity. They could move quickly on frozen soil and rivers, but with the snow already melting in March, their armored troops and heavy siege engines got stuck in the mire. Snowmelt also flooded the pastureland on which Mongol armies relied to feed their animals. This explains why it took them four winters to subjugate the kniazia and why Batu and Subötei departed suddenly for Europe in 1241, leaving unfulfilled their plans for Novgorod and other targets.[43]

The Hungarian Campaign

In March 1241 the Mongols crossed the Dnieper with as many as 130,000 mounted warriors, entering the Kingdom of Hungary. At the time, King Béla was then in his royal residence of Buda. Having heard the news of the Mongol attack against the Rus, he had sent his military chief, the count palatine, to guard the Verecke Pass in the Carpathians. It didn't work. King Béla was informed by a messenger that the Mongols had invaded, that the palatine's army had been unable to stop them.[44]

The attack on Hungary was a direct consequence of the Qipchaq and Russian campaigns. By welcoming Qipchaq and Russian elites fleeing the Mongols, Béla had come to embody the resistance to the Mongols. He was not, like Bashman, an active foe. But in 1239 he had granted asylum to Köten, the Qipchaq khan, and his men. Doing so increased Béla's personal prestige, as the Qichpaq were converted to Christianity under his patronage, an act of proselytism that was praised by the pope. Absorbing the Qipchaqs also bolstered Béla's military power, for the newcomers were integrated into his army. They constituted an efficient cavalry that responded directly to Béla, independently of the feudal barons, who were sometimes reluctant to commit their own forces to the king's causes. But the costs were high. Not only did Béla's hospitality earn him the Mongols' enmity but it also created internal tension, as Hungarians did not easily accept their king's decision to support and protect the Qipchaqs.[45]

The Mongol invasion was a carefully planned affair, befitting Sübötei's strategic acumen. He coordinated five parallel operations across Central and Eastern Europe, against the Czechs, Poles, Germans, and Hungarians. Several armies passed through the Carpathian Mountains simultaneously, along multiple routes: Batu and Sübötei took the Verecke Pass into Hungary; Orda took the northwest route into Poland; and the other armies advanced from the south and southeast. But the target all along was Hungary. The operation was designed to surround Béla's forces like wild animals caught in a battue hunt.[46]

Béla realized that he faced a formidable foe, but he had immense difficulty responding. He urged his barons and bishops to assemble their armies in Pest, a big city and a major crossing point on the Danube. But the barons and bishops showed no haste. According to Master Roger, an Italian prelate who witnessed the invasion, they instead dithered over what they thought was a mere "rumor." And Béla's own defensive efforts proved largely ineffective at slowing the invaders. According to Archdeacon Thomas of Split, who would soon experience a Mongol siege himself, King Béla "had long barricades built, blocking with felled trees all the places where transit seemed easiest." But Batu sent scout troops with axes to demolish the defensive works, "removing all from the places of entry." The Mongols even set about "cutting down forests" and "laying roads" to clear and ease their path.[47]

The Mongols quickly gained ground, and soon small Mongol groups were appearing around Pest and harassing villages throughout the region. Béla did not immediately react. In fact, he forbade his men to respond to the enemy provocations. He knew that the Mongols, like other steppe nomads, excelled at luring enemies into traps and figured that the Mongol contingents were baiting his forces. Yet, demonstrating the serious lack of coordination that hampered the whole Hungarian defense, the Archbishop of Kalocsa did not comply with Béla's nonengagement order. The archbishop fell for the Mongol deception and lost many of his forces as a result.

It was clear that King Béla was unable to fully mobilize Hungary's forces.[48] Lacking sufficient internal support, he appealed to his neighbors for help but found himself isolated—just as the Mongols had planned. King Wenceslas of Bohemia and Duke Henry of Silesia, Kraków, and Greater Poland were already fighting the Mongols in their own territories and could provide no aid. Only the Austrian Duke Frederick of Babenberg, Béla's cousin, committed reinforcements. But Frederick arrived in Pest with a small escort, for it was impossible to mobilize a large army on such short notice. Besides, Frederick's intentions were ambiguous. After killing a "Tatar," capturing another one, and inciting an anti-Qipchaq mob, he left Pest before any battles took place. Later, when Béla was defeated and in flight from the Mongols, Frederick tried to extort money from his cousin in exchange for sheltering him.[49]

Worse still, in the course of war preparations, King Béla lost his strongest ally: Khan Köten and his Qipchaq riders. Unlike many of the Hungarian nobility, the khan had responded to Béla's call, ordering his horsemen to prepare for war. They were a formidable force; according to Master Roger, the Qipchaqs in Hungary numbered 40,000, of whom a majority would have been warriors. Modern scholarship cannot confirm the accuracy of that number, but what is clear is that the Qipchaq population was large enough to get on the locals' nerves. Hungarian villagers feared that the nomads' "enormous amount of cattle" damaged "the pastures, crops, gardens, orchards, copses, vineyards." And the barons felt threatened by the Qipchaq warriors, whose power they could not control. To appease the anger against the Qipchaqs, Béla scattered them throughout the Hungarian plain and moved Köten first to his palace in Buda and then to Pest. This way he could show the Hungarian people that he was keeping a close eye on the khan. He could also shelter Köten from unruly Hungarians who blamed him for the Mongol invasion—after all, it was the Qipchaqs the Mongols had come for. But Béla's efforts came to naught. When the Mongols approached Pest, a crowd of Hungarians forced their way into the palace and killed Köten, his family, and retinue. In the countryside, too, Hungarians and Germans turned against the Qipchaqs; in the eyes of these Europeans, Qipchaqs and Mongols were one and the same. And yet only Köten's horsemen could have stopped the Mongols. The Qipchaq warriors who were supposed to fight on the Hungarian side left for Bulgaria, destroying what they could in their path.[50]

In spring 1241 the Mongols defeated the Germans, Polish, and Hungarians in two key encounters that took place in Poland and Hungary almost concurrently. On April 9 Orda's army demolished Duke Henry and his German and Polish cavalry at Leignitz (Legnica). Two days later, 420 miles southeast of Leignitz, Batu's and Sübötei's armies confronted King Béla at the River Sajó in the Plain of Muhi. Despite all the mishaps so far, the Hungarians were in a good position. They were guarding the only bridge over the river, and they knew they outnumbered the Mongols, whose small Mongol camp could be seen on the other bank of the river. But the Mongols did not need a bridge to cross a river, and they knew how to beat larger armies. The Mongols found fords, crossed them overnight, and fell on the Hungarians. Master Roger writes that, on April 11, 1241, "at dawn, [the Mongols] surrounded the entire royal army and started shooting arrows like a hailstorm." In a few hours, the Mongols captured the bridge and forced the Hungarians to retreat into their own camp, where they were caught as though in a net. Thomas of

Split, who had spoken to eyewitnesses, reported that "the Tatar army completely surrounded the Hungarian camp, as if in a ring-dance. They drew their bows and set about firing arrows everywhere, while others circled the camp and sought to set it on fire." The Mongols allowed panicking Hungarians to flee, deserting the army; the Mongols "opened up among themselves a point of exit where they did not shoot," Master Roger reported. A great number of Hungarians rushed into the opening and ran off. The Mongols then methodically destroyed the shrinking remainders of the Hungarian army. Béla himself escaped to a forest, while many of his prelates and warriors drowned in a nearby swamp with the Mongols on their heels.[51]

After their defeat, some of the Hungarian military elite fled, while others entrenched themselves in Pest. But it was only a matter of days before the Mongols arrived. Béla's younger brother Coloman announced that "everyone should look out for himself" and retreated beyond the Danube. Like the overwhelming majority of Hungarian cities east of the Danube, Pest lacked stone walls; its earthen barricades would never withstand the Mongol catapults.[52]

In January or February 1242, the Mongols crossed the frozen Danube, entered western Hungary, and stormed the royal seat of Esztergom with some thirty siege engines. From there they advanced into Austria and Dalmatia in pursuit of King Béla, who was hiding on the Dalmatian coast, in Split. But suddenly, in March, the Mongols halted. Batu and Sübötei ordered all the forces to withdraw—an incomprehensible decision from the standpoint of the locals, who could see that the Mongols were preparing for a lengthy occupation. Some Split residents had even begun to collaborate with the Mongols, assuming the nomads would be their new masters.[53] What the Hungarians, Poles, Croatians, and other Europeans did not know was that in December 1241, Great Khan Ögödei had died. The members of the golden lineage, as well as the army commanders, needed to go back east to join a quriltai and decide on Ögödei's successor. Friar Plano Carpini, a papal envoy who traveled through Central and Eastern Europe and Central Asia on his way to Qaraqorum in 1246, suggested that this was the main reason for the Mongols' withdrawal from Hungary.[54]

Recent scholarship has offered additional explanations for the sudden retreat. One factor may have been resource scarcity in Hungary. Several

White Sea
Baltic Sea
Novgorod
RUSSIAN
Moscow
PRINCIPALITIES
Kiev
POLAND
HUNGARY
Danube
BULGARIA
BYZANTIUM
Black Sea
CAUCASUS
SELJUQ
ANATOLIA
Tabriz
Rayy
Tigris
Euphrates
Mediterranean Sea
MAMLUKS
Nile
Red Sea
The Gulf
Arabian Sea
ULUS OF JOC
MONGO
Bulgar
Ural
Volga
Sarai
Caspian Sea
Aral Sea
Syr-Daria
Jand
KHWAREZM
Amu-Daria
Otr
Bukhara
Samar
Balkh
Mongol Empire, c. 1250
Conquered by c. 1260
Ulus of Jochi, c. 1250
CAUCASUS Area of Shared Revenue
POLAND Other Power
0
500
100
20°
40°
60°

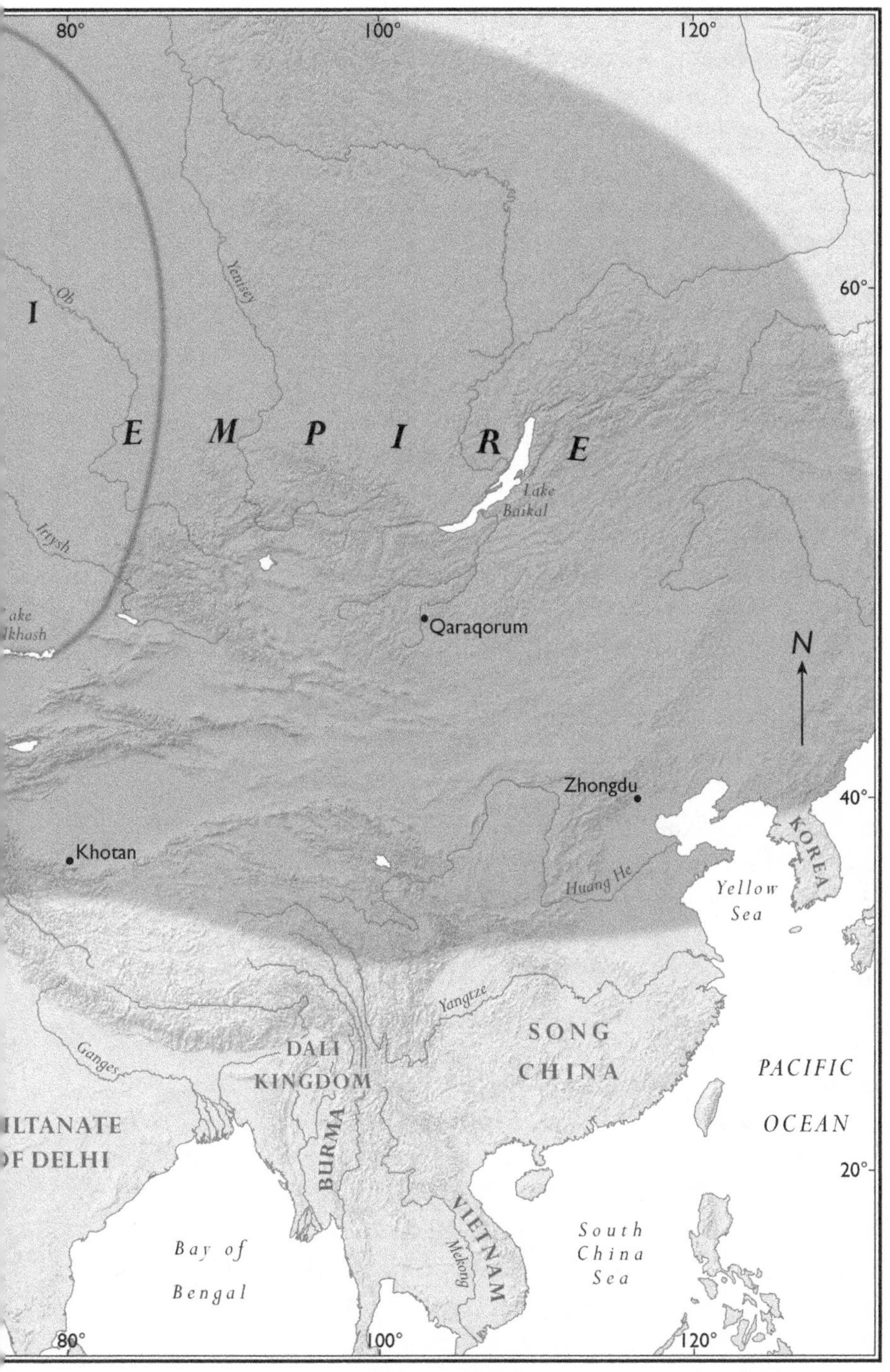

By the mid-1200s, the Mongol Empire covered nearly half of Eurasia.

modern historians argue that the Hungarian plain could not sustain the Mongols' numerous camps, herds, and cavalry horses. Notably, the Mongols, who tried as hard as possible to be self-sufficient, were obliged to ask locals for provisions for troops and animals.[55] The winter of 1241–1242 was particularly cold. While the freezing temperatures helped the Mongols cross the Danube, heavy snowfall reduced their mobility elsewhere and prevented them from accessing a number of cities and castles. The harsh winter was followed by heavy rainfall, which caused harvest failure, widespread famine, and rapid depopulation. Villages that had supported the Mongol occupation since spring 1241 could no longer do so. In Dalmatia the thaw turned the ground into mud fields, forcing the Mongols to retreat because they could not pull their siege engines and carts.

Another factor explaining the Mongols' retreat was likely the military challenge of the campaign. In western Hungary, at least twelve cities and castles successfully repelled Mongol assaults. When the Mongols left after two months, the region was almost untouched and reconstruction had already begun in Transylvania where, according to Master Roger, "many people had survived" Mongol assaults. The Mongols had lost a significant number of men and faced an acute leadership problem, as Batu and Sübötei disagreed with each other on strategy. According to Sübötei's biographers, Batu made several poor decisions during the battle of Muhi and even wanted to abort the operation.[56] But the tension between Batu and Sübötei went beyond strategy; it also reflected discord between the branches of the golden lineage. Sübötei's biographers were pro-Toluid; they sought to paint the Jochids in a bad light, for in the 1240s relations between the Jochids and the other branches of the golden lineage were growing more strained, as the powerful Jochids grew to resent the authority the Ögödeids exercised over them. The withdrawal from Hungary reflected the familial tension: Batu went home to the Qipchaq steppe and Sübötei to Qaraqorum. In 1246, after a five-year regency under Ögödei's chief wife, their eldest son Güyük was elected great khan. Sübötei joined the election quriltai and supported Güyük, but Batu refused to attend. He stayed in the Qipchaq steppe to consolidate his horde and would never return to Mongolia.

Home in the Qipchaq Steppe

The Qipchaq integration into the Mongol Empire had started around 1210 and was completed in 1240. The conquest had led the Mongols to Hungary, the western end of the Eurasian steppe belt that forms a grass highway between East Asia and Europe. It was no accident that the Chinese called the Mongols' military offensive of 1236–1241 the Qipchaq campaign: the primary goal of Chinggis Khan and his sons was to subjugate the steppe nomads, not to annihilate the "civilization" of the sedentary peoples—Russians, Poles, Hungarians, and others. The Mongols wanted to inhabit, control, and populate the steppe; their onslaught against the Russians and their invasions of Hungary, Poland, and Austria were side effects of a war among nomads. The Russians and Hungarians had allied with the Qipchaqs, and the Mongols made them pay for their choice.[57]

Historians have pointed to a number of advantages that enabled the conquest. One is the Mongol mastery of cold-weather warfare, whereby they fought when their enemies were unprepared and, when their enemies were better prepared, retreated to distant and well-defended camps to recover. The western steppe was not ideally suited to this strategy; the early thaw severely compromised the Mongols' military efficiency. But they adapted to climactic differences, moved to more hospitable terrain, and modified their goals to ensure that they focused on the key, winnable battles. In doing so, they constrained their enemies to participate in a new form of warfare for which the Mongols had set the rules.[58]

The Mongols not only disturbed their enemies' seasonality, but they also forced their enemies to rush into poor strategic decisions, as they did at the battle of the Kalka River, in Vladimir, and in Muhi. The Mongols' tempo was fast and tight, catching sedentary people off guard. While Central and Eastern European lords spent months mobilizing their forces of peasant farmers, the Mongols were continuously conscripting and mobilizing. Throughout their campaigns, the Mongols forcefully brought people in their ranks. Finally, the heavy and slow European knights and armies were no match for mounted archers and siege experts equipped with the most technologically advanced weapons. The ability to attack and withdraw in a flash became the hallmark of

Mongol strikes. Experienced commanders like Sübötei were able to take instant decisions, including his timely retreats from Russia and Hungary.

Mongol strategy was effective in part because it paired large-scale military operations with pastoral economics, combat acumen with effective resource management. In all their military campaigns, including the Westward operations, warriors brought along their families, tents, baggage, and herds. Servants, workers, herders, women, and children all took an active part in daily logistics and made the final conquest of the Qipchaq steppe possible.[59]

The Qipchaq campaign exemplifies the political ambition so often missing from conventional wisdom concerning the Mongols. The Mongols did not fight in the western steppe for the sake of fighting, nor of plunder, nor even of revenge, although revenge was an element of their motivation in taking on the Qipchaqs. More important was the effort to colonize the entire steppe belt. Batu accomplished his father Jochi's unfinished task and fully integrated the Qipchaq territories into the Mongol Empire. With this conquest, the Mongols dominated the nomadic world; there was no more steppe to conquer. In a short time, the descendants of Jochi would establish a durable and powerful political community in the western steppe. That community was the Horde, an independent actor on the world stage that drew on Mongol traditions but developed its own ways of life and governing institutions and took a foremost role in the future of its Russian, European, and Mediterranean neighbors.

3

New Hordes

Batu was the leader of the *ak orda,* the white horde, and his brother Orda led the *kök orda*—the blue horde. The colors marked the two princely hordes that dominated the others. The *Chinggis Nāme,* a sixteenth-century collection of oral narratives on the history of the Jochid ulus, records that the natives of the Volga-Ural still remembered the political birth of the ak orda and kök orda. The locals said that Ejen Orda (Lord Orda) and Sayin Batu (Batu the Good) were the sons of Jochi, born of a woman of the Mongol elite. When Jochi died, Orda wanted Batu to sit on the throne of their father, although Batu was the younger brother. But Batu could not simply agree to ignore the birth order: permission was needed from their grandfather, Chinggis Khan. The two heirs, accompanied by seventeen of their brothers, brought the case to Chinggis and the begs. The *Chinggis Nāme* notes that the *yasa,* the khan's law and teaching, "gave Sayin khan the right wing with the regions surrounding the River Itil [Volga], and he gave Ejen the left wing with the regions near the Syr Daria River." The natives said that Chinggis reserved for Batu the best share, but Batu could not accept his inheritance before it was confirmed by a quriltai. But what was Orda's motivation? This the people could not explain.[1]

Although the stories circulating among the people of the lower Volga probably do not get every detail right, they do capture the essential point that Jochi had left no indication of how his succession should proceed, which meant that his father would have to settle the matter. Chinggis's decision reflected both tradition and iconoclasm. On the one hand, he followed tradition by selecting an heir from the two sons of Jochi's Qonggirad wives; all Jochi's other sons were by different mothers. On the other hand, Chinggis's decision went against the principle of seniority, which created political tension between Batu, Orda, and their followers. Jochi's succession became a major turning point, as it split his horde in two. Batu assumed military and political leadership, but Jochi's warriors were divided between the two brothers. Batu and Orda parted to avoid an internecine war, Batu pursuing independence and Orda remaining closely tethered to the Mongol center. When necessary, steppe peoples knew how to split on good terms and thereby prevent bloodshed.[2]

Batu benefited from the open-ended territory Chinggis had granted him. The great khans officially recognized that Batu, as the Jochid chief, had a claim on all territories lying beyond the Irtysh River, which, in Batu's view, meant that any land and people of the far northwest belonged to him and his children. This expandability was Batu's great advantage over Orda, who received a huge but bounded territory, with no possibility of enlargement. Orda's territory was surrounded by territory of other Mongols, so he could not move outward without attacking his next-of-kin. Batu, on the other hand, was poised to complete the conquest of the Seljuq Sultanate, the Georgian kingdom, and the numerous principalities of Syria and Iraq.[3]

Orda was the eldest of Chinggis Khan's grandsons, an ambitious and highly esteemed man who had taken active part in the Qipchaq campaign. In 1236 he joined Sübötei in fighting the Bulgars, in 1237 he participated in the siege of Ryazan, and in 1240 he took part in the conquest of Kiev. A few months after taking Kiev, Orda commanded the army that successfully attacked Leignitz. Thus in the decade after Chinggis Khan had chosen Batu, Orda proved his worth on the battlefield. Great Khan Ögödei, Chinggis's successor, seems to have considered Orda the equal of Batu, granting both of them lands in northern China.[4]

But Orda and Batu were not equal in their political leanings. Orda was faithful to Great Khan Ögödei and maintained good relationships with the most powerful members of the golden lineage, while Batu turned away from the empire and instead focused on ulus Jochi. As we saw in the last chapter, Batu refused to go to Qaraqorum after Ögödei died in 1241; Orda, however, was there. Then in 1246, as the regency of Ögödei's khatun was drawing to a close, it was Orda who represented the Horde at Güyük's election quriltai. Not only that, but Orda served an important role at the quriltai. After Ögödei's death, his uncle, Temüge Ochigin, had attempted a coup; during Güyük's enthronement quriltai, Orda was entrusted to investigate Temüge Ochigin's power grab. Orda was assisted by Möngke, who was the eldest son of Tolui and was renowned for having captured and killed the Qipchaq chieftain Bashman. Together Orda and Möngke questioned a number of witnesses and ultimately ordered the execution of their great uncle.

The elevation of Güyük rather than an elder such as Temüge Ochigin—like the elevation of Batu over Orda—reflects the combination of tradition and pragmatism that Chinggis Khan promoted during his rule. As a matter of tradition, the political body of the Mongols constituted two generations: *aqa,* elders, and *ini,* juniors, and the elders were the superiors. This system was modeled on steppe food-sharing customs: during a meal, senior herders were served first. But elders could choose to give their share to the juniors. The same was true of politics. Elders did not necessarily get to make every decision or act with impunity, and there was room for power-sharing with juniors. Chinggis had combined respect for seniority with a willingness to break genealogical hierarchy. This, too, was a steppe tradition. Under the Türks, contenders to the throne could yield their claims, thereby legitimating the rule of their juniors and demonstrating that seniority alone did not dictate politics. Orda participated in this tradition, according to early sources, when he "gave his consent to Batu's becoming ruler and seated him on his father's throne." By providing avenues for claimants to withdraw and accede to their younger brothers, Chinggis and other steppe rulers sought to prevent fratricide and the wider conflicts that could result.[5]

To better promote peaceful transfers of power, newly enthroned khans made overt demonstrations of humility, while the elites established their consensus surrounding the enthronement. The sources contain vivid and extensive descriptions of Güyük's enthronement, which emphasize this performance of harmony. Rashīd al-Dīn's *Compendium of Chronicles* reports

> after discussion the princes and begs agreed to enthrone Güyük. As was customary, he refused and offered the job to every prince, using his illness and weak constitution as an excuse. After the commanders insisted, he said, "I will accept on condition that henceforth the emperorship remain among my offspring." All agreed to this and gave *möchälgäs* [written pledges], saying, "So long as there remains of your progeny a piece of flesh a dog wouldn't take if it were wrapped in fat and a cow wouldn't accept if it were wrapped in grass, we will give the khanate to no other." Then a shaman's pole was erected, the princes doffed their hats, loosened their belts, and sat [Güyük] on the khan's throne.

Rashīd al-Dīn describes a similar process at Ögödei's enthronement, with his brothers rejecting the supreme power and the new khan declaring that he was carrying out the orders of his family.[6]

These rituals of acceptance and consensus were crucial to Mongol government, for they confirmed that the khan was legitimate and would enjoy authority over his people, including old adversaries. It was essential that the whole political body—meaning the aristocracy, not the entirety of the empire's subjects—assemble and designate a candidate unanimously. The enthronement rites demonstrated subjects' loyalty, while signals of consent, which were carried out before witnesses, made it clear that power had not been seized by force. The candidate offered the throne had to refuse it and claim that others were worthier. Serious additional contenders had to be named. All of them had to publicly declare that they did not want the throne, or that they gave up any claim to it. Only then was the consensual candidate free to accept the position. At least two members of the golden lineage would take him by his arms, carry his belt, and lead him to the throne, where they would seat him. These supporting men were often the chief runners-up to the throne. In the case of Güyük, the supporting men were Orda and a son of Chagatay.[7]

These rituals were not some fig leaf. Under Chinggis's system, genealogical and political hierarchies were important but were not immutable, which meant that competition for power within the golden lineage was real. Any male descendant of Chinggis Khan with a high maternal pedigree had a right to claim the throne, so that there was always a range of legitimate contenders and thus several aspirants had to abandon their claim in order for the group to achieve consensus. One of the purposes of the election and enthronement quriltai was to dramatize the tension among competitors and also definitively salve that tension. Face-to-face unanimity, accompanied by acceptance and withdrawal from competition by the runners-up, were fundamental principles of steppe law.

The Horde's political culture was a hybrid of Chinggis's rules, steppe institutions such as the keshig, quriltai, and tümen, and pragmatic Jochid innovations. Orda represented the elders and Batu the juniors. Together they established a consensus that would hold for generations. Each had his horde and a distinct territory: the Batuids' centered on the lower Volga in the West, and the Ordaids' centered on the middle Syr-Daria and upper Irtysh in the East. Each horde created two different pools of contenders for the Jochid throne, shaping two separate lines of succession. In the early Horde, the descendants of Orda and Batu could not claim each other's assets, territories, or peoples.

When Güyük was elected, Batu and Orda abandoned their right to claim the position of the great khan. Batu was not a contender, because he was absent from the quriltai. After Orda, none of Jochi's descendants would emerge as strong candidates for Chinggis Khan's throne. Yet the Jochids had other means of shaping the political life of the empire, as they would soon demonstrate.

In time the Jochids would come to rule a hugely diverse empire of their own, and they showed a particular genius for ruling a multiethnic population. Like Mongols generally, the Jochids were pragmatic about cultural differences. The Jochids both cajoled and threatened their vassals. Sedentary workers were accommodated and exploited. They enslaved some sedentary subjects and allowed others to go on with the lives they had known, taking part in crafts, warfare, animal husbandry, administration, entertainment, religious services, and medicine. Some conquered peoples experienced little social change—they might not have known they were dominated, except that they had to pay taxes to the Mongols. Other local peoples were thoroughly incorporated into

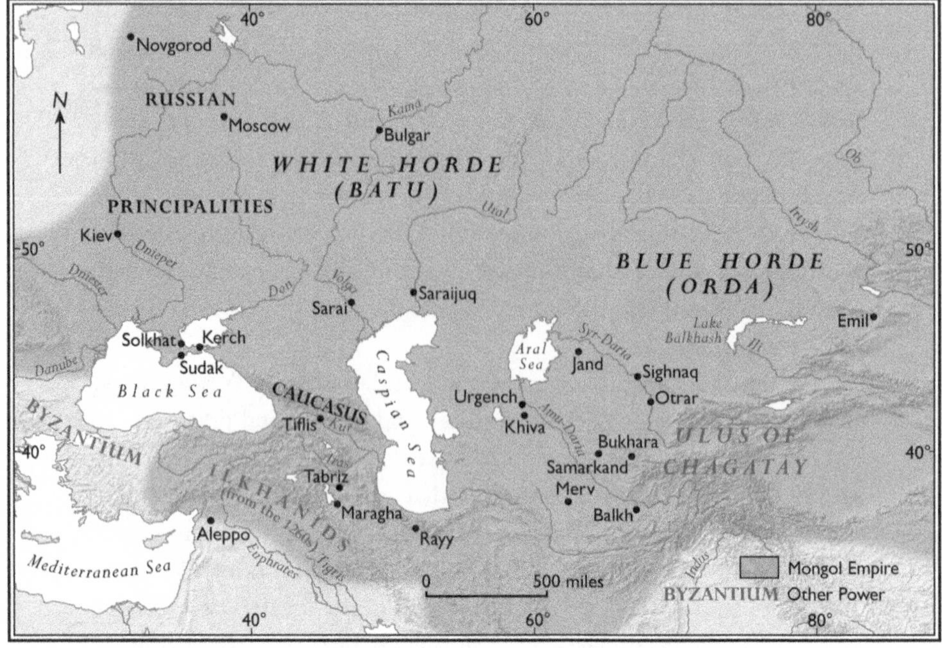

Major divisions of the Horde. The White Horde (Batu) controlled the modern territories of Russia and Ukraine in the west; the Blue Horde (Orda) held the modern territories of Kazakhstan, Uzbekistan, and Turkmenistan in the east.

the hordes, requiring constant effort, organization, coercion, and tolerance. Old loyalties needed to be broken and new ones forged to ensure the stability of the varied and expanding Horde.

The Birth of the Jochids

The great khans' nominations, such as those of Ögödei, Güyük, and later Möngke, reveal that the Mongols had established patterns of succession. The candidates were all Chinggis's descendants though the male line, and they were also grown men whose fathers had died and who needed the support of other members of the elite. As these were the only requirements, a large number of individuals could compete for the throne. Juvaynī explained the rule for ranking: "According to the custom of the Mongols the rank of the children of one father is in proportion to that of their mothers, so that the child of an elder wife is accorded

Decorated bowl showing a Mongol couple (Kashan, Iran, early thirteenth century). The Mongols were the ruling group in Iran at the time this piece was created. (David Collection, Copenhagen, Denmark/ Pictures from History/Bridgeman Images)

greater preference and precedence." In this system, the khatun, the khans' wives, had a crucial role. But what the Mongols meant by "elder wife" was again not a simple matter of seniority.[8]

The status of a khatun was based on multiple factors. One was her date of marriage: the earlier in her husband's life, the higher her rank. A second marriage often gave the first khatun greater responsibilities. The khatun's age was also important: younger wives obeyed older ones. Character and reputation counted, too. And, finally, the wife's personal pedigree and extended social network were of utmost importance. Chinggis Khan considered Qonggirad, Kereit, and Oyirad women the highest-ranking, not least because these peoples were key political allies. His sons carried on the tradition.[9]

In 1237 Ögödei went a step further and established a preferential marriage system between the male and female descendants of Chinggis Khan and the Qonggirad. Imperial chief wives were thus supposed to be of Qonggirad origin, although Ögödei's order was not rigorously followed. The decision probably reflected the fact that Börte, Chinggis Khan's first wife, was the daughter of Dei Sechen, chief of the Qonggirad. A khan had many khatun because marriage was a political partnership, but only few of the women were chief wives, with their own extended households. Secondary wives and concubines often stayed with chief wives who controlled them. The chief wife could be highly influential; she might have her own court of secretaries, treasurers, and traders and sit at the quriltai.[10]

The customs of the Horde, including patterns of succession and marriage, were influenced by those of the old Mongol Empire. The people of Jochi considered the sons of the Qonggirad khatuns the preferred candidates to the throne, and, in the long run, the Qonggirad remained the primary *quda,* marriage partners, of the Jochids. Eight of Jochi's wives are mentioned by name in the old genealogies. Among them, Sarqadu-khatun of the Qonggirad was the eldest and was the mother of Jochi's first son, Orda. One of his younger wives, the daughter of a Qonggirad noyan, gave birth to Batu. These princes would both rule. So would a third, Berke, who was the son of Jochi and Sultan-khatun, a daughter of the Khwarezmian shah. Berke would have to fight harder than his brothers for a place on the Jochid throne, owing to his mother's lower rank.

No record states exactly how many descendants Jochi had in the 1250s, but Rashīd al-Dīn writes that "he had nearly forty sons and innumerable grandsons." The Jochids thus flourished quickly. In only two generations, their house had grown to include several hundred people. They were born of an alliance between the Qonggirad and the Borjigid through the male line of Jochi.[11]

The Shift Men

Thirty years after Chinggis Khan had given 4,000 men to Jochi, the same warriors and their descendants still lived with their families in the

Qipchaq steppe. They were forever attached to the service of the Jochid khans. The Mongols called these loyal servants *keshigten,* the shift men. In the steppe world, there was no khan without a keshig.[12]

Following the structure installed by Chinggis, Batu organized his shift men according to a cycle of twelve days—monkey, hen, dog, pig, mouse, ox, tiger, hare, dragon, snake, horse, and sheep days. Batu had four shifts and four keshig elders, one to lead each shift. Every three days one of Batu's keshig elders took over and commanded the shift men on duty. The four shifts were the stem cells from which the Horde originated; they protected and served the khan by administrating and controlling his people.[13]

The shifts were divided into night guards, day guards, and quiver-bearers. Batu might have had as many as 1,000 night guards, 2,000 quiver-bearers, and 8,000 day guards. Their numbers varied over time, and the Jochid khan had smaller shifts than did the great khan, but both keshigs were organized the same way. All Mongol keshigs, Jochid and otherwise, also included cooks and stewards as well as chancellery members such as secretaries, accountants, and translators. The keshig was neither a warband—a small nomadic force—nor an army. It was the khan's government.

The *kebte'ül,* the night guards, were vital, for they were in charge of the khan's household. Their primary task was to run the supply system that provided the court with food, drinks, games, and music. While the horde was settled down, the night guards watched the *ordo geren,* the khan's tents, and set everything in order. The khan had a giant palace-tent, which the Mongols called the golden tent. Around it was a security perimeter called the *ordo:* a precinct where shift men were stationed and where they ate. The precinct was an independent unit within the camp, with its own rules and administration. The ordo was mobile and followed the khan's migration route. In general, Mongol camps were malleable structures, the layout of which could morph as needed to regulate the circulation of people and goods. In the case of the khan's headquarters, the organization could be altered to permit selective access to particular tents and to court assemblies.[14]

Khans were close to their shift men, some of whom would be known to the khans throughout their lives. An heir apparent—in fact, any important member of the golden lineage—began to recruit his own keshig in his youth. They rode together and engaged in manly activities and would exclude all others from their hunting parties. A new khan would inherit a part of his predecessor's keshig, which he would combine with his own. When a khan died, his night guards normally stayed in his horde, which would be turned over to the command of his chief widow. These loyal followers worshipped their master's soul for the rest of their lives. A horde survived its founder through the night guards, who became the founder's memorializers.[15]

Official positions were kept in families and transmitted from father to son or nephew, so keshig elders could bequeath their role to the next generation. A keshig elder often attempted to control his own succession and when assigned a faraway mission such as delivering a diplomatic letter or overseeing tax collection, he would delegate his shift responsibility to a son or to another subordinate who could replace him if he did not come home. But a new khan still nominated his own men, although he might favor existing shift men. Batu renewed at least half of Jochi's keshig.[16]

While the keshig collaborated with and served the Jochids, the two groups were genealogically distinct. The descendants of Jochi did not belong to the shift men, and the keshig elders did not typically marry princesses from the golden lineage. When intermarriage did occur, it did not result in familial political alliance. To preserve the balance of power, Batu kept the Qonggirad and other powerful in-laws away from influential keshig positions. In this respect, he followed Chinggis Khan's rules of kinship control, which affirmed the idea that a family-run empire would be a stillborn empire. It was essential, therefore, that elite families have their separate tasks and expectations. It was also with power-balancing in mind that khans manipulated lineages, interfering with genealogy in order to promote those family members loyal to themselves while ensuring that rival family members would not accrue too much influence. For political reasons, khans could convert a junior into a senior and grant a teenager a keshig elder's position.[17]

Keshig elders were among the begs, the aristocracy. In the Horde the elders and other non-Jochid officials were also known as *qarachu,* the western steppe term for bo'ol. The qarachu begs were the elite of the subordinated peoples, serving the golden lineage and given charge of important management and military positions. Even in the sixteenth century, most of the qarachu begs claimed to descend from Jochi's four original minggan, the regiments of elite steppe warriors Chinggis had gifted his son. As outsiders to the golden lineage, the qarachu begs were strictly prevented access to the supreme position, but the khans could never rule without them.[18]

Each Jochid horde had its own keshig, whose members did not necessarily come from their chief's family. Again, this structure served to prevent the emergence of power centers independent of the khan, for keshig members would be grouped through a kind of military structure, not by family or ethnicity. The shift men were recruited from anywhere in the empire, as a group or on an individual basis. Many came from the conquered peoples—Qipchaqs, Alan, Russians, Hungarians, and others seized the opportunity to become Mongol shift men.

In addition the keshig included elite hostages from afar—future leaders, whom the khan held as a token of their noble relatives' loyalty. Batu's keshig, for instance, counted a large number of sons of kniazia.[19] The hostage-taking practice was deeply alien to Westerners like John of Plano Carpini, a Franciscan friar who traveled the Mongol Empire and learned of the hostage-taking program. Plano Carpini perceived the practice as a means to destroy foreign aristocracy. "Of those whom they allowed to return they demand sons or brothers and they never afterwards give these their liberty," he wrote. "This is how they have treated the son of Jerozlaus and a chief of the Alans and many others," a reference to Alexander Nevsky, son of Kniaz Ieroslav of Vladimir-Suzdal. In fact Plano Carpini was wrong. The Mongols did not keep their elite hostages for life. Rather, the Mongols trained their hostages both to lead and to obey, so that they could return home as vassals, ruling their homelands in the name of the khan—with his full support, including military assistance and proof of investiture. Taking hostages was an old steppe diplomatic institution that processed outsiders into the nomads' social systems and built long-term political relationships. Chinggis's success with the practice had confirmed that the loyalty of the vassals originated with their physical presence in the ruler's court. Once more, the Jochid khans copied Chinggis's imperial methods.[20]

The quriltai was another linchpin of Mongol political life, which the Jochids retained. The Jochids assembled in quriltais at least twice a year: at the lunar new year, which coincided with January or February, and during the sixth lunar month, which began toward the end of June. Thousands of people assembled under a huge tent, including male and female descendants and next-of-kin of Jochi; their in-laws; the keshig elders; and a number of shift men, especially secretaries, accountants, and stewards. Each attendee could bring a limited number of guests. The rest of the keshig watched and served the assembly. Attendees entered, sat, ate, and toasted according to strict precedence; women took their seats on the khan's eastern side and men on his western side. The guests brought gifts to the khan, and he granted them cloth, silver, and gold. The assembly divided itself into aqa and ini, older and younger brothers. The aqa were more influential than the ini but could not rule without them, as both groups had to validate the khan's decisions in order to make them law.[21]

A quriltai was a closed-door meeting. The Mongols did not share internal politics with foreigners, who were denied access to crucial meetings and rituals. Given that foreigners provided most contemporaneous written accounts of Mongol life, it is hard to say exactly how the Jochid assembly functioned, and in what way its rules might have differed from those used in the East, which were established by Ögödei in 1229 and codified in 1234. What we do know is that attendees ruled on judicial cases, consequential marriages, key investitures, rewards, war, and diplomacy.[22]

In the mid-thirteenth century, the new elites Chinggis Khan had shaped began to crystallize socially. In the Horde, these elites helped to establish the Jochids as a distinctive group, albeit one whose robust political institutions—quriltai, keshig, patterns of succession, and so on—mirrored those of the empire as a whole. As we will see later, the sons of Jochi maintained these institutions even as they achieved self-governance. The Jochids also modified the institutions they inherited, learning to apply Mongol political theory and practice under novel conditions and drawing on tradition to support their evolving regime.

The Seasons of the Khan

Batu's residence in the lower Volga was in many ways ideal. It was safe, about five hundred miles from the Dnieper River, where the Lithuanians often conducted devastating raids, and from the Caucasus, where rebellious Alan and Circassian groups hid in the mountains. The lower Volga also provided excellent pastures and salt, as Sübötei and Jebe had discovered when the Westward first wintered there in 1222–1223. In spring, when insects proliferated in the humid delta, Batu moved his horde two hundred miles upriver, where the air was cool and healthy. And the whole area of the lower Volga was a crossroads of water and land routes. In winter the frozen rivers became a constellation of roads that converged in the lower valleys of the Dnieper, Don, and Volga. In summer riverboats connected the hordes and Russian villages and towns within a day or two's travel.[23]

Yet there would soon be limits to the seemingly unstoppable push of the Mongols, and the allotment of the territories fixed during the time of Orda and Batu would remain unchanged over the next generations. The routes of seasonal migrations also varied little, but the number of tents increased every year, and the areas of the winter and summer camps attracted ever more permanent settlers. The growing population was not a result of conquest, for the Jochids were largely at peace during the first decade of Batu's and Orda's rule. Rather, demographic increase was both the cause and the result of intensive pastoral activities. The growth was also supported by expanding trade opportunities, for, while at peace, the Jochids had no other way to obtain the luxury goods necessary for diplomacy and for sustaining the sharing system that bound elites to the khan and commoners to elites, as I describe in detail below. A combination of commerce and sophisticated herding techniques bolstered the Horde when it could not rely on the spoils of war.[24]

A basic challenge was to achieve economic efficiency while also enabling the social interaction that was so crucial to Mongol politics. The hordes had to be mobile in order to allow sufficient grazing, lest overgrazing in one spot damage the steppe ecology. But, at the same time, they had to convene in order to carry out political meetings. Another pitfall was the difficulty of grazing at a scale sufficient to support the population. Doing so required heavy labor. To solve their economic challenges while enabling political life, the Mongols developed several tactics. First, war captives—when available—and outsiders without status were forced to contribute to the collective workload. Second, they multiplied satellite camps and markets that helped to supply the hordes. Finally, they turned seasonality into a political instrument, scheduling their political activities during times of year when their subsistence needs were most easily filled. They also accepted that sometimes political demands would result in economic losses.[25]

Why so? Because when it was necessary to hold a political gathering, the Mongols would leave a part of their herds behind and force the rest to travel faster. The people of the hordes, who lived far away from one another, consumed a lot of energy to attend yearly trade fairs and festivals of political significance. These included quriltai, colossal gatherings organized at least twice a year. These interactions were as crucial to Mongol life as healthy herding, leading inevitably to friction between politics and herding. When a chief wanted to delay a quriltai, he would argue that his animals needed to fatten, preventing him from traveling. This was not a metaphor.

The new strategy for sustaining population growth began with Great Khan Ögödei and his successors. Their basic pastoral needs grew to such an extent that local resources were becoming exhausted, so Ögödei built a formidable infrastructure to supply Qaraqorum and his people's hordes. Ögödei achieved efficiency far beyond of earlier pastoral production. But there was more to Ögödei's program than efficiency: he turned the subsistence strategy of his forefathers into a power strategy, in which the movements of his hordes followed not only the demands of grazing but also of politics, even when mobility was costly to the herds. Ögödei and his descendants developed a system in which they could tolerate economic losses as they focused on politics—gathering to perform rituals, talk, eat, and drink.[26]

Like the great khans in the east, the Jochids developed efficiencies, markets, and political practices that enabled them to supply a vastly larger population than those of traditional nomads while still convening the dispersed hordes. Batu's supply camps were perhaps modeled after Ögödei's *tergen yam,* the relay supply system for heavy loads, which delivered to Qaraqorum five hundred wagons of food and drink every day. The Jochid logistics were less spectacular and more mobile, as Batu never accumulated the resources and manpower of Ögödei. Still, Batu did everything necessary to implement the new style of pastoral economy and politics. He expanded trade activities, allowed a huge number of workers in his horde, and organized drinking festivals to which the horde's people were able to travel in spite of the costs of migration. Batu's shift men were conscious of the dangers of overgrazing and responded to them by multiplying the number of satellite camps.

The fattening of horses and camels during periods of calving and milking was crucial to the pastoral economy. During these months, usually from May to September, the herds needed to rest. When the mares were milking, they did not march with the khan's horde. The Mongols used this five-month-long season not only to relax—these were essentially peaceful stretches—but also to organize extensive political meetings and take governing decisions. It was no accident that the Mongols planned enthronements and great quriltai during the drinking festival they held in summer.

Batu's satellite camps provided the court with horses, sheep, cattle, and enormous quantities of dairy and meat products. All of it was the property of the golden lineage. In the western steppe, the satellite camps marched separately and usually preceded the khan's camp so that supplies could be organized at an agreed-upon stopping point before the khan arrived. One satellite camp was reserved for keepers of birds of prey; khans collected falcons, for they were symbols of rule and powerful weapons in the hunt for birds, rabbits, marmots, foxes, wolves, and small Saiga antelope. The Mongols hunted not only for meat but also for skins and furs. Shift men separated falcon farming, herding, and other supply camps from the horde; they also supervised the khan's hunt. Keeping distance between satellite camps and hordes was a valuable sanitation practice, and the dispersal of animals and people helped to prevent overgrazing around the khan's horde.[27]

Besides supply camps, the Jochid hordes had mobile markets. These were likely under the supervision of night guards. Markets stood at the extreme ends of a given camp; in the khan's camp, one needed a horse to travel from the orda, the ruler's precinct, to the market. The Franciscan missionary William of Rubruck noted that "a market always follows Batu's orda, but it was so far away from us that we could not go to it." In the steppe, families knew how to sustain themselves and had no need to visit the markets every day. Poor visitors at the margins of the social system relied exclusively on the generosity of others to access food and drink for survival.[28]

The nomads knew that politics and the pastoral economy had divergent schedules, and they manipulated both dynamics with the other in

Illustration of a bronze mirror with Arabic inscription (Iran or Anatolia, twelfth or thirteenth century). Mirrors were paraphernalia of the steppe aristocracy well before the Mongol conquests, and the Jochids supported further production, using mirrors for divination or as talismans.

mind. In the case of the great khans, recent scholarship has shown that their mobility was largely driven by politics rather than herding and that we have to distinguish between pastoral mobility and "imperial itinerance." Empire-building nomads moved to project power. The Jochids, too, focused less on herding efficiently than on asserting control over their society and extending power over their neighbors.[29]

If the Mongol economy was powerfully shaped by politics, it also interacted with their belief system, for both the belief system and the economy were deeply entwined with the natural world. The Mongols did not consider humanity superior to nature, and humans were not the masters of the environment. Mongols saw animals, plants, terrain, and insects as lifeforms to be feared and respected. They believed in the "land masters"—the intangible entities of the land, defined by the anthropologist Grégory Delaplace as "localised at a certain place, commanding such diverse phenomena as weather, luck for hunting, and environmental conditions in general." And the Mongols handled the earth and wildlife with great caution, as these entities could be vengeful and hostile. Mongols worshipped nature and cared for it deeply.[30]

The Source of Life

The milking season, which arrived at roughly the same time in the eastern and western steppes, was a source of rejoicing throughout the empire. People celebrated with music, archery, and wrestling competitions, and by drinking *kumis* or *airag*—fermented mare's milk. The kumis festival was the largest and most elaborate of the Mongol gatherings. It was also the time when herders came to the khan's horde to pay tribute to the khan. "Baatu has thirty men within a day's journey of his camp, each one of whom provides him every day with such milk from a hundred mares," Rubruck recorded. "That is to say, the milk of three thousands mares every day, not counting the other white milk which other men bring. For, just as in Syria the peasants give a third part of their produce, these men have to bring to the orda of their lords the mare's milk of every third day."[31]

Along with paying the milk tax, herders were required to lend out mares, as determined by the tümen system. Mongol chiefs would lend mares to their khan, which he would keep for a year or more. In turn, chiefs borrowed mares from herders of lower rank. The mare circulation reflected the Mongol's socioeconomic order: they shared everything, but redistributed possessions and resources according to people's status, with more going to higher-status individuals. Lending and borrowing animals was common at all levels of society. The shift men and wealthy herders dispersed their herds to avoid overgrazing in their locations, and poor men would raise some of these animals in other locations, supplementing their own much smaller herds. There was no question of ownership: animals belonging to the elite were branded with a *tamga,* a lineage mark, and stealing them was punishable by death. Poorer herders simply milked animals owned by others, and then delivered upward a portion of their production. In this way a poor herder could more easily feed himself and his family, and the society could take advantage of its animals without damaging the productive capacity of any particular location.[32]

Much of the milk produced at every social level was turned into kumis. Preparing kumis required experience, skill, and patience, for it entailed stirring or churning raw mare's milk for hours. It was also a symbolically loaded task that only men were allowed to perform. A fizzy drink, kumis typically had an ethyl alcohol content of between 1 and 2.5 percent, but the level could be raised if the milk fermented longer. *Kara kumis,* reserved for the khan and the elites, was a special mixture that remains unknown; it might have had a higher alcohol content than normal kumis. There was no kumis in the cold season, but in the summer, kumis replaced water, which could become lethally contaminated in the heat.[33]

The season of the drinking festival brought visitors from across the hordes to the khan's court, and the guests expected to have unlimited access to kumis and kara kumis for weeks on end. In June 1254, at Great Khan Möngke's drinking festival, Rubruck counted five hundred carts and ninety horses laden with mare's milk. Only five days later, the court took a similar delivery. The old sources can at times be more vivid than accurate, but these figures are realistic. In the course of one milking season, a mare produced up to 3,300 pounds of milk, of which about half was left to the foals and the rest used to make kumis. Given the size of Mongol herds, there would likely have been enough production to support the population's thirst. And considering that an adult can digest up to 340 fluid ounces of kumis a day, a large supply would have been needed.[34]

Drinking kumis was more than a shared tradition. It was also a vital part of the Mongol diet. Shamans knew kumis was an unparalleled

Illustration of a golden bowl with a dragon protome on the handle, intended to dangle from a belt (Horde, mid-to-late thirteenth century). Dragon protomes show non-Mongol influence—possibly Khitan, Jin, or Song—but the workmanship is Jochid.

energy booster and used it in various rituals. Recent studies confirm the drink's health benefits. In particular, researchers have shown that kumis from animals milked around June—exactly when the drinking festival was in full flow—yields especially high levels of vitamin E, niacin, and dehydroascorbic acid, a form of vitamin C. Drinkers would have been able to partake of the kumis when it was maximally nutritious, as the producing camps were never far from the court, ensuring that the supply was fresh.[35] Fresh kumis strengthens the immune system and treats and prevents typhoid, dysentery, and other diseases that were common at the time of the Mongol expansion. Kumis also has antibiotic properties and is still used against bacterial infections. The Mongols recognized that kumis was useful in treating kidney stones, which was likely a prevalent ailment. As avid meat-eaters, the Mongols probably had elevated levels of uric acid, which leads to painful afflictions such as kidney stones and gout. Reportedly, both Batu and his brother Berke suffered from gout.[36]

Kumis was vital to the flourishing of Chinggis Khan's descendants in the mid-thirteenth century. They multiplied their herds, increased the production of milk, and drank huge amounts of the stuff. The population rose, and their children grew stronger.

Let Them Receive Their Share of the Empire

"His bounty was beyond calculation and his liberality immeasurable," the Persian historian Juvaynī wrote of Batu. "Merchants from every side brought him all manners of ware, and he took everything and doubled the price of it several times over." Like other outsiders—and even some Mongols—who witnessed the khans' generosity, Juvaynī was at once impressed and bewildered: Batu was paying the merchants twice what they asked for.[37]

But Batu's generosity should not be confused with magnanimity. He was generous because generosity made him powerful. Batu needed to draw in traders in order to make his economy and political system function, especially when conquest was not supplying spoils to distribute. Hoping to win merchants' favor, he emulated Great Khan Ögödei, who had ordered that "merchants be paid a premium of ten percent over the total of their sold merchandise." According to Rashīd al-Dīn, Ögödei's *bitigchis* (secretaries) warned him that he was already buying their goods for more than their value. "Merchants deal with the treasury in hopes of a profit," Ögödei replied, "and they have an expense to pay off you bitigchis. It's the debt they owe you I'm discharging lest they come away having taken a loss in dealing with us." In another instance, "Someone brought [Ögödei] two hundred bone arrow heads. He gave him a like number of bars (of silver)." This was more than a matter of prestige. Mongol leaders were cautious not to slow down the circulation of goods and, knowing that merchants could not be coerced or controlled, instead seduced them. Mongol officials imposed light taxes on commercial transactions and promised safety for merchants and protection for their goods. The khans and their officials also allowed traders to access the *yam*—the Mongol's impressive supply and communication network, which I detail below.[38] Mongol leaders also competed with one another to attract traders and merchandise, offering privileges such as tax exemptions for traders and entrepreneurs. For Batu, as we will later see, this policy had already begun to bear fruit in the 1250s.

As contemporaries noticed, the purpose of the Mongol khans was not to accumulate wealth but to dispense it. Rashīd al-Dīn reported of Ögödei, "One day, when he had laid the foundations of Qaraqorum, he went into the treasury and saw nearly a hundred thousand bars [of silver]. 'What benefit do we derive from all these stores?' he asked. 'They have to be constantly guarded. Have it announced that everybody who wants a bar should come and take one.'" According to several other anecdotes, Ögödei gave silver and gold bars to his people in order to bankroll their business and trading efforts. Ögödei was confident that what he gave to his subjects would come back to him sooner or later. In the Mongol economy, circulation brought more resources than retention.[39]

The khans did accumulate wealth—through the products of their personal domains, servants, herds, gifts, taxes, and war. But trade served a different function. It was not meant to enrich the khan, who did not actually engage in trade or seek profit, as he was above the human world. Khans could only give or receive; they did not buy but instead granted, which also is reflected in their demonstrative generosity. No, trade was not intended to benefit the khan personally but rather to provide health for the empire and welfare for the people—health that was measured as much financially as spiritually, for circulation was intimately tied to the Mongol belief system.

The Mongols saw commodities as receptacles or mediums of something immaterial, and circulation of this immaterial something was essential to the cosmic balance of the world. Specifically, the *qubi,* the redistribution system, supported not only the living but also the dead, whose spirits needed to be continuously appeased in order to protect the living from negative interference by the "ill dead." Circulation was said to appease these spirits. What is more, the Mongols believed in the rebirth of their souls, and redistribution increased one's chances of an optimal rebirth. Thus, when a host shared his earthly goods with a large number of guests, he would bring happiness and prosperity to the living, the dead, and to himself in his afterlife. Through this complex interplay of the imminent, the transcendent, and the reborn in this world, the Mongols conceived of the things they shared, apportioned, and circulated among themselves as having a direct impact on the wellbeing of the society. Circulation of the commodities obtained through trade, taxation, and war was therefore key to maintaining social order and to repairing social disorder. It is hard to reconstruct how the medieval Mongols defined collective happiness, but they certainly believed that the circular movement of things was crucial in producing it. And that meant that the khan could hardly have a more important task than ensuring the fluidity of the redistribution system.[40]

None of this is to say that accumulation of wealth did not happen. Far from it; accumulation was widely accepted. Yet wealth only made sense in terms of its redistribution, which was carried out according to the qubi, a system of shares itself based on the tümen. The khan gave gifts—many obtained via trade and diplomacy—to the commanders of tens of thousands, who in turn gave gifts to the heads of thousands, and so on down the line. This was the Mongol circulation system at work. The khans did not need luxury goods for their subsistence economy—they needed them for their political economy. They used the goods to reward elites and bind them to the court, and the elites used the same goods to retain the loyalty of the common people. Silver ingots, gold, precious textiles, furs, pearls—all these were constantly reassigned. The khan's redistribution took place during quriltais, in plain view. The shift men supervised, registering the goods and counting them behind the scenes. It was all an elaborate project on behalf of maintaining a cohesive political body and a benevolent cosmic order.

The Jochids did not intend to let the great khan govern them. To maintain their independence, they had to compete. That is what Batu did; he competed with the great khan in every area—the market, politics, patronage. Batu quickly recognized the huge potential of the lower Volga, and in a few years, turned the region into a dynamic trade hub by attracting merchants from Kiev, Sudak, Novgorod, and farther north. His cousin Büri, from the rival line of Chagatay, protested publicly that Batu's territory should be shared. Batu had him executed. The Jochid khans would never allow other members of the golden lineage to claim the Qipchaq steppe.[41]

Mongolizing Space

The Mongols believed that mountains, lakes, and valleys possessed cosmological power. On those sites they built their palaces and *qoruq*—burial grounds. As we saw, the great khans harnessed Qaraqorum's spiritual nexus, the Orkhon Valley. They also made a memorial for Chinggis Khan in Burqan Qaldun, an old spiritual site in eastern Mongolia's

Khentii Mountains, where the locals had celebrated the cult of the ancestors before the Mongols came. Most likely, Chinggis's body was moved from the Tangut territory to Burqan Qaldun. The mountain captured their leader's *sülde,* his charisma and vital energy. At Burqan Qaldun, the Onon, Kherlen, and Tuul rivers had their source, and the riverbeds were seen as mystically connected to the birth of the Mongols. This was also the native region of Temüjin, and the place where he held the quriltai of 1206. The addition of his burial ground turned Burqan Qaldun into the most sacred area of the empire.[42]

In the far west, the descendants of Jochi had built their own landmarks. Under Batu, they started to construct sacrificial sites, palaces, religious edifices, and qoruq. The original location of the khans' burial ground remains uncertain. A late tradition identified the area of Saraijuq, on the Ural River, with the Jochid khans' qoruq. Indeed, the lower Ural was the original nuntug Chinggis Khan granted Batu, before Batu was put in charge of the Qipchaq campaign. According to this tradition, Batu founded the city of Saraijuq, which became a spiritual center. In fact, Saraijuq dated to the tenth century, but the story of Batu as founder speaks to Saraijuq's emergence as a key Jochid spiritual site. Among the spaces the Jochids created was a royal cemetery. This cemetery has never been discovered, as Mongols did not want anyone to know where their khans were buried. Jūzjānī, a contemporary source, recorded that the place of Batu's burial "is covered up, and horses are driven over it, in such a manner that not a trace of it remains." What we do know is that there was a strong connection between the site where a khan was enthroned and his final place of rest. The majority of the Batuid khans were invested with their powers in Saraijuq area. Just like Chinggis Khan made the area of Burqan Qaldun his enthronement site and ancestors' sanctuary, Batu turned the lower Ural into a sacred land where his descendants would perform the rites of the ancestral cult and be buried with their next-of-kin.[43]

Guards watched over the qoruq of elites and commoners alike; Plano Carpini relates an episode in which he accidentally entered a commoners' burial ground and was caught by the watchmen. Secret, protected, and forbidden to foreigners, burial sites mattered to the Mongols more than cities did. The decision on a burial site thus said a great deal about which places truly mattered within Mongol societies. Thousands of Mongols died during the Hungarian campaigns, and their bodies were repatriated from Europe to Mongolia. But at some point during Batu's rule, the Jochid practice changed, and the dead were laid to rest in the lower valleys of the west. The Jochids no longer needed to move the bodies of their deceased, because their home was now the Qipchaq steppe.[44]

The Sitting City

Around 1250 Batu sponsored the construction of permanent structures at a location the Mongols recorded on their coins as Sarai, meaning palace or city. Local nomadic groups had occupied the place from time to time, but no major settlements existed there before Sarai. The khan's palace was probably an enormous reception hall designed after the golden tent or another ceremonial tent. The palace was surrounded by buildings of mud bricks, ceramic, and stone, and large stone statues were erected nearby on mobile platforms. The palace stood almost halfway between the northern and southern limits of the migration route followed by Batu's horde. The city was unwalled.[45]

Not much is known of Sarai's original shape, organization, and size. Rubruck, who visited in October 1254, paid little attention to it. He mentioned in passing "a new city, that Batu has built on the Itil"—that is, the Volga—and noted that "Saraï and Batu's palace are on the eastern bank of the river." Plano Carpini did not mention the new city, which suggests that the khan's palace was built after his visit in 1246.[46]

Historians disagree over the exact function of Batu's complex. It is a common mistake to compare Sarai to a classical imperial city, for the khan would neither live within four walls nor have his mausoleum constructed there. He also did not try to impress his people with buildings. Sarai probably served a function similar to that of Qaraqorum, "the sitting city" Ögödei had founded two decades earlier. Qaraqorum was an enclosed, brick-walled town with two districts, one for Muslim merchants and one for Chinese craftsmen. Next to the great khan's palace, there were a number of palaces for the court secretaries, twelve Buddhist temples, two mosques, and a church. Like Qaraqorum, Sarai was a meeting point for outsiders, with mudbrick houses and well-organized districts. Sarai hosted traders, travelers, secretaries, artisans, and religious men, who found there the comforts of sedentary life. True, Mongol cities were completely different from what the westerners were used to; Rubuck noted how small Qaraqorum was—"not as large as the village of Saint Denis, and the monastery of Saint Denis is worth ten times than that palace"—and Sarai was smaller still. But Mongol cities were nonetheless welcoming. The khans went out of their way. Great Khan Güyük even had a palace built in his new city of Emil for the benefit of important foreign travelers—a palace in which he would not himself live.[47]

Sarai was thus not unique within the empire, and nor was it within the Horde. Settlements burgeoned along the Jochid hordes' seasonal rounds, under the court's sponsorship and control. The Jochids had thousands of war captives, and they wanted to settle some of them, especially craftsmen whose work or art required long-term stays or permanent installations. This was not always an easy proposition, as forced settlement led to uprisings. Plano Carpini heard that Russians forcibly settled in a city in the Qipchaq steppe rebelled against the Mongols. The Jochids also used cities to accommodate Franciscan and Dominican friars and other sedentary emissaries, who could not cope with the demands of nomadic life, as well as merchants and travelers who needed storage for their goods. And the Jochids financed the construction of shrines and religious buildings; Sartaq, Batu's eldest son, ordered a Nestorian church built in the new settlement he founded on his horde's route. Indeed, new towns popping up across the Mongol Empire between the mid-1230s and the mid-1250s were filled with temples, churches, monasteries, and mosques. These were permanently occupied towns. They bustled with activity when the khan was around, but they were never quiet.[48]

Mongols themselves considered sedentary residences less comfortable than their tents, which were warmer, soft, and more intimate. But even if the immobile cities were primarily the Mongols' answer to the needs of their increasing population of sedentary subjects, the new cities served their own people, too. Palaces hosted quriltai and other major gatherings. As a center of trade, religion, and craft, Sarai helped to advance the political and economic goals of the Horde and, as it grew, elevated the khan's prestige. What Sarai was not was an administrative center. Mongols ruled on horseback.

The Moveable City

Hordes covered huge swathes of land. A massively elongated city, a single horde could contain thousands of people. When conditions were ideal, the numbers could reach a hundred thousand. Everything the people of the horde needed was portable: homes, workshops, palaces, shrines, statues. A horde was a self-sufficient unit that moved with its supply system, which included enormous numbers of horses, goats, sheep, oxen, and camels. Herding was always central to the operation of a horde, though over time the hordes diversified their subsistence strategies to sustain their ever-growing populations. Seasonal diets were a byproduct of mobility. Mongols hunted and fished throughout the year, but winters demanded special arrangements. As the cold season progressed and the animals lost weight, the nomads relied more on carbohydrates. Herdsmen exchanged sheep and skins for grains; the Jochid elite supplemented their diets with millet and wheat from the many villages near their wintering grounds in the Volga delta and lower Don. Villagers sold produce at the hordes' markets and seasonal trade fairs.[49]

Year after year, the Jochid hordes moved up and down the great rivers of their territory. During the communal migrations, people rode horses and carts or walked. Women, including khatuns, knew how to ride, but only did so for short distances, work, and leisure. When the horde migrated, women perched on their two-wheeled carts and drove them. Along the bank of the Volga, "one woman will drive twenty or thirty carts," Rubruck marveled. He explained how the women tied together, one after the other, carts drawn by oxen and camels. A cart might be piled with trunks of goods or might carry a substantial tent. Within the first decade after settling in the western steppe, the Jochids had become almost entirely dependent on a particular type of tent, known as a tent-cart. The traditional Mongol trellis tent (yurt or *ger*) could be dismantled and packed onto a cart; in the case of the tent-cart, the tent was permanently embedded in a flat bottom. The tent-cart could be moved from a flatbed cart to the ground, but it could not be disassembled. In the east, Mongols frequently used tent-carts when the ground allowed it, but they never replaced the trellis tent. The western terrain, however, was more accommodating of tent-carts. The biggest ones needed more than twenty oxen to pull them.[50]

Illustration of a belt ornament (Horde, mid-1270s). This ornament was one of at least seventeen on a single belt, among them a piece bearing the *tamga,* lineage mark, of Batu Khan. The inclusion of the khan's tamga demonstrated the princely status of the belt's owner.

The Jochids refined their transportation system in order to accommodate the great wealth they had amassed during the last Qipchaq campaign—clothes, fabrics, pelts, weapons, jewelry, tools, and other household utensils. Not only did they begin to make more tent-carts than trellis tents, but they also raised more oxen and camels, which were strong enough to pull or carry their heavy chests of goods. The camels were also trained to cross rivers while laden. In the 1250s a wealthy Jochid had between one hundred and two hundred chests filled with belongings.[51]

Some of the hordes were as impressive as the khan's. "It seemed to me as if a large city was approaching me," Rubruck wrote when he first saw a horde in early June 1253. This horde, migrating along the western banks of the Don, was led by one of Batu's delegates. Rubruck learned that the delegate had no more than five hundred men under him—the rest of the people were families, workers, religious men, captives, and others. The difference between imperial and other hordes lay in the size of the keshig, for the khan's camp was the seat of power.[52]

To recover the political landscape of the Horde, we need to understand the political geography of the nomads, a geography that had little to do with administrative division. Places like Sarai and Qaraqorum were not essential to Mongol power. Sources produced by sedentary people, who gauged the grandeur and sophistication of empires by the size and number of their cities, vastly overestimate the significance of sitting Mongol capitals. In reality those capitals were but small enclaves in a vast political universe. The capital was the khan's horde.

Hordes—the khan's and the others'—were more strictly organized than any sedentary city of the day. Moving in massive numbers required extreme discipline from humans and animals. Mongol horses were especially impressive. When dismounted, these horses were trained to follow their riders and could return to camp on their own. Mongol horses also did not need fodder; they fed themselves in winter by seeking grass under the snow, allowing them to survive where no other horses could. Westerners compared them to dogs, a compliment concerning the horses' resourcefulness.[53]

When setting camp, people knew exactly where to pitch their mobile homes. The tents were always positioned with the entrance door facing south. The camp formation was designed to regulate people and animals and ensure that everyone respected each other's status. A settled horde integrated precedence of rank and lines of descent into its layout, with the khan's tents in the center and other tents lined up west and east. But the organization was not only a matter of status, for the camp layout bore a symbolic meaning. By positioning themselves according to the cardinal directions, inhabitants oriented themselves in space, society, and the cosmos. Birth, death, and politics altered the configurations of the moveable cities. Their flexibility made them more adaptable to changing circumstances than were sitting cities. The layout of a settled horde reflected its shifting social organization, and one could read from its plan whether the people were at war or peace.[54]

The defense system of the Mongol camps was based on a circular layout called *güre'en,* the ring. To protect themselves against enemies and strangers, the Mongols camped in a circle, with the horde's chief in the center. The Jochids settled in ring-camps during hunting parties and wars or when a small group had to travel across the steppe. In times of peace, they opted for the linear layout with the khan's tents in the center. When needed, the horde could turn into a war machine almost instantly, providing the mobility required for swift attacks and strategic retreats.[55] Contemporaries thought the horde was the safest place on earth. Not only did the circle provide protection against marauders, enemies, and wild animals, but the location of hordes near rivers also limited the effects of fires. The shape of the horde further served to diffuse social discord by avoiding concentrations of people in overpopulated districts. The moveable city could always be extended to accommodate more people. Shift men kept watch day and night, but a horde was not a military camp, and women and children always outnumbered armed horsemen. In the early 1250s the Jochid hordes enjoyed peace after half a century of nearly constant warfare, and they adapted their moveable cities to take advantage of that peaceful life.

Work in the camp followed strict gender roles. Men were responsible for a number of tasks associated with herd management and animal slaughter. They also hunted, and they crafted bows, arrows, tents, carts, harnesses, and horse-riding equipment. As for the women, their activities fascinated travelers. "Their women make everything," Plano Carpini wrote. "Leather garments, tunics, shoes, leggings and everything made of leather; they also drive the carts and repair them, they load the camels, and in all their tasks they are very swift and energetic. All the women wear breeches and some of them shoot like the men." Rubruck noted that "the orda of a rich Mongol will look like a large town, and yet there will be very few men in it," an observation that reinforces the key role women played in operating the camp.[56]

Not only did women run the camp, they also owned the households. They would host their husbands regularly, as a husband had to switch homes often to visit each of his wives. This was a common practice at all levels of society, reflecting both the design of Mongol camps—

prioritizing mobility—and of the decision-making power invested in women of all social classes. Rubruck noted that Batu's twenty-six wives each had her own "large house," and these were accompanied by smaller ones serving as "chambers in which their attendants live." Sartaq, meanwhile, had six wives and his eldest son two or three. Rubruck counted "a good two hundred carts" belonging to each wife's home. Spouses had assigned places in the camp layout reflecting their rank: the chief wife at the extreme west and the last wife at the far east.[57]

Because the camp could be extended, the Mongols were able easily to accommodate newcomers, including traders, diplomats, wandering scholars, and religious men, any of whom would immediately be assigned homes. The security and social order within the camps impressed these visitors, who were used to city life. "Fights, brawls, wounding, murder, are never met with among them. Nor are robbers and thieves who steal on a large scale found there," Plano Carpini observed. "Consequently their dwellings and the carts in which they keep their valuables are not secured by bolts and bars. If any animals are lost, whoever comes across them either leaves them alone or takes them to men appointed for this purpose." Plano Carpini noticed that, in general, the Mongols were unusually respectful of each other.[58]

Plano Carpini was also amazed that people did not enter the great khan's pavilion through the large gate reserved for the ruler, even though the gate was unguarded at the time. Plano Carpini was astute in noting the discipline of the horde's people. The Mongols had a strong sense of social hierarchy and numerous taboos, which guided and constrained them in their everyday lives. Theft, adultery, and revealing certain secrets were capital offenses. Even speaking to foreigners was, if not prohibited by law, discouraged as a matter of social norms. When ordinary Mongols did communicate with outsiders, they might withhold information or spread false rumors, lest they break the norm. Mongols rarely transgressed these basic rules and made sure that foreign visitors understood them.[59]

The camp reflected the changing Mongol world and society in microcosm: as the empire and the individual hordes thrived, their camps took on new markers of success. Military victories, for instance, could bring considerable novelties. Celebrating khans commissioned the construction of special ceremonial tents made of silk and felt, which might accommodate thousands of people. The Mongols also adapted the tents they seized from vanquished enemies; after overcoming the Hungarians, Batu took over and inhabited the white tents of king Béla, demonstrating his superiority over the defeated ruler. In general, the size and grandeur of tents and carts reflected lineage, status, and wealth. Thus Great Khan Güyük's red, white, and golden tents could hold two thousand people, while the smallest tents in a given horde were around five and a half yards in diameter and housed perhaps five adults. Only felt of the highest quality was naturally white; typical felt was gray, so the women who owned the tents coated their felt with lime, white clay, or powdered bone to brighten it. Commoners also carefully painted and decorated their homes. They sewed into the walls pieces of colored felt representing "vines and trees, birds and animals." Married women also made ornate carts for themselves. Even humble possessions could be beautiful.[60]

The Great River Valleys

The people of the Horde saw in the landscape things that escaped the eye of sedentary people. The rivers and the mountains were not frontiers but rather ways to harness space and touch the heavens. Rivers, in particular, were defining features of the Jochid domain. They were highways through the steppe, crossable—for the Mongols—at almost any point. And they provided winter camp sites, as hordes settled on the frozen surfaces.

The territory of the Jochids stretched from the Irtysh River to the Dnieper River. To the east lay the great khan's territory; to the west the lands of the Lithuanians, Poles, Hungarians, and Teutonic Knights. The core of this huge territory was a belt of four hundred miles that ran along the lower Volga. This area was reserved for Batu's horde. His next of kin, noyans, and begs inhabited other parts of the Qipchaq steppe. The various groups apportioned among themselves the banks of the Ural, Volga, Don, and Dnieper, the four largest rivers that crossed the steppe. Their hordes moved up and down the banks, stopping now and then in places they found advantageous for purposes of provisioning, herd management, and politics.

Visitors witnessed the Mongols' riverine nomadism. Plano Carpini, who traveled across the Qipchaq steppe between February and April 1246, reported, "All these chiefs go down the river towards the sea in winter, and turn upriver, in summer, towards the mountains." A decade later, Rubruck confirmed that, from January to August, Batu's horde moved north along the eastern bank of the Volga to Ukek, the modern Saratov. From August to December, Batu's horde followed the course of the river southward to the delta. Sartaq, Batu's eldest son, had his own horde on the western bank of the Volga and moved in parallel with his father. Only a few days' march separated their camps. Modern scholars have likened the Jochids' seasonal circuit to what is known as vertical transhumance, whereby herders in mountainous regions will switch between higher elevation—and cooler temperatures—in summer and foothills or grasslands in winter. The Horde's transhumance is similar in that they went north to cooler places in summer and south to warmer places in winter. But in the western steppe, the Jochids marched on the flat, steady ground of the great river basins, allowing them to move with their possessions in addition to their animals.[61]

The seasonal round was a march of approximately 370 miles each way. People would move regularly every two or three days, making for "a very slow pace," Rubruck reported, "as a lamb or an ox might walk." The nomads probably traveled between five and twelve miles a day depending on ground conditions, requiring five to seven months to cover each leg of the circuit. To protect their herds from fatigue, the Mongols rested frequently and gave the animals access to fresh grass. This method also avoided overgrazing in any given area. "Each captain, according to whether he has more or fewer men under him, knows the limits of his pasturage and where to feed his flocks in winter, summer, spring and autumn," Rubruck added.[62]

In winter, the herds, beasts of burden, carts, and Mongols crossed the frozen rivers. The Volga was an icy corridor that Rubruck described as four times wider than the Seine. Plano Carpini wrote that it took him and his companions several days to cross the Dnieper, which he considered amazingly vast—like all the great rivers of the steppe. The Mongols would set up tents on the frozen surfaces, live there, and fish through holes drilled into the crust. Presumably, staying close to the riverbanks also secured access to water and prevented the Mongols and their herds getting lost.[63]

In summer sedentary people could cross the Volga at the level of Ukek, where the Mongols had arranged fording points for carts. This allowed the Mongols to supervise foreigners and sedentary locals as they journeyed through the region. The nomads, however, needed no such infrastructure to cross rivers. They had portable boats: a light and circular piece of leather, pierced all around, through which they threaded a cord to make a pouch. They filled these pouches with their belongings and put their saddles on top, then tied the pouches to the tails of strong horses. A man swam in the front to drive the horses, while others sat on the pouches themselves. The Mongols sometimes used oars to cross faster. They switched frequently from one bank to the other, impressing sedentary peoples who were stuck fording rivers at fixed spots.[64]

Knowing where and how to ford a fast-flowing river was one of the Mongols' most important skills. It provided a huge advantage over settled people. The local Russians, for instance, navigated the same rivers but could not cross them with the ease of the nomads. The Russians could travel up and down the waters themselves, but the Mongols controlled the few crossing points and did not let locals pass when and where they wanted. Locals were forced to waste time traveling to the crossings, where they also had to pay fees to the Mongols. For the Mongols, harnessing the rivers meant not only making use of them but wielding them as a tool of power over their subjects and neighbors.

Intersecting Mobilities

The Jochid hordes were spread all over the steppe belt. In addition to Batu's and Sartaq's, there were at least seven other big hordes: one on each side of the Dnieper; one near the Don, led by Batu's sister and her husband; one on each side of the Ural, led by military commanders; one led by Berke, Batu's younger brother, and located in Transcaucasia; Orda's horde, near the city of Emil; and, in the region of Lake Ala Köl, Jochi's horde, which, after his death, was under the control of one of his wives.[65]

Although some hordes, like Batu's and Sartaq's, were neighbors, others could be separated by hundreds of miles. They communicated through the yam, a chain of official posts that allowed a horseman to go from the Volga to the Irtysh in eight weeks. The yam was a multifaceted system, which served the whole Mongol Empire in myriad ways. The Mongols used the yam to spy on enemies, carry goods and messages between far-flung locations, and supply military camps, cities, and hordes. Development of the yam began under Chinggis Khan, although equestrian communication networks long predated him. Since at least the seventh century, Türks, Kitan, Uighurs, and other Central Asian rulers had implemented messaging systems. The Mongols merged these regional networks and fit them to their own ambitions. By the mid-thirteenth century, the yam was fully operational.[66]

There were hundreds of yam stations, small camps run by Mongols and locals, where official travelers and emissaries could obtain food and fresh mounts. The cost of maintaining the stations fell on the local people, who were required to provide horses, water, food, and clothing and to accommodate official travelers, foreign emissaries, and their escorts. The *yamchi,* postmen, who staffed the stations did not give away horses but rather exchanged them for horses that the travelers had received from a previous station. Mongols were selective about horses. They distinguished between pack, post, and war horses and between those suited to long distances and sprinters useful for urgent missions across short distances. The army controlled the whole yam system.[67]

In the Qipchaq steppe, yam stations were located roughly a half-day's distance from each other. Their facilities, equipment, and size varied. Yam posts near villages and cities were better supplied, while posts located deeper in the steppe were sometimes rather poor. All the yam horses belonged to the empire; the yam operated like a state-run horse rental company that covered the whole Mongol territory.

The yam combined the Mongol supply and communication networks. To function effectively, it required mastery of diverse technologies of transportation and mobility, braiding together three subsystems. The *tergen yam,* comprising carts pulled by oxen, camels, and strong horses, moved heavy loads and covered only portions of territories, like the area around Qaraqorum. The *morin yam,* the regular postal route, was limited to riders on horseback, and ran through the whole empire. And via the *narin yam,* a secret communication system, a messenger could travel more than a hundred and twenty miles a day. This ability to combine different forms and patterns of mobility explains how fewer than a million Mongols scattered over huge distances could rule an empire almost a continent in size. The yam made the steppe smaller.[68]

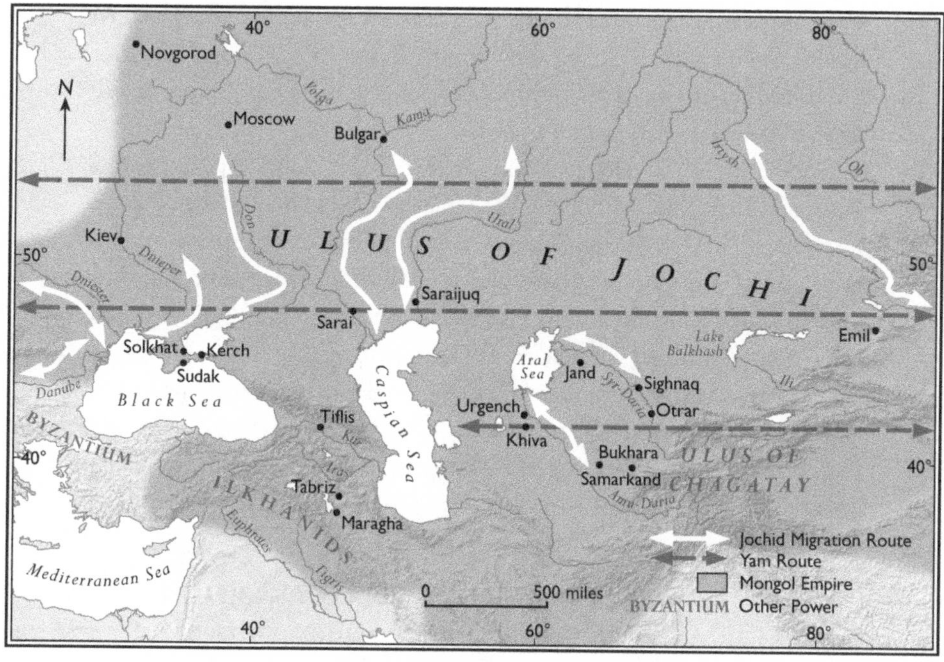

Movements of the Jochid hordes, showing intersecting yam routes.

By making fresh mounts available to horsemen who also knew how to cross the great rivers, the Mongols not only gained firm control over their new territories but also developed a unified transportation system. The yam enabled east-west mobility, which intersected with the north-south migration routes of the hordes. The horizontal mobility of the yam was fast and flexible; a rider could take advantage of the yam at any time and travel in either direction. The vertical mobility of the hordes along the great river valleys was slower and seasonally directional.

The intersecting horizontal and vertical mobilities were like the fast- and slow-twitch muscles of the empire: they worked because they were complementary. Vertical mobility enabled the slow, long-distance march of the annual round, while horizontal mobility enabled sprints across the empire and jumps from one horde to another. The yam routes were also mobile, to ensure that they intersected the hordes as they made their rounds: yam routes ran along more southerly latitudes in winter and more northerly ones in the summer. East Asian nomads might have known from long ago the powerful dynamics of intersecting mobilities, but the Mongols maintained this system over generations at a previously unseen level of complexity.

The Mongols developed and completed the colossal projects that Chinggis Khan had launched. They had learned to absorb ideas, skills, institutions, and people in order to create new infrastructure and project their power. The yam relied on the Mongols' knowledge of ecology and animal biology, on their ability to move fast and endure long-distance rides, and on secure written communication enabled by the Mongol bureaucracy, which created special seals and paper formats, registered translators and emissaries, and issued passports. The yam grew with the empire itself, both reflecting and enabling imperial practice. It was an effective system, and the Mongols were proud of it.

Come Out So That We May Count You According to Our Custom

The Qipchaqs gave themselves up to the Mongols. Around 1245–1246 the Qipchaqs returned in large numbers to their homeland, leaving Bulgaria and Hungary, where they had been attacked, enslaved, and otherwise mistreated by the local populations. Their old territory was now ruled by Batu's horde; the Qipchaqs would never take power again. Instead, their reappearance increased the Jochids' manpower. Some of the Qipchaqs entered the tümen system and became, at best, low-status members of the Horde. Hundreds of others ended up on the slave market; the most fortunate of these were bonded to the Mamluk courts of Delhi and Cairo.[69]

The Jochids had replaced the Qipchaqs and created a new order. The Mongols imposed their laws, and their tümens atomized the old kinship groups and established a pyramidal hierarchy. The level of governance and social control were previously unseen in the western steppe, but nomadic and sedentary subjects alike had no choice but to accept it and integrate into the Mongol socioeconomic system. Qipchaqs and Russians submitted to the new regime, but only the Russians survived the Mongol embrace with a sense of distinctive peoplehood intact.

In the 1240s there was no unified Russia but instead a range of principalities. Most of the Russians who submitted to the Mongols were fishermen, craftsmen, and peasants dwelling in small forest towns. The former Russian capitals of Kiev, Vladimir, and Suzdal had suffered severely during the conquest and remained half empty. Trading cities—especially Novgorod, which the Mongols had left untouched—fared better. Only a few days' boat ride separated these northern towns from the khan's camp; a growing number of Russians took advantage by seeking work in the Jochid hordes as servants, translators, artisans, and priests. The most numerous of the Jochid subjects, Russians could immediately find a role in the Mongol economy, a vast new world that stretched from the Black Sea to the Pacific Ocean. But at the same time, the Russians faced considerable uncertainty as to what they could expect from Mongol domination. They only knew that dramatic changes were taking place.

The bad news came in winter 1257 and spread quickly in Novgorod and the surrounding region. The Tatars, as the Russians called the Mongols, had come to levy taxes. The khan's envoys, protected by Kniaz Alexander, arrived in town to collect taxes in cash, fur, and young people. The Novgorodians were waiting for them. They welcomed the envoys, talked peace, and offered gifts for the Tatar tsar. Eventually the Novgorodians convinced the Mongols to accept the gifts and suspend the payment. But the envoys considered the gifts a mere advance on what was owed. The Mongols would be back, and the next time they would be less merciful.[70]

In 1259 the envoys returned in winter, the Mongol season of war. The chief tax collectors settled in the area of Novgorod with their wives and warriors. They counted houses and levied taxes, provoking a "great tumult." The inhabitants turned against the Mongols, who warned Kniaz Alexander to "give us guards, lest they kill us." Alexander was in a difficult position. By 1259 he was a major political figure—not only the prince of Novgorod, but also the grand prince, with authority over all the other princes of the Russian principalities. Novgorodians and others expected him to live up to his reputation as their defender: in 1240, at just nineteen years old, he had gained the sobriquet "Nevsky" by successfully leading Russian troops against Swedish invaders at the Neva River. But while Alexander was an esteemed leader and fighter, he also knew what the Mongols were capable of. He was present during the conquest of the 1240s and had spent several months at Great Khan Güyük's court. Indeed, Alexander's father was reportedly poisoned by Güyük's mother during her son's enthronement festivities. But while Güyük's party had threatened Alexander and his family, Batu had always shielded him from the great khan.[71]

Alexander convinced the Novgorod boyars to protect the tax collectors, but the commoners rebelled and refused to be counted. They knew that the purpose of the *chislo,* the census, was military conscription and taxation. The greater the number of Russians counted, the more the tribute would cost. Ultimately Alexander himself led the Mongols into town with the help of the boyars, who "thought [the tax] would be easy for themselves, but fall hard on the lesser men." According to the *Chronicle of Novgorod,* "the accursed ones," that is, the Mongols, then "began to ride through the streets, writing down the Christian houses." The Mongols made their count, fixed the tribute, collected the payment, and left. Alexander marched alongside the tax collectors as they returned to the khan's horde. Allowing the tax collectors to leave the city empty-handed would have meant war, and Alexander would rather fight Swedes than Mongols. Alexander played Batu's game in order to fulfill his own long-brewing ambitions.[72]

For the Mongols, census-taking was a key technique of rule. It was essential to both the tümen and taxation, not least because people themselves constituted one form of payment the Mongols collected. Already in Chinggis's time, the Mongols counted the households of conquered peoples in order incorporate subjects into the tümen and eventually the military. According to the *Secret History,* Chinggis ordered his adoptive son Shigi Qutuqu to keep the population register, known as the Blue Register *(köke debter),* in proper order. Quite likely this primary form of registration developed into the tax census. Many scholars have argued that the Mongols learned registration practices from the Chinese, but persuasive evidence shows that the Mongols borrowed their method from the old steppe empires.[73]

We know that, as the Mongols gained ground in the west in the early 1240s, they made a systematic effort to count Russians, because *Basqaq* and *darughachi*—tax collectors—were sent to the yielding Russian cities. As soon as the inhabitants surrendered, the Mongols asked them to "come out so that we may count you according to our custom." In 1245 Batu ordered the first census of the Russian principalities. His letter to the kniaz of Kiev, recorded in the *Sofijskaya Chronicle,* ordered all subjects, including fugitives, to register for the *dan',* the tribute. New subjects were also required to enroll in the Horde's troops and perform community service, such as herd management and maintenance of river fording points.[74]

The Mongol tithe required 10 percent of everything—people, goods, and animals. While traveling in Russia, Plano Carpini heard that a Mongol tithe collector—a Muslim, perhaps an old administrator of the Qara Khitai—was demanding from every Russian family he counted one boy out of three. He also apparently took unmarried men and women and poor people. According to Plano Carpini, other items collected as taxes included "the skin of a white bear, a black beaver, a black sable, a black fox and the black pelt of a certain animal." Those lacking such goods would have to pay in other ways. "Whoever does not produce these things is to be led off to the Tartars and reduced to slavery among them," Plano Carpini wrote.[75]

The Mongols adapted the tümen system to sedentary populations. In the Horde, contingents of Russians, Alans, Bulgars, Magyars, and others were divided into units of 10, 100, 1,000, and 10,000, a task that fell on census takers. Their job was thus not only to survey but also to maintain the redistribution system by organizing the people into groups to which revenue shares were directed. The 1245 census was intended for use by the Jochid hordes and by the empire as a whole, a double assignment that allowed Batu to create a much-needed embryonic administration for the new territories, although he never managed to complete the first census.

At that time tax collection was the empire's main source of revenue, more lucrative than trade and other moneymaking ventures. As the Mongols took over foreign territories, they quickly realized that it was more useful for tributes to be paid in local goods and currencies: raw silk in the east; fur-based currency or silver ingots in the pagan and Christian north; and dinars and dirhams in the city of Bulgar, the Caucasus, and Central Asia. The Mongols actually created new local coins because existing ones in conquered places bore the symbols of the rulers whom the Mongols deposed. Thus Ögödei implemented fiscal reforms around 1231–1232 and issued new coins for Central Asian taxpayers. Later he issued separate coins for merchants and craftsmen settled in Qaraqorum. The first Qaraqorum coin featured Ögödei's tamga and combined words in Arabic and Uighur scripts.[76]

Ögödei's new coins were different from the earlier coins struck under Chinggis Khan. Reflecting Mongol conquests of Muslim lands, for example, some of Ögödei's coins contained the Islamic profession of faith; mentioned khānī or qānī, meaning "imperial"; and included the name or simply the title of the Abbasid caliph al-Nāsir li-Dīn Allāh, though he was deceased. The familiar name of the caliph was meant to reassure the Sunni Muslims who used these coins. The Mongols were appropriating one of the foundational rights of Muslim rulers: the *sikka,* the right to mint coins.

The Mongols manufactured the money in which their subjects had to pay tribute. In 1243 the Mongol general Baiju conducted the census in Georgian and Armenian lands; the following year, the Mongols started minting coins in the same area. In 1246–1247 the Georgians were reportedly paying the Mongols a tribute of 40,000 bezants. The coins had a mounted archer engraved on them, along with the inscription *ulugh Munqul ulush nyk,* meaning "one great Mongol nation." In keeping with the Georgians' participation in Muslim-dominated trade networks, the inscription was in Arabic script. In 1248 the same coin was issued in the city of Bulgar, on the Volga. The Mongols were turning their new subjects into taxpayers as quickly as they could.[77]

The Mongols had good reason to issue coins featuring Islamic signifiers: they wanted to enter the Islamic mercantile system. Founded on trust in a political order nominally headed by the caliph, the Islamic system was the most extensive and integrated commercial network in Eurasia, stretching from the Qara Khitai to the Mediterranean and including a large section of Africa. Abbasid dinars and dirhams were used, and often imitated, from Sweden to North Africa. In the crusader kingdoms, the Franks used Fatimid dinars and minted both dinars and dirhams bearing the Muslim profession of faith. The Mongols successfully conformed to the existing system. With the aid of Muslim advisers whom they pressed into service—including Qara Khitan and Khwarezmian financiers and the best minters of Baghdad, Tabriz, and

Balkh—the Mongols produced coins that Muslims instantly identified as acceptable means of payment.

The new issuance of Islamic coins roughly coincided with Great Khan Güyük's second census, taken in 1247. This census was of a much larger scale than its 1245 predecessor. The Mongols planned to register the sedentary populations of China, Central Asia, Iran, and the Russian principalities. Due to the complexity of the process and local resistance, they succeeded only partially. In the western wing, where Batu did not comply with Güyük's orders, a proper census would not take place until around 1254, when a new great khan, Möngke, had ordered again that the entire population of the empire be counted. This time Batu decided to cooperate.[78]

The great census would finally be completed in 1259. In 1257, according to the *Yuan shi,* Möngke nominated a chief darughachi for the Volga region. A number of counters—*chislenitsi,* in the Russian sources—assisted him. They covered Crimea, the Caucasus, the Qipchaq steppe, and the north, possibly up to southern Siberia. They counted the population of Suzdal, Ryazan, Murom, and Vladimir. The region of Novgorod came last, in 1259. The Mongols sent only a few men to supervise the tax collection and relied heavily on local elites to convince hostile cities and villages to comply. Andrei, who preceded Alexander Nevsky as kniaz of Vladimir, also became a spokesman for the Mongol census, as he too understood that helping the census takers would bring favor.[79]

The Jochid census operations took around five years, a surprisingly long period in comparison with the rest of the empire. It may be that Jochids counted things other Mongols did not—not only houses but also animals, cultivated fields, vineyards, orchards, barns, and mills.[80] Bitigchis, imperial secretaries, developed a writing system for administrative purposes like the census. They also created a centralized chancellery and archives to assist in tracking people, goods, and lands. Lists of these items were sent to the great khan's administrators, who compiled from them a comprehensive record of resources at hand. The Mongols counted houses and tents rather than individuals, although they did note people's professions and social status. They especially valued craftsmen, metalworkers, jewelers, traders, translators, religious leaders, musicians, and those who could read and write.[81]

As a general rule, the Mongols exempted clergymen from the *kupchir,* the main tax, and from a number of secondary obligations like supplying the yam. Tax exemptions were highly advantageous. Mongol leaders granted them not only to Christian, Muslim, Buddhist, and Taoist religious men, but also to those who had contributed to building the empire, such as Chinggis's close circle and their descendants, military men, and literati. Those exempted were called *tarkhans.* The tarkhans became a new category of influential people who had nothing in common except their protected status and a strong interest in seeing the Mongol regime prosper.[82]

The Mongols maintained their old sharing system until the end of Möngke's reign in 1259. While the system was in force, the descendants of Jochi had to share the Russians, Bulgars, Alans, Armenians, Georgians, and Qipchaqs with other members of the golden lineage. They also shared their three most lucrative sources of income, including the per-household tax and the yam supplies. In exchange the Jochids received revenues from China, Afghanistan, Iran, and Azerbaijan, which more than compensated for their losses. In addition to redistributing wealth and manpower, administrative undertakings coordinated at the level of the entire empire, like the censuses, helped to knit the empire together. The census also created new linkages on the ground between the hordes and their sedentary subjects, as the Jochids' relationship with the kniazia revealed.

The Beginnings of Mongol Domination in Russia

Before the Mongol conquests, both Kiev and Novgorod enjoyed special status. Unlike the other Russian principalities, they had no local dynasty of princes. The Russians were bound to a centuries-old system in which Kiev was granted to the senior kniaz, according to the lateral succession system that determined the hierarchy of the kniazia. The rivalry over rulership in Kiev governed the kniazia's political agendas and fostered fierce conflicts among them. The Novgorodians, meanwhile, distanced themselves from the other Russian principalities. Having established their own sophisticated system of governance, they hired a prince to rule them but granted him only limited powers and forbade him from levying taxes on Novgorod and its lands. The free artisans, merchants, and boyars of Novgorod collected their taxes themselves and fixed the amount they paid, in the form of furs, to their kniaz.[83]

The Mongols brutally terminated the old order of succession in Kiev as well as the freedom of the Novgorodians to choose their own kniaz. Now Batu's horde was the capital. Batu signed off on the kniazia's selection for grand prince, who technically had authority over all the kniazia, and the grand prince was, in turn, supposed to appoint governors to rule Novgorod. By disrupting the Kievan regime, the Mongols broke the Russians' system of tax collection to create a new one. Novgorodians resented the enforcement, all the more as they had not been militarily defeated. After Alexander's death in 1263, they negotiated relentlessly to regain their unique status until Alexander's brother Iaroslav, the new grand prince, agreed to let the Novgorodians organize tax collection themselves. The Mongols allowed this as long as they received their own payments. In less than twenty years, a new structure of government had emerged in the Russian lands. This structure drastically changed the balance of power among the kniazia, as now it was the favor of the Mongols that decided who would be designated as grand prince and granted authority to collect taxes.

Hordes had multiple ways to incorporate dominated people, and the Jochids managed to navigate between political centralization and local autonomy. They tolerated Russian micropolitics as long as it sustained their own politics, which played out on a grander scale. The Russian principalities were at the margins of the Jochids' domain, sedentary societies that bordered the steppe, which was the Horde's center. These clusters of outlying villages and towns were nonetheless integrated into the empire through the yam and trade routes. For peasants and citizens, taxation was more acceptable than violent domination. The Mongols initiated a longstanding social, cultural, and political entanglement with the Russians, who understood that the Mongol regime would be more supple and stable than the Kievan. That engagement would have profound consequences for the development of Russia.

4

The Great Mutation

The Mamluk emissaries had been on the road for more than two months. Starting in Cairo, they sailed the Nile to Alexandria and crossed the Mediterranean, where they entered the Byzantine Empire. Just two years earlier, Emperor Michael Palaiologos had taken Constantinople back from the Crusaders. An ally of the Mamluks—the warrior-dominated sultanate encompassing Egypt and Syria—Michael gave the Mamluks his blessing and allowed them to pass the straits of the Dardanelles and the Bosporus. From there the emissaries crossed the Black Sea and reached the southern Crimean coast, arriving in the fortified harbor of Sudak. Soon the Jochids learned that foreign envoys were in town. A deputy of the khan came to see the emissaries and provided them horses from the yam, armed escorts, and a guide, for the Mamluks were traveling deep into the steppe to a place they had never seen.

As the envoys approached the banks of the Volga, the number of tents, people, and herds kept growing. Russian boats and caravans from many corners of the world, loaded with food, drink, and goods, were slowly converging on a single point. That point was the envoys' destination, too: the horde of Berke Khan. As the envoys approached, a high official welcomed them. They were assigned a tent and given food. Soon they were taken to the khan's precinct and instructed on proper behavior in the ruler's presence. They were to leave their weapons, including knives, outside the tent, and they were not to keep their bows in their cases, leave them strung, or put arrows in their quivers. On pain of death, the Mamluks were not to touch or walk on the threshold of the khan's tent.

Berke's tent was lavishly decorated, its white-felt walls lined with silk and carpets embroidered with gems and pearls. The tent was also enormous and packed with people—as many as five hundred horsemen, according to the envoys' reports. The guests entered the tent from the left side and found Berke sitting on a throne. He wore a Chinese silk robe and donned, by way of a crown, a Mongol hat. The envoys made a note of his thin beard and his hair gathered in braids, revealing the precious stones set in gold rings in his ears. His belt, too, was inlaid with gemstones. The envoys saw no sword on his side; instead Berke was adorned with black horns hooped with gold and a purse of green leather. His boots were made of red velvet, and his feet rested on a cushion, as if he were suffering from a gout attack. His chief wife and two other ladies were beside him. More than fifty begs were seated in a semicircle, all staring at the visitors.

The emissaries handed over their letter. The khan seemed intrigued and asked the high official to translate it. Only then did the khan allow the envoys to pass to the right side of the tent, where they kneeled down against the felt walls. This was likely an indication of their acceptance. Berke questioned the envoys about Egypt and the Nile. Satisfied with the answers, he ordered his servants to bring the foreigners kumis, meat, fish, and mead. The Mamluk envoys stayed in the khan's horde twenty-six days. They were invited several times to be in the presence of the khan and his chief wife. The ruling couple offered them food, drinks, gifts, and cash and kept enquiring about elephants, giraffes, and the Nile and its floods. Finally Berke gave them an answer to bring to the sultan.

The emissaries headed back to Cairo with joyous news, confirming what the sultan had heard through merchants: the khan, together with his wives and horsemen, had indeed converted to Islam. Berke's horde hosted muezzins, imams, and shaykhs, and it had mobile schools where children learned to read the Koran. The rest of the khan's reply was perhaps even more consequential, for the khan agreed to an alliance with the sultan and promised to sell slave warriors to the Mamluks.[1]

Illustration of a silver buckle depicting a fantastic creature (Horde, thirteenth century), which was part of a rawhide belt including twenty-nine decorative pieces that are still preserved. Such belts were produced in Jochid workshops until the mid-fourteenth century.

Berke was a transformative figure in the Horde. He was the first khan installed exclusively by the Jochid begs, without confirmation by the great khan. This was a signal of what was to come, as Berke solidified the Horde's independence from the Toluid-dominated Mongol center. He also redirected the Horde toward Islam, dramatically altering its internal culture and politics and reorienting its place on the world stage by pivoting toward Muslim rulers and traders. Yet, for all his divergence from Mongol traditions, Berke maintained a distinctively Mongol regime, one that prioritized commerce and redistribution, acceptance of diversity, and rule through vassalage. It was not always easy. Competition with other Mongols, in particular the Ilkhanids to the south, nearly suffocated the Horde economically. Yet the Jochids persevered, thanks in large measure to their engagement with the Mamluks and other new trading partners. In his person and his policies, Berke epitomized the adaptiveness of Mongol ways of life and rule.

Berke

Batu died in 1255, most likely. He had lived on the banks of the Volga for ten years, was nearly fifty years old, and had become one of the most influential figures of the Mongol Empire. He had succeeded his father early. When the other grandsons of Chinggis Khan came to rule, Batu was the oldest khan in the empire, which granted him an unquestioned authority. Mongol official sources reported that during quriltai nobody dared to oppose him. Yet he had always been second after the great khan.[2]

Batu entrusted the throne to Sartaq, his first-born, but Sartaq died soon after the great khan had confirmed his position. Möngke then nominated Ulaqchi, a direct descendant of Batu, to lead the ulus of Jochi. Ulaqchi was either Batu's fourth son or the son of Sartaq. But Ulaqchi, too, lasted just a short time as khan. A year after Batu's death, the Horde had lost two more leaders, leaving the job to Berke, who was enthroned in 1256. Berke was Batu's half-brother. Already in his forties, Berke had the status of an elder. But he was a controversial choice, both within the Horde and beyond it. A Muslim and the grandson of the Khwarezmian shah, Berke had forged deep ties with fellow Muslims in Central Asia and Anatolia. Even Batu had grown to fear his brother's influence. And nothing indicates that Berke visited the great khan before he sat on Batu's throne.[3]

Berke took Batu's penchant for independence to a new level. While Batu enhanced the Horde's autonomy, he never openly contested Toluid power. Berke, by contrast, resisted the Toluids, even though they were the most powerful branch of the golden lineage. The Toluids had been ascendant since the death of Güyük, when they mobilized against the Ögödeids in an effort to wrest control of the throne. Batu, with the support of Orda and fellow Jochids, had sided with Tolui's line and supported Möngke for the office of great khan. On the other side, the candidate was Ögödei's grandson Shiremün. After the Toluids discovered a conspiracy against Möngke, they carried out a massive purge against the descendants of Ögödei and Chagatay. One generation after the Jochids lost their claim to the supreme office of great khan, two other branches of the golden lineage were also pushed out. Only the Toluids remained in the race for the imperial throne. But throughout the 1250s, the Jochids were emerging as a counterweight, and more forcefully under Berke.

The 1260s finally brought the clash between the Jochid and Toluid lines, leading to the partition of the old empire. This was the consequence of a series of disagreements concerning succession and conquest. The empire grew explosively in the 1260s, but the growth was uneven. The Toluids maintained an aggressive expansionist posture, but the Jochids did not. Having left their native valleys and mountains for a flat country and more temperate climate, the Jochids were busy making the Qipchaq steppe their own and needed time to acclimate to their new environment. Around the same time, the Toluids, still centered on Mongolia, prepared large-scale attacks against China, northwestern Iran, and the Middle East. The empire suddenly was riven by clashing political dynamics. In the west continued conquest was in Toluid interests but endangered the consolidation of Jochid power; in the east conquest was a necessity for consolidating Toluid power but offered the Jochids no benefits. Eventually this divergence split the Mongols. Their empire assumed a new shape, with the Horde de facto autonomous and stronger than before, and a new Toluid ulus, referred to as the Ilkhanate, in parts of the Muslim world. The Ilkhanids were established and first ruled by Hülegü, Great Khan Möngke's brother and Chinggis's grandson. Hülegü was a formidable political figure and warrior, whose war with the Jochids precipitated the first great transmutation of Chinggis's empire since 1206.

The Dismemberment of the Central Islamic Lands

In 1251 Möngke entrusted Hülegü to finish the work Chinggis had started when he sent Jochi, Sübötei, and Jebe to take over the Khwarezmian Empire and pursue the Qipchaqs. Now it was time to press even farther west, to Iraq, Iran, Azerbaijan, Greater Armenia, Anatolia, and Egypt. Möngke ordered two in every ten Mongol warriors to enroll under Hülegü's command. Historians have estimated that there were between 70,000 and 170,000 Mongols in Hülegü's army of 300,000 fighters; even the lowest estimate demonstrates that the Mongol leaders had mobilized their manpower on a vast scale. In addition the number of siege engineers had increased from Chinggis's times, and the siege engines had improved.[4]

The Middle Eastern campaign began in 1256. First, the Mongols targeted eastern Iran, where they dismantled the fortresses associated with the sect of Nizari-Isma'ili and captured the group's master. Next they subjugated the Lurs and the Kurds, nomadic peoples living in the western part of the region. In the winter of 1257–1258, the Mongols moved on to the Abbasid Caliphate based in Iraq. The conquest of

Baghdad took them less than a fortnight. The Abbasids were supposed allies of the Mongols, and Caliph al-Musta'sim had sent envoys and gifts to Güyük a few years earlier. But al-Musta'sim rejected the Mongols' demands for formal submission and refused Hülegü's request for military support against the Nizari-Isma'ili, Lurs, and Kurds. The caliph simply could not support operations against Muslims anywhere, even though he formally controlled only Baghdad. Owing to his position, which implied universal sovereignty over Muslims, he felt moral obligations far beyond his domain. Spurned by al-Musta'sim, Hülegü sacked Baghdad and had the caliph executed.[5]

Berke's men took an active part in the siege of Baghdad but not in the looting of the city or the execution of the caliph. Historical records also indicate that Hülegü never consulted Berke on these actions, neither of which appears to have been included in the plan the two leaders had agreed to. Whether Berke disagreed with Hülegü's violent moves is, however, unclear. As a Muslim Berke may have opposed executing the caliph, who was understood to be a sanctified person and the successor of the Prophet Muhammad. But as a Mongol prince, Berke perhaps respected Hülegü's right to punish al-Musta'sim, who had broken his promises to his Mongol allies. What we can say is that Berke's supporters claimed he opposed the looting and execution, although this might well have been an attempt to clear the khan's name in front of a Muslim audience that was critical to his popularity and power.

After the submission of Iraq, Hülegü enjoyed the milking season in Azerbaijan and wintered in the Mughan steppe. He concentrated his next campaign on the Muslim Ayyubid dynasty that Saladin had founded nearly a century earlier in Syria, Palestine, and Egypt. By the time Hülegü attacked the Ayyubids in 1259, they had lost control of Egypt to the Mamluks, but Hülegü had his sights on the Mamluks as well. The central Islamic lands, including the still-Ayyubid areas of Damascus, Aleppo, and Hama, held enormous geopolitical and symbolic significance. Hülegü quickly dispatched the Ayyubids, elevating Mongol power to a new level.[6]

Hülegü's conquests strengthened the empire, bringing in new subjects and their wealth. But the gains were concentrated in Toluid hands, often at the expense of the Jochids. Möngke had reoriented imperial policies to strengthen Toluid interests. For instance, while spoils were still shared according to the traditional qubi system, the process was directly supervised by the Toluids through a new central secretariat they created. Möngke also turned over Jochid lands to members of his own lineage; after entrusting the Caucasus to Berke in 1251, the great khan reassigned the territory to Hülegü in 1254. Not only that, but the new conquests limited the Jochids' potential future expansion into the dominions Chinggis Khan had set aside for them. Hülegü's armies took position in Khorasan, Georgia, Iraq, Syria, and east Anatolia, preventing the Jochids from pushing outward their southern borders.[7]

It seems that, in spite of all this, Berke remained on peaceful terms with Möngke throughout the 1250s. As a senior member of the golden lineage, Berke had to take an active part in the Middle Eastern campaigns, and Jochid troops contributed to the onslaught against the Lurs, Kurds, Nizari-Isma'ili, Abbasids, and Ayyubids. Berke expected to receive a substantial share of the spoils and, being Jochi's heir, to rule at least some portions of the new conquered territories: after all, Chinggis Khan had entrusted the West to his eldest son and his descendants. Thus when the Syrian campaign began in fall 1259, Berke was still supporting Hülegü's war efforts.[8]

The sudden destruction of the Ayyubids put the rest of the Middle East on notice, and shockwaves quickly reached the Mamluk sultan in Cairo. With the age-old Ayyubid power extinguished, the regime in Cairo became the last defender of the Muslim faith. The Mamluks were also the Mongols' next target. But before the Mongols could begin their assault, Möngke died, and Hülegü departed eastward to take part in the election of the next great khan. He ordered Ked-Buqa, his most trusted general, and a contingent of scout troops to hold the newly conquered peoples in Syria and Palestine and wait for the return of the mass army.[9] In 1260, before leaving for the east, Hülegü sent envoys to Cairo to inform the Mamluks that they must submit or be destroyed. His message boasted that no one could escape the Mongols, who had received from Tengri the right and the task to rule the world. It was a deep insult to the Mamluk sultan, Qutuz, who was a respected warrior and who of course did not recognize any right granted by Tengri. The message also mocked Qutuz personally, recalling his origins in the Khwarezmian Empire, where he had been sold into slavery following the Mongol conquest. Finally, Hülegü denigrated Qutuz as the usurper of the Ayyubid throne in Egypt.[10]

Incensed, Qutuz took the bait. He ordered Hülegü's envoys killed and their heads hanged on Bab Zwayla, one of Cairo's southern gates. The Mongols now had their justification for war, but the sultan was not about to wait to be attacked. He assembled a sizeable army, not less than ten thousand horsemen, reinforced by Turkmen, Bedouin, and Kurds as well as recruits fleeing Mongol domination. In spring 1260 the Mamluk army entered Palestine. In the process, they crossed territory held by Frankish crusaders, but the Franks allowed them to pass. The Franks had recently clashed with Ked-Buqa's men, who had retaliated by sacking Sidon. It seems some of the crusaders saw the Mongols as a more immediate threat than the Mamluks. The Frankish leaders of Acre even gave supplies to the Mamluk army.

When the Mamluks entered Palestine from the west, Ked-Buqa was on the eastern side of the Jordan River. Upon learning of the approaching Mamluks, he crossed the river to confront them. He had no choice but to face the Mamluks with only one tümen and less-than-dependable allies. The battle took place in Ayn Jalut, north of Jerusalem, on September 3, 1260. After several hours of fighting, the Mamluks crushed the tümen and killed Ked-Buqa. The Mongols suffered badly from the untimely defection of the Ayyubid prince al-Ashraf Musa, whose troops were supposed to reinforce Ked-Buqa's left wing but instead departed the battlefield at the very moment the Mongols most needed them. The defeated warriors escaped where they could, with the Mamluk emir Baybars and his horsemen on their tails. Baybars's men followed Ked-Buqa's retreating forces up to northern Syria and killed almost all of them.[11]

News of Ked-Buqa's defeat spread quickly. Immediately upon learning of the Mamluk victory, Mongols in Damascus, Aleppo, and Hama fled, and soon the Mongols had abandoned the whole of Palestine and Syria. The locals avenged themselves by plundering Mongol camps, chasing and killing runaways, and capturing women and children who had been left behind. Most of Syria was now in the hands of the Mamluk army. It was a resounding defeat, but the Mongols had experienced those before. One of the main motivations of Mongol warfare was, after all, revenge. They always struck back, and they never forgave. From the day the Mamluks marched on Ked-Buqa, they became the blood enemy of the Mongols, who knew they would need to mobilize their full forces to defeat the sultan. When Hülegü returned from the east, he declared the destruction of the Mamluks an absolute priority. But carrying out his wish would not be easy. Not only had he lost one of his most trusted generals, but, as I describe below, the quriltai to elect Möngke's replacement had spurred Mongol infighting that threatened one of Hülegü's key support: the partnership with the Jochids.

Asphyxia

Succession struggles engulfed the empire after the death of Great Khan Möngke in August 1259. His brothers Arigh Böke and Qubilai each claimed the mantle of the great khan and organized their own enthronement quriltais. Both enjoyed strong support among the Mongols and their allies. Since neither was willing to withdraw, one would have to defeat the other in battle to claim the throne.[12]

Berke sided with Arigh Böke. First Berke had a new Bulgar coin minted under Arigh Böke's name. Then the ruler of the Horde contacted Qubilai's enemies. In 1260 Berke sent his envoys to the Delhi Sultanate, whose rulers had always refused Mongol's demands for allegiance. Berke's support for Arigh Böke put him on a collision course with Hülegü, who backed Qubilai. In 1261 the tension between Berke and Hülegü finally boiled over. For a decade, Hülegü had been slowly making gains at the Horde's expense, taking territories that Chinggis had set aside for the Jochids. Now Hülegü was trying to take the Jochids' share of revenues from Iran. With support from Qubilai, Hülegü installed a delegate in Herat, where the taxes and tributes of eastern Iran were centralized before being distributed to the members of the golden lineage. Berke responded by ordering one of his commanders, Negüder, to defend his share. Negüder chased out Hülegü's men, ensuring that the Jochids would receive their due and that Berke and Hülegü's cold peace was now a hot war.[13]

Hülegü accused Berke's commanders of treachery and witchcraft and began to purge Jochids from the Mongol armies under his command. In particular, Hülegü struck at Tutar, a grandson of Jochi who led a contingent of warriors that operated in Iran under Hülegü's nominal supervision. Tutar and Hülegü had come to loggerheads over the Herat revenues, and now Hülegü accused Tutar of plotting against him. It is not known if in fact Tutar was planning any foul play, but Hülegü produced what was apparently convincing proof. Berke could not oppose Tutar's trial and execution. The result was another blood feud, as Tutar's son Nogay—a seasoned commander close to Berke, who would later become a major figure in Jochid history—never forgot what Hülegü had done to his father.[14]

After targeting the Jochids, Hülegü attacked other Mongol delegates who had commanded in the Middle East. Hülegü's goal was not only to curtail the authority of the old delegates but to also inject Toluids into the administration from Afghanistan to Anatolia, at all levels of governance. Carrying out such an effort meant severe internecine warfare. For instance, high on Hülegü's hit list came Baiju, a respected and experienced warrior of enormous pedigree: he was close kin of Jebe, one of Chinggis's key generals, and his father had belonged to Chinggis's keshig. Baiju had also led the first invasion of the Seljuq Sultanate and ruled for ten years over Azerbaijan and Anatolia. Baiju did not support the Jochids, but he also neither respected nor feared Hülegü. What he wanted was to maintain his power and autonomy. Hülegü would not have that; his men killed Baiju, through poisoning or execution. For the first time, the Mongols were conquering at the expense of their own.[15]

Berke decided to strike back. Although Berke made no formal declaration of war, in the winter of 1261–1262, he and his warriors pushed deep into the Caucasus—former Jochid territory, now under Hülegü's authority. The Jochid troops crossed the Terek River, advanced along the Caspian coast, and took possession of Derbent and Shirvan. Berke's aim was to secure access to Tabriz, on the other side of the Caucasus, because the Horde's elites had strong financial interests in the city. Tabriz was western Iran's equivalent of Herat: the center of fiscal administration. The Jochids received up to 30 percent of Tabriz's revenues, making the city a critical pressure point. In addition Berke's *ortaqs,* his licensed traders, had trading posts and clients in Tabriz, where they made lucrative transactions in their khan's name.[16]

On August 20, 1262, Hülegü left his summer pasture of Ala-dagh, near Van Lake, to confront Berke at Shirvan. It was early in the war

Hülegü chases Berke, painting from *Livre des Merveilles du monde et autres récits* (illuminated manuscript, France, c. 1410–1412). The manuscript, concerning relations between Western Europe and Mongol Asia, speaks to Europeans' interest in and knowledge of Mongol politics. (Bibliothèque nationale, Paris, France/Bridgeman Images)

season, but the situation required a forceful response. The Jochids had already smashed his vanguard, meeting little or no resistance. Once Hülegü's forces arrived on the scene, though, fortunes turned quickly. In November his army pushed the Jochids up to Derbent. In December Hülegü himself arrived at Derbent, expelled Berke's men, and chased them beyond the Terek River.

Berke's campaign was a failure. Within two years, the Jochids had lost their positions and influence in the Caucasus, Khorasan, the Seljuq Sultanate, and Baghdad. The Jochids also were in a difficult position in Khwarezm. They controlled northern Khwarezm, but the southern part of the region was in the hands of Alghu, the grandson of Chagatay. Alghu was initially appointed the leader of Chagatay's ulus by Arigh Böke, but in 1262 Alghu switched sides and turned to Qubilai. Alghu expanded the Chagatayids' territories, incorporating areas that belonged to the Jochids, while progressively taking full control of Bukhara and

Samarkand, which had historically been under the joint administration of the Chinggisid houses.

Alghu's defection from Arigh Böke had serious consequences, as it led to Arigh Böke's surrender and Qubilai's victory. If this was not bad enough for the Jochids, who had supported Arigh Böke, Hülegü also cancelled the Jochid share that had flowed from Tabriz since the times of Batu and had the Jochid ortaqs expelled from the city. Berke's military operations also put the Jochid troops under Hülegü's command in a dangerous position, though Berke managed to extract them. In the summer of 1262, many of these Jochid refugees rallied around Negüder near Ghazni, in Afghanistan, where they fought against other Mongols allied with Hülegü. But Negüder quickly lost ground and then his men. Hülegü seized the moment to appropriate the Jochid tax income sent from Herat.[17]

Berke's army retaliated, forcing Hülegü's men to retreat to Shirvan in January 1263. By spring, the milking season had arrived, and the war was halted. But aggressive diplomacy was in full swing.[18] In May Berke sent his first embassy to Cairo to coordinate with the Mamluks against their mutual enemy. Hülegü had transgressed yasa, Berke explained—the sacred law of his own people. "His only aim is to slaughter the human beings with hate," Berke wrote. The khan asked the Mamluks "to send an armed force in the direction of the Euphrates in order to block Hülegü's passage." Unable to defeat Hülegü himself, Berke needed serious help, wherever it came from—even if that meant allying with non-Mongols against Mongols.[19]

Over the next few decades, the region between the Terek and the Kura rivers would be contested by the descendants of Jochi and Hülegü, but the threat Hülegü posed was not primarily territorial. It was economic. What mattered most to Berke and his shift men was maintaining tribute and trade. Hülegü was systematically severing the routes by which tribute and goods reached the Horde. In doing so, he was cutting off the redistribution system that was the lifeblood of any Mongol regime. If there were no more luxuries to distribute, the fuel of the system would dry up, and the whole society would collapse. Hülegü was strangling the Jochids.

The Mamluk Alliance

The Mamluk Sultanate is an oddity of history: a regime ruled by emancipated slaves. Historically, Islamic armies purchased slave warriors who

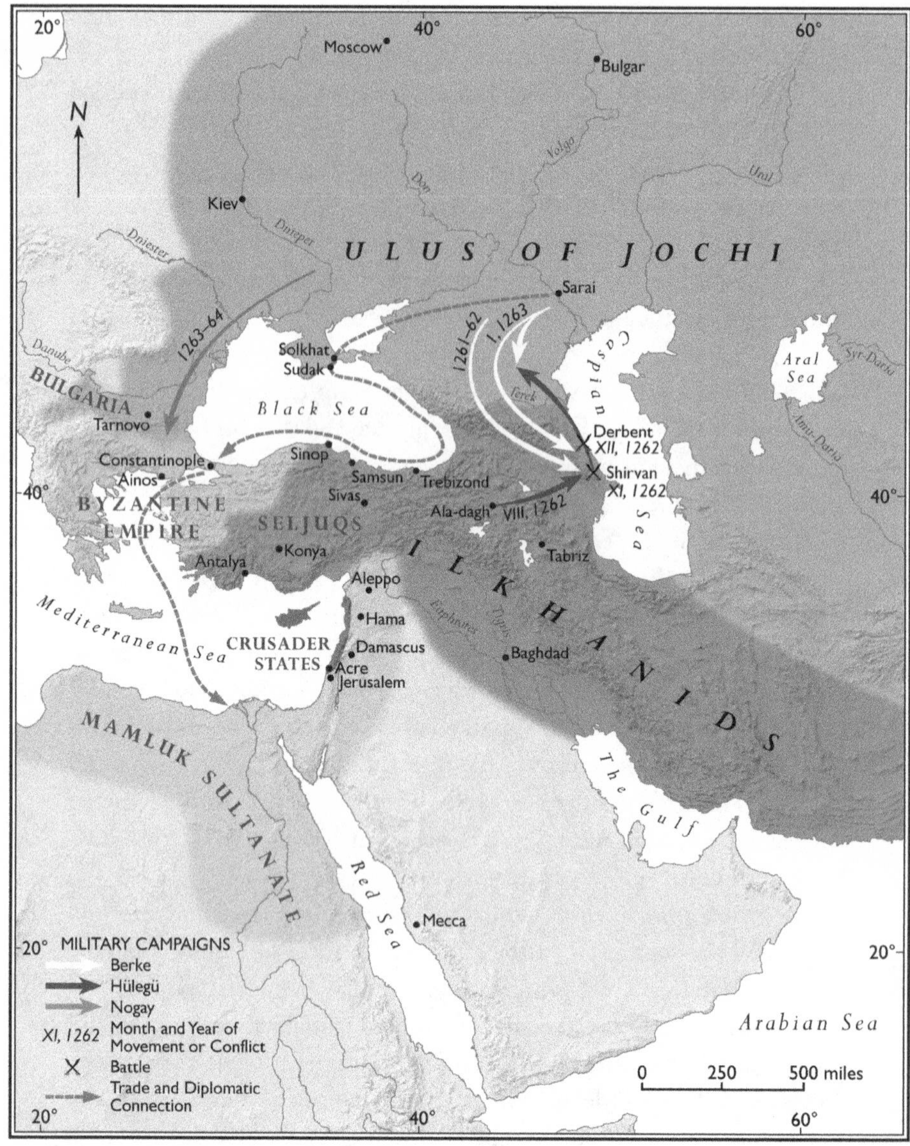

Movements of the Berke-Hülegü war, 1261–1264.

were called mamluks, the "owned." The last Ayyubid rulers bought mamluks in large numbers on Seljuq markets, especially in the Anatolian city of Sivas. Most of the slaves were young men born in the northwestern steppe or in the Caucasus. They came through the trade circuit that crossed Crimea, where merchants bought and sold them for textiles and furs. Batu had allowed this old circuit to grow, producing ample tax revenue for the Horde. But Hülegü disrupted the system when he ordered his armies to enter Anatolia and conquer the Seljuq Sultanate.

It wasn't the first time Mongols had invaded the Seljuq regime. In 1243 the Seljuqs had submitted after defeat at Köse-dag in eastern Anatolia. They were reduced to paying an annual tribute of clothing, horses, and gold. The Jochids considered 'Izz al-Dīn the sultan, and his people their own. But 'Izz al-Dīn in fact shared power with his brother Rukn al-Dīn, who had gained the support of the Toluids. In 1256 Hülegü arrived on the scene with the great army, siege engines, carts, and animals. He promptly appropriated the Mughan steppe, the region's best winter pasture, and ordered Baiju to move deeper into Seljuq lands. Sultan 'Izz al- Dīn's immediate reaction was to refuse entry to Baiju's men, for accepting them would have required relocating his own people. The Seljuqs had paid tribute; they had an agreement with the Mongols, and that agreement did not include allowing an occupation. But 'Izz al-Dīn could not fight Hülegü or Baiju and had to submit again.[20]

The colonization of eastern Anatolia was even more significant than the first Mongol campaign against the Seljuqs thirteen years earlier. This time Hülegü's annexation of the steppe belt from Mughan to Van Lake was definitive. Like the Jochids who made the Qipchaq steppe and the lower Volga their own, Hülegü's descendants kept this area for their ruler's horde. Their decision to populate Azerbaijan would also prevent, for nearly a century, any Jochid expansion to the south.[21]

The defeat of the Seljuqs gained Hülegü a reluctant partner. The Seljuqs participated in his campaign in Syria, culminating in the capture of Aleppo in February 1260. But in September the news of the Mamluk advance on the Syrian border and the Mongol defeat at Ayn Jalut gave 'Izz al-Dīn hope. He contacted Baybars, the Mamluk sultan, seeking an alliance against Hülegü. Yet it was too late for 'Izz al-Dīn. The Mongols had forced him to take out loans from their imperial treasury, and they were demanding reimbursement. In April 1261 a large army sent by Hülegü came after 'Izz al-Dīn. He fled and sought asylum in the empire of Nicaea, one of the successor states that emerged from the dissolution of the Byzantines.[22]

Michael Palaiologos, the emperor, welcomed his old friend. ʻIzz al-Dīn, whose mother was a Byzantine princess, had good relations with the Byzantine elites and had hosted Michael a few years earlier. In July 1261 the sultan participated in the military operations that allowed the emperor to take back Constantinople from the Latins. At roughly the same time, ʻIzz al-Dīn communicated with Hülegü's enemies, asking both the Jochids and Mamluks to send him troops. ʻIzz al-Dīn planned to go back to his former capital Konya and restore his power, and he offered to make Baybars the overlord of half of his sultanate. ʻIzz al-Dīn did not offer Berke anything and did not need to, for the sultan was a vassal of the khan by marriage—ʻIzz al-Dīn wed a Jochid princess, and his daughter was one of Berke's secondary wives. The alliance entitled ʻIzz al-Dīn to the Horde's protection.[23]

Baybars appreciated the Seljuq sultan's offer, but what he needed most was manpower to fight both the Crusaders and Hülegü. Only the Jochid khan could provide that: Berke had young men, widely considered superior mounted warriors, from the Qipchaq populations the Mongols had subjugated in the first half of the thirteenth century. But even if Berke agreed to sell the Qipchaqs, it would be hard to get them to Egypt because in 1262–1263 Hülegü's blockade set in. In the Caucasus, the Jochids could not move beyond the Kura River. Hülegü also installed checkpoints and flooded roads, preventing merchants from entering and leaving the Horde. The only way Jochid goods could escape Hülegü's blockade was for traders to push through the Black Sea to Constantinople. Given this, the next challenge for Baybars was to secure shipping rights through the Bosporus and Dardanelles, so that the slaves, sold at the old Crimean harbor of Sudak, could reach Egypt. To this end, Baybars concluded an agreement with Michael Palaiologos as soon as Michael had regained Constantinople. Michael agreed to let the sultan's envoys and merchants pass from the Black Sea to the Mediterranean through the Dardanelles and Bosporus straits, and the Byzantines received substantial income from the Mamluk trade in the form of taxes and gifts. In addition, Michael and Baybars opened a route from Alexandria to Constantinople, which allowed the Mamluks to bypass the Seljuq circuits cut off by Hülegü.[24]

The negotiations between the Jochids and Mamluks were carried out through the mediation of Alan merchants, probably slave traders. Sweetening the pot, in October 1262 Jochid refugees fleeing Hülegü's armies arrived in Damascus asking for Baybars's protection. Baybars welcomed them and sent lavish gifts to Berke. A few months later, Berke agreed to a pact with Baybars, 'Izz al-Dīn, and the Byzantine emperor Michael Palaiologos, along with Michael's allies the Genoese. The khan promised the Mamluk Sultanate young men from the heartland of the Horde, although they would mostly be tax defaulters, war captives, criminals, and poor workers. The new alliance between Berke and Baybars extended the trade route from Constantinople to the lower Volga, a journey that took two months or more depending on political and weather conditions.

Berke's decision to side with the Mamluks, the Toluids' main rivals in the Middle East, had an immediate effect: it stopped Hülegü on the Syrian border. The Mongols never reached the Mediterranean shore. They would have to rely on Greeks, Seljuqs, Armenians, Italians, and other go-betweens to bridge the Black Sea and Levantine coast to Europe. This explains why both Hülegü and Berke would allow a range of small maritime powers to emerge on their European borders. Venetians and Genoese started to send traders, ship owners, and lawyers to the Horde and to Hülegü's lands.

Even more significant, the Mongols' internal strife transformed the geopolitics of Islam, reorienting its Eurasian centers toward Cairo and the lower Volga. In less than a decade, the Mongols had destroyed the Abbasid state, caliphate, lineage, armies, and allies; reduced Baghdad to a small provincial town; and finished the Ayyubids. Suddenly Jochid leaders converted to Islam, provided military manpower to the Mamluks, and adopted Islamic symbols. In the lower Volga, Berke welcomed Muslim elites from everywhere. Before the end of the century, Sarai and Cairo would surpass Baghdad in political importance. By disrupting the *dar al-islam,* the Abode of Islam, and interfering with what was probably the largest socioeconomic system of the time, the Mongols brought about massive shifts in the Afro-Eurasian balance of power.

In July 1263 Baybars dispatched a new embassy to Berke. But the Mamluk envoys were stopped en route, in Constantinople, on Michael

Palaiologos's authority. Now Michael wanted to slow down the war between Hülegü and the Jochid-Mamluk alliance. Hülegü not only led Mongol armies, controlled Baghdad, Tabriz, and the Seljuqs, but he was also the emperor Michael's close neighbor—a force to be reckoned with on the Byzantines' doorstep. Michael had to choose: Would he maintain his promises to the Jochids, or would he break his promises to them to avoid antagonizing Hülegü? Michael chose the latter. He detained Sultan 'Izz al-Dīn, the Mamluk envoys, and the huge gift package the envoys were carrying to the Jochids. The gifts were worth several thousand dinars (gold coins); holding them outraged both Baybars and Berke.[25]

The Jochid reaction was immediate and brutal. Nogay, Berke's general, led the attack against the Byzantine Empire. As the son of Tutar, the senior commander Hülegü had executed about four years earlier, Nogay considered any ally of Hülegü's a personal enemy. Michael Palaiologos may not have been a treaty partner of Hülegü's, but the Byzantine emperor was at the very least appeasing Hülegü. With the cooperation of the Bulgarian king, Nogay destroyed several villages and cities in the Byzantine territory of Thrace. Eventually Michael agreed to free 'Izz al-Dīn and pay a heavy tribute to the Jochids. 'Izz al-Dīn was then relocated to Crimea, where Berke created a micro sultanate under 'Izz al-Dīn's patronage.[26]

Nogay's task was not only to rescue 'Izz al-Dīn and impose a tribute on Michael Palaiologos. Nogay was also to bring under firm control the lower valleys of Central Europe, and he accomplished this, his horde colonizing the area from the mouth of the Danube to the Dniester. Nogay thus brought the Jochids geographically nearer to the Byzantines, so the Horde's warriors could watch the Dardanelles and Bosporus and intervene in any activities that might foreclose access by the Jochids and their trade partners. Nogay also took control of the land route through Bulgaria, which compensated for Hülegü's closure of the roads through the Caucasus and northern Syria.

Fighting for Economic Independence

Nogay's conquests extended and reinforced Jochid authority over the lands north of the Black Sea, fulfilling crucial economic goals. The primary objective was to assert control over salt extraction. West of

Perekop, the isthmus connecting Crimea to the mainland of what is now Ukraine, salt was produced in large quantities. Salt was critical to nomads and sedentary people alike. They used the stuff to preserve food, enhance its flavor, and cure diseases. They also understood that adding small amounts of salt to water could prevent dehydration. People came from the Russian lands to purchase salt at the Perekop Isthmus, as Rubruck noticed in 1253:

> At the far end of this province there are many large lakes, on the shores of which are salt-water springs; as soon as the water from these runs into the lake it turns into salt, hard like ice. Baatu and [Sartaq] draw large revenues from these salt springs, from men come thither from the whole of Russia for salt, and for every cartload they give two lengths of cotton valued at half an *yperpera* [Byzantine gold coin]. Many ships also come by sea for the salt, all giving payment according to the amount each takes.[27]

Like Batu before him, Berke was keen to keep a firm hand on the salt-extracting regions. The lower Dnieper was one of them, and the only competition within hundreds of miles was the lower Volga, which was also Jochid territory. The Jochids thus established exclusive control over the production and trade of salt from western Asia to southeastern Europe.

As profitable as salt was, furs were even more lucrative. Historians estimate that the people of the far north provided more than half a million pelts a year, including those of sables and other martens, ermines, steppe foxes, beavers, squirrels, and hares. Archeological sites in northern Russia also reveal hunting of polar foxes, lynx, otters, badgers, woodchucks, ferrets, wolves, and wolverines, which provided yet more furs. The lands of darkness, as contemporaries called the far north, was the largest supplier of precious furs in Eurasia. The region was in Jochid hands.[28]

Fur was vital to survival in cold weather, but its commercial value lay also in its role as a luxury item. Furs were the standard luxury goods of the Islamic world. Already in the eighth century, the Abbasids considered furs a social marker par excellence. The Muslim elite adored *Burtasi,* the black and red fox furs used for hats, coats, and caftans. In the tenth century, a black Burtasi—so named for the Burtas people who hunted them—could cost more than a hundred dinars, a considerable sum. Wealthy Abbasids commonly had tent decorations and interior walls made of precious pelts. In the thirteenth century, the demand for furs in Iran, Central Asia, Mesopotamia, and North Africa was huge.[29]

When the Jochids took over the Ural and Volga valleys, the fur market was old and dense, featuring a good deal of long-distance trade. The market had always been shared across ethnic groups and was fiercely competitive. Volga Bulgars, Qipchaqs, and Russians from Rostov and Novgorod dominated the traffic. The Volga Bulgars channeled a great part of the trade through their cities and relied on well-established caravan routes to export toward Central Asia. They received furs directly from the hunters, but also from Russians who sailed to the middle Volga to sell pelts they had obtained through raids, tribute collection, and trade.[30]

The Qipchaqs developed an alternate route, which did not involve the far north and bypassed both Bulgars and Russians. They dealt directly with the Burtasi hunters and transported furs from the hinterlands of Volga Bulgaria to the harbor of Sudak. There, merchants arrived from the Seljuq Sultanate to exchange fabrics for slaves and pelts. Ibn al-Athīr recalled how the Qipchaqs used the harbor to export furs and other items to the Muslim world just before Mongol rule set in. Sudak "is a city of Qipchaqs," he wrote, "from which they receive their goods because it lies on the shore of the Khazar [Caspian] Sea and ships with clothing come to it; the clothing is sold for girls, slaves and Burtas furs, beaver, squirrel, and other items that are found in their land."[31]

The Qipchaqs, like the Volga Bulgars and the Russians, were middlemen. None of them were hunter-trappers. Hunting in the northern forests required specialized skills. Trappers had to master the terrain, ecology, and climate in order to survive the far-northern winter. They learned how to build and manipulate skis, dogsleds, and traps that would kill a target without ruining its pelt. They knew when the best time was to hunt and how best to ship the pelts to the merchant middlemen. The Jochids, for their part, did not need to worry about securing the pelts or even transporting them. Mongol involvement lay in control of the transit routes and markets. Hunters brought their pelts from the forest to the middle Volga; from there the pelts were sent to the lower Volga

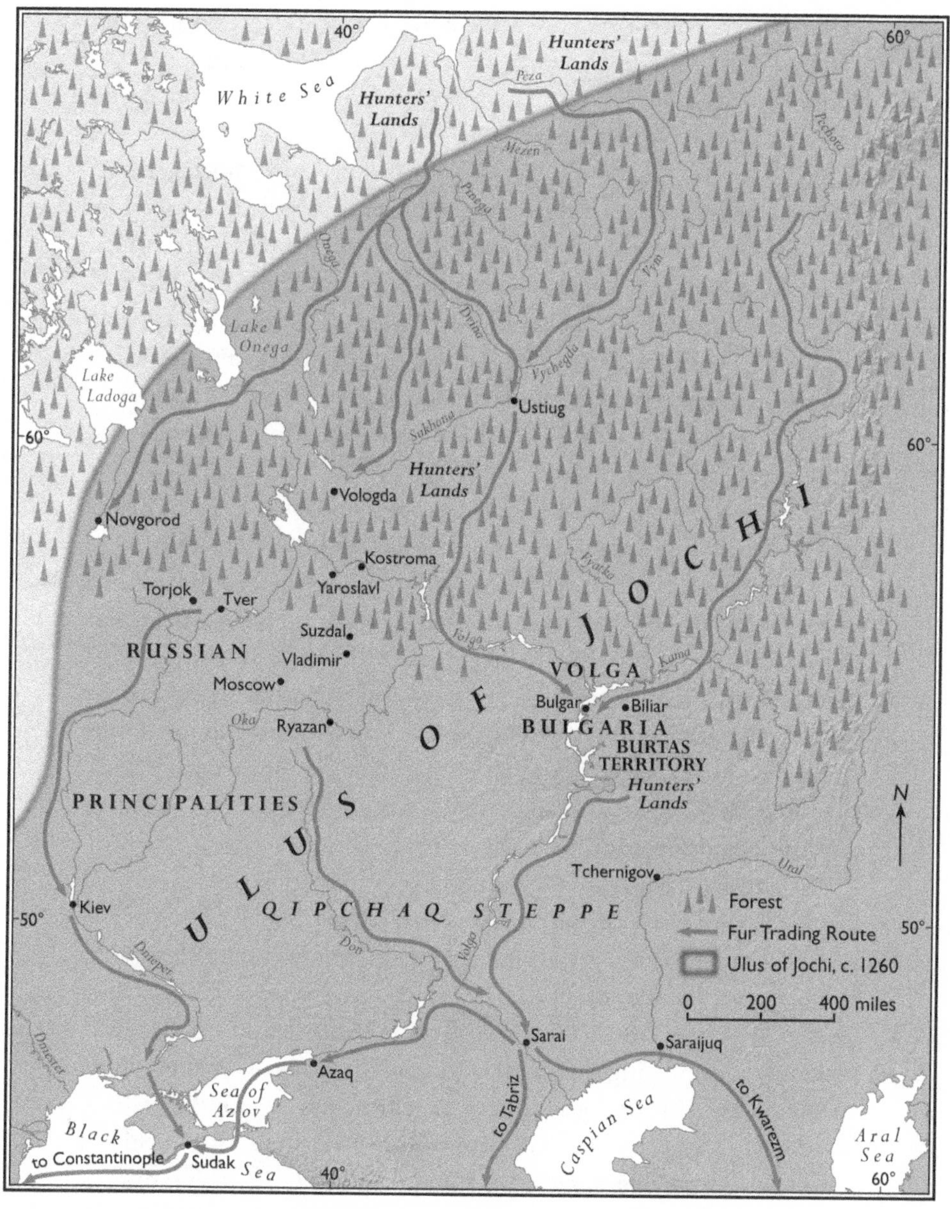

Fur trading routes along the Volga River and its tributaries.

and finally were dispatched by caravans to Crimea, Eastern Europe, and Urgench—the old Khwarezmian capital that now belonged to the Jochids. Russian merchants also transported furs along the Dnieper to Kiev or along the land route to Sudak. In other words, the top of the fur chain lay at the mouths of the Volga, Don, and Dnieper rivers, were the Jochids ran the ports and markets. Everything shipped by water passed through those ports, and a large volume of land traffic fed through the Horde's markets. When the Jochids realized that old fairs and regional markets in Volga Bulgaria were still attracting valuable cargo, they took over the markets and turned them into collection spots where furs would be packed and redirected toward their own camps. The Jochids also taxed the middlemen—the collectors and distributors.[32]

Through the fur trade, the Jochid hordes integrated Volga Bulgaria and the Russian principalities into their own political economy. As in other conquered lands, the Mongols did not destroy local subsistence systems; rather, they appropriated a share of the output. The Jochids intensified the north-south fur traffic, as it was in their own interests that the circulation between the Pechora River Basin and the lower river valleys remained fluid. The political gain lay in the contribution of furs and fur profits to the qubi, the sharing system. The shift men centralized furs, silver ingots, and other kinds of tax revenue, which the khan redistributed during quriltai and court banquets.

The fate of Sudak is indicative of the transformations in commercial life that occurred after Berke's conflict with Hülegü flared up. Sudak had long been an important harbor and it remained so under Batu's control. It continued to play that role under Berke, but changes had come. Southern Crimea now was closely linked to Constantinople and the Mediterranean world, turning Sudak into the main gate between the Horde and the West. This was one effect of the agreement among the Jochids, Mamluks, Byzantines, and Genoese, which had assured the Jochids a route through the Dardanelles and Bosporus straits, compensating for the loss of access to Tabriz, Sinope, and other commercial centers Hülegü had taken. The trade from Sudak also involved different players than it had decades earlier, with the Qipchaqs no longer in charge. The consequences of the trade alliance were far-reaching, despite its goal having been a short-term one: to circumvent Hülegü's blockade. Once the

Jochids took control, they did not let go, and the core of the Eurasian fur business remained in their hands for a century.[33]

The Mongol war of succession ended in 1264. Arigh Böke, Berke's candidate for the office of great khan, was forced to surrender to Qubilai and died in captivity within two years. Qubilai was elected great khan during a quriltai held without Jochid leaders. Toluid sources claim that in 1263 Qubilai had issued a *yarlik,* a notice of imperial order, bestowing on Hülegü the territory from the Amu-Daria River to Egypt, including Syria. Hülegü's new status allowed him to create an ulus, although he died just a few months after having fulfilled his ambition. His descendants, who became known as the Ilkhans, would rule over Azerbaijan, Iran, most of Anatolia, and points east extending as far as modern-day Pakistan—a long belt of territory, on the southern border of the Horde. As Toluids, the Ilkhans would show nominal obedience to the great khan.[34]

The Jochids lost the war against the Toluids, in the sense that their preferred candidate was kept off the imperial throne, while Hülegü took over territory that, per Chinggis's will, was destined for Jochid control. But the Jochids were able to persevere and even bolster their ulus. By protecting the routes that connected the Horde to Europe, the Mediterranean world, and Egypt, the Jochids managed to evade Hülegü's blockade, secure new sources of wealth, and assert their control over the lucrative slave, salt, and fur trades. The Jochids did more than stave off economic warfare. They also replaced the loss of income from the old empire-wide redistribution system, enabling lasting independence from the Mongol center.

We Have All Converted to Islam

Berke was steeped in Islam. His mother was a Muslim and a Khwarezmian elite, and, as a young man, Berke's religious choice was influenced by Sayf al-Dīn Bākharzī, a shaykh from Bukhara and a disciple of the leading Khwarezmian Sufi Najm al-Dīn al-Kubrā. As an adult, Berke continued to forge deep ties with Islamic communities from all over Eurasia. In the early 1250s Berke's horde dwelled in the Northern Caucasus, "which is on the route of all the Saracens coming from Persia and Turkey," Rubruck noted, using a then-common European term for

Muslims. "On their way to Baatu" Muslim envoys "pass by [Berke] and bring him gifts," Rubruck observed. "He pretends to be a Saracen and does not allow pork to be eaten in his orda." Batu took notice of Berke's popularity among Muslims. At one point Batu had asked Berke to oversee the Seljuqs and the Syro-Palestinian emirates, but the khan soon changed his mind, for he worried that Berke's Muslim connections would bring him too much power.[35]

Many of Berke's contemporaries considered him a Muslim before he assumed the throne, though it was only when he became khan that he officially converted to Islam. Conversion rituals or ceremonies must have taken place in his horde. Adopting Islam was a way to assert his position as a leader of Muslims and orient his foreign policy toward the dar al-islam. Berke sent letters to the various sultans sharing the news of his conversion. His letter to Baybars was read aloud in front of the Mamluk emirs in Cairo. Berke's letter read, "As for myself, I together with my four brothers, stood up and fought [Hülegü] from all sides for the sake of reviving the light of Islam and returning the abodes of the True Religion to their old state of prosperity and to the mention of the Name of God, the call to prayer, the reading of the Qur'an, prayer, and avenging the Imams and the Muslim community." No sooner had Berke been elected khan than his court began attracting visitors from Iran, Central Asia, and Afghanistan. Berke quickly gained a reputation as a strong defender of the Muslim faith.[36]

Other Jochid elites, including khatuns, noyans, keshig elders, and qarachu begs followed Berke in converting to Islam. In his second letter to Baybars, Berke wrote, "We have all converted to Islam, tribes, clans, individuals, soldiers, big and small people, namely: our younger and elder brothers with their sons." He went on to list the names of the influential Mongols who now followed him. Among them were the leaders who had been part of the Mongol imperial administration in the Middle East before Hülegü shattered it.[37]

The Islamic turn brought the khan and his regime a new form of legitimacy as well as much-needed allies in the intra-Mongol conflict. Although there was no religious strife among the Mongol leaders, religion became a means for the Jochids to contest the power of the Toluids, who supported Christians in the Middle East. The falls of the caliph and the Muslim rulers had created a power vacuum, which

Hülegü exploited by allying with King Het'um of Lesser Armenia and Prince Bohemond of Antioch, both of whom were Christians. Hülegü also ostentatiously favored Christians over Muslims in Baghdad and Tabriz. His commander Ked-Buqa, a well-known Christian, acted similarly in Damascus. Doquz Khatun, Hülegü's chief wife, was a fervent Nestorian and was said to support Christian priests. She had a portable church made for her and, when settled, placed the structure at the gate of her precinct. From there, the priests called people for prayer. By contrast, Berke's chief wife would appear in public accompanied by her muezzin and imam and had her own portable mosque.[38]

The political effects of the Jochid conversion were enormous. Just a few years after Batu had supported a Toluid war in the Middle East that brought the Jochid armies to the doorstep of the Mamluks, Berke parlayed his Muslim connections into a powerful and durable alliance with the Mamluks. The alliance not only fostered wealth and security for both the Jochids and Mamluks, it also changed the scale of military slavery. The Mamluks now had a direct line to their principal source of military manpower, as their warrior slaves arrived mainly from the Qipchaq steppe. Baybars and his followers called their *dawla,* their regime, "the armed wing of the Islamic world." In fact, Mamluk success was a side effect of a Mongol-on-Mongol war.

The political consequences of the Jochid conversion were felt within the Horde as well, not just in its relations with Muslim powers. Among ulus Jochi, Islam became a source of collective identity that bloomed outside the boundaries of Mongol imperial law and culture. The Jochids thereby found a way to overcome their loss of status within the golden lineage, legitimizing their independence from the Mongol center by adopting a faith and practice different from that of the great khan himself. Much as an independent foreign policy and war posture enabled the Jochids to escape the political and economic constraints of Toluid domination, an independent culture buttressed their claims to rule regardless of competition with the Toluids. This is not to say that the Jochids abandoned their Mongol heritage. Islam offered a rich pool of new symbols and rituals that could be added to their old ones. Berke became sultan but remained khan: he governed in accordance with the yasa, Chinggis Khan's rules, and he upheld the sharia, the sacred law of the Muslims.

Not all the Jochids became Muslims. Sources do not reveal how many of Berke's herders followed him, but we do know that, for most Mongols, Allah and Tengri were the same: a god whose belief in the Mongols was revealed in the force they possessed—force with which they dominated the world.

Unity

In 1266 or 1267, Berke died at the age of nearly sixty. Members of the Jochid lineage and begs assembled in a quriltai to elect their new khan. Berke had no heir apparent, and the assembly decided to use the opportunity to solidify the Horde under Batu's line by electing one of his grandsons—not a descendent of Berke. From this point on, only Batu's lineage would have rightful claims to the throne. Concentrating power in Batuid hands was a play for unity. Ulus Jochi had evolved into a political power in its own right, but its future was still tied to that of the Mongol Empire from which it emerged. It was Batu whom Chinggis Khan had selected to succeed Jochi, and it was Batu's line that would go on ruling.[39]

Still, the separation from the Mongol Empire was real and brutal. It was a story that unfolded over many years, beginning when Jochi and his descendants were permanently ejected from the imperial throne. The war between the Jochids and the Toluids could have been the end of the Horde, as Hülegü's blockade nearly destroyed it. But instead the internecine conflict proved to be another obstacle the Horde overcame, as the Jochids persisted and, in doing so, asserted that much more independence from the Mongol center. This was a seismic moment in global history, as it set up the next century of Jochid influence in Europe and the Mediterranean, detailed in later chapters. From the standpoint of steppe peoples, though, the battle between Berke and Hülegü was no great rupture in history, for nomads often separated and reassembled. They had done so throughout Chinggis Khan's life, turning against him, siding with him, succumbing to him. Now his descendants were engaged in similar power plays. But the Horde was also different from other Mongols. The Jochids' level of organization, geographical reach, and internal cohesion set it apart among Eurasian empires. It would go on to outlast the Mongol Empire of which it was an autonomous part.

What emerged from the war of 1260–1264 was both Mongol and not, both Batu's Horde and something new. Under Batu the Horde had grown tremendously, expanding to at least nine big riverine hordes and incorporating hundreds of thousands of conquered subjects, of whom more than half were sedentary. The Horde's political economy proved successful, as the regime dominated trade in its region, mastered its environment, and imposed a lucrative taxation and conscription scheme across its territory. Yet, throughout Batu's time, the Horde remained dependent on the qubi system, which meant that it was still tied financially to the wider Mongol Empire. Under Berke, the Horde broke away economically, politically, and culturally. What came after Berke, after the Mongol-on-Mongol war, was a novel hybrid. The Horde was now culturally both Mongol and Muslim. The Horde practiced Mongol-style economics—focused on subsistence, tribute, trade, and circulation—but without ties to the Mongol treasury. And the Horde traced power to Chinggis's chosen successor, Batu, yet defied the orders of the Mongol center.

By the mid-1260s, no Mongol could dispute Jochid supremacy over the western steppe. They had lost the war with the Toluids, but even the great khan had to recognize that the Horde was a consolidated power, a diverse but integrated world of Mongols, Russians, and Caucasians; pagans, Christians, and Muslims; city-dwellers and herders: a nomadic kingdom unto itself.

5

The Mongol Exchange

After Berke's death, three hordes rose to dominate the ulus of Jochi. Each of them had its own keshig and territory, but together they constituted a single regime, sharing tax revenues and other resources. The central, Batuid horde belonged to the khan; the eastern horde to the descendants of Orda; and the western horde to Nogay, the Horde's highest-ranking military officer. For many years, these primary hordes were at peace with each other and ran the ulus of Jochi in concert.

The resulting time of prosperity, from the mid-1260s until the mid-1300s, is often referred to as the Pax Mongolica. During the first decade of this period, Khan Möngke-Temür, who succeeded Berke, oversaw a sophisticated system of government that reflected the evolution of Mongol traditions. Far from static, Mongol governance adapted to conditions on the ground. Möngke-Temür drew on Chinggisid institutions, but he applied them to circumstances that his predecessors in the east could not have envisioned. The flexibility built into those institutions was on full display as Möngke-Temür balanced power among rivals within the empire, imposed Mongol-style law and order on sedentary subjects with unfamiliar political cultures and ethnic traditions, and fostered a trade network that knit together Central and Eastern Europe, the Mediterranean, Siberia, and the Black Sea. This was truly the *Mongol* exchange; the various participants knew it was the Horde that made the network run, and they courted the khan in hopes of improving their own fortunes. In this period the Ordaids also became leading players in the Siberian fur trade, and Nogay's expanding horde brought in new wealth from his highly productive territory girding the Danube River. The results included growth in the Horde and major consequences for the geopolitics of the day, as the Jochids asserted their influence over Christian and Muslim powers.

But the Horde's three-legged political structure always involved a tenuous equilibrium, which shattered with the death of Möngke-Temür in the early 1280s. The Horde continued to prosper and play its critical role as a globalizer. Yet within, the Horde was riven by power struggles, as ambition clashed with principle, ego with law. Möngke-Temür's weak successors allowed rivalries to metastasize. In particular, Nogay could not be contained. Finally, in the closing decade of the thirteenth century, a civil war broke out within the Horde, pitting Nogay against Toqto'a, a khan whom Nogay had helped to place on the throne. Ultimately Toqto'a would emerge the victor, but only after the Jochid elite came to his rescue.

This, then, became another turning point: the rise of the begs, the leading members of society. That new political forces could repeatedly arise within the regime only further emphasizes the dynamic character of Mongol governance. Yet the irony is that the begs were not looking for change. A conservative force, they hoped to ensure the continuation of the wider Mongol imperial system, based on the social and political hierarchy elaborated by Chinggis and ordained by Tengri—a system that both Nogay and Toqto'a threatened in their own ways. Thus did the begs become a power center of their own, with an agenda that was both historically unusual and yet legible within the universe of Mongol political theory and practice.

When we dig into the story of the Pax Mongolica, we find how inadequate that concept is. The Horde, and the Mongols in general, did not "settle in" to a golden age. Prosperity did not entail stability. Rather, it was the Horde's plasticity that enabled its continuing success. Even as the regime grew wealthier, it became that much more politically fractious; internal tensions were not incompatible with economic success.

Ulus Jochi was a living, breathing entity, whose leaders constantly calibrated their policies in order to achieve public and personal goals and thereby created new conditions that spawned further transformations. The Pax Mongolica story encourages us to see the Horde as a state that rose, peaked, and fell—an empire that gained all it could from its strengths, burned through its good fortune, and then failed to develop further in the face of a changing world. The truth is far more interesting.

Peace in the Horde

The Blue Horde, led by the descendants of Jochi's eldest son Orda, was a key factor in the peace the Horde enjoyed in the final third of the thirteenth century. During this period, the Blue Horde grew in numbers. A few thousand warriors and their families became ten thousand or more. In addition to Orda's direct family, his keshig and horde gathered women and men of various origins, including Qonggirad, Merkit, Kereit, Arghun, Oyirad, Naiman, and Kinggut. The Kinggut was a large military group who descended from the original *minggan:* the unit of a thousand warriors Chinggis had given to Jochi, which Orda inherited.

Also in Orda's horde were the Jalayir warriors. Orda probably acquired the Jalayir during the Hungarian campaign of the early 1240s. These seasoned warriors comprised four minggan and obeyed a powerful Oyirad family. But that was not all: on Orda's territory there still lived the peoples of the four sons of Jochi who had followed Orda when his horde had separated from Batu's. Together, these Mongol groups shaped the "left-hand wing" of the Horde—possibly the largest nomadic population of Mongol Eurasia.[1]

Ordaids and Batuids were of the same flesh and blood. They worshipped the same ancestors and trusted one another. Yet there were some differences. Marco Polo saw the peoples of Orda as "the proper Tartars," who strictly followed the yasa and the steppe spirituality. They believed in Tengri and *Etügen,* Earth, and they made offerings to *Etügen Eke,* Mother Earth. They made *ongon*—felt effigies that they rubbed with mare's milk, food, and grease. The Ordaids sacrificed to the mountains, the lakes, the rivers, and the ancestors. Batuids also performed these rituals, but Marco Polo singled out the Ordaids as purists. Nothing indicates that, on the eve of the fourteenth century, there were Muslim or Christian populations in the left-hand wing of the Horde, a stark contrast to the diversity of the Batuid khan's and Nogay's hordes.[2]

The peoples of Orda stretched across the western Siberian plain, the world's largest swamp. In the south, they controlled the main valleys from the Ural River to the Irtysh River. Through the eyes of foreign travelers, most of these lands were wild, empty of human-driven development. Marco Polo reported that the Ordaid ruler had "neither city nor castles; he and his people live always either in the wide plains or among great mountains and valleys." Yet there were in fact new settlements in the foothills of the Ulugh Tagh Mountains, in the lower Syr-Daria, and in the valleys of the Chu, Sari-su, Turgai, and Ishim rivers. These settlements confirmed that Orda's Mongols had colonized these regions. Although the western Siberian plain was dominated by nomads, brick buildings popped up, as they did everywhere under Jochid rule.

The Ordaid territory lay in the middle of Mongol Eurasia, surrounded by other Mongol hordes. To the west were the Batuids; to the southeast the heirs of Ögödei; in the southwest, the descendants of Chagatay; and in the east, only the Irtysh River separated the Ordaids from the lands of the Toluid great khan. The Ordaids watched their neighbors closely, as changes in the surrounding world could affect the Blue Horde quickly and profoundly. The Ordaids were repeatedly involved in the challenges of the Ögödeids, Chagatayids, and Toluids and were key players in Jochid affairs. From their central position, the Ordaids were always the first to know about the hordes' controversies, alliances, wars, droughts—whatever happened to the Mongols, the Ordaids got the news.[3]

The Ordaids not only occupied the center of the Mongol Empire but also did so peacefully. They were experts in multilateral diplomacy and maintained constant communication with the other Mongol leaders. The sons of Orda fostered lines of contact between the Horde and the other Mongols, dispatching envoys to inform the Jochid khan and the begs of events elsewhere in the empire. Most importantly, the Ordaids never exhibited expansionist tendencies. Although they were born of bloody conquests, the descendants of Orda were not themselves belligerent; they sought order and happiness among the Mongols.

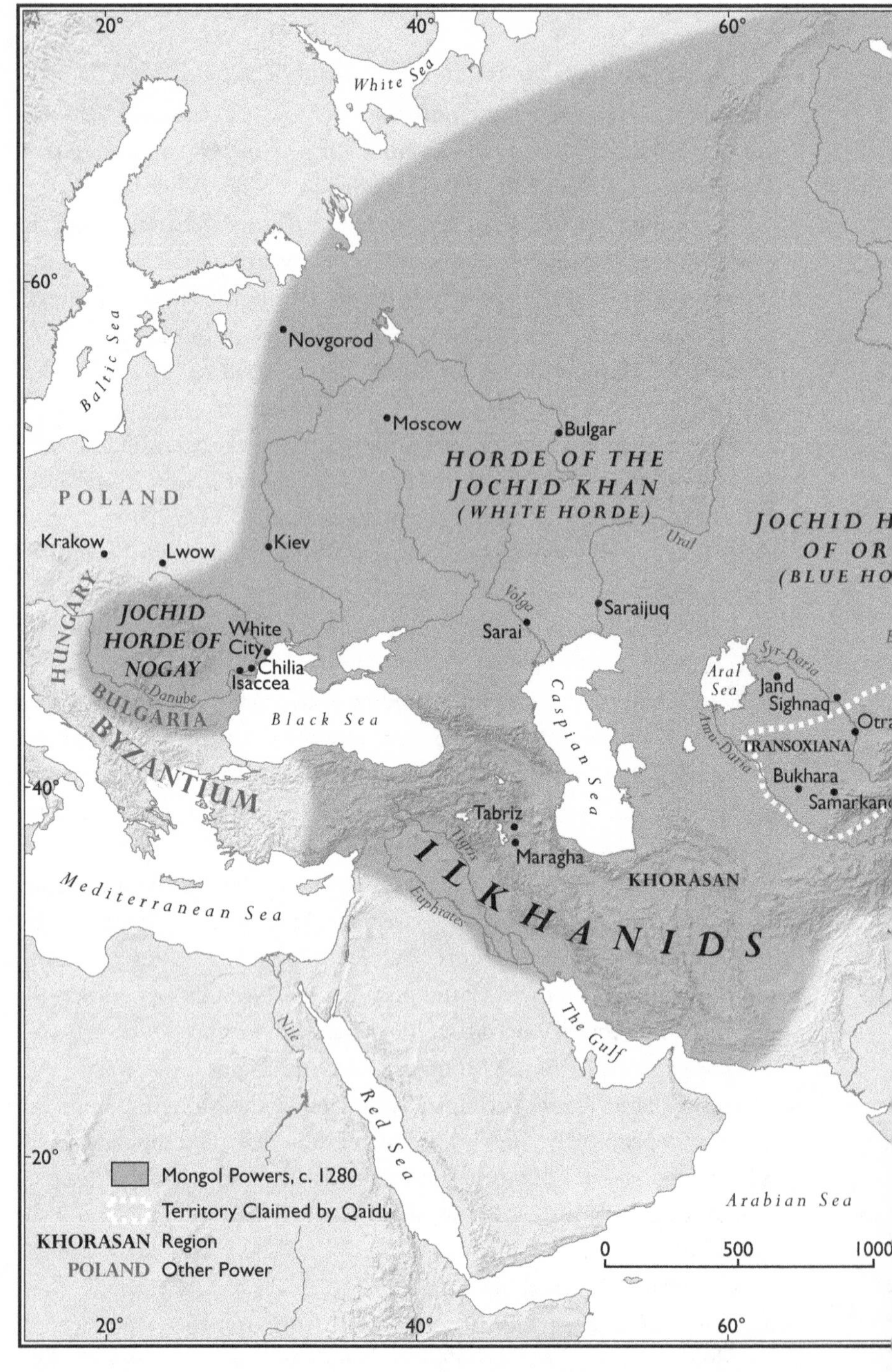

20°
40°
60°
60°
40°
20°
White Sea
Baltic Sea
Novgorod
Moscow
Bulgar
HORDE OF THE JOCHID KHAN (WHITE HORDE)
POLAND
Krakow
Lwow
Kiev
Ural
JOCHID H
OF OR
(BLUE HO
HUNGARY
JOCHID HORDE OF NOGAY
White City
Chilia
Isaccea
Danube
BULGARIA
BYZANTIUM
Black Sea
Volga
Sarai
Saraijuq
Caspian Sea
Aral Sea
Syr-Daria
Jand
Sighnaq
Otra
Amu-Daria
TRANSOXIANA
Bukhara
Samarkan
Tabriz
Tigris
Maragha
KHORASAN
ILKHANIDS
Euphrates
Mediterranean Sea
Nile
The Gulf
Red Sea
Arabian Sea
Mongol Powers, c. 1280
Territory Claimed by Qaidu
KHORASAN Region
POLAND Other Power
0
500
1000

The three major Jochid hordes, 1270–1299, showing the White Horde of the Jochid khan, the Blue Horde of the Ordaids, and the horde of General Nogay. Also noted is the territory claimed by Qaidu, the heir of Ögödei.

Political stability was also important at home, and the Ordaids achieved it due in part to their structural advantages. Unlike the other Mongols, the Ordaids did not share their territory with populous sedentary communities such as the Russians, Iranians, and Chinese. Consequently, the frictions common to interactions between nomads and sedentary peoples were limited. (To the extent that there were subject populations, the Ordaids treated them much as the Batuids treated their own subjects: both leading houses were less interested in regulating the daily lives of subjects than in enhancing their productivity.) The left-hand wing also enjoyed privileged access to the fur market of the far north. While the Batuids controlled the Pechora River fur network, the Ordaids oversaw the Siberian market.[4] The Ordaids were beneficiaries and practitioners of the longstanding Mongol policy of ruling through trade, an approach they took toward the highly fragmented societies of the far north.

Key among these subjects were the Samoyeds, the hunters and reindeer herders of the Sayan Mountains. Mongol scout troops had established contact with them during northward explorations that may have brought the nomads as far as the Arctic Ocean. The Mongols forced a tributary relationship on the Samoyeds, who provided their new masters with the furs of Siberian black foxes, sables, ermines, and white bears. Furs were some of the most sought-after commodities in Eurasia. Over time the Ordaids became the exclusive buyers and so were able to purchase furs at a convenient price. They also taxed hunters, trappers, and traders in kind. But, in turn, the left-hand wing was largely dependent on the wider Mongol trade system, because the major markets were operated by the Batuids in the west and the Toluid great khan in the east.[5]

Of their own accord, the Ordaids aligned their politics with the Batuids' and respected the Jochid khan. When necessary the Ordaid elite assembled with the other Jochid leaders, and they made political and military decisions together. Carrying out their diplomatic role, the Ordaids represented the Jochids at quriltai with the other branches of the golden lineage. All the Mongols agreed that the Ordaid leader was no one's vassal. As a rule, the Horde's Batuid khan neither appointed the Ordaid leader nor meddled in the internal business of the left-hand wing. Yet the Ordaids and Batuids were deeply intertwined. The Ordaids "ruled their ulus in autonomy," Rashīd al-Dīn reported, but their leaders also understood that they "should recognize Batu's successors and write their names at the top of their decrees."[6]

The first of those successors had been Berke. The next was Möngke-Temür, one of Batu's grandsons. When the Horde's elite elected Möngke-Temür at a 1267 quriltai, they expected him to walk in the footsteps of his founding ancestor Jochi, and they were not disappointed. Möngke-Temür maintained the Horde's independence, refusing upon his enthronement to visit Great Khan Qubilai. Instead Qubilai's ambassadors had to come to the lower Volga to bless the new Jochid leader, who welcomed the envoys and accepted the gifts they carried. In effect Möngke-Temür was announcing his autonomy without acrimony. He was a cautious ruler who would make overtures for peace, as long as doing so benefitted the Horde. This was Möngke-Temür's principal goal: not conquest or vengeance but prosperity. His people loved him and called him Kölüg, Strong Horse, a name that signifies "the best khan."[7]

Although he could not occupy Chinggis's throne, Möngke-Temür had a strong claim to the position of primus inter pares among Mongol leaders. He was a descendant of Chinggis's eldest son Jochi, ruled the largest Mongol territory, and had no personal enemies within the golden lineage. On top of this, the Jochid army was large, growing, and well-equipped, and warriors enjoyed high social standing. They were loyal to their khan, who could command them to go to war at any time. The other Mongols, including the great khan, respected the Jochids under Möngke-Temür.

To bolster the wealth of his people and publicize his rule, Möngke-Temür launched a major monetary reform early in his khanship. He issued new silver coins bearing his name, title, and tamga (his seal); there was no mention of the great khan, which signaled that Möngke-Temür ruled his ulus without deference to any higher authority. Möngke-Temür also increased the number of mints and, in an effort to respect the diverse interests of his subjects, ensured that region-specific coins were issued across his domain. Coins minted in Khwarezm were valid in the Horde's eastern territories; coins issued in Sarai circulated in the central lands; Bulgar coins circulated in the north; and coins minted in Qrim were used in the west. Regional coinage supported a kind of federal system that combined political centralization with clear-cut local distinctions. The Horde's leaders controlled the mints and centralized the tax revenues; coins minted without the khan's authority were officially worthless. But the system also allowed local economies to develop independently. The benefits were manifold. For one thing, preventing economic concentration centered on the khan's court helped to keep the population of his horde relatively low, sparing his grazing grounds. For another, regional autonomy within an overarching Jochid system protected local trades without cutting them off from the main circuits of exchange. The inhabitants of northern Khwarezm, the lower Volga, the northern Caucasus, and Crimea realized that working within the Mongol regime was in their interest.[8]

Not everyone needed coins, and coins did not need to circulate everywhere. Demand tended to be seasonal, following the schedule of trade fairs and tax collection. But coins could be issued wherever and whenever they were needed to conduct business. This meant that, although the khan was the only one who could authorize the design of a coin or determine where it would serve as legal tender, the minting could come at the request of a trader, taxpayer, or foreign traveler—anyone who owned silver bars and wanted to make coins out of them. One just had to bring the silver to the mint, pay the cost of fashioning the silver into coins, and pay a fee to the khan.

Officials feared capital flight, so they tried to attract and retain coins within their regions. The laws of the Horde seemed intended to salve these anxieties by discounting the value of a coin beyond its production area: a Bulgar coin bought more in the north than in Sarai region, for instance. But this rule had the effect of driving up demand for silver, whose value remained stable from one region to another. Thus, while it was unlikely that coins would travel far, silver did, becoming a kind of universal currency within Mongol-dominated territories. Silver was the easiest means of transferring, transporting, and multiplying capital. It was easy to carry, accepted by everyone, and nonperishable. Produced massively in Europe, the Russian principalities, Volga Bulgaria, and Central Asia, silver bars were like modern-day traveler's checks. They were converted into local coins for small or medium-sized transactions and used as a direct means of payment in large commercial operations. In the 1270s the Horde had both a booming economy and increasing economic needs. Möngke-Temür's reform helped to fuel the boom, so that the needs could be met.[9]

Möngke-Temür understood that the Horde's prosperity depended not only on shrewd internal economic management but also on maintaining and improving the Jochids' political position within the frequently tense political environment of the empire at large. A pragmatist, Möngke-Temür prioritized power balancing over personal ambition. Rather than try to force himself onto the throne—the Jochids had long since lost any lawful claim to the great khanship—Möngke-Temür wanted to limit the Toluids' authority without weakening the overall Mongol regime. By the late 1260s, the Toluids were clearly ascendant, controlling the great khanship under Qubilai and the Ilkhanids under Abaqa, Hülegü's successor. Möngke-Temür played both sides with respect to Qubilai, sometimes pressing his own independence from the great khan and sometimes courting his favor. And, even as Möngke-Temür openly preached peace, he tried to undermine Abaqa. The Ilkhanids continued to pose a threat to the Horde; their conflict had ended, but relations along the border were tense, and the two regimes competed for access to trade and markets. The peace Möngke-Temür pursued was not necessarily friendly: it was a balance of power that favored the Horde's capacity to benefit from the Mongol system of economic domination. Like his grandfather Batu, he intended to see the Horde—and his family—profit by capturing the dynamics of exchange. For the Jochids, Möngke-Temür was a guide through politically fraught waters.

Balancing Power

In sharp contrast to the peacefulness that prevailed in West Asia, Mongols were killing each other in Central Asia. Around 1267 a conflict broke out between Qaidu, the heir of Ögödei, and Baraq, the heir of Chagatay. Qaidu and Baraq were neighbors, and both had expansionist views. Möngke-Temür and his associates found a way to exploit the situation for the benefit of the Horde, simultaneously enriching their people, striking an economic and diplomatic blow against the Toluids, and settling the feud between the other two houses of the golden lineage.

Imperial politics had put Qaidu and Baraq on a collision course. In the course of the rise to power, the Toluids had severely undermined their predecessors on the throne, the Ögödeids. Qaidu knew the sting of the great khan's ruling methods: a few years before open fighting broke out between Qaidu and Baraq, Qubilai had gifted Baraq claim to territories conquered by Qaidu, but Qaidu refused to give them away. In an effort to rebuild his strength, Qaidu hoped to take Samarkand and Bukhara, the wealthiest cities in Central Asia, which were under Baraq's administration. Baraq and Qaidu's first battle took place on the banks of the Syr-Daria River. Baraq won, and Qaidu turned to Möngke-Temür, who was a natural ally. The Jochids understood that a victory for Baraq would be disastrous because Baraq had the great khan's support, which meant that his success would only enhance Qubilai's influence. Moreover, the Jochids were suspicious of Baraq's expansionist tendencies, as he was their eastern neighbor. Möngke-Temür agreed to help Qaidu, sending him fifty thousand warriors under the leadership of Berkecher, Berke's brother.[10]

With Berkecher's forces at his side, Qaidu led an effective counterattack against Baraq, driving Baraq's dying army into the agrarian region of Transoxiana, where Bukhara and Samarkand lay. Baraq hoped to restore his forces by requisitioning local resources and enrolling arms makers. At this point, Möngke-Temür, Berkecher, and Qaidu could have finished off Baraq's army, but the allies understood that doing so might mean the destruction of Transoxiana, a high price considering the area's importance as a center of trade, crafts, and food production. Rather than crush Baraq, the allies decided to negotiate for his surrender. In their view, Baraq had no reasonable choice but to accept peace terms.[11]

In the spring of 1269, Berkecher led a Jochid delegation to the Plain of Talas, where Qaidu was organizing a quriltai to settle the conflict with Baraq. Qaidu did not invite Qubilai; Abaqa, the Toluid chief of the Ilkhanids; or any of the other Toluid leaders. Qaidu and his allies wished to negotiate with Baraq alone. The quriltai opened with a week of festivities, during which the attendees enjoyed fresh kumis, wrestling competitions, music, and horse races. Then, Berkecher, Baraq, and Qaidu—representing the descendants of Jochi, Chagatay, and Ögödei, respectively—held their council.

What happened next exemplifies the power-balancing at which the Jochids excelled under Möngke-Temür. Rather than humiliate Baraq, who had lost the war, Berkecher and Qaidu brought him into an agreement that mostly hurt Toluid interests. Per the treaty, the parties decided that they would collect all of the imperial tax revenues from Transoxiana, while Qubilai received none of the share that had previously flowed to the great khan. Qaidu and the Jochids claimed one third of the revenues for themselves, leaving two thirds to Baraq and the Chagatayids. The agreement also put pressure on the Ilkhanids by motivating Baraq to make war on them. As part of the treaty, Baraq's army was expelled from Bukhara, so he needed a new location to station his forces. Baraq decided to seize pasturelands in Khorasan; the region was under Abaqa's jurisdiction, but Baraq claimed that the Ilkhanids had no inheritance rights there. Möngke-Temür and Qaidu supported Baraq's position on Ilkhanid usurpation and agreed to back his war. For the Jochids, the results of the treaty could hardly have been better. They gained revenues at the expense of the great khan and formed an alliance with Qaidu and Baraq that could bring long-awaited victory over the Ilkhanids.[12]

The Talas quriltai was a significant meeting. By dividing up territories and tax income without consulting the great khan, Mongol leaders were taking both the great khan's share and his authority for themselves. This was more than an assault on Qubilai's financial interests; fellow Mongols were denying him his status as supreme ruler. In essence, the quriltai established equality where previously there was hierarchy. Möngke-Temür, Qaidu, and Baraq were asserting that Qubilai was a khan just like themselves, and that none of them could command the others. Behind the scenes, though, each of the allies had his own plan, and these plans were not mutually compatible. Möngke-Temür wanted to eliminate the Ilkhanid threat, to which neither Qaidu nor Baraq objected. But Qaidu sought to take over Baraq's ulus, then to claim Qubilai's throne, while Baraq intended to regain enough strength to expand again, potentially at the expense of his new partners.

The divergence in these goals became obvious during Baraq's war on the Ilkhanids. A few months after the Talas quriltai, Baraq, with the aid of reinforcements sent by Qaidu, attacked Abaqa as planned. But Baraq quickly lost ground, and Qaidu recalled his men. Not only that, but Qaidu then switched sides, offering to support Abaqa. At the battle of Herat in July 1270, Abaqa defeated Baraq and the Chagatayid army for good. Baraq died soon after, and his commanders, advisers, and court

Glazed ceramic bowl with a bird figure (Horde, fourteenth century). The Jochids produced glazed ceramics in large numbers.

staff went to Qaidu and offered to serve him. Qaidu had abandoned Baraq; now Qaidu integrated Baraq's people into his own, achieving one part of his goal.

For Möngke-Temür, the Ilkhanid victory over Baraq was a humiliation, but it did not lead to a fundamental change of strategy. Möngke-Temür went on balancing power; what changed was the relative power of his competitors. Whereas Möngke-Temür previously used Qaidu to check Abaqa and Qubilai, now the Jochids had to be more concerned with Qaidu, who had gained much by absorbing Baraq's former ulus and had clear intensions on the great khanship. With respect to the Ilkhanids, then, Möngke-Temür swallowed his pride. In November 1270 the Jochid khan congratulated Abaqa on his victory, sending a gift of falcons and hawks, which in the language of gifts could be read as an acknowledgment of the two khans' status as peers.[13]

Möngke-Temür flexed his power-balancing muscles again in the fall of 1276, when a coalition of Toluid princes rebelled against the great khan. The princes accused Qubilai of violating Chinggis's rules and becoming pro-Chinese after having moved the empire's capital from Qaraqorum to the Chinese city of Shangdu. The allegations were mere excuses; what really concerned the rebel princes was installing their preferred Toluid on the throne in place of Qubilai. The rebels captured one of Qubilai's generals and Qubilai's son Nomuqan. Seeking to enlist the support of other Mongol leaders, the rebels sent the general to Qaidu and Nomuqan to Möngke-Temür, possibly via Qaidu. In either case, Möngke-Temür had a decision to make. He could have Nomuqan killed, pleasing Qaidu, who was still technically Möngke-Temür's ally. Or the Jochid khan could send Nomuqan home, scorning Qaidu and embracing Qubilai. Would Möngke-Temür back the great khan or the man who would be the great khan?

Möngke-Temür chose neither option. He saw no benefit in supporting Qaidu over Qubilai, potentially upsetting the imperial center. But, at the same time, returning to Nomuqan to Qubilai would have meant throwing away a valuable bargaining chip. To ensure a balance of power that favored only the Jochids, Möngke-Temür did what was best for the Horde, not for Qaidu or Qubilai: he kept Nomuqan as a hostage. The brilliance of this move would become clear nearly a decade later, when, amid new power dynamics, Möngke-Temür's successors decided to release Nomuqan in order to break with Qaidu and court Qubilai. But though the Horde's allegiance shifted, its goal remained the same: to buttress an imperial system that served Jochid goals.[14]

It might seem that Möngke-Temür got little in return for the ample support he offered Qaidu in his war with Baraq. Undoubtedly, the Jochids provided Qaidu military and political help he badly needed; Baraq would have crushed Qaidu without Berkecher's intervention, and it was Möngke-Temür's agreement at the Talas quriltai that allowed Qaidu to legally confirm his victory over Baraq. Perhaps most importantly, the Jochids decided not to oppose Qaidu's seizure of Baraq's ulus. But the Jochids were always looking out for their own interests. These interests did not include controlling Bukhara and Samarkand, so allowing Qaidu to take over was no loss. What the Jochids did need was trade connections with the cities and surrounding region. As long as Qaidu kept the area stable and respected the Horde's trade rights in his domain, that was enough for Jochid leaders. Möngke-Temür's instrumental role in Qaidu's rise helped to assure that the Jochids would keep their trade status. The Jochid khan also gained a position of superiority over his ally, Qaidu, who was his protégé and debtor. Möngke-Temür therefore had ample reason to remain on good terms with his eastern neighbor.[15]

But the alliance with Qaidu also bore rotten fruit. By providing Qaidu with troops and equipment, Möngke-Temür emboldened Qaidu to challenge the great khan, fostering a lengthy war among Mongols. The tension between Qaidu and Qubilai would become a critical constraint on Jochid foreign policy in the 1280s, as I discuss below. On top of that, Möngke-Temür's alliance with Qaidu did nothing to temper the Ilkhanid threat. The Ilkhanids remained a thorn in the Jochids' sides throughout the 1260s and 1270s. Such was the game of alliances: it came with benefits and downsides.

For the most part, the Jochids negotiated skillfully, though. This was true outside the confines of the Mongol Empire as well. Under Möngke-Temür's rule, the Jochids became key players in Europe and the Mediterranean, shaping regional politics and commercial relations in an effort to enhance their own security and prosperity. Relations with sedentary populations inside the Horde and beyond were highly complex, but the Jochids knew how to make the best of their opportunities. They applied the longstanding Mongol playbook based on trade, tribute, and elite cooptation, evolving the steppe tradition to meet the challenges of their domain and its neighborhood.

A Geopolitical Leader

To sustain their power, the Jochids needed to adapt to circumstances alien to their forebears. The Horde had inherited the yasa and the varied heritage of steppe nomads. But the Jochids ruled sedentary Europeans including Hungarians, Bulgars, and Russians. Some Jochid subjects practiced steppe spirituality, while others were Christian, Muslim, or Buddhist. And from their place on the edge of Europe, the Horde interacted with many peoples beyond their rule, including Slavs, the Byzantine Empire, Genoese and Venetian merchants, and the Mamluk sultan in Cairo, across the Mediterranean. The pope and the metropolitan—the head of the Russian Orthodox church—were both important pieces on the Horde's diplomatic chessboard.

The khans and their officers learned to work with these and other players—how to rule them, directly and indirectly; how to trade with them and encourage them to take advantage of the Mongol-run trade network; how to insert themselves into foreign interests; and how to make the interests of foreigners align with their own. Of course, Mongols had a history of dominating foreigners in the east and in Central Asia, but Europe and West Asia were different and required different political strategies. The Jochids thus had to innovate in order to prosper. Under Möngke-Temür and his successors, the Jochids did just that, but they also maintained the key political structures underlying their ulus. In the final decades of the thirteenth century, the Horde proved how flexible Mongol governance was, as the regime invented new strategies of rule on the basis of age-old principles.

A case in point was the eastern Slavs, primarily Russians. Russians were the most numerous among the Horde's sedentary subjects. Their governing institutions were unlike those of the Mongols, as were their economic priorities. Not only that, but Russians and other Slavs were hardly analogous to the Central Asians and Chinese the Mongols had earlier learned to rule. Politically, the Russians were fragmented, subject to layers of feudal rule and lacking central leadership. The Russians were also mostly scattered among small villages; there were a few major cities, but the urban lifestyles of China and Khwarezm were largely unknown. On top of all that, the Russian principalities were agriculturally poor, their output unstable and varying drastically from year to year. The Russians subsisted largely on fish, small game, and berries, and produced some finished agricultural products such as honey and alcohol. But there was not much surplus they could turn over in tribute. Other items, such as furs and crafted objects, became the focus of Mongol taxation.

The Jochids created for the Russians a type of governance befitting their political and economic particularities and cultural sensitivities. The overall approach was supervisory and indirect. The khan did not place garrisons in Russian towns, nor did the Mongols attempt to absorb the Russians into their hordes en masse, as they had the Qipchaqs and other dominated peoples. Instead the Jochids worked with existing Russian elites to enact policies that kept the public contented enough to abide the regime and pay their taxes.

The two major power centers among the Russians were the ruling elite—including the princes and the boyars—and the church. The Mongols communicated with and coopted both. The khan and his advisers had frequent exchanges with the kniazia, especially the grand prince of

Vladimir, who was required to visit the khan's court regularly. Mongol envoys also brought orders and messages to the metropolitan. Princes and religious officials alike would sometimes respond to messages through the Mongol envoys, but the Russians also at times used their own men—a sign that the relationship with the Mongols was a two-way street rather than merely an exercise in top-down control. Partnership was key to Jochid rule over the Russian principalities, not least because the Mongols relied on Russian elites to collect taxes for them. This reflected the evolution of the Horde's governing practices under Möngke-Temür. Prior Mongol leaders had sent their own tax collectors right into Russian towns, where the collectors faced huge local opposition. Starting in the 1260s, the Jochids took a different approach. Now it was local notables who would gather taxes from the commoners. The notables would then turn the payments over to Jochid envoys who were instructed to await delivery at the fringes of population centers.[16]

To keep the Russian boyars on their side, the Mongols learned to respect the sources of their wealth and influence. Although boyars usually lived in cities like Novgorod, where political decisions were taken, their status was based on the sizeable landed domains they owned. The Mongols left these lands be. In one sense, this was not unusual, for the Mongols never taxed property directly. Instead they taxed craft and agricultural production, sales, trade, and households; demanded levies on particular resources such as water; and collected supplies for the yam. The Russian boyars did have to pay these taxes, but they were also permitted to keep their lands. This is what was unusual: the lack of interference in landholding itself. In China and Central Asia, the Mongols were much more interventionist, redrawing property lines and redistributing ownership. By allowing the thousands of Russian landowners to keep their domains intact, the Jochids were making clear that they intended to share the fruits of their conquests with the sons of those they had vanquished.

The Horde took other measures as well to maintain the trust and affection of the boyars, even while imposing their own methods of social control. As we have seen, life in the hordes was unusually safe and secure, surprising European visitors. The Jochids tried to ensure similar order in the Russian principalities, so that the people could achieve the economic output and population growth that would fuel the khan's regime. To this end, the Mongols regulated Russian subjects much as they did their own, banning Russians from carrying weapons and riding warhorses, while deputizing local rulers to provide security. Princes, boyars, and their guards were allowed to be armed, provided that they showed loyalty to their Mongol masters. Thus, in exchange for supporting the regime, Russian elites were empowered at the local level, enabling them to maintain their traditional place in the hierarchy with respect to ordinary Russians. This was a critical governing maneuver. Slavic elites were accustomed to clear distinctions of status and could not accept relegation to the common herd. To confirm the positions of local rulers, the Mongols granted them *yarliks*—written diplomas, which had long been used across the empire to make formal announcements.

At the same time, the Mongols did not forget about unarmed elites. Artisans, merchants, and religious leaders were also critical to the Horde's political economy. While artisans and merchants generated wealth, the clergy had great influence over the public and the princes, whose own power was difficult to maintain without the backing of the church. To support the work of these unarmed elites, the Mongols granted some of them—especially clergy—tarkhan status.[17] The conferral of tarkhan status began with the metropolitan and the Orthodox priests. As tarkhans, the clergy and their institutions were exempt from taxation, and the clergy themselves were exempt from military conscription. In exchange for these legal protections, the clergy supported the legitimacy of the Mongol regime. In effect, by accepting tarkhan status, the Orthodox Church was announcing that it backed Mongol sovereignty, a substantial political victory for the Mongols. The imprimatur of the church helped to keep the kniazia from rebelling and asserting authority that many of the princes felt was rightfully theirs. The system would prove highly advantageous for the church as well. The Orthodox Church was elevated while other Christians in the Horde, such as Catholics, Armenians, and Greeks, were not initially granted tarkhan status. The financial benefits allowed the Orthodox clergy to establish new properties, while the conscription exemption boosted the church's work force, as individuals chose to join the church rather than be sent away to war or to labor in Mongol camps. The benefits of the conscription exemption were perhaps clearest in the fortunes of Orthodox monasteries, which gained many recruits and prospered.[18]

The structure of the tarkhan privilege helps to clarify the ways in which the Jochids under Möngke-Temür maintained a specifically Mongol scheme of rule. Alternatively, instead of the tarkhan system, the Horde might have implemented the dhimmi system of religious toleration practiced in Muslim polities. After all, though Möngke-Temür was not Muslim, his predecessor Berke had been and had turned the Horde in the direction of Islamic ruling practices. So the Horde might well have applied the dhimmi system. But Möngke-Temür must have reasoned that the tarkhan approach better suited his political needs: whereas the purpose of the dhimmi system was to integrate subjects, the goal of the tarkhan system was to coopt elites. Under the dhimmi system, non-Muslims paid a special tax but were allowed to practice their faith. Under Mongol governance, religious tolerance was presumed; the khans did not care what faiths and rituals their subjects practiced, as long as these subjects contributed the taxes and labor expected of them. Möngke-Temür determined that the Russian peasants would obey the boyars whose land they worked and the religious leaders who protected their souls, so his advantage lay not in mollifying the general population—as the dhimmi system did—but in coopting the elites. If the khan could keep the boyars on his side by respecting their domains, and the clergy by bestowing tarkhan privileges, then it would not matter that the kniazia were restive. Without the clergy, the aristocracy, and the public on their side, the kniazia could never mount a serious challenge to the khan.[19]

The tarkhan system allowed the Russian clergy to establish new landed properties. The Orthodox monks prospered, too: they were not conscripted nor sent away, and monasteries prospered. Unlike the dhimmis, the tarkhans were exempt from paying taxes; for the Mongols, elite loyalty was enough. This soon proved to be a very advantageous system for the Orthodox churches and monasteries as they started to grow their capital.

It was not only by means of incentives that the Horde won support of the Russian elite. The Jochids also wielded superior strength of arms, which was appealing to Russian elites who understood that Mongol protection could be beneficial for them. This advantage was perhaps most obvious in Novgorod, which was the most important commercial center of northern Russia but also subject to economic and military pressures that made life precarious.

Located on the banks of the Volkhov River, Novgorod sat at the intersection of popular east-west and north-south trade routes. From Novgorod, merchants could link up to a network of rivers that carried their goods to the Baltic Sea, the Volga Valley, Kiev, and the Black Sea. What is more, Novgorod teemed with skilled artisans. But the city was hampered by a lack of raw materials. Iron could be found locally, but otherwise the boyars who owned the craft workshops had to import metals from Europe. Craftsmen also needed high-quality wood from the Caucasus, amber from the Baltics, and gemstones from the east. The Novgorodians paid for the raw materials with salted fish, wax, honey, and furs—commodities whose production was likewise controlled by the boyars.[20]

The elites of Novgorod and its surrounding region were thus deeply invested in trade, which meant that they were exposed to shocks affecting the region's trade networks. And such shocks were not uncommon. Novgorod had to cope with two serious military threats, both from the northwest. Despite their defeat in 1240 against Alexander Nevsky, the Swedes continued to compete with Novgorod for the control of the Gulf of Finland, a key area for the Baltic trade. On top of this, in the late 1260s Teutonic Knights were beginning to colonize the Baltic shores and expand toward Novgorod. In 1269 the Novgorodians defeated the knights at Rakvere, in Estonia, bringing peace to Novgorod's western border. But the truce was temporary, and everybody knew it.

Under duress from the northwestern sea powers, the Novgorod boyars accepted Mongol protection, which guaranteed favorable trading conditions. This meant the boyars would have to acknowledge subordination to the grand prince—he was, after all, the Mongols' vassal—which was historically unusual, as the Novgorodians had always maintained independence. But subordination was a small price to pay in exchange for protection and noninterference in their business, especially since it was mostly for show. The boyars had merely to welcome and host the grand prince's officials, who had no real power. Under Mongol auspices, the boyars reached an agreement with the grand prince that prevented him from owning lands and delivering justice in the Novgorod principality. Most importantly the Novgorodians obtained the right to collect the Mongol tribute themselves. This would help to avoid tensions of the kind that beset the Mongol census under Alexander Nevsky, who, as grand prince, had tried to mediate between the Mongols and the Novgorod elites and commoners who refused to pay taxes. With the boyars overseeing tax collection directly, the Mongol levy would seem less of an imposition.

The Novgorod agreement proved beneficial to both the Jochids and the Russians and arguably had a catalytic effect on economic development across Europe. With the Mongols set to referee disputes, relations between Novgorod and German traders improved, facilitating a durable, large-scale commercial alliance involving Novgorod, Riga, Lübeck, Hamburg, Cologne, Visby, Bergen, and other northwestern cities. Together, merchants in these cities formed what became known as the Hanseatic League. For centuries to come, the league's trading houses dominated the vital fish and salt businesses of the Baltic and North seas and shaped exchanges between Northern Europe and the wider world. The Mongols thus enlarged the commercial horizon and multiplied the trade prospects of their northern subjects. In doing so, the Mongols had profound effects on the future of the region. In the last decades of the thirteenth century, the Russians recovered from the devastations of conquest and built new stone churches. By 1302 the Novgorodians began erecting a stone kremlin to replace their old wooden fortress. Such developments might have been impossible without the Mongols' protection, political acumen, and liberal trade policies. Security and free passage for merchants and goods; privileged treatment for elites, clergy, traders, and artisans; carefully planned tax and land regimes; and mostly indirect governance were the stuff of prosperity, for Russian subjects and Mongols alike.[21]

Like its treatment of its Russian subjects, the Horde's foreign relations were dominated by the demands of commerce. Möngke-Temür wanted peace with his neighbors, as long as they agreed to trade with the Horde on terms favorable to his people.

With this in mind, the khan sought early in his rule to reestablish peaceful tributary relations with the Byzantine Empire, relations that had frayed after Nogay's deep incursion into Byzantine lands to rescue the Seljuq sultan ʿIzz al-Dīn in 1263. In the aftermath, Emperor Michael Palaiologos's attempts to win over Berke had been rejected. But around

1266, after Berke's death, Michael tried again, sending Möngke-Temür a large tribute of textiles. To seal the deal, Michael also offered the khan one of his daughters. Möngke-Temür welcomed the Byzantine princess and married her to Nogay, whose horde was closest to the Byzantines. From this point forward, the Horde and the Byzantine Empire would regularly communicate on rules of exchange and regional politics.

The new peace with the Byzantines reflected the recent improvement of relations between the Jochids and the Ilkhanids. The Byzantines had allied with the Ilkhanids, resulting in a crushing Byzantine defeat at Nogay's hands. But with relations between the Jochids and Ilkhanids normalizing under Abaqa and Möngke-Temür, there was no reason for the Horde to continue standing against the Byzantines. That said, while the Horde and the Ilkhanids claimed to be on peaceful terms, Möngke-Temür had men stationed in the northern Caucasus watching the border on the Kura River. On the other side, Abaqa had ordered a wall and ditch built along the river. His warriors, too, watched the border day and night. Only caravans of merchants could pass; an armed horseman crossing the Kura would have meant war. So both parties kept the wary peace. For the time being, it was in the Jochids' interest to honor the terms of the peace with the Ilkhanids and allow diplomatic envoys and caravans to come and go.[22]

Möngke-Temür also maintained the alliance with the Mamluks of Egypt and Syria. For the entirety of Möngke-Temür's rule, merchants could navigate from the Volga to the Nile, developing a lucrative trade channel. The alliance was beneficial for both the Jochids and Baybars's Mamluks, who did not seem to care that Möngke-Temür had no apparent interest in following Berke along the path of Islam. What mattered was the exchange, for each party had something to offer the other. Each side desired special novelties, what Mongols called *tangsuq* and Mamluks called *tuhaf.* Möngke-Temür requested medicines—anything that could heal, protect, or extend life. The khan, in turn, sent Baybars what the Mamluks wanted most: slaves, furs, and hawks. The alliance with the sultanate had deep geopolitical consequences. The threat of a possible counterattack from Baybars's Jochid allies prevented Abaqa from concentrating his forces and conquering Mamluk Syria, while the sale of young men to the Mamluk Sultanate refreshed Baybars's armies, which also served to keep Abaqa at bay.[23]

Another key Jochid alliance was with the Genoese, who wished to establish a port in Crimea, the westernmost domain of the Horde. Crimea was an old commercial nexus, inhabited by both sedentary and nomadic peoples. For Western Europeans, Crimea was the main door to the steppe landmass now under Mongol domination. The Genoese were familiar with the region and the Mongols, having previously traded at Sudak and taken part in Berke's first embassy to Baybars. The Genoese understood that they could profit from the alliance between the Horde, the Byzantines, and the Mamluks, provided that the Genoese had their own harbor from which to run their business. At Sudak the Genoese had to share resources with Greeks, Jews, Alans, Venetians, and others. But the Genoese were tired of sharing. Seasoned and ambitious merchants, they had fought against the Venetians and the Greeks to expand their business, and they wanted to control their own destiny.

Möngke-Temür let the Genoese know that they were welcome to settle on his lands as long as they paid taxes and followed his rules. We do not have records of the negotiations, but we can surmise that, by 1281, the khan had allowed the Genoese to occupy Caffa, an old Greek settlement on the southeastern coast of the Crimean Peninsula. The new Genoese settlement was small and only seasonally active, for every year between December and March, heavy winds prevented sailors from navigating the Black Sea. But the Genoese hoped to expand their commercial activities and eventually turn the settlement into a permanent fortified position to rival Sudak and the harbors controlled by their Venetian rivals.[24]

For their part, the Jochids wanted more out of the Genoese than taxes. The Jochids also wanted a seafaring partner. Mongols were avid surveyors, who made the best use of their land and riverine resources and had an eye for defensible locations. However, it was not enough to project power over spaces they could reach on horseback, so the Jochids had to rely on middlemen on the coasts, who could connect them to the world beyond. Caffa was a strategically privileged location in this regard. Through the Genoese, the Mongols could control the nearby strait of Kerch, which connects the Black and Azov seas. Whoever controlled the strait controlled Black Sea access to the Horde.

Other sea routes important to the Horde were secured by the Byzantines and Venetians. The Byzantines oversaw the Bosporus and Dardanelles and thus the trade channel between the Mediterranean and the Black Sea, while the Venetians occupied the eastern bank of the Azov Sea soon after 1268. From there, the Venetians could reach the mouth of the Don River, a water highway 1,162 miles long that flowed from the Russian city of Ryazan and traversed the Horde. Through treaties, military threats, and regular contacts, the Jochids were the overlords of these critical passages, as well as Kerch. The alliance system was a diplomatic jewel, which saw the Jochids benefiting from competition among the very parties with whom the Horde allied. But diplomacy of this sort was also a tricky balancing act. The Jochids had to be cautious that their allies did not settle their own differences and combine forces against the Horde.

For the Horde itself this had important implications: while the alliance with the Byzantines had strengthened the Jochids' control over Black Sea access and allowed its people to exit and enter through the Bosporus and Dardanelles, the alliance with the Mamluks gave the Jochids access to the Nile and the Red Sea. Whether Genoese, Pisan, Venetian, Greek, Armenian, or Egyptian, sea traders and coastal powers became essential strategic partners for the Jochids.

Another key to Jochid commerce under Möngke-Temür's reign was southeastern Moldavia. Notably, the Jochids did not just obtain access to the region—they controlled it directly, installing Nogay as its ruler. Southeastern Moldavia was essential to the Jochids for at least two reasons. First, from southeastern Moldavia they could watch the end points of the Dniester and Danube rivers. These were critical trade routes that connected the Black Sea to a galaxy of inland ports. Second, portions of southeastern Moldavia—specifically, the Bujak steppe and the region of the Danubian lakes—were ideal for winter camps. A large corridor between the Dniester and Danube rivers, the Bujak steppe provided more than 3,800 square miles of grasslands. Since the Bronze Age, it was mostly a nomads' land, and in the first half of the thirteenth century, Qipchaqs dominated the native peasants and semi-sedentary herders. The Mongols knew from the Qipchaqs where to find the best winter and summer grasses. Southeastern Moldavia was a place where Mongols could live, which meant they needed to govern it directly, not through intermediaries as in Russia.[25]

Moldavia was also an ideal location from which to develop industries producing tradable commodities. For one thing, the region was one of the most profitable salt production centers in Europe. The salt came from western Perekop, the eastern Carpathians, Transylvania, and saline lagoons stretching between the Dniester and Danube. Salt fueled local economies and was exported to northern Russia, Anatolia, Poland-Lithuania, and territories deep within the Horde. In addition to salt, Moldavia produced wheat, wine, honey, horses, wood, pigs, cattle, fish, fish oil, caviar, and wax. All were exported from the cities along the lower Danube and Dniester. Many other commodities were imported and traded in those cities, including cotton, silk, and woolen textiles; glassware; metalwork; and fur. On top of that, human trafficking remained a prosperous business throughout the region and attracted dealers from far away.[26]

To solidify their territorial control, the Jochids sponsored the construction of permanent settlements. In Moldavia these often developed on older urban locations like Isaccea, a trade hub on the Danube delta and the site of Nogay's capital. From Isaccea it was easy to cross the Danube and go from Moldavia to the hilly plains of Dobruja, where Bulgarian, Alan, and Seljuq populations lived. The Jochids had two other key towns: Kilia, a Danubian hub, and Cetatea Alba or White City, on the lower Dniester. These trade centers blossomed under the Mongol regime, attracting ever more settlers. The Jochids also created entirely new settlements along the Danube and Dniester, such as Orheiul Vechi and Costeşti. These towns had mosques, shops, baths, workshops, and houses of stone, brick, and earth. As in the lower Volga two generations earlier, the Jochids protected the sitting cities that emerged on their territory, serving natives and merchants and bringing in new subjects.[27]

From the Bujak steppe, one could access an extensive land and water network connecting the Black Sea coast and Europe. One part of this network was the Dniester River, which offered the most direct route from White City to the principality of Galicia-Volhynia and to Poland. Yet the river was navigable only in its middle and lower courses, which meant traders needed a land route for part of their journey. This land and water network was known as via Thartarica, the Mongol road. It emerged after the Mongol arrival, helping to connect the Black Sea littoral to Lwow on the Poltva river, at the other extreme of the Dniester, more than 400 miles northwest of White City. Part of the Hanseatic League, Lwow was a German-dominated hub, from which traders could make connections to Braşov, Krakow, the Baltic, and even Bruges, in Flanders. It was precisely on this route that German merchants met their primary trade partners, the Genoese. Through the via Thartarica, there was the prospect of linking from the Horde all the way to Western Europe.[28]

In the case of the via Thartarica and elsewhere, we see the Jochids operating as a high-level facilitator of a large-scale trade network. Mongols financed and carried out trade themselves, but they also supplied the nodes and connections—ports, roads, river routes, fords, merchant-friendly settlements—that others used to transport goods. For the Jochids, their emergence as facilitators of Eastern European and Mediterranean trade circuits could not have come at a better time. In the second half of the thirteenth century, the Crusader kingdoms along the eastern Mediterranean coast were in continuous decline, costing the Genoese key trading posts. The Genoese needed access to new harbors, and the Black Sea market was particularly enticing thanks to the 1261 Treaty of Nymphaeum, which the Genoese had signed with the Byzantines. In exchange for Genoese aid in the Byzantines' war with the Venetians, the treaty granted the Genoese trade-tax exemptions and rights to acquire land, creating highly favorable conditions to develop their business in the Byzantine Empire. But at this point, half of the Black Sea coast belonged to the Jochids, limiting the value of the agreement. So the Genoese established contact with the Mongols around 1263 and finally, during Möngke-Temür's rule, secured their Black Sea position, first at Sudak and then at Caffa by 1281. The historical records suggest that the Genoese quickly established themselves at Caffa and, within months of arriving, had a thriving business at the mouth of the Danube. Soon after, they created trading posts at the Mongol cities of Kilia and White City, which the Genoese linked to Constantinople, Europe's most urbanized location.[29] The Genoese were not alone in taking advantage of the Jochid network, which also linked Germans, Slavs, and Greeks. Greeks in particular had a large presence at Kilia. Between them, Greek and Genoese traders bought most of the crops grown in the Bujak steppe and sent large quantities of grain to Constantinople.

Throughout the network, encompassing the Black Sea littoral and the lower river valleys from the Danube to the Don, the Mongols were in command, bringing together the scattered merchants of Europe. The Jochids supervised and taxed all this trade. They also monetized it; as usual, the coin dies were theirs. Byzantine coins were also used, but to a much lesser extent than Jochid coins. The Jochids created the tools of exchange and reaped the rewards in taxes, fees, and tributes. Not only that, but the Jochids turned long-distance traders and local elites into loyal proxies. Germans, Genoese, and other fragmented but dynamic groups of European settlers attached themselves to the Mongol giant and kept the Horde booming.[30]

The Jochid Civil War

The Jochids' commercial and political success in the late thirteenth century was undeniable and far-reaching, and the Horde's impact in Europe and the Mediterranean is testament to the empire-building skill of Möngke-Temür and his associates. But growth came with costs. The enormous benefits of settlement and trade were not evenly distributed, and new wealth produced new centers of power within the Horde, which fostered internal competition and eventually civil war.

One of the emergent power centers was Orda's horde, which benefited from the politics of commerce. Overland trade routes were a key arena of competition between the most powerful Mongol lineages: the Jochids dominated the northerly east-west routes, traversing Ordaid lands, and the Toluids dominated the southerly routes, which ran through Ilkhanid territory. With this in mind, Möngke-Temür sought to promote the northern connections at the expense of the southern ones by persuading foreign businessmen that the Horde's route was quicker and safer than the Ilkhanids'. By following the Ordaid route, known as the Siberian Road, traders could also avoid Qaidu's territory. Qaidu's lands offered the shortest path from the Persian Gulf trade hotbed of Hormuz to the Chinese capital of Zhongdu, but Qaidu's constant fighting with Qubilai and frequent tensions with the dominated Chagatayids made for insecurity along the route.

Under these circumstances, the Ordaids were able to take full advantage of their dominant position in the far-northern fur trade. The Siberian Road connected Bashkir land to Qaraqorum and northern China, ideal endpoints for a trade based on furs. It wasn't just merchants who thrived. Along the route, the horde set up collection and delivery stations where caravans stopped and transacted, benefiting locals. And the khan collected fees from the caravans as they made their way across the Siberian plain.[31]

Boosted by the flourishing economy, the Ordaid leader, Qonichi, became a more important figure in Mongol politics.[32] Qonichi had his own keshig, which governed the people, organized supplies, guarded the court, regulated markets, and collected taxes. But he did not challenge the khan. Like his Ordaid predecessors, Qonichi followed the Batuids' foreign policy. Yet, around 1282, the balance of power within the Horde changed drastically because of the sudden death of Möngke-Temür. In the absence of the beloved Strong Horse Khan, two non-Batuid chiefs saw opportunities to consolidate power: Qonichi and Nogay. As non-Batuids, neither could obtain the begs' agreement to become khan, but they could try to install a puppet khan who would not get in the way of their own plans. On Nogay's advice, the Jochids enthroned Möngke-Temür's brother Töde-Möngke, a man of high status but low political stature, who showed no interest in governing.[33]

Under Möngke-Temür, the Horde had scrupulously balanced between Qaidu and Qubilai, while maintaining frosty but largely peaceful relations with the Ilkhanids. Qonichi upended this grand strategy, for he felt he had more to gain from connections with Qubilai and the Toluids than by continuing to back Qaidu. Qonichi brought together Nogay and Töde-Möngke to formulate a common policy that would realign Jochid efforts, and at a 1283 quriltai the parties agreed that it was time to reconcile with the Toluids. As a token of good will, the Jochids released Qubilai's son Nomuqan, who had been a hostage of the Horde for some eight years. The great khan sent gifts in return, publicly expressing his desire to normalize relations with the Jochids. Over the next few years, relations between the Ordaids and the Toluids continued to improve. In 1288 Qonichi received from the great khan thirty-three pounds of silver, a neckless of pearls, and beautiful embroidered clothing—generosity that was soon extended to Qonichi's warriors via the sharing practices common to all the Mongol hordes.[34] As for the Ilkhanids, Qonichi saw no benefit in maintaining the cold war.

Unlike the Batuids, whose territory bordered the Ilkhanids' along the Caucasus, the Ordaids felt no threat from the Ilkhanids. Qonichi sent envoys carrying a message of "sincere friendship" to the Ilkhanids. He even proposed forging alliances against Qaidu.[35]

The new Jochid friendship with the Toluids was an outcome of a joint decision among the principal Jochid hordes, but, for the first time, it was an Ordaid, Qonichi, who initiated foreign policy. The Batuids followed. This is not to say that the Jochids were entirely unified, though. Nogay's ambitions outstripped Qonichi's. While Qonichi pursued prosperity and security for his already-well-established horde, Nogay wanted more. He wanted to expand and deepen the realm, solidifying the Horde's power in the west. And he wanted to be the Jochid khan. It was Nogay's ambition that ultimately led to a civil war within the Horde.

Nogay was the Horde's senior commander. In practice he outranked all the other begs, making him the first Jochid beglerbeg, although apparently he never wore the title. He was stationed along the Jochids' western border, a strategically essential location demanding constant, calculated military presence. Since the Hungarian campaign of 1241–1242, Bulgarian rulers had oscillated between war and peace with the Horde, threatening to cut off Jochid access to the inland trade route to Poland and to the lavish grasslands of the western steppe. The inland route was crucial to the Horde's wider foreign policy, as it not only gave the Jochids access to the European hinterlands but also compensated for fluctuations elsewhere: the Crimean road to the Middle East opened and closed subject to the Mamluks' goodwill, while the Caucasian road was dependent on the Ilkhanids. In addition, there was the constant possibility that the Byzantines would choke off the Black Sea straits. A firm hand in the west was therefore necessary to control the Byzantines, too.

That hand was Nogay's. The commander was ideally positioned for the task. He was a descendent of Jochi, although not through the prestigious lines of his sons Batu, Berke, or Orda. Nogay had fought, and lost an eye, on the Caucasian border, helping to establish a fearsome reputation. And he had led the war against the Byzantines in 1263, earning the respect of a major neighboring power. Nogay turned southeastern Moldavia into his headquarters, and from there brought the Byzantines and the Bulgarians into greater dependency on the Horde.

Nogay's horde prospered from its location on the Danube, benefiting from trade, commodities production, the influx of conquered peoples, and climactic conditions suited to the nomadic herding life. But Nogay's status fell during Möngke-Temür's reign. Nogay had been a close ally of Berke's, even joining the khan in converting to Islam. But after Berke's death, Nogay was removed from the center of power. With the Batuids established as the exclusive heirs to the Jochid throne, Nogay's pedigree took a blow; all of Möngke-Temür's brothers, sons, and nephews ranked higher in the line of succession, dramatically limiting Nogay's horizons.

Still, Nogay tried to amass decision-making power during Möngke-Temür's reign. In 1270 Nogay contacted the Mamluk sultan Baybars in an effort to forge his own alliance with the Mamluks without involving the khan. Nogay also sought to appropriate the extravagant gifts the Mamluks delivered to their Mongol allies. To win over the sultan, Nogay invoked his own Muslim faith. Nogay also referenced his partnership with Berke, Baybars's close friend. Most likely Nogay was present in the ceremonial tent with the begs when Berke received the Mamluk ambassadors for the first time. Just like Berke, Nogay offered to extend his friendship to the sultan and fight the Mamluks' enemies.[36]

Yet Baybars resisted Nogay's outreach. For one thing, the sultan was suspicious of Nogay's low status in the Jochid line. For another, Baybars's main enemies were the Ilkhanids, whereas Nogay had worked long and hard to make peace with them, at times contravening Möngke-Temür's own policy. Recall that, in 1270, Möngke-Temür was allied with Baraq against Abaqa, until the Ilkhanids definitively defeated Baraq. Möngke-Temür responded with grudging overtures to the Ilkhanids, remaining embittered toward them. Nogay, however, was enthusiastic about allegiance with Abaqa. Indeed, Nogay's chief wife went in person to Abaqa's court to negotiate a marriage between their son Büri and the Ilkhan's daughter. Büri stayed with his wife's family as a proof of the ties that united Nogay and Abaqa. Nogay's embrace of the Ilkhanids did not endear him to Baybars, and it was not until the 1280s, when Nogay's power became impossible to ignore, that he and the Mamluk sultan had any further exchanges.[37]

One key demonstration of that power came in 1283, when Nogay went so far as to replace Grand Prince Andrei of Vladimir with a preferred kniaz. Töde-Möngke Khan, freshly installed after the death of Möngke-Temür, supported Andrei but did not have enough influence to impose his own will. Nogay pushed Andrei from his throne and installed Andre's elder brother Dmitrii. This was clear interference with the khan's prerogative to appoint his own vassal, an unmistakable signal that Töde-Möngke was only nominally in charge.[38]

Nogay's foreign policy was similarly independent of the khan's. As a border commander, Nogay often got information before the rest of the Jochid leaders, and he did not always share what he knew. What is more, Nogay made high-level military decisions on his own. His horde's location was ideal for acquiring more people, land, wealth, and prestige; he could expand his territory to the north, south, and west without fighting other Mongols, and he did not care to wait for the khan's approval when it came to conquest. Nogay also had no compunction about raiding even in areas he already dominated. In the 1280s Nogay led the only truly expansionist horde. The Ordaids remained peaceful, and the Batuids focused on maintaining a cold peace with the Ilkhanids on their southern frontier.

Nogay organized several raids in Poland and Lithuania, with conquest in mind. He also wanted to supervise more directly southern Russia, a Jochid tributary area. And Nogay demonstrated his power by inviting Jochid vassals to obey him rather than the khan. For instance, he invited the kniazia of Suzdal and Bryansk to visit him, not the khan. In 1285 Tsar George Terter of Bulgaria minted coins bearing Nogay's name and paid tribute to him. In turn, Nogay offered military aid. Nogay even struck out on his own to strengthen relations with the Byzantines. He married Euphrosyne, daughter of Emperor Andronikos II, who was Michael Palaiologos's successor. The contemporary Greek historian Pachymérès reported that the emperor Michael had also curried favor, continually sending Nogay gifts including luxurious clothing, fine food, barrels of spiced wine, and gold and silver cups. Nogay was delighted with everything Michael had sent him, apart from the clothing, which he accepted only when he was told that the garments bore magical powers. Otherwise, a Mongol warrior would never dress like a Byzantine.[39]

Such was Nogay's strength that foreign leaders would abandon their allies in favor of vassalage to him. Thus, in 1284–1285, Nogay's army entered Hungary at the invitation of King László IV, who needed help to crush a rebellion among the Hungarian barons. Nogay was happy to oblige: László's kingdom was geopolitically crucial as part of the borderland between Europe and the Horde—precisely the region that Nogay intended to control. In choosing to ally with Nogay, László was choosing a Muslim over his existing Christian partners, an extremely bold move. Hungary lay on the eastern frontier of Latin Christendom, and Catholics hoped to integrate the territory into their own sphere of influence. To ally with the Horde, László had to cut ties with his own House of Angevine and with the Roman Catholic Church. But allying himself with the Horde served László's best interests. Unlike the pope, Nogay could provide the military help László needed. The pope was left furious with both the Hungarian king and the Jochids, whose ambitions he feared.[40]

Töde-Möngke Khan was not involved in Nogay's military campaigns in Hungary, Poland, and Lithuania. The khan had a reputation for being disinterested in politics—making him a lunatic or a saint, depending on the source's point of view—and did not appreciate Nogay's appetite for war. Soon enough, other high-ranking Jochids were flocking to Nogay's side. Even the khan's nephew Töle-Buqa took his orders from Nogay, participating in the Hungarian campaign.[41]

In 1287 Töde-Möngke abdicated. Nogay forced him out in favor of Töle-Buqa. But while Töle-Buqa had the right lineage—Batu was his great-grandfather—and the title of khan, he lacked the ruling prerogatives of his predecessors. Under new arrangements, Töle-Buqa had to share power with his brother Könchek, with Möngke-Temür's sons Alghui and Toghrilcha, and with Nogay. The Jochids were now governed by a council, of which the khan was merely one member. Relations between Töle-Buqa Khan and Nogay quickly deteriorated, as the khan suffered several military failures while carrying out plans developed by Nogay. Indeed, already during the Hungarian campaign of 1285, Töle-Buqa had lost large numbers of troops amid a devastating retreat across Transylvania. Then, in 1287–1288, the Jochids launched military operations in Poland but were unable to capture Sandomir and Krakow, as planned. The khan lost more men, war equipment, and horses and, again, his army was forced to withdraw under difficult conditions.[42]

Other military failures were likely Töle-Buqa's alone. In 1288 and again in 1290, he tried to lead the Jochid army into Ilkhanid territory, but the frontier was well guarded, and Töle-Buqa's warriors were stopped each time. Nogay did not take part in the attacks; nor did Qonichi, whose Ordaid horde was at peace with the Ilkhanids. But Nogay must have known about at least the first assault. In April 1288, just before Töle-Buqa's attack, Nogay offered the Ilkhanid ruler a *sharil,* a Buddhist relic. Arghun—Abaqa's son, who had succeeded to the Ilkhanid throne in 1284—was extremely pleased with the gift. Nogay wanted to make clear that he had nothing to do with the aggression that was to come.[43]

Nogay's policy toward the Ilkhanids should not be misunderstood as a sign of rapprochement, much less friendship. Nogay still considered the Ilkhanids rivals; he was merely pursuing his own approach to victory, an approach that, for the moment, did not involve direct aggression. While Töle-Buqa wasted troops against Arghun, Nogay sought to undermine his adversary through diplomacy involving his Christian neighbors. In the late 1280s, Catholics were balancing between Jochids and Ilkhanids—exploring relations with both, for reasons spiritual and political. For the Jochids, the stakes were high. If the pope were to ally with the Ilkhanids, the Horde might lose its Latin trade partners. More generally, the Horde would find itself weakened in European, Mediterranean, and Middle Eastern markets. And no matter the trade effects, the Jochids would have to deal with the Ilkhanids from an inferior position. So Nogay decided to divide the Ilkhanids and the pope.

Nogay's wedge would be the Franciscans. Franciscan friars had been circulating among the Jochids since the mid-thirteenth century. The Franciscans Plano Carpini and Rubruck had been among the first Westerners to visit the Mongol Empire and to describe the Horde, and their reports informed missions of later years. Dominicans also visited the Jochids, but the Franciscans were more involved in the life of the Horde. Initially, the friars used their connections to the Italian Black Sea trade network to gain influence with the Mongols. The Franciscans traveled with the nomads, trying to convert them on the road and learning their languages, habits, laws, and social norms. Thus when the Franciscans arranged their first permanent missions at Sarai and Caffa around 1280, the nomads were already familiar with them. Soon after, the friars established themselves in Nogay's capital. They were instantly popular, for they were letter writers, secretaries, interpreters, and healers. Reportedly, they undertook all these services for free.[44]

Around 1287 Nogay got his chance to bring the Franciscans over to his side. A Franciscan church and bell tower in the Crimean settlement of Solkhat had been destroyed by local Muslims, and heads of the Horde's Franciscan community wanted justice. They brought a petition before the Jochid authorities. Seizing the opportunity to show publicly that he was a friend of Catholics, Nogay sided with the Franciscans. He delegated a Muslim envoy to inform the Muslim community of Solkhat that they would have to pay for the construction of three new bell towers, and he sent the friars a large amount of money to cover damages. At the same time, Nogay's chief wife asked the Franciscans to baptize her at a Crimean holy site called Qirq Yer. To reward the friars and show them favor, she authorized them to build a monastery in Qirq Yer and ordered local officials to protect them.[45]

At this point Nogay had lived close to Christians for more than twenty years and had learned from his interactions with them. He knew that the Christian world was fragmented, and he would need to choose the right allies among its multiple and overlapping sovereignties in order to gain the pope's esteem. Those allies could not be the Russian Orthodox, to whom the Jochids had already shown favor through conferral of tarkhan status and support for the construction of Orthodox bishoprics at Sarai and Sudak. Backing the Franciscans would tamp down Orthodox influence within the Horde and potentially win over European Catholics. Nogay thus intended to support a new Catholic bishopric, or an institutional equivalent, on his own territory. With the Franciscans as his loyal proxy, Nogay would have a pipeline to the pope, helping to turn Catholics away from the Ilkhanids.

By the late 1280s, Nogay was closer than ever to becoming khan of the Horde. The final step was to unseat Töle-Buqa and the council. To this end, Nogay joined forces with an ambitious young warrior named Toqto'a. Toqto'a was the son of Möngke-Temür and his chief wife Öljeitu. As such, Toqto'a had a strong claim to the Jochid throne. But Toqto'a faced obstacles. His uncle, Töle-Buqa, and his brothers Alghui and Toghrilcha, omitted him from the council, for fear that he would try to take the throne himself. Toqto'a was brave, strong, and popular among the Horde's fighting men; other high-ranking Jochids were keen to keep him in check. Seeking a protector and ally who could elevate him to his desired position, Toqto'a called on Nogay. The supreme commander obliged. While their goals were ultimately at odds—both wished to become khan—in the near term, the men were aligned. They began to orchestrate a coup to overthrow Töle-Buqa and the council.

The moment came in 1291. Feigning serious illness, Nogay made what seemed to be a hero's dying request: he asked that the Jochid leaders gather in a quriltai with him, at which all would lay down their arms and toast to peace within the Horde. As a child of the conquests who had known Batu and Berke and become the Horde's most revered commander, Nogay could not be refused; the leaders would collect their hordes and meet at the khan's location along the Volga. En route to the Volga, the supposedly ailing Nogay prevented suspicion by accepting visitors who would report on his condition. He lay in his tent with his guests, spitting congealed animal blood that he had stuffed in his mouth. The plan worked: news spread in advance of Nogay's horde that the old commander was not long for this earth. Then, when he was close enough to the khan's camp, Nogay sent word to Toqto'a to assemble his troops and get ready for the onslaught. Their timing had to be perfect.

When Nogay reached the banks of the Volga, he made camp and invited the khan and the councilors to join him at his tent. They entered unarmed, while their guards most likely stayed outside. Still coughing blood, Nogay reminisced about his forty years of service to the khans and insisted on the need for harmony among the descendants of Jochi. Moved by Nogay's words, the assembled Jochids praised the commander's wisdom and courage. Then, suddenly, Toqto'a and his men attacked. They killed Töle-Buqa and all the ruling council members apart from Nogay, starting with Toqto'a's elder brother Toghrilcha.[46]

This was something new in Jochid history: a political murder with the aim of seizing the throne. To solidify his claim, Toqto'a married Toghrilcha's chief wife. In the Mongol world, it was not unusual for men to marry their fathers' or brothers' wives. This was a way to protect a widow and keep her estate within the family. But there was more at stake in Toqto'a's case. By appropriating his elder brother's chief wife, Toqto'a intended to highjack the lineal succession. Toghrilcha's seniority made him a more legitimate candidate to the throne; to assume Toghrilcha's claim, Toqto'a had to do more than kill his elder's physical body. The younger had to replace the elder in the genealogical tree.

Toqto'a got his wish and was soon made khan of the Horde. Once on the throne, he maintained close ties with Nogay. They spent two years purging Töle-Buqa's keshig and followers, even those who were close relatives. Such a large-scale political purge was also new to the Horde, although not to the Mongols in general. Significant purges had occurred under Great Khan Möngke, for instance. A purge was an extraordinarily violent means of erasing internal resistance, but killing potential enemies all at once was preferable to a lengthy hunt for rebels.

Such actions were bound to provoke resentment, and Toqto'a's Batuid relatives turned their ire on Nogay. The khan's inner circle knew that Nogay, seasoned politician that he was, was pulling the strings, and they urged Toqto'a to break off from the supreme commander's influence. In 1293 the khan did so, demonstrating his autonomy by restoring Kniaz Andrei as grand prince of Vladimir. Ten years earlier, Andrei had been forced out and replaced with his brother Dmitrii, per Nogay's wishes and against those of Töde-Möngke Khan. Now Toqto'a sent troops to eject Dmitrii. Dmitrii fled to Pskov, in far northwestern Russia, and the troops raided Moscow and thirteen other towns. Russian sources describe a harsh campaign, with widespread terror and a high death toll. These reports may be exaggerated, but the kniazia nonetheless decried Toqto'a's show of force. The khan was making clear that he intended to rule them closely. He was not going to continue Töde-Möngke's hands-off approach. Nor would Toqto'a allow Nogay to openly make political decisions in place of the khan.[47]

The turf war over administration of the Russian principalities was the beginning of the end for Nogay and Toqto'a's alliance. Their conflict came to a head around 1297, owing to a Mongol familial squabble. The tension began with Nogay and one of his in-laws, Salji'üdai Güregen. Salji'üdai was not a prince, but he was a powerful leader of the Qonggirad, the Jochids' oldest and most prestigious marriage partners, and he was a member of Toqto'a's inner circle. Salji'üdai was descended from the uncle of Chinggis Khan's chief wife, Börte, and was at this point married to Kelmish Aqa, Toqto'a's grandmother. A highly influential figure herself, Kelmish Aqa was Qubilai's niece and had family ties and political connections with the Toluids in China, Iran, and Azerbaijan.

Mongol ruler on campaign, illustration from an early fourteenth century copy of Rashīd al-Dīn, *Jāmiʿ al-tawārīkh*. The footman at left appears to carry a *gerege*, a tablet inscribed with an official notice of safe passage. (Pictures from History/Bridgeman Images)

Salji'üdai was therefore a force to be reckoned with, and his children were desirable marriage partners. But they were not necessarily well suited for their spouses, as Nogay's daughter discovered soon after marrying Salji'üdai's son. While Nogay's daughter converted to Islam, her husband retained his religion, which was likely Buddhism. Rashīd al-Dīn reported that before long the couple were fighting "over religion and beliefs" and could not stand each other.

The daughter complained to her father, who saw an opening to interfere. Pointing out Salji'üdai's status as a qarachu—an elite, but not a member of the golden lineage—Nogay pressed Toqto'a to banish Salji'üdai from his inner circle and either send him back to his ancestral land in northern Khwarezm or turn him over to Nogay himself. Toqto'a refused. This was unusual for multiple reasons. For one thing, Nogay, unlike Salji'üdai, was both a Jochid and supreme commander:

by lineage and by office, Nogay outranked his in-law, in spite of Salji'üdai's own undoubtedly noble extraction. In addition, Nogay was accustomed to calling the shots, albeit behind the scenes. But this time, instead of carrying out Nogay's will, Toqto'a went his own way. Toqto'a was firm in his decision. Nogay may have been his protector, a descendent of Jochi, and the most feared and respected Mongol in the west. But the khan had no intention of igniting a quarrel with the Toluids and Qonggirad, who gave him military support.[48]

With Toqto'a asserting himself, Nogay was facing the very real possibility of consignment to same role he had played under Möngke-Temür: that of an influential commander with great autonomy—but, still, just a commander. Indeed, the present circumstance was worse than that, for Nogay could no longer afford to bide his time. He was in his fifties, possibly older, an advanced age among Mongol warriors. He knew that the end might come soon. So he did something radical: he declared himself khan. To make his claim real and legal, he issued coins bearing his tamga. He also tried to solidify his legacy by choosing his eldest son Cheke as his primary heir.[49]

There could not be two Jochid khans at the same time. The only question was how the dispute would be settled. Would resolution come via quriltai or war? As a Batuid and the enthroned khan, Toqto'a might have seemed the more legitimate choice of ruler. Certainly there were begs who thought so. But he had numerous enemies among the Jochid families, and several begs sided with Nogay. In the old days, such contests for power inevitably inspired the Jochids to part ways; the western steppe was big enough for many powerful hordes. But this time no consensus was reached, and neither side trusted the other enough to back down. So war it was.

In the winter of 1297–1298, on the lower Don, the two hordes fought their first battle. Nogay emerged the victor, forcing Toqto'a's army to withdraw toward the Volga. But the battle was not decisive, so Nogay developed a wider strategy. His next step was to take control of Crimea. The peninsula formed an enclave within the Black Sea territory, and Nogay feared that the inhabitants would stay loyal to Toqto'a. Nogay targeted the Genoese of Caffa, whom he accused of holding back his share of tax revenues. To make the Genoese pay, he sent mounted archers under his grandson's command, but the grandson was killed during his stay in Caffa. Outraged, Nogay called on his warriors and allied begs to punish the culprits. The sources do not mention whether the troops were successful in finding the grandson's killers, but the sources do indicate that Nogay's allies killed, robbed, and enslaved Muslim, Alan, and Frankish merchants around Crimea.[50]

Plundering merchants was a lucrative business, and when the begs who fought in the Crimean raid returned to Nogay, their hearts were filled with glory and their carts were loaded with spoils and captives. But then Nogay did something none of his commanders anticipated: the old leader released the prisoners. The Crimeans were not, after all, Nogay's enemies. Indeed, most of them were his trading and political partners, and he had no intention of undoing his carefully cultivated alliance with the Franciscans. He simply wanted to show who was in charge. Releasing the prisoners was, however, a disastrous miscalculation. The begs who had fought to avenge Nogay's grandson deserved to be rewarded. Their earnings were taken from them, a humiliation and a violation of Chinggis Khan's law. The dispossessed begs left Nogay at once and joined Toqto'a's camp.[51]

The final battle took place on the Kügenlik River in southeastern Moldavia. This had been the core of Nogay's territory, but without the begs, he could not hold the area, allowing Toqto'a to move his horde and his warriors in. Toqto'a's men destroyed Nogay's army. Nogay managed to escape the battlefield but was soon caught and fatally wounded by a Russian cavalryman fighting for the khan. Nogay's sons picked up the fight against the Batuids, but his horde nearly disintegrated, its people fleeing to the Balkans, Poland, and Lithuania. His heir was finally killed in Bulgaria. In the meantime, the khan successfully established his authority over Nogay's former territory. Toqto'a installed one of his son's hordes at Isaccea, where Nogay's capital had been.[52]

The civil war lasted three long years and deeply shook the Horde. When it finally ended in 1300, thousands of skilled horsemen had died and thousands of others had been sold into slavery in the Middle East and Europe. The war made a deep impression on contemporary observers as well. Conflict was in full swing in 1298 when Marco Polo, locked in a Genoese jail, told the writer Rustichello da Pisa of the large numbers involved in the war, the appalling level of violence, the masses of dead bodies. According to Polo, whose *Travels* ends with Nogay's initial victory over Toqto'a, the supreme commander was the greatest "Tartar" leader in Europe. After all, for more than thirty years, Nogay had sustained the Mongol imperial order on the western border, and it seemed he was about to emerge triumphant once more.[53]

After Nogay's death the Jochids maintained their control over the bordering Bulgarians and Byzantines, but exchanges with the Hungarians and Balkan peoples waned. The descendants of Nogay remained in Eastern Europe, where they slowly lost the authority that Nogay had accumulated. In the early fourteenth century, the great river valleys of the Dniester and Danube were still safe places for nomads, but the command center of the Horde had been moved back to the lower Volga.[54]

Nogay faced several disadvantages in his war for supremacy over the Horde. For one thing, he was isolated, his territory cut off from the distant Mongol uluses, where he might have found allies. To reach the descendants of Chagatay, Ögödei, and Tolui, Nogay's envoys had to cross the Jochid or Ilkhanid hordes. Nogay's interactions with the eastern Mongols were thus sporadic. By contrast, Toqto'a could rely on old partnerships that connected him to nomadic elites across the entirety of Mongol Eurasia.

A second disadvantage lay in Nogay's comparatively humble position, which constrained his popularity among the begs. The war between Toqto'a and Nogay forced the begs to choose a camp, and Nogay was unable to hold their allegiance. Since the time of Chinggis Khan, top-down diffusion of wealth had been essential to the khan's maintenance of elite support, but even supportive begs worried that Nogay, with his limited network, could not satisfy them. When he revoked their spoils, he seemed to prove that he was not an able provider.

Nogay faced one more disadvantage: the Qonggirad were on Toqto'a's side. The Qonggirad were influential and superbly wealthy. Since the rule of Batu, the Qonggirad had been kept away from key keshig positions, but they still had access to the khan through the Jochid princesses whom they married, and the Qonggirad used these connections to amass significant power. Indeed, the Qonggirad were elites in northern Khwarezm, one of the most prosperous regions of the Horde. Endowed with its own coinage, the area was a vital section of the northern trade route. Through their commercial enterprises, the Qonggirad accumulated money and manpower, which was at Toqto'a's disposal.[55]

The Power behind the Throne

Supporting the Qonggirad begs over Nogay was a fateful move. It meant that, while Toqto'a had firmly restored the Batuids as the leaders of the Horde, he also had upset age-old rules of governance. By backing the qarachu Salji'üdai over the Jochid Nogay, the khan opened a door that had been closed since the death of Chinggis. For the first time, a direct descendant of Jochi and member of the golden lineage—who was also the highest-ranking commander of the Horde, above even the keshig elders—could not impose his will upon a qarachu. The supremacy of the golden lineage had started to crack.[56]

The threat to the priority of Chinggis's house, surely, is one reason why many Jochid princes and begs initially backed Nogay over Toqto'a, only abandoning Nogay after he gave away their rightful spoils. In the world of the Mongols, social and political hierarchy were not just vital, they were also sacred: the supremacy of the golden lineage was acknowledged by Tengri, who had bestowed strength on Chinggis Khan and his heirs. To refuse the laws of social hierarchy, as Toqto'a had when he supported Salji'üdai, was a matter of life and death; doing so endangered the whole community. Nogay is often viewed by historians as rulebreaker, but he was in fact following a conservative impulse: he tried to preserve the larger regime of Mongol law and tradition. In the view of Nogay and his followers, the war stemmed from rivalry between a Jochid leader—Nogay—and the Qonggirad; the choice was between the golden lineage and the qarachu. Underlying social tensions in the Horde were becoming exposed, especially among the begs, who struggled to decide which leader to back given their commitments to the Mongol world order—Toqto'a, their rightful khan, or Nogay, whose rights vis-à-vis the Qonggirad were being denied.

Although Nogay was defeated, he left a deep mark on the political culture of the Horde. Importantly, he showed that the Horde could survive with a weak khan by devolving power. Working through the governing council and as the power behind the throne, Nogay was a genuine leader who enhanced ulus Jochi's wealth and strength. And Nogay nearly took de jure power himself by mobilizing the begs, a highly unusual maneuver that made clear the increasing power of the aristocracy.

Nogay's experiments in governance failed in that he never became khan. But the results of his efforts endured. In the wake of the civil war, the begs became that much more forceful. They had elevated Nogay and then destroyed him by coming to Toqto'a's rescue, with the immediate result being in most respects a return to the status quo ante: Jochid khans asserting their authority. But when the next great succession battle came in the mid-fourteenth century, it would be qarachu begs at the center of the power that emerged. The ever-evolving Horde had more uncharted territory to navigate.[57]

6

The Northern Road

If you're traveling from Venice to the great khan's capital in China to do business, take my advice. First, you must grow a long beard. Once you reach Mongol territory, you will melt into the crowd like a Muslim merchant. Second, in addition to your merchandise, bring several hundred silver bars, which you can exchange when you need local coin. And, finally, never take the southern road.

What you want is the northern road. The entry point is at the harbor of Tana, which stands at the mouth of the Don River. There, hire a *drogman,* a translator, and choose a good one no matter the cost. You also need at least two male servants who speak Qipchaq, the language one hears most in West Asia. In addition to male servants, you may hire a woman, but make sure she speaks the language too. After Tana, the next stop is Hajji Tarkhan, where the Volga flows into the Caspian Sea. You will need ten to twelve days to get there with a horse-drawn carriage, and twenty-five if you are traveling with an oxcart. To prepare for this trip, stock up on dry, salted fish and flour, but don't worry about meat. You will find it everywhere along the way.

The route from Tana to Hajji Tarkhan goes through the steppe. You may see many Mongol warriors. It can be unsafe, and it is wise to walk with other people—ideally a medium-sized caravan of sixty horsemen.

Once you arrive at Hajji Tarkhan and the Volga delta, get rid of your carts and take boats: you will go faster and pay less to ship your goods. Sarai, the great Mongol settlement, stands upstream a day or so. The river flows fast and divides into several navigable tributaries; follow the branches eastward, through the next valley and out to Saraijuq—the little Sarai. Saraijuq is the biggest Mongol trade center on the Ural River. It is also where the Mongols come together to worship their ancestors.

In Saraijuq exchange your horses for camels and continue toward the chalky road to northern Khwarezm and the old Muslim cities that once belonged to the sultan Muhammad. From Saraijuq to Urgench, the capital of Khwarezm down in the Amu-Daria Valley, it takes twenty days on camel carts. This is a long, dry road across a high plateau, but Urgench and the surrounding valley are worth the trip. The city is one of the main commercial crossroads of the region, and the crowd is so thick on market days that you can't ride through on horseback. If you want to sell some of your goods, this is the right place. People come to buy everything, especially silk.

From Urgench, follow the road eastward to the next river valley—a forty-day journey by camel carts. Eventually you will reach Otrar, on the Syr-Daria. The city was half destroyed when the Mongols conquered it in 1220, but now it is blooming again. Otrar stands on the border between the Jochids and Chagatayids; it is the eastern limit of the Horde. You have now traveled a distance of roughly two thousand miles, and you are halfway on your journey. From here, the northern road merges with a branch of the southern and continues to the Chagatayid city of Almaliq, then up to China.

On the northern road, you don't need to pay much for shipping. If your merchandise does not exceed 25,000 golden florins in value, you will need only sixty to eighty silver bars in total to reach Khanbalik (Beijing), and it may cost you even less on the way back. Always invest in small, easily packed luxury items, such as silk, because you'll need to trade some of it for silver when you return home. That's because, in China, the Mongols will ask you to exchange your metal bars for banknotes. It's the only money they accept in this area. After you turn around, stop again in Urgench to exchange your silk for new silver bars.

Don't worry about thieves; the Mongol laws protect foreign merchants and harshly punish robbery. But certain precautions are necessary in order to ensure that the law is on your side. Most importantly, don't venture into Mongol lands without a business partner. If you die on your trip, everything you bring with you goes to the khan—unless you have a companion who can claim your goods. Also, make sure you get the news from the Mongol lands, because when there is no khan—or if many khans are fighting for power—the roads are hazardous for foreigners. Otherwise, the northern road is safe day and night.[1]

Such was the advice of Francesco Pegolotti, a merchant working for the Compagnia dei Bardi, a Florentine banking company. We know very little of Pegolotti, except that he stayed at various Bardi trading posts and wrote a handbook for traders some time between 1335 and 1343. Based on his own experiences and the oral reports he heard from long-distance traders, he compiled a set of recommendations—paraphrased above—for those who wished to journey into the Horde and on to China.

In the fourteenth century, merchants had a choice between two long-distance routes that crossed the Mongol landmass, a southern and a northern route. The southern route, by land and sea, was mostly in the hands of the Ilkhanids and the Toluid great khan. The trip from Tabriz to Khanbalik was exhausting and unpredictable—it could take as little as three and a half months and as long as three years. The way was also perilous and the itinerary ever-changing, thanks to political upheaval underway in the Toluid territories throughout the early fourteenth century. A trader could never be sure which markets would be open, which yam stations would be in operation, and which roads would be passable. The northern steppe route, controlled by the Jochids, was safer and more predictable, although it could be tricky when passing through the fractious territory of Qaidu. The trip from Tana to China lasted seven to eleven months, but contemporary travelers considered this fast enough. Most importantly, the itinerary was fixed, and so were the taxes and shipping costs, which were kept low. Based on Pegolotti's reports, we can estimate that the tax was equal to no more than 1.6 percent of the value of the goods.[2]

Pegolotti had good advice, but he did not know about the Siberian Road, the far-northern caravan track through Ordaid territory and on to Qaraqorum and China. The Siberian Road branched off the northern route Pegolotti described, but his sources would never have been able to survive the cold and snow. Only nomads, fur hunters, and seasoned trackers had the skills and equipment—including dog-sleds—to take advantage of the far-northern route, which skirted the Arctic Circle. The stations of the Siberian Road are not recorded, but the route must have linked the Ural River to the Irtysh River and passed through the Altai Mountains. By means of the Siberian Road, one could reach or exit Yuan China without having to worry about the political situation in Qaidu's land.[3]

Today we commonly speak of a Silk Road that connected east and west, but in truth the Silk Road was several routes, two of them controlled by Mongols: the northern, Jochid-dominated route and the southern one, which was largely under Ilkhanid control. The entirety of the northern road, including its subarctic offshoot, was one of the keys to Jochid power. In the fourteenth century, Jochid rulers continued to prioritize commercial relations, operating flexibly to preserve their tax base and productive capacity among sedentary subjects while using soft and hard power to maintain leadership of the Eurasian trade network—all in support of the circulation and redistribution that enabled political strength and the balance of the Mongol universe. In the first half of the 1300s, the Horde firmed up its domination of the kniazia, with major consequences for the future of Russian politics. The Jochids masterfully manipulated the Mamluks, Genoese, and Venetians, enriching themselves and their subjects. And, finally, the Horde came away with the biggest prize of all: freedom from the Ilkhanid threat. Between the 1330s and 1350s, the Ilkhanids collapsed, ending competition from the southern road and leaving the Jochids the undisputed masters of trade in Eurasia. At least for a time.

Toqto'a Consolidates Power

In 1298 the Ordaid horde lost its leader, Qonichi. Qonichi had been a very large man. According to Rashīd al-Dīn, "day by day he grew fatter," to a point where he could no longer ride a horse and had to travel in a cart instead. Qonichi's contemporaries claimed he was crushed to death by the excess fat around his neck. Historically obesity was rare among

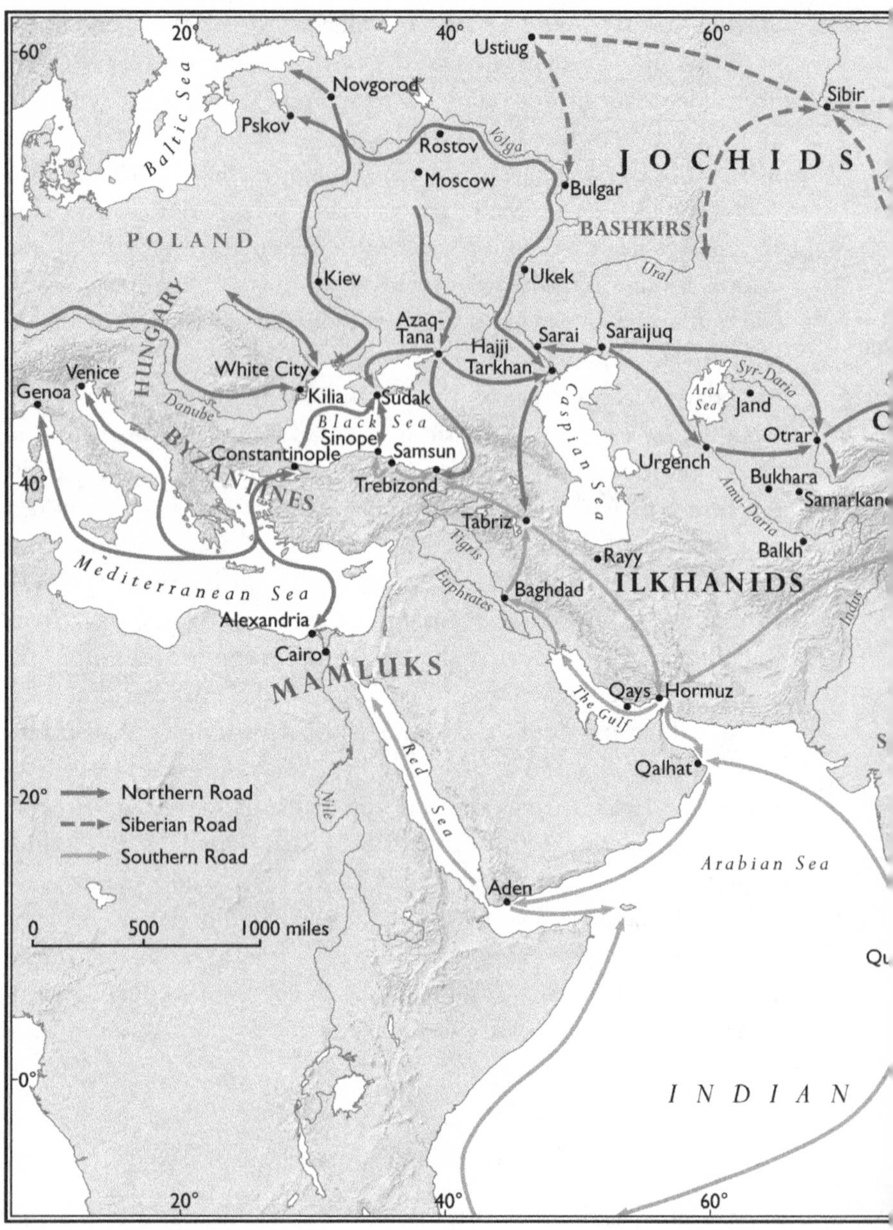
Baltic Sea
Novgorod
Pskov
Ustiug
Sibir
Rostov
Volga
Moscow
JOCHIDS
Bulgar
BASHKIRS
POLAND
Kiev
Ukek
Ural
HUNGARY
Azaq-Tana
Hajji Tarkhan
Sarai
Saraijuq
White City
Venice
Genoa
Kilia
Sudak
Danube
Black Sea
Sinope
Samsun
Constantinople
BYZANTINES
Trebizond
Caspian Sea
Aral Sea
Syr-Daria
Jand
Otrar
Urgench
Bukhara
Amu-Daria
Tabriz
Tigris
Rayy
Balkh
Mediterranean Sea
Euphrates
Baghdad
ILKHANIDS
Indus
Alexandria
Cairo
MAMLUKS
Qays
Hormuz
The Gulf
Qalhat
Red Sea
Nile
Northern Road
Siberian Road
Southern Road
Arabian Sea
Aden
0 500 1000 miles
INDIAN
60°
40°
20°
0°

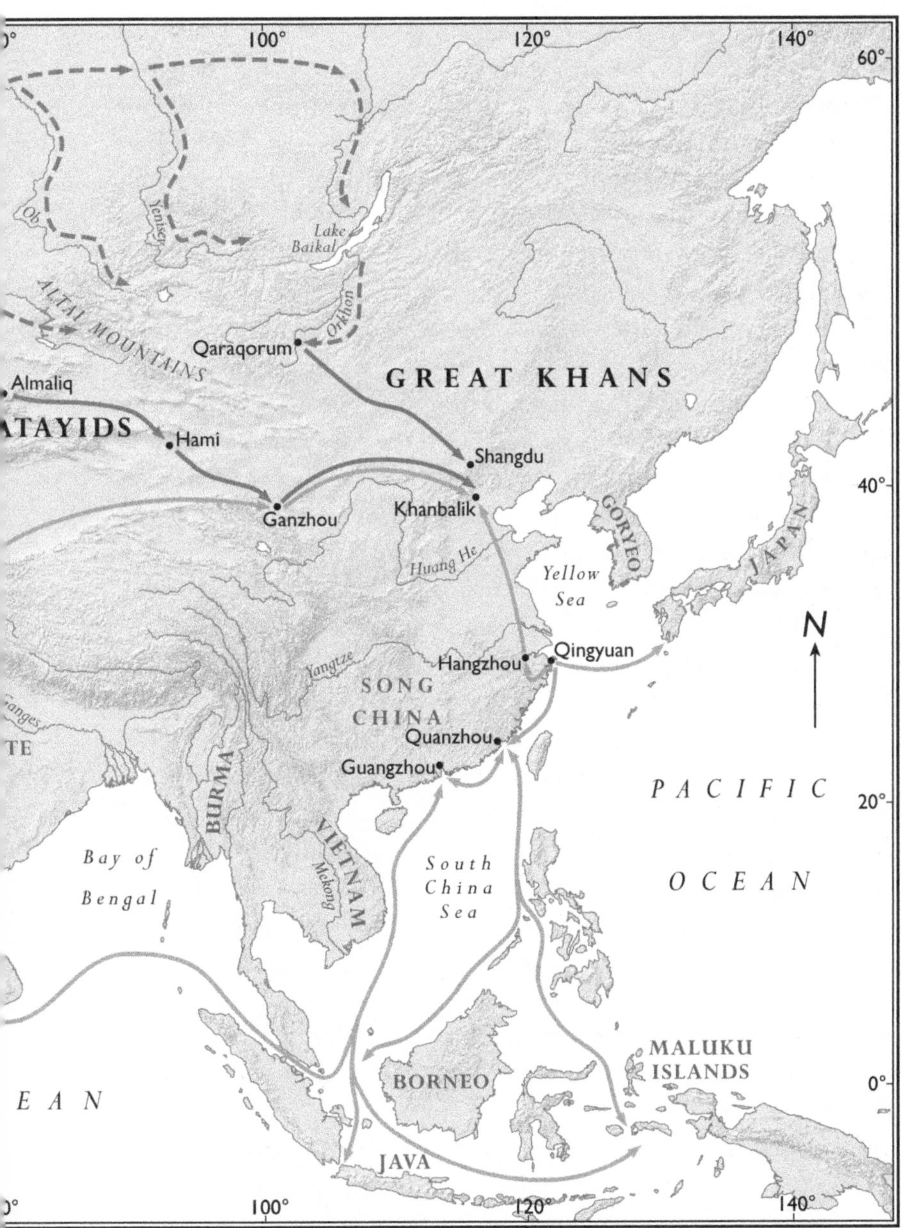

The Mongol exchange, c. 1300–1330.

nomads, though more common among the wealthy city inhabitants who stayed within their four walls. But at this point the nomadic elites were so prosperous, and their supplies so well organized, that the mobile courts consumed as much food and drink as the biggest cities of Eurasia. Mongol diets had also changed, too rapidly incorporating goods such as sugar introduced by traders.[4]

Qonichi's heirs clashed over succession, and they soon involved their Mongol neighbors in the conflict. The Ordaids had been peaceful for half a century; their abrupt fighting sent a shockwave across the whole of Mongol Eurasia. Qaidu and the Chagatayids supported Qonichi's cousin, but the Jochid khan Toqto'a and the great khan in the east supported Qonichi's son Bayan. Each camp provided warriors to support their candidate. In 1304 the Mongol leaders agreed to a general truce. But the official peace did not fully dissolve the tensions among the Ordaids, and sporadic fights continued for several years. It was only when Qonichi's grandson Sāsī Buqa inherited the throne, around 1312, that the conflict truly ended and the Ordaids reunited.[5]

The truce, however, had purposes other than ending the Ordaid war. The primary goal of the peace was to reassert the domination of the Toluids and Jochids over Mongol Eurasia. By 1304 Qaidu was dead, and it was clear that the Jochid Toqto'a and the Toluids formed a powerful coalition, far stronger militarily than any of the other Mongol groups. Together, the Jochids and Toluids were the decision-makers. Other members of the golden lineage were reduced to a subordinate position: they could either submit or rise up and rebel. Thus, in 1304, the Ilkhanid ruler, a Toluid, wrote, "We . . . descendants of Chinggis Khan spent forty-five years recriminating against each other. Now, under the protection of Tengri, we elder and younger brothers have reached a mutual agreement. Our states are one, from southern China, where the sun rises, as far as the Talu Sea."[6]

Qonichi's death, and the general truce, provided an opportunity for Toqto'a to assert himself. With Qonichi and Nogay out of the picture, the Jochids faced a power vacuum, which Toqto'a rushed to fill. Meanwhile the agreement among the Chinggisid rulers enabled Toqto'a to expand his trading partnerships throughout the empire. He used the Mongol roads to reach deeper into the Eurasian landmass, ensuring that the Horde remained the chief beneficiary of the Mongol exchange.[7]

Toqto'a also restarted the pressure campaign against the Ilkhanids. Unlike Nogay, Toqto'a insisted that the descendants of Hülegü had usurped the lands of Arran and Azerbaijan and that the Jochids had to take them back. Through diplomacy, Toqto'a persuaded the Ilkhanids to reopen the Caucasian road south of Derbent. But he wanted more than that: he wanted full access to the southern road, extending to the Far East. This would require more than diplomacy, so in 1304–1305 and again in 1306–1307 Toqto'a sent envoys to the Mamluk sultan urging him to attack the Ilkhanids. The Ilkhanid ruler Öljeitü struck back by offering the sultan an exchange of prisoners and promising to let Mamluk merchants trade in his territory. Keen to send their traders to Tabriz and Baghdad, the Mamluks agreed to a temporary truce with their old enemies, the Ilkhanids. Soon after, the Mamluks officially rejected Toqto'a's plan for a joint campaign.[8]

A few months later, in November, Toqto'a punished the Mamluks for supporting the Ilkhanids. He ordered the Genoese—the Mamluks' best middlemen—chased out of the Horde and had their goods seized. Toqto'a did not go too far: he wanted to change the Mamluks' minds, not permanently sour relations, so he allowed Mamluk envoys themselves to continue visiting the Horde. To justify evicting the Genoese, the khan publicly accused them of trading children on his territories and selling them to the Mamluks. In the Latin world, this was a grave accusation. Not only did the Catholic Church prohibit human trafficking, but the Pope also excommunicated anyone who provided Muslim rulers with weapons, wood, and soldiers.

By May 1308 the Genoese abandoned Caffa. They had been under siege for about seven months, were short on supplies, and could no longer defend the harbor. Indeed, throughout the northern shore of the Black Sea, Italian business was on hold, tensions with the Mongols were high, and Christian conversions decreased, to the detriment of the entire Latin network. All this unnerved the Franciscans, who blamed the Genoese merchants, accusing them of practicing illegal trading activities, spying on the Mongols, and feigning loyalty simultaneously to the Mamluks, Ilkhanids, and Jochids.[9]

Unlike his predecessor Möngke-Temür, Toqto'a did not see the Genoese as key trade partners. Their expulsion was therefore not a significant issue. Toqto'a's attention was directed at the lower Volga and the flourishing central Eurasian economy that buoyed the region. Toqto'a's horde was in the middle of the northern route and, more specifically, a trade corridor that reached from northern Khwarezm to the northern Caucasus. This long stretch of land was the khan's private domain; his keshig exerted direct control over it. To contemporaries it was Ulugh Kul, the Great Center.[10] Situated at the intersection of the east-west Silk Road and north-south fur road, the Great Center was a series of thriving nodes, where the nomads of the Eurasian hinterland traded weapons, tools, grains, animals, and clothes.

To better exploit his advantageous position in the Great Center and encourage more trade, Toqto'a began implementing monetary reforms in 1306–1308. The commercial situation had changed since the last monetary reform in Möngke-Temür's times, and the coinages of the four most productive Jochid regions needed significant reconfiguring. Foreigners often complained that their silver bought them old coins of lesser value than the more recent ones. There was also a problem of standardization. Old coins had been struck according to various metrics of weight and material purity. As a result, not everybody agreed on the value of a given coin, which led to disputes. There were too many different monetary issues in circulation, creating an urgent need to standardize the weight system.[11]

The khan's advisers, accountants, and ortaqs (official traders) came up with a plan to tackle the most important issues: replacing old silver coins with newly minted and better standardized ones, ensuring that foreigners used local currency when they traded in Jochid territory and dissuading people from taking Jochid coins across the border. All of this would be achieved without eliminating the benefits of diversity, which the Mongols had long recognized. While new standards were implemented, Toqto'a never sought to establish a common coin for the entirety of the Horde. Rather, he unified the monetary and weight systems in each region so that regional systems would be internally coherent but would still differ from each other. And while Toqto'a banned the use of foreign coins in much of the Horde, they could still be tendered in border settlements. Finally, the new, standardized coins largely maintained earlier regional variations in shape, size, and markings, which bolstered people's trust in both the currency and the regime. As ever, merchants and taxpayers felt more comfortable using coins referring to their own traditions and belief systems, and Toqto'a left in place the Turkic, Muslim, and other symbols and scripts that users preferred.[12]

The goals of Toqto'a's reforms were not purely economic. They were also political, which is why he had his tamga, his lineage mark, removed from the coins struck in the Great Center. Whereas previous Jochid khans felt the need to assert their authority over lands in which Mongols were an alien presence, by this point, no one doubted who was in charge of the territory ruled directly by the khan, leaving Toqto'a no reason to publicly claim what was indisputably his. On top of his lineage rights, his military successes made him powerful, safe, and confident in the mandate that Tengri had bestowed on him. Only the coins issued in the city of Bulgar and in Crimea, the lower Don, and the lower Danube showed the khan's mark, for these were the Jochid borderlands, where the khan's authority was indirect.[13]

A final political goal of the reform was to balance Jochid power against the Ilkhanids. Toqto'a's reform came as a response to the Ilkhanid ruler Ghazan, who had just launched his own currency policy. The Horde did not comply with the new exchange rules implemented in Azerbaijan and Iran, the Ilkhanid regions that bordered the Jochid territories. Instead the Horde reinvented its own system to be more competitive against the Ilkhanids'.[14]

It took the Jochids almost thirty years to complete Toqto'a's reform. Beginning in Khwarazm and Crimea, and later in the lower Volga and Bulgaria, old coins were recalled, repurposed as jewelry, or melted and recycled into new coins, tools, weapons, and other everyday utensils. The Jochids took their time because they understood the importance of continuity in assuring economic growth and political stability. Making people change their habits required persuasion, diplomacy, and patience, and Toqto'a, his associates, and his successors were willing to invest the necessary time and effort.

Around 1311 the cold war that had prevented the Mamluks from trading with the Horde via the Genoese came to an end. To show that the khan was eager to reopen commercial relations, his envoys presented the sultan a hundred slaves and a pile of luxury furs. It was a clear message that Mamluk trade was welcome again in the Horde. The news spread that the khan had reconciled with the sultan and that the Jochid coin

The Mongol ruler Ghazan, seated on the throne with his wife, from a c. 1430 edition of Rashīd al-Dīn, *Jāmiʿ al-tawārīkh.* The royal couple is placed on equal footing, a Mongol rule that also applied in the Horde. (De Agostini Picture Library / Bridgeman Images)

system had been improved, offering better conditions for trade, resulting in renewed growth in human trafficking in Crimea. Delighted, the sultan sent the khan envoys carrying a thousand pieces of armor including headgear, belts, and barding. But when the envoys arrived at the khan's camp, they discovered that Toqto'a had recently died, apparently drowned in a shipwreck on the Volga. Keeping to business as usual, the Mamluks gave the gifts to his successor.[15]

Controlling the Competition

Some of Toqto'a's contemporaries claimed that his drowning was in fact a murder and that his nephew Özbek was involved. Özbek's role is uncertain, but it is not hard to see why he might have had a vendetta against the khan. During the coup of 1291, Toqto'a killed Özbek's father Toghrilcha. Adding to the list of grievances, Toqto'a had married Bayalun, Toghrilcha's chief wife and Özbek's stepmother. In the view of some Mongols, Toqto'a's fratricide and usurpation of the throne marked him for revenge. Whatever the case may be, his transgressions weighed on the next generation and resurfaced when the time came for a transfer of power.[16]

The question was whether the next khan would be Toqto'a's chosen successor, his son Tükel Buqa, or else Özbek. As a youth Özbek had been banished from the khan's court, and most likely spent his time in northern Khwarezm, where he held a position in the army. Tükel Buqa, by contrast, had enjoyed the honors, resources, and gifts bestowed on him by his father, thereby gaining much political prestige. Even so, Özbek had his supporters. Preliminary debates over the succession, most likely held at Sarai, were heated. Some of the Jochids and the qarachu begs supported the rights of Toqto'a's house and others the rights of Toghrilcha's. Influential religious elites interfered, exacerbating tensions. Buddhists supported Tükel Buqa and Muslims Özbek, who, according to Muslim sources, promised that he would publicly convert to Islam upon taking the throne. Indeed, it was the head of the Muslim begs, Qutluq-Temür, who invited Özbek to return to Sarai and vie for the throne. Özbek also had the support of Bayalun, newly widowed once more. In the eyes of his followers, Özbek would restore Möngke-Temür's direct line of succession, which Toqto'a had misappropriated.

In early 1313, with the lunar new year approaching, the hordes converged on the lower Volga for festivities and the enthronement of their new khan. But no consensus had been reached. During the festival Özbek learned that, in the event he was enthroned, his opponents were preparing a coup against him. Upon hearing the news, he rushed out of his tent, gathered his men and allies on the outskirts of the festival site, and then returned in full force. Outpacing his enemies, Özbek slayed Tükel Buqa, while Özbek's men killed the begs and princes who opposed him. Özbek seized the throne, and in the succeeding months, he and Qutluq-Temür chased the fleeing members and supporters of Tükel Buqa's house. More than a hundred were executed.[17]

Soon after taking the throne, Özbek married his stepmother Bayalun. By doing so, he reestablished his deceased father in the direct lineal succession, erased Toqto'a and his descendants from the line, and tightened his own control over the ruling lineage. As a Muslim, Özbek was forbidden from marrying his stepmother, but the khan's jurists circumvented the issue by claiming that Bayalun's previous marriages were not valid, because her former husbands had not been Muslim. Such creative legal thinking was to Özbek's benefit but also Bayalun's. She was no passive instrument of legitimation; on the contrary, Bayalun had been at the center of power for more than twenty years, and she was keen to maintain her influence.[18]

Özbek's ambition went beyond simply establishing himself on the throne. He also sought to ensure that, among all the branches descending from Möngke-Temür, only his own could produce candidates for the next generation of khan. Thus Özbek killed not only Tükel Buqa but also the descendants of Toqto'a's younger brother. In doing so, Özbek eliminated all of the grandsons of Möngke-Temür with claim to the throne equal to his own. This was intended to guarantee that no one could emerge as a competitor to Özbek's direct descendants.[19]

Özbek's rise to power by means of murder and political purges was not unique, but that is precisely why it was momentous. That Özbek, like his predecessor Toqto'a, won the throne by killing his rival demonstrates that, at least within the Horde, the Mongol succession system was breaking down. Chinggis Khan had developed a political process that tolerated competition among potential successors, assuring that matters would be settled by negotiation and consensus rather than violence. But with each transfer of power among the Jochids, the process was strained further. Since the days of Batu and Orda, interregnum periods had shortened, a clear sign of the Jochids' decreasing willingness to negotiate with one another. Long gone was the time when defeated candidates accepted the decision of the quriltai and publicly gave up their claim to the throne.

Of course, Özbek did not reach the throne by himself. The assistance of Qutluq-Temür was crucial, and Özbek repaid that assistance by granting Qutluq-Temür authority unprecedented for a qarachu, an elite not from the golden lineage—a decision with transformative implications for Jochid governance. From the time of Batu, the political regime of the Horde had relied on distinctions among the elites, intended to prevent families outside the golden lineage gaining too much power and to prevent the khan's relatives from toppling him. To this end, both Jochids and Jochid in-laws had been kept out of the keshig. Over time, however, conflict and competition among the descendants of Batu changed this system of distinctions and the leadership positions that individuals could hold. The first major change was the creation of the beglerbeg position, which devolved a great deal of power to a single agent beneath the khan and above the keshig elders. The beglerbeg was the khan's deputy, referred to in Arabic source as *nā'ib al-qān*. Nogay was the first to hold this position, meaning that a Jochid was allowed in the khan's official ruling circle.[20]

Özbek went farther, installing Qutluq-Temür as beglerbeg. This was a drastic change because Qutluq-Temür was a güregen, an imperial husband; his chief wife, Turabak Khatun, was a wealthy Jochid princess. In addition, Qutluq-Temür was made governor of Khwarezm, another role previously unavailable to in-laws, who were prevented from governing hordes and administrative divisions of the ulus. Meanwhile Qutluq-Temür's brother 'Isa also entered the ruling group after marrying the khan's daughter. 'Isa's own daughter became the khan's fourth wife. 'Isa used his kinship ties to strengthen his own position, becoming the second most powerful beg after Qutluq-Temür.[21]

Özbek's ruling circle was unusual for other reasons, too. His in-laws were Muslims, adding a new dimension to the keshig and the beglerbeg position. And the criterion for their membership was not their honored place in Mongol society or their skill in military command but rather the political, financial, and military support they provided the khan. Özbek's qarachu in-laws had backed his election and now they were ruling begs. Perhaps reflecting the historic rupture that Qutluq-Temür and 'Isa represented, Özbek changed the name of his ruling cadre: they were no longer keshig elders but ulus begs. There were also eight of them, rather than the original four.

The Jochids immediately perceived the threat of the khan's new way of governing: Özbek was subordinating his blood relatives to preferred appointees who traditionally were barred from the sorts of offices he bestowed on them. But there was nothing the Jochids could do. Qutluq-Temür had more to offer Özbek than they did—specifically, military support and the political allegiance of a powerful Muslim leader, whose partnership was vital to governing Muslim populations and maintaining stable relations with the Horde's southern neighbors. Qutluq-Temür remained a central figure of the government until his death around 1335. For more than twenty years, he commanded in the lower Volga and in northern Khwarezm, while 'Isa ruled Crimea and stood in for Qutluq-Temür as beglerbeg when necessary.[22]

Merging the ranks of the ulus begs—the former keshig—and the Jochid marriage partners was Özbek's most significant innovation. The bond between Özbek's and Qutluq-Temür's families in time became generalized into a new framework of governance that transcended lineage. In this new system, the qarachu begs took over many former functions of the Jochids and other Mongols and helped the khan centralize power under a single, all-embracing administration.

All Hordes in One

One of the first acts of Özbek's government was to appropriate and redistribute the Jochids' assets and power. The khan divided the territories and peoples of his horde into a number of groups, each administered by one of his loyal qarachu begs rather than by a Jochid. The Jochids also no longer ruled sedentary subjects directly and did not collect taxes themselves. Instead, the khan's deputies collected the taxes and deposited them in the treasury. The khan continued to distribute cash and gifts to the Jochid princes, but their authority had been highly constrained.[23]

The armed forces had always answered ultimately to the khan, and that did not change under the new system. What did change was the hierarchy beneath him. Now the Jochid princes no longer commanded the forces in their territories. Instead, the ulus begs did, helping to ensure that armed horsemen from all the Jochid territories would gather upon the khan's call, for Özbek had eliminated the possibility that a resentful Jochid prince might act independently. Ibn Battuta reported that the ulus begs headed seventeen tümen commanders, each of them leading up to ten thousand warriors. Another source claims that Özbek was able to mobilize more than seven hundred thousand horsemen, a massive army that was invisible in times of peace but suddenly took shape when ordered.[24]

The shift toward qarachu authority was especially pronounced in the khan's horde, where historically the Jochids had been even more dominant among the elites than in other hordes. But Özbek took more direct control of other hordes, too, including the Ordaid horde in the east. The left-hand wing lost considerable autonomy after 1321, when a new ruler, Irzan, took over. Irzan was the heir to powerful Ordaid predecessors, who had brought prosperity to their horde and even. In the case of Qonichi, an Ordaid had even become the de facto leader of the Horde. But while Irzan benefited from the wealth and capacity others had generated, he wanted more: he claimed the great cities of the lower Syr-Daria Valley, including Otrar. This was a clear encroachment on Chagatayid territory. Such ambitions were beyond even the considerable abilities of the Ordaids, which led Irzan to call on the help of Özbek. The khan provided his Ordaid relatives with military and political support in exchange for commitment to his policies and to himself. The political status quo ante between the Batuid and Ordaid hordes was thus restored, with the Ordaids the clear subordinate. At quriltais, Irzan followed Özbek's lead, never raising his voice against the khan's wishes. Indeed, the eastern horde was perhaps more dependent than ever, as the economies of the two hordes became more integrated and the Ordaids began to adopt Islam.[25]

The territory of Orda's descendants had been expanding for decades, inching closer to and eventually encompassing Muslim-occupied lands. By the time Özbek and Qutluq-Temür were ascendant in the Horde, the Ordaids bordered Khwarezm in the west—Khwarezm with its Muslim beglerbeg, local Muslim administrators, and the Islamic splendor of its capital, Urgench. Rebuilt by the Jochids, the city was a hub of the fur trade and therefore the site of much interaction with the Ordaids. In Urgench the Ordaids encountered the mystical aura emanating from religious buildings, among them the mausoleum of the Sufi leader Najm al-Dīn al-Kubrā, whose teaching had influenced Berke Khan's conversion. Both Qutluq-Temür and his chief wife had their own religious and funerary buildings. Further Islamic influence came from Özbek himself. Influential officeholders of the central Horde were now mostly Muslims, as evidenced in their names, buildings, and burials.

Two Mongol men studying the Quran, from an early fourteenth century edition of Rashīd al-Dīn, *Jāmi' al-tawārīkh*. Mongol hordes featured tent-mosques, tent-churches, Buddhist monasteries, and mobile Islamic schools. (bpk Bildagentur / Photo: Ellwardt / Art Resource, NY)

We do not know if officials converted en masse or whether the officials were recruited because they were Muslims. We do know, however, that under Özbek Islamic faith and practice became a necessity for those seeking a political career. Merged more tightly with the central horde, the Ordaids followed suit, and herders in the left-hand wing began to convert to Islam or, more precisely, to conflate Tengri and Allah.[26]

Irzan was said to be the first Ordaid leader to sponsor Islamic institutions. Under his rule madrasas, mosques, and Sufi lodges were built in the towns of the Syr-Daria Valley. Irzan was also said to be buried in Sighnaq, a site on the eastern bank of the Syr-Daria River that had previously been settled by urban and agrarian Muslim communities and that would become the center of the eastern horde. Together, the Ordaids and Batuids reinforced local Islamic establishments, promoting and securing connections between Muslim-dominated areas, including the Ordaid Syr-Daria region and regions directly controlled by the khan, such as the Bulgar towns on the Volga. Crucially, Özbek granted tarkhan status to Muslim elites across the Jochid realms. As the Muslim tarkhans used their financial protections to build and fund more schools—through which they taught, healed, and fed the poor—the Muslim community of the Horde grew in size, wealth, influence, and visibility. And as Islam secured a more important place within the Horde, the Muslim Özbek became that much more powerful. He was knitting himself more thoroughly into the lives of his diverse subjects. Many who previously saw themselves as dominated taxpayers became loyal followers of a ruler who was a kind of spiritual father.[27]

Almost concurrently, at the western end of the Jochid territories, the Danubian horde also came firmly under the control of the central horde. Under Nogay, the Danubian horde had enjoyed considerable independence, but Toqto'a and then Özbek saw to it that the west was brought to heel. Around 1300 Tsar Theodore Svetoslav of Bulgaria, following orders from Toqto'a, murdered Nogay's eldest son and successor, Cheke. Cheke had been Theodore's brother-in-law and ally, yet Theodore carried out his mission to eradicate what was left of Nogay's rule. There were to be no followers, no legacies, no memories of Nogay—all had to be wiped out. Cheke was strangled and beheaded, to make clear that Nogay's lineage had been cut off for good—the bones had been broken. Soon after, and again on the authority of the khan, Theodore conquered the "Black Tatars," as the Slavs called the nomads of the Bujak steppe. The Black Tatars were a mix of Qipchaq and Mongol families and warriors who had followed Nogay; Theodore harshly repressed any resistance among them.[28]

Özbek's Balkan policy continued Toqto'a's. Both khans seemed to consider Bulgaria the westernmost part of the Horde—not an ally, but a territory. Indeed, Jochid armies attacked the Byzantines at least five times during Özbek's rule, while the Bulgarians were never attacked—a clear sign that Jochid rule ended at the border between Bulgaria and Byzantium. Confirming this, Özbek authorized Theodore Svetoslav's southward expansion, which came at the expense of the Byzantines. Theodore was also allowed to expand northward to the Dniester River, giving him power over the former lands of Nogay, which were Jochid regions. Specifically, the Bulgarian tsar was allowed to rule the areas of Dobruja and Bujak. Theodore and his successor George Terter banished from the Danubian horde the final remnants of Nogay's heirs and followers.[29]

After George Terter died in 1323, Özbek established firm, personal control over the west. The new Bulgarian ruler, Tsar Michael Shishman, hoped to create a more ambitious Bulgarian dynasty, but he did not get the chance. Nogay's legacy was no longer a threat, and Özbek had no further need for Bulgarian mediation. Instead Özbek supported the formation of a small principality known as the Romanian Land or Walachia. In exchange for Özbek's protection the Romanian leader, Besarab, a former vassal of the Hungarian king, was to reinforce the Jochid frontier, especially against expansionist Hungary. The Romanians proved themselves in 1330, when they crushed the Hungarian army at the Battle of Posada. Walachia had once been the core of Nogay's territory, and the wealth gained there through trade and economic development redounded to the Romanians who took over—a legacy that would help to drive Walachia's growth and consolidation for generations to come.[30]

The role an empire assigns to its borderlands says a lot about its imperial dynamics. Some peripheries are largely forgotten, but the Jochid khan saw his borders as crucial. Walachia and Bulgaria were the Mongol gateways to Central Europe and, thanks to their empowerment by the Horde, key bulwarks against Hungarian and Byzantine expansion. Vassalage supported the interests of both sides—the khan and his subordinates. Until the death of Özbek in 1341, Catholic Romanians and Orthodox Bulgarians maintained the Horde's border, and through them the khan's name resonated with fear and respect deep into Western Europe. Meanwhile, the two statelets—Walachia and Bulgaria—developed into durable regimes of their own, ultimately outlasting their Mongol masters and going on to play key roles in Balkan politics throughout the next centuries.

The Rocky Rise of Moscow

The history of Mongol rule in the Russian principalities was largely one of hands-off relations—until Özbek. Özbek's influence on Russian politics was profound, leading to world-historic change. In particular, his support of the princes of Moscow fueled the transformation of a backwater town into the enduring center of Russian power and reset the ruling lineage of the eastern Slavs.

When Özbek took the throne, the state of relations among the Russian princes was as it had been for decades. The principalities were small and fragmented. Each was led by a kniaz responsible for defending his domain and administrating and sustaining the local economy. Although scattered, the kniazia were unified under the power of the grand prince, who was the overarching leader of the Russians. This was true when the grand prince had his court at Kiev and when the court moved to Vladimir. The grand prince was selected according to the *lestvitsa,* a principle of succession whereby the eldest kniaz became grand prince, provided that his father or grandfather had also served in the role.

For the Jochids, the Russian system worked well. Each kniaz collected taxes from his territory and sent the receipts to the grand prince, who in turn distributed the entirety of the revenue to the Mongols. The Mongols preferred to oversee a centralized administration rather than handle directly a constellation of villages and cities led by rival princes. As for how that central administration functioned, the Mongols were happy to leave the grand prince in charge. They had enough experience in state building to know that hierarchy was essential to effective administration, and the grand prince was the traditional occupant of the top of the hierarchy. The grand prince needed to have two qualities: he needed to be loyal to the khan, and he needed to command the confidence of the Russian people; otherwise he would face difficulty collecting the Mongol taxes. To better assure the people's confidence, the Mongols largely allowed the traditional succession process to hold sway. The title of grand prince technically was confirmed by the khan, but Mongol appointments were largely consistent with the lestvitsa. Tension between the old Russian pattern of succession and the Horde's authority was therefore rare.[31]

Both sides—the Jochid and Russian elite—sought to uphold each other's governing prerogatives because both benefited from their relationship.

The kniazia sought the khan's support because the khan's trust and material backing were key to their power. And the khan courted the kniazia because the khan needed to determine who among the kniazia was a reliable ally. Over the years, mutual respect formed between the two sides, and they communicated well. Russian princes could even marry Mongol princesses, a sign that the nomadic lords trusted their northern vassals. Unlike Byzantines and others who routinely used their daughters as diplomatic gifts and tokens of political allegiance, Mongols were reluctant to cut off their daughters from the steppe world, so the Jochids' willingness to marry their daughters to non-nomads was a sign of their high esteem for the Russians. One of the few instances outside Russia proves the point: as I describe below, in 1320 Özbek married his niece to the Mamluk sultan, an unprecedented kinship relationship between Jochids and Mamluks.[32]

A balance formed as Russian and Mongol elites became mutually dependent. Russian elites kept their populations under control and funneled tax receipts to the Mongols. Russians also subordinated themselves. In hopes of winning Mongol favor, kniazia visited the khan's horde as often and for as long as needed—at least six months and sometimes a year or two. Through these visits, a prince could enhance his stature, expand his network, and deepen his military strength. For their part, the khans never visited the kniazia; the khans did not go to their subjects except in cases of war. The khan's movement always required a higher motivation. When the Russians came to him, the khan would, at least sometimes, resolve their conflicts. This further enhanced the khan's prestige while helping to maintain stability among the Russians. In exchange for the Russians' deference and material support, the khan offered protection: if the grand prince needed military help, the khan could not turn him down. The Jochids were the overlords, but they knew their duties.[33]

Under Özbek's rule, this balance shifted in favor of the khan's authority, and the Russian tradition of succession was severely disrupted. The transformation was precipitated by changes in Russian politics following the Mongol conquest of the 1240s, long before Özbek's rise to power. In the course of the conquest, major centers such as Kiev and Vladimir were ruined economically, and their elites were decimated. The princes of Moscow and Tver rushed to fill the vacuum. Both towns had recovered relatively quickly, in part by taking in laborers fleeing from the devastated areas. Situated on the upper Volga, Tver was the first northeastern town to show signs of resurgence. By the 1280s inhabitants were already building the monumental Church of Transfiguration.[34]

For its part, Moscow had a great deal of catching up to do. Despite its growth in the wake of the conquest, it was, in the early fourteenth century, still something of a backwater. Its walls were made of earth and its kremlin of wood. Compared to important cities such as Novgorod, Tver, Vladimir, and Kiev, Moscow looked modest and rural. But the rulers of Moscow were ambitious. According to the old succession pattern, the princes of Moscow, descendants of Alexander Nevsky's youngest son Daniil, did not have priority for the position of the grand prince. Yet the Daniilovichi were about to seize the throne and turn Moscow into the most powerful principality in northeastern Russia.

The Muscovites' first opportunity came in 1304, during the reign of Toqto'a Khan. That year, Grand Prince Andrei died, and two candidates vied to replace him: Iurii of Moscow and his uncle Mikhail of Tver. They asked the khan to decide between them, and Toqto'a chose Mikhail. Mikhail was a loyal subject of the Mongols, and as Iurii's senior and the son of a former grand prince, he had a proper claim according to the lestvitsa. Yet Iurii did not accept the result, and Moscow rebelled. It took Tver two military campaigns to call Moscow to order and finally assert Mikhail's authority. For the time being, Iurii had to give up his claim. But the mere fact that the Moscow line was ineligible, and yet tried to appropriate the throne, marked a critical turn in Russian politics.[35]

The next major development came soon after Özbek replaced Toqto'a, in 1313. Grand Prince Mikhail traveled to the lower Volga to pay his respects to the new khan and have his grand princely rights confirmed. Mikhail stayed for two years in Özbek's horde, a lengthy absence of which Iurii took advantage. In 1314 Iurii made a play for Novgorod, which though not the seat of the grand prince was under Mikhail's direct control. Iurii's men entered Novgorod and captured Mikhail's lieutenants. During subsequent negotiations, the Novgorodians offered to turn their throne over to Iurii. Enraged, Mikhail returned to his domain—with the khan's permission and a contingent of Mongol troops—to punish the Novgorodians. In 1315 Mikhail stormed Novgorod and reaffirmed his rights there. To settle the issue, the khan ordered Iurii to present himself at the Horde's court.

Iurii came as called, but when he returned to Moscow, he did so in unexpectedly grand fashion: he brought with him Özbek's envoys, twenty thousand mounted archers, and a Mongol document conferring on him the title of grand prince. A clever politician, the kniaz of Moscow had sworn total loyalty to the Mongols during his time at the khan's court. Iurii convinced the khan that he was a more suitable grand prince than Mikhail because he, Iurii, could deliver taxes more efficiently. Özbek also understood that elevating Iurii would mean the grand prince was in his debt. The bond between them was sealed with the wedding of Iurii to Konchaka, Özbek's sister.

Building on his success, Iurii launched a campaign against Tver in 1317 and faced Mikhail on the battlefield. Mikhail won the contest, forcing Iurii to flee, and captured Konchaka. Mikhail intended to release the Mongol princess, but she died in a Tver jail. The death had been an accident, but Özbek summoned Mikhail to be tried anyway. Under other circumstances, a party believed responsible for the death of a khan's sister might have been executed forthwith, but Mikhail was the Mongols' old friend and a former grand prince, so caution and deliberation were required. The outcome, however, was foreordained. After a trial lasting several months, Mikhail was publicly declared guilty on a number of charges, including withholding taxes, treason, and rebellion. He was executed around November 1318.[36]

With Mikhail removed and the khan's authority behind him, Iurii became the first grand prince to bear the title in opposition to the old dynastic rules. But he had lost the respect of his peers and struggled terribly in his efforts to collect taxes for the Mongols. Iurii also faced attacks from Mikhail's sons, Dmitrii and Alexander, princes of Tver. In 1322 Özbek had no choice but to remove his confidence from the house of Moscow and transfer the grand princely title back to Tver, restoring the old system of succession. Özbek first confirmed Dmitrii, but after Dmitrii avenged his father by murdering Iurii in 1325, Özbek withdrew the title and turned it over Alexander.

Tver would not have the upper hand for long. Like Iurii before him, Alexander of Tver had difficulties collecting taxes. In 1327 Özbek sent his deputy to Tver to test the grand prince's loyalty and obtain the amount due. But the inhabitants of Tver refused payment and instead revolted, killing the deputy and his delegation. The Tver uprising infuriated the khan, all the more so as the murdered deputy had been his relative. This was a major transgression, for which Alexander had to be expelled from the throne and his people severely punished. Özbek dispatched a Russian-led punitive force, which sacked the city and drove out Alexander, who fled to Lithuania. Later Alexander would, with Özbek's blessing, reestablish himself in Tver. But the khan's forgiveness was short-lived, and Özbek had Alexander and his son executed in 1339.[37]

The Russian who led the Mongol force that defeated Alexander was Ivan of Moscow, Iurii's brother. Ivan had no right to the throne by virtue of the lestvitsa, but he knew that the true power to confirm the grand prince's appointment came from the khan and so pursued Özbek's favor. At some point between 1327 and 1332—the sources are unclear on the exact date—Ivan presented himself before Özbek, lavished the khan with precious gifts, and was granted the title of grand prince of Vladimir. The khan once again was raising the Daniilovichi above the other ruling families, despite the old ways of succession. The question was whether the new line would hold, for of course Iurii had been elevated by the same means, only to lose the khan's indulgence.[38]

To secure his position, Ivan expanded the Daniilovichi territories through military means, land purchases, and marital and religious alliances. The land purchases enabled Moscow to absorb surrounding principalities, a policy reflected in Ivan's distinctive sobriquet: Kalita, meaning money bag. Ivan Kalita developed strategies to turn the Daniilovichi lands into rich and well-protected dominions that would attract people and produce the resources the Daniilovichi needed to sustain their influential position.

Ivan's ties to the Orthodox Church proved especially profitable. The seat of the metropolitan had moved from Kiev to Vladimir in 1299, and from Kiev to Moscow in 1325. The following year Metropolitan Peter joined with Ivan to embark on the most impressive construction program ever launched in Moscow. They sponsored the building of the Church of the Assumption and four additional stone churches, all erected in Moscow's kremlin. Byzantine and Slavic craftsmen would later add wall paintings and install massive church bells. The buildings' magnificence announced Moscow's piety as well as the city's claim to the legacies of Kiev and Vladimir.[39]

Ivan Kalita's heirs maintained good relations with the Orthodox Church, for the church brought them what they badly needed: an image of legitimacy, prestige, and morality. Yet the church had its own agenda, and the successors of Metropolitan Peter remained cautious. They supported the Muscovite grand prince as long as his policies served the unity of the Russian church, which worked diligently to assert itself over and above the division of the principalities. Thus, on the one hand, the metropolitans accepted land grants and cash donations from the Daniilovichi. On the other hand, the church was careful not to openly promote Moscow's interests over those of other princely houses.

Indeed, the interests of many kniazia diverged from those of the Daniilovichi, whom other princes saw as usurpers. It was easier for these kniazia to accept the khan's authority than Moscow's. Resentful princes from Tver, Pskov, Beloozero, Iaroslavl, Rostov, and elsewhere allied against the Daniilovichi, trying to prevent them from collecting taxes and complaining to the khan. But, in spite of the opposition, the Daniilovichi under Ivan Kalita and his successors paid the khan in a timely manner. Critical to their ability to do so was armed domination of Novgorod, the main location through which northern European silver entered Russian lands. The Novgorodians, who historically had supported the grand prince and accepted his direct authority, rejected Moscow's rule. Yet the Novgorodians lacked the military power to contest the Mongol-backed Daniilovichi. So while Novgorod's elites tussled with the Daniilovichi politically, the Novgorodians also paid the silver. Novgorod was thus the Daniilovichi's key to the Mongol door. As long as the silver flowed, the Daniilovichi could count on the support of the khan's army, whom none of the disaffected kniazia dared face. In Jochid terms tax delivery was proof of loyalty, and the Jochids were loyal in return.[40]

The rise of the Daniilovichi was never a smooth and linear process. Under Ivan Kalita's sons and successors, Moscow's authority eroded, and the grand princes were often unable to convince other kniazia join their military campaigns. When Ivan II died in 1359, Moscow's territorial expansion had stopped and Daniilovichi rule was tenuous. Still, the house of Moscow cultivated their relationship with the Mongols by actively involving themselves in the Horde's domination system, strengthening kinship ties, and communicating in face-to-face meetings. The bond Ivan Kalita and Özbek shared was passed on to their heirs. But the Daniilovichi also knew that bond would be severed as soon as the grand prince proved unable to deliver the tax receipts the Mongols expected. After all, Özbek had temporarily withdrawn his confidence from their family when Iurii, the first Muscovite grand prince, had failed to perform his tax-collecting duties. The khan's displeasure was a sword of Damocles hanging over Moscow.

Trading Far and Wide

Özbek capitalized on Mongol fame. He knew that his horde was powerful because he received gifts from exotic kingdoms. The rulers of faraway lands sent *tangsuq*, the marvelous and unusual things that delighted Mongol elites and demonstrated the esteem in which the Horde was held. If diplomacy and trade were expressions of one's position in the world, then in the first decades of the fourteenth century, the Horde was secure in its place of prestige.

Security, though, did not come automatically. The game of power was complicated and required investments of time, effort, money, and sometimes blood. Özbek's greatest predecessors—the likes of Batu, Berke, and Möngke-Temür—knew this, and so did Özbek himself. No matter how powerful he was, he faced foreign-policy challenges that had to be handled delicately. One consistent difficulty was control of the Caucasian passes, which the Jochids and Ilkhanids shared. Özbek sought to wrest undivided authority over the passes. On two occasions during Özbek's rule, in 1318 and 1335, the descendants of Hülegü faced succession crises, and the Jochids attacked during both of these moments of weakness. The Ilkhanids repelled them both times. Between attacks, though, Özbek took a more peaceful approach and managed to build alliances among the Ilkhanid elite. For instance, around 1330 he married his son Tinibek to the daughter of an influential Ilkhanid emir. This could be seen as part of the Jochid plan to seize control of the Transcaucasian passes, by obtaining kinship rights.[41]

While negotiating with, and sometimes assaulting, the Ilkhanids, Özbek appeased the Toluids in the Far East in an effort to protect long-distance commerce along the east-west axis—the Silk Road. He promoted peace with the great khan and openly refused an invitation from the Chagatayids to ally against the Yuan, the Toluid dynasty Qubilai had founded in 1271. Özbek distrusted his Chagatayid neighbors and preferred to see them stuck between the Toluids and himself.[42] In the west Özbek strengthened his ties to the Mediterranean world, especially the Mamluks and the Italians. In 1316 he pardoned the Genoese, whom Toqto'a had expelled from the Horde in 1307–1308, allowing them to return to Caffa and rebuild the city. Özbek offered them the best possible terms to trade and travel in his territories, and in exchange he expected them to orient the flow of goods toward Jochid commercial hubs rather than Ilkhanid ones.[43]

Within a few years, the fortified harbor of Caffa was again a prospering trade center and seat of Franciscan activities. And once more, Franciscans extended their missions to the Horde's center, integrating themselves into the seasonal circuit of the khan's court. The friars even reached out beyond the Volga and claimed numerous conversions among the herders of western Siberia. Taking advantage of the Mongol politics of tolerance, the missionaries founded at least ten convents in Özbek's territories. From the khan's perspective, as long as the Italians brought wealth and fortune, they were welcome to penetrate the deep steppe.[44]

Özbek intended to use the Genoese as go-betweens to strengthen his ties with the Mamluks. This was a longstanding role for the Genoese. Since the 1260s they had worked for the Jochids and Mamluks mostly as freelance seafarers, and some of the most successful among them became ambassadors of a sort. For instance, the merchant Segurano Salvaygo was close with both the sultan and the khan and often stayed at the khan's court, where he conducted business for the sultan, the Mongols, and himself. His activities helped secure the Horde's commercial connections.

In 1315, in an unexpected turn of events, Mamluk sultan al-Nāsir Muhammad requested a bride from the khan. If the deal was sealed, it would constitute the first kinship-based alliance between Jochids and Mamluks. It took three years for the parties to come to terms, but finally, in spring 1320, Tulunbāy Khatun reached Alexandria, where she was to be wed. She was accompanied by a retinue of three thousand, including Salvaygo. The princess was probably Özbek's niece, but she was introduced to the sultan as the khan's daughter.[45]

Although the marriage was established with great care, it was ill-fated from the start. The trouble was that Mamluks and Jochids had very different ideas about what marriage alliance meant. Al-Nāsir Muhammad thought he was boosting his stature by marrying a Chinggisid heiress, but the Mongols believed the sultan was offering himself as their vassal. After all, the few other non-Mongol husbands of Jochid daughters were among the Horde's most trusted vassals. The misunderstanding bore considerable consequences, as the Jochids now saw the Mamluks as debtors and immediately demanded financial and military favors. To begin with, the khan required that the sultan pay a bride price and wedding costs amounting to 27,000 dinars, a sum the Mamluks were forced to borrow from the khan's traders. And the wedding ceremony had hardly ended when Özbek asked the sultan to ally in a war against the Ilkhanids.

Al-Nāsir Muhammad saw the bride price as pure extortion, and he had no intention of resuming the Mamluks' longstanding rivalry with the Ilkhanids. In fact, he had just initiated peace talks with the Ilkhan, and the two rulers would soon sign a commercial treaty. Al-Nāsir Muhammad refused to join Özbek's campaign and even warned the Ilkhanids that the Jochids were planning an attack. If there was a war plan, it must have been called off, as there is no evidence in the sources of a Jochid attack on the Ilkhanids in the 1320s. Instead, an angry Özbek struck back at the Mamluks by forbidding traders in the Horde to sell the Mamluks slaves. Özbek also ordered Salvaygo captured and executed: someone had to pay for the failure of the wedding. Al-Nāsir Muhammad divorced Tulunbāy Khatun around 1327 and arranged for her to be married to a Mamluk emir.[46]

Despite the frictions, Özbek and al-Nāsir Muhammad continued to exchange embassies. The Mamluks hoped to resume the slave trade because they still depended on the Jochids to acquire skilled warriors. And the Jochids were not so insulted that they were willing permanently to forgo the financial benefits of a relationship with the Mamluks. Moreover, there was always the possibility of a future alliance against the Ilkhanids because the peace between the Mamluk sultan and the Ilkhan seemed precarious. The threats and intemperate actions Özbek and al-Nāsir Muhammad exchanged were part of their complex dance, as each sought the best possible terms of partnership for his own people. The two leaders never became enemies; such a breach would have resulted in profound changes to the world order, but it did not come to pass.

In general, commerce was a rough-and-tumble line of work, and traders went on engaging with the Mamluks and Jochids no matter their conflict. Even the killing of Segurano Salvaygo did not dissuade the Genoese, who continued to ply their merchandise in the Horde and take advantage of the robust Jochid web of trade. Throughout Özbek's reign, Europeans were major players in the lucrative human-trafficking and grain businesses. The best wheat in central Eurasia grew in the fertile lands of the Danube Valley, where farmers also cultivated barley, rye, oats, millet, sorghum, and peas for local consumption and trade. In the early fourteenth century, the center for this trade was the Jochid settlement of White City, at the mouth of the Dniester River. The other main granaries were located to the west, in Crimea and the area of the Azov Sea. To reject the Jochids was to reject access to the breadbasket of the entire Black Sea region and thereby lose out on an opportunity to supply the population centers of the area, above all heavily populated and grain-hungry Constantinople.[47]

Although the Jochid territories were full of productive granaries, the Mongols themselves rarely grew and consumed grain, except for millet. They also did not trade the grain themselves. Instead, in keeping with their expertise in developing and exploiting trade networks, the Mongols facilitated trade carried out by others, mainly Genoese, Germans, and Greeks. The Jochids levied taxes on every transaction. Taxes were light, but there were several of them, including customs duties, weighing fees, and levies on shipping and sales. Moreover, as grain, slaves, and other goods were purchased and resold over their long journeys from the Horde to their far-off destinations, the Jochids collected their fees several times on the same merchandise. Collectively the taxes yielded substantial profit.[48]

The ecological endowments of the Horde's territory ensured that it would be a force to be reckoned with when it came to grain sales, but that did not mean the Jochids could simply allow nature to take its course. Özbek used hard power to prevent merchants from diverting to Ilkhanid and Chagatayid markets, going so far as to kill brokers and

Court scene, from a 1314 edition of Rashīd al-Dīn, *Jāmiʿ al-tawārīkh*. Court attendants wear Mongol caps and characteristic Islamic signifiers, including beards and turbans. Elements of Byzantine and Chinese traditions round out the multicultural milieu. (With kind permission of the University of Edinburgh / Bridgeman Images)

burn down marketplaces. The Jochids also tried to prevent the Mamluks from dealing directly with the other Mongols and from developing alternative routes. And the Horde prevented the Italians from trading too independently. The Jochids were never able to secure truly exclusive control over the grain and slave trades, though. The Ilkhanids, strong and equally determined, stood in their way.

But, over time, Özbek and his administrators found other ways to hamper the Ilkhanids—and serve their own needs in the process. As the Horde's population grew in the first half of the fourteenth century, the Jochids needed yet more trade in order to meet the demand for luxury products. That demand would be met by pivoting toward the Venetians and peeling them away from the Ilkhanids.

In 1332 Özbek welcomed the Horde's first ever ambassador from the Venetian Senate, who hoped to obtain a piece of land where Venetian merchants could build a trading post. Previously the senate had invested in the Ilkhanid route, much to the displeasure of merchants who worried about the insecurity of Tabriz and the road to Hormuz. Eventually the senate changed course, though, and tried find a safer route as well as trade hubs where Venetian traders could enter Mongol markets before any competitors. In particular, the Venetians hoped to set up trading settlements deep in the Horde, allowing them access to goods before the Genoese, who were at the periphery of the Horde on the Black Sea.[49] In less than a year, the Horde and Venice finalized the negotiations. The khan permitted the Venetians to rent a large quarter in Azaq, a steppe settlement with easy access to the mouth of the Don River and to the Azov Sea. Azaq was an old Greek harbor; the merchants called their quarter Tana, after the Greek name for the Don. At Tana the Venetians could live permanently, build their churches, grow their own food and wine, and carry out their business. Özbek guaranteed light taxation, and when a transaction took place, both Mongols and Venetians supervised the weighing of goods. The Venetians also received a grant of jurisdictional flexibility: if they were embroiled in trade disagreements, they could choose to have either the Venetian consul or a Mongol deputy intervene, whereas Mongol traders could turn only to Mongol officers. Crucially, the khan guaranteed that the Venetian merchants could be held liable only for their own debts, a promise they had begged for, as the Mongols had in the past made the Venetians pay the debts of other Italians.[50]

The deal with Venice was but a piece in Özbek's larger plan. Tana would bring more business to the Horde and more tax money. It would also trigger competition among the Italians by breaking the Genoese monopoly over the Black Sea littoral and southern Crimea. Even more significantly, the agreement would weaken the Ilkhanids and hurt their political economy by diverting the trade northward. Despite the low tax rate, the deal was highly profitable for the Horde, and the Jochids would renew it seven times during the next twenty-five years.[51]

When it came to trade and the diplomacy surrounding it, Özbek was an avid practitioner of the longstanding Jochid strategy of playing friend against friend, shifting alliances, and retaining flexibility in the face of a changing world. He intermittently blocked key sections of trade networks, resulting in frequent lurching between war and peace. He manipulated Italians, Mamluks, and others, switching from policies of appeasement—treaties, marriages, and diplomacy—to outright extortion, blockades, and military pressure. This explains why even in the most economically active areas of the Horde—including Moldavia, Crimea, the Caucasus, the lower Volga, and Khwarezm—trade traffic never settled into a steady flow. The exchange vacillated between booms and busts according to the Jochids' political interests.

New Cities

By the 1330s continuing economic growth had transformed Sarai into a huge city. It took half a day on horseback to cross from one end to the other. Sarai had open space but also densely populated districts with uninterrupted rows of gardenless houses. They ran along large streets bordered with *aryks,* deep irrigation ditches and water pipes most likely serving bathhouses and ceramics workshops. The most crowded part of the city hugged the edge of the Akhtuba River, a tributary of the Volga, for two miles or so. Groups of brick houses and nomadic dwellings also peppered the surrounding plains for several miles, shaping a wide suburban zone.

Located on a cliff, Sarai was safe even when the water level rose. The Volga overflowed sporadically, turning the area into a large gulf connecting to the Caspian Sea. When flooding happened, the landscape of Sarai changed. The roads were inundated and the city became a series of islands connected by riverine channels. During these periods, mostly in spring, Sarai served as an upstream harbor that offered quick access to the Caspian. Indeed, Sarai had a sophisticated water system. Two kinds of pipes ran across the urban settlement: one, made of ceramic, supplied water, while the other, made of wood, carried sewage, which probably discharged into the Akhtuba. The city also had a number of wells that provided water for household use, although not for drinking. Drainage systems were a commonplace in Central Asian cities, likely well before the period of Mongol domination. Under the Mongols, Central Asian urbanites moved to the Volga region and built there the same infrastructure they were familiar with in their hometowns.[52]

The people of Sarai called the khan's palace altun tash, Turkic for "golden stone." The palace sat on the cliff, possibly at its highest point, and the massive solid-gold crescent perched on top of the structure could be seen from far away. As ever, the palace was not the khan's home, but he stayed there during his annual visits to the city. While the khan was in town, he held a feast with games and collective rituals in which the city's multiethnic population participated. Following the old Mongol tradition, during the festivities, the khan distributed robes and other gifts to elites, including his Muslim emirs. On the outskirts of the city, the khan hosted archery, wrestling, and horseracing competitions.

Sarai amazed Ibn Battuta. A traveler familiar with the centuries-old cities of the Middle East, he marveled at the well-maintained Mongol metropolis, where there were no indications of ruins. Indeed, every sign pointed to growth and prosperity. Since Batu had ordered the city built almost a century earlier, people had continuously arrived and settled there. In the fourteenth century, Sarai's population might have exceeded 75,000.[53]

The city was conspicuously diverse, with a population comprising Mongols, Qipchaqs, Russians, Greeks, Syrians, Egyptians, Alans, Cherkess, and other Caucasians. Ibn Battuta reported thirteen large mosque gatherings on Fridays and countless smaller prayer meetings. There were churches, monasteries, hermitages, and other sorts of temples, too. Muslims coexisted with Christians, Buddhists, and Tengri worshippers. But Sarai was not a melting pot, exactly, as groups of foreigners tended to live in their own clearly demarcated districts. For example, merchants from western Iran, the Baghdad region, the Syrian-Palestinian coast, and Egypt had their own walled neighborhood.

Sarai boasted several marketplaces, but its economy was based on more than trade. The city was primarily a production center, with permanent infrastructure useful to a range of artisans. An industrial complex contained kilns for bricks and ceramics, as well as workshops where craftsmen built wells, assembled drainage piping, glazed ceramics, and prepared glass. Blacksmiths, potters, jewelers, bone carvers, and many other artisans lived and worked with one another in the western part of the city, close to the merchants.[54]

For all its charms, Sarai was not enough for Özbek. Sometime in the 1330s, he began construction on a palatial complex about seventy-eight miles north of the city, on the same side of the Volga. As soon as people heard of the new palace being erected upriver, they started to move there, and a new town emerged quickly. The city was named Sarai al-Jadid, New Sarai, as indicated on the thousands of coins the Jochids minted there. And the city was new indeed, as the site had been a wasteland before the Mongols began building there.

By the time Özbek commissioned the palace, he had sat on the Jochid throne for more than twenty years. Strange though it may seem that a nomadic ruler who already had a palace would build another, this was the decision of a seasoned leader whose wealth had bourgeoned and whose political ambitions had matured. He had his reasons for constructing a new capital. For one thing, the old Sarai had become enormous; it made sense that a new city would more easily accommodate additional cohorts of craftsmen, workers, and traders. And New Sarai was well located. Unlike Sarai, New Sarai required no infrastructure to protect it from sea flooding, because it was more than 155 miles from the Caspian. New Sarai was also, like Sarai, on the route of Özbek's seasonal round, so the nomads could draw on the developing city as a supply station. Steppe cities provided the Mongols' necessary food, fodder, water, and people, and New Sarai was no different in this respect. Water was the key; it was essential for most crafts, particularly for the many metallurgists based in New Sarai. The Jochids had workers build a complex irrigation system at New Sarai involving an artificial lake. They also created infrastructure for waste disposal and drinking water.[55]

Within two decades or so, New Sarai shared the same features as the other cities of the Horde—not just Sarai, which continued to be active, but also major settlements on the khan's round such as Hajji Tarkhan, Ukek, and Beljamen. In all these places, the Jochids owned craft workshops, sizeable farms, and fruit and vegetable gardens. Most houses were made of bricks and wood, and wealthy people decorated their dwellings with glazed, colored ceramics. On the outskirts of the towns, residents erected temporary wooden structures, such as ceremonial pavilions for the khan and his family to use while passing through town. Many settlements grew during Özbek's reign, and new ones went up. There were large areas of urbanization and simple hamlets. The Jochids followed a careful plan when building settlements in the Volga Valley. They selected spots at the mouth of the river in the south, on the eastern bank of the Akhtuba up to the Volga elbow, and then on the other bank of the river heading north.

The Jochids also left their mark on the pre-Mongol cities of the Horde, especially those they had conquered in northern Khwarezm. The most notable building boom was among religious sites. The number and variety of Muslim institutions in the region, including mosques, schools, hotels, and bathhouses, amazed Ibn Battuta. In Urgench he visited the

197-foot-tall minaret that Qutluq-Temür had restored and the mosque and mausoleum his wife Turabak Khatun had commissioned.[56] The focus on religious buildings spoke to the effects of toleration practices and to the ease with which assorted creeds blended into the nomads' beliefs, taboos, and rituals. Özbek, himself a Muslim, bestowed tarkhan status on religious elites of every variety, including wealthy Mongols who converted to Christianity and Islam. These converts then financed the construction of churches, mosques, monasteries, and shrines, ensuring that there were more and more places to pray, teach, and rest in the afterlife. The construction of religious sites in turn spurred further urbanization, as people congregated around spiritual centers. While the new cities of the Horde were built mostly with mud, bricks, and clay, their religious buildings were made largely of stone. Sponsored by the highest-ranking Mongols, these structures were built to last.[57]

By the middle of the fourteenth century, there were more than a hundred riverine and hinterland settlements in the Horde. Most were established on sites that had been useless for sedentary people but were great spots for herders. None of the Jochid towns had fortifications. They had internal walls to demarcate districts and protect sacred spaces—religious institutions, cemeteries, the khan's moveable headquarters and immobile palaces. But every Jochid city was open to the outside.[58]

Lords of the Earth

Urban development was closely tied to land ownership, a concept that evolved in the Horde as the Jochids deepened their relations with dominated peoples. Traditionally both the Mongols and their sedentary subjects enclosed lands, but they did so for different reasons. While sedentary people understood themselves as owners of land, building fences and fortifications to mark and defend their holdings, Mongols believed that the spirits were the true lords of the land on which they dwelled. The nomads poured libations over the earth, in hopes that the spirits, duly honored, would protect them and bring prosperity and happiness. When the Jochids fenced off land, their concern was not to protect themselves against burglars or enemies but to repel the souls of the ill-dead.[59]

The Jochids did not try to impose their vision of the land on sedentary peoples. When called upon to settle disputes, the khan's judges usually respected local laws, including customary Slavic and Islamic law. The inhabitants of the sedentary enclaves—mainly the Russian principalities, Volga Bulgaria, and Crimea—were free to make private real estate transactions, as long as their acquisitions did not reduce available pasturage or otherwise encumber the herders. Sometimes the khan's representatives specifically authorized these transactions, and sometimes the Jochid administration was not involved at all.[60]

Many sedentary landowners were tarkhans, especially those landowners involved in religious institutions. These property holders grew wealthy thanks in part to their tax and service exemptions. In the Jochid realms, tarkhan-owners included Orthodox Christians but non-Orthodox too, particularly Franciscans. The Jewish community benefitted as well, as did Muslim dignitaries. Rich landowners who were not tarkhans could also gain the benefits of the status by hosting or endowing a protected religious community on their property. The result was that religious establishments were braided into agrarian life, developing alongside the farms, vineyards, orchards, and sawmills that provided them food, drink, and fuel. In addition, wealthy Mongols purchased lands in order to found religious institutions and sponsored several monasteries in the Russian northeast, especially in Rostov and Kostroma.[61]

No overarching law governed transactions between Mongols and sedentary peoples. Instead what was expected was mutual respect of one another's rules for measuring and selling plots, which involved the exchange of verbal oaths and written contracts and performance of culturally appropriate gestures. The Russians practiced *otvod,* an alienation ritual in which they might walk the limits of a property and swallow a clump of its soil. Mongols gave offerings to appease Mother Earth and tame the spirits. But though the rituals, oaths, languages, and worldviews were different, both parties shared the general sense that ownership of land did not depend on a single person but on a family or a group of people, including ancestors and unborn generations. Mongols understood that every land transaction was made on behalf not only of oneself but of one's lineage, including ancestors, those living, and those not yet born. The Russian alienation ritual, meanwhile, indicated the release of traditional familial rights. Ordinarily, Russian families had rights to buy back land even if their ancestors had sold it; an alienation ritual made the sale permanent. When it came to land transactions, whether for religious, spiritual, or legal purposes, all agreed special care was needed.[62]

While there was no all-encompassing Mongol land law, Mongol administration clearly enabled a development boom, for wherever Mongol law provided financial benefits, predictable kinds of growth followed. The boyars of Novgorod were so driven by the prospect of exchanging church construction for tax exemptions that, at one point in the fifteenth century, the city was home to eighty-three churches, most of them built of stone. More generally, the tarkhan system provided a legal framework that safeguarded people's estates. The *yarlik,* the document the khan granted to tarkhans, was considered irrefutable proof of ownership, allowing descendants to inherit their family estate in its entirety, although each inheritor would have to obtain a yarlik of their own. The Tarkhan system therefore ended up supporting the burgeoning of private landed property in Russia, where the earliest private land ownership records seem to go back to the fourteenth century. Private landed property probably existed as a legal concept in Russia before the Mongol domination, but there can be little doubt that the Mongol approach led to a dramatic expansion in both ownership and development capacity. The result was considerable growth in urban and agrarian areas alike.[63]

Of course, protecting private property was not the purpose of the tarkhan system. This outcome is simply another demonstration of the evolving nature of Mongol institutions. Mongol law and practice were changed by the encounter with the other, and the other was changed, in enduring ways, by the encounter with Mongol law and practice. Flexibility was the key. The Mongols had no need to encroach on nonthreatening local ways of doing things; the khan could demonstrate his absolute sovereignty when required. In everyday life, then, interactions between nomads and settled people were fluid and negotiable. From the ordinary processes of existence across borders—geographic, cultural, political—unforeseen novelties emerged.

The Collapse of the Ilkhanids

By the 1330s Özbek and the Jochids were riding high. The khan had long since overcome the questions of legitimacy that surrounded his enthronement, and his controversial political reforms had only augmented his power. He had successfully meddled in Russian affairs to the Horde's benefit, establishing the princes of Moscow as loyal vassals while skillfully using the tarkhan system to maintain the support of the other Russian princes—even as Moscow's usurpation left them feeling alienated. He had established productive relations with Central European, Russian, and Italian Christians and with Muslims in the Caucasus, Central Asia, and the Middle East, and he masterfully manipulated the competing trade communities to ensure that the Horde never lacked for tax revenues and the luxury goods indispensable to the Mongol political and spiritual order. Özbek's aggressive diplomacy ensured continuing Jochid leadership of massive and lucrative commercial networks extending from the Mediterranean to the Black Sea, the Volga, Siberia, and on to the Far East.

One problem still bedeviled the Horde, though. Directly to the south, the Ilkhanids maintained the competing southern route, hampered mobility in the Caucasus, and countered Jochid interests at the Mamluk court. And there was no reason to believe the longstanding rivalry with the descendants of Hülegü would end any time soon. The early fourteenth century had been a time of crisis for the Ilkhanids, as high-ranking officials battled each other for control while a child Ilkhan, Abū Saʿīd, awaited his opportunity to rule. But the regime survived, and in the 1320s Abū Saʿīd rose to the occasion, asserting himself on the throne and improving relations with the Mamluks and Venetians. His domains were vast, including the present-day countries of Armenia, Azerbaijan, Georgia, and Iran and parts of what are now Turkey, Iraq, Afghanistan, and Pakistan. Even when Özbek stole the Venetians away in 1332, no one would have thought that the breakdown of Abū Saʿīd's regime was imminent.

But then, in November 1335, Abū Saʿīd died at the age of thirty-one, likely from poisoning. He left multiple wives and at least one daughter but no son. The Ilkhanid succession had often generated conflicts, but this time no descendant of Hülegü was strong enough to compensate for the lack of an heir. That left the throne to contenders from secondary lines. At least three princes and one princess, Abū Saʿīd's sister, as well as high officials from various Mongol families asserted claims. Even the Mamluk sultan interfered with the succession crisis, backing his own candidates. There were capable people among the contenders; the Mongol officials had considerable administrative and military experience, and they were Muslim, which was an important source of legitimacy. But the contenders were not members of the golden lineage, making Abū Sa'īd's succession the first in which nonmembers of the golden lineage dared claim the throne of a key Mongol territory. Ultimately none of the contenders possessed enough prestige, warriors, or money to assume leadership. The Ilkhanids fragmented, never to regain their former unity. As contemporaries put it—reflecting both the Muslim and Mongol view that khans prospered under a divine dispensation—the Ilkhanids had lost the mandate of heaven.[64]

Several causes lay behind the abrupt collapse of the Ilkhanids, some of which were deeply rooted in the structure of the regime. In particular, the Ilkhanids had always been disjointed, as eastern Anatolia, the Caucasus, and Iran constituted a dizzying patchwork of lands, peoples, and powers. The Mongol regime kept them together for almost a century, but regional divisions remained strong, fostering endless competition among ambitious emirs and noyans and denting the ruler's prestige. The dysfunction was clear before Abū Sa'īd's death and was one of the causes of the wars that marked his childhood. These frictions among cities, regional forces, and nomadic elites were much more intense in the Ilkhanid territory than in the Horde, where relations between the Jochids and their sedentary subjects, especially the Russians, fostered stability. Internal competition was not the only factor to blame for undermining the Ilkhanid regime, but it cannot be dismissed either. Regionalism certainly complicated the task of central administration and, notably, the powers that emerged from the ashes of the ulus often broke along the same lines as the Ilkhanid provinces. That regional rivalries became geopolitical ones suggests that the Ilkhanid state had not been terribly cohesive to begin with.[65]

Internal pressure was joined by external pressure from the Horde. The growing success of the northern route in the 1330s meant the decline of the southern route. With the southern route faltering, there was little common cause for the Ilkhanids' Mongol commanders and regional elites to rally around. The economic loss meant that the top of the hierarchy could not afford to uphold the downward redistribution system, further alienating dominated parties. The dissolution was slow but by the late 1350s, the Ilkhanid regime had completely lost its hold on military power and its once-conquered territories.

The end of the Ilkhanids was an opportunity for the Jochids. Not only were they free of the encumbrances caused by their longstanding rival, but they also had a chance to take over their former rivals' lands. Under Janibek, Özbek's son and successor, the Jochids led an army through the Caucasian pass of Derbent-Shirvan in winter 1356–1357. The Jochids followed the coastline of the Caspian Sea down to Tabriz, in Azerbaijan, the last Ilkhanid capital and the door to the southern route. The Azerbaijan region was ripe for the taking, having fallen under the control of the despised Malik Ashraf. The grandson of a powerful Ilkhanid commander, Malik Ashraf was rejected by Muslims as both sinful and illegitimate, and the people of the region rallied around the Jochids. According to a number of sources, Azerbaijani Muslim elites even requested that Janibek depose Malik Ashraf, which is precisely what the khan did.[66] The conquest of Tabriz marked the first time since Batu's rule that the Jochids were rewarded for their military operations beyond Derbent. The Jochids captured other cities, too, along with the surrounding grasslands, which had been the Ilkhanids' winter grazing territory. For the Jochids, this was revenge a century in the making.

The contemporary author Abū Bakr al-Qutbī al-Ahrī celebrated the Horde and its massive display of force, claiming that the khan had raised up to 300,000 warriors. Today's scholars believe the number was perhaps a third of that, but whatever the number, the campaign was a stunning success. Now that the Toluid family had lost their western territories, the Jochids expected to take the lead in the Mongols' world empire. To promote his victory, Janibek ordered coins bearing his name minted in Tabriz, and he bragged to the Mamluk sultan.[67] The khan headed back to the lower Volga with substantial spoils and captives. He left his son Birdibek in charge of Tabriz, the Azerbaijan region, and its people. Malik Ashraf had been hanged, and most of the Azerbaijani emirs had submitted to the Horde. Their vassalage was still superficial, but in time Birdibek would overcome the insubordinate emirs and complete the conquest of the Ilkhanid heartland.

A major effect of the Ilkhanids' decline was a boost in trade in the Jochid territories and the revival of connections that had been neglected while merchants took southerly routes. Traders now prioritized the long-distance road that linked Otrar and Almaliq, the Jochid-Chagatayid border cities, to the Horde. This was the pivotal route that the Florentine merchant Pegolotti described in his handbook for traders. The road went to northern Khwarezm and up to Saraijuq and the Ural Valley. The journey between Urgench and Saraijuq was a harsh and dry one, yet caravansaries—roadside inns—and wells popped up to support travelers. In the 1330s there were at least fifteen caravansaries located at a distance of roughly eighteen miles from each other, just like yam stations.[68]

With the northern road flourishing as never before, and the far-northern Siberian Road now connected to the clear favorite of the Silk Road's two main thoroughfares, the Jochids firmly controlled the crossroads of Eurasia. They dominated the north-south fur road and the east-west Silk Road, consolidating their economic dominance. At last the Jochid-Ilkhanid rivalry that belied the so-called Pax Mongolica was over, and the Horde had become the uncontested gravitational center of the Mongol exchange. Yet, while the collapse of the Ilkhanids removed a formidable and longstanding opponent, enabling further Jochid thriving, that collapse also created a power vacuum on the Horde's southern border. This would challenge and change the Horde in unexpected ways.

7

Withdrawal

In September 1343 a street fight overturned the Horde's relations with the Latins. Hajji 'Umar, a Jochid beg, had humiliated Andreolo Civran, a Venetian nobleman and merchant, in Tana. Seeking revenge, Civran and his men ambushed Hajji 'Umar and killed him along with his followers and family. Venetians, Genoese, Florentines, and Pisans—Janibek Khan immediately ordered all of them expelled from their trading posts on the Don and the Black Sea. The khan also confiscated their goods and ships. The merchants sought shelter in the Genoese fortress at Caffa, but Janibek's armies pursued them and laid siege to their refuge. The murdered beg was an important official—a tax collector—and the khan could not let the killers escape without punishment and serious compensation.[1]

The Venetian Senate condemned Civran and a few others for their roles in the murder. All of them were temporarily exiled from Venice and forbidden from returning to Tana. Then the Senate sent envoys to negotiate with Janibek. Negotiations went slowly, but by April 1344 the envoys brought home news that the khan was ready to reach an agreement. Janibek was open to granting the Latin traders a new contract, but he also demanded that a Jochid court judge Andreolo Civran's case according to Mongol rules, a condition the Venetians could not accept.

To compel Janibek to agree to their terms, the Genoese and Venetians temporarily allied and enforced a *devetum,* a trade embargo, on the Horde. The khan responded by placing his own embargo on the Latins and by again sending troops to besiege Caffa in 1345. Janibek also prohibited grain exports, a blow to the Genoese and Venetian economies and the cause of bread shortages in Constantinople. Caffa withstood the siege thanks to its harbor, which received supplies the khan's troops were powerless to intercept. Janibek raised a fleet of thirty ships in order to expand the blockade to the sea, but the Genoese, superior sailors, destroyed one Mongol vessel after another. There were high losses on both sides. At the end of 1346 or in early 1347, Janibek lifted the siege and negotiations resumed, soon producing a new agreement.[2] The Venetians received authorization to resettle in Tana, but Janibek also raised the *comerclum,* the trade tax, from 3 percent to 5 percent.[3]

It was never the khan's goal to expel the Venetians and Genoese. Rather, he wanted to show that he was in charge. The Genoese, in particular, were obstinate: they considered Caffa their own, claiming it did not belong to Janibek's empire. The khan would lay siege to Caffa again in 1350, to remind the Genoese that they were guests on his lands. And as guests, they were subject to the khan's will. He could change the terms of their welcome, demanding higher taxes and using force of arms to ensure that he collected. Janibek's embargo was effective in spite of his fledgling navy; his ground troops cut Caffa off from the grain loads that typically arrived from points north, enforcing the prohibition on grain exports. But Janibek's objective was no more to starve Constantinople than to eliminate the Latin presence in the Horde. It was all business.[4]

It was not quite business as usual, though, because the Horde was facing a challenge far greater than insubordinate Italians. The Horde was also facing the plague—the Black Death. Gabriele de' Mussi, an Italian notary, recorded that during the siege of Caffa, an epidemic broke out in the Jochid ranks. The mortality rate was so high that, reportedly, no more than one in twenty Mongol warriors survived. Mussi also provides an early account of biological warfare, as the Jochids apparently catapulted infected body parts into the fortress. Unable to defend themselves from land-based attackers, the Caffans eventually abandoned the city then sailed to Pera, their trading post in the suburbs of Constantinople, and from there sailed into the Mediterranean, carrying with them "the darts of death" with which the Mongols had assaulted them. Mussi claimed this was how the plague spread from Asia to Europe.[5]

Mussi's story is almost certainly untrue in important respects, although it is nonetheless revealing. We can be confident of its inaccuracy for several reasons. First, Mussi witnessed none of the events he described. At the time they supposedly transpired, Mussi was in his hometown of Piacenza, north of Genoa. As a notary, he probably heard stories secondhand, through Genoese arriving from the Black Sea. Second, it makes little sense that Mongol warriors would have handled plague-infected bodies. If they understood that the infected dead could be a weapon—as Mussi's story implies—then they would also have known the risk of interacting with the bodies. And there is indeed evidence that the Mongols understood the danger of contact with infected people and so avoided them. On top of that, Mongols normally showed deep respect for their own dead, even during war campaigns. Finally, the epidemic struck Crimea in fall 1346, yet it reached Constantinople only in September 1347, Alexandria in October, Genoa in November, and finally Venice in February 1348. The gap in outbreaks rules out the possibility of a direct spread from Caffa to the Mediterranean via germ warfare. The plague did cross the Black Sea and penetrate the Mediterranean, but not as a result of the Caffa siege.[6]

If Mussi painted an inaccurate picture of "mountains of dead . . . thrown into the city," his fears of transmission were certainly understandable. In late 1347 and early 1348, when the plague reached Italy, locals grasped that Asia had already been struck and further understood that the epidemic could have reached them via places like Caffa and Tana, the portals connecting Western Europe to the Mongol colossus.[7] In early spring 1347, the embargoes were over and goods were leaving Tana for Europe again. Those goods were very likely contaminated: a year earlier, a Byzantine source reported that Tana was a plague-infected harbor. Food supplies were a major means of plague transmission, especially from the Horde's Italian-operated ports. Warehouses were full of previous seasons' harvests, as the embargoes had prevented grain from circulating for more than two years, and rodents had proliferated in the stores. The trade ships from the Horde that reached Italy in summer 1347 carried not only grain but also infected rats, mice, and fleas.[8]

For the Jochids, the second half of the fourteenth century was the polar opposite of the first. The plague, combined with disastrous internecine conflicts elsewhere in the Mongol Empire, enervated the Horde. By the 1360s, the ulus of Jochi would crack into three parts: the remnant of the khan's horde in the center and, to the east and west, larger and more powerful clusters of hordes that picked over the bones of declining cities like Sarai. But it was not just external pressure that undermined the Horde. Also significant was the Jochids' changing political culture. Under Toqto'a and Özbek, authoritarianism and centralization had seeped into the Horde's governance, replacing the old, stabilizing institutions of consensus-building and power diffusion. Meanwhile the khans' political purges hollowed out the golden lineage, leaving the Horde without a ruling class strong enough to assert itself and opening the ulus to rebellion, secession, and schism. The result was a period of unstable governance and social and economic deterioration known as *bulqaq*—anarchy.

It turned out that the Ilkhanids' gradual collapse between the 1330s and 1350s was just a harbinger of the most consequential global political phenomenon of the fourteenth century: the disintegration of the Mongol Empire. The Horde succumbed to infighting, the ulus of Chagatay split, and the Yuan, the Toluid regime in the far east, was ejected from China. All these changes were hastened by the Black Death, which revealed weaknesses in the larger world system stewarded and relied on by Chinggis's heirs. With the global economy shattered by the pandemic, trade and circulation—the lifeblood of the Chinggisid regimes—drained away. By the end of the fourteenth century, there was still a Horde, there was still a Yuan dynasty, and there was still a people that called themselves the ulus of Chagatay, but all of these looked dramatically different from the sturdy polities of decades earlier.[9]

The Black Death Spreads

Yersinia pestis, the bacterium that causes plague, is an age-old organism carried by the burrowing rodents of the Eurasian steppe. *Y. pestis* does not transfer easily from wild animals to humans, who are not its natural hosts. To spread across species, the bacteria require an assistant, some other animal that serves as a vector from the rodent body to the human.

Historically that vector has been fleas. After fleas feed on plague-infected blood, they may transmit the bacterium to their next target, and while fleas prefer the blood of rodents, they will settle for any mammal when they must—as, perhaps, when they find themselves in the bowels of a ship, far from the soil and its creatures. This is how *Y. pestis* escaped the wild and became the most dangerous source of disease humanity has ever known. The Black Death was not humanity's first encounter with an outbreak of disease caused by *Y. pestis*—that was the Plague of Justinian, in the sixth through eighth centuries. But the Black Death was far more acute, killing perhaps twice as many people in just a few years.[10]

The strain of *Y. pestis* that caused the Black Death arose sometime between 1196 and 1268, owing to genetic mutation. But it was not just the new strain that was responsible for the extent of the sudden outbreak of the mid-fourteenth century. Something pushed it along. Indeed, several things: the entire system of human relations with the natural world would have to have changed in order for the mutant strain to become so consequential. In this respect, it would be fair to say that Mongols were at least partially responsible for the spread of plague, even if they did not fling infected corpses at European traders.[11]

The natural environment of *Y. pestis* was disrupted by earthquakes, wildfires, climate change, and human activity. During the Mongol conquests, long sieges, mass migrations, and the movements of armies—with their herds of camels, horses, and heavy carts furrowing the ground—all disturbed the plague's habitat. And Mongol interference did not end with conquest; the development of Chinggis Khan's gigantic empire made for lasting environmental change. Through the movement of goods, animals, and people, the Mongols brought an increasing number and diversity of ecological zones into contact. There was also a great deal more interaction between humans and other animals as herds grew, hunting intensified, and the fur trade blossomed.[12]

The fur trade was particularly hazardous, as it put the Mongols and other steppe and forest peoples into proximity with a huge variety of potentially infected marmots. The gray marmots of the Altai Mountains, steppe marmots, and the Tarbagan marmots of northern China, Mongolia, and southwestern Siberia all could harbor plague. Humans could contract the disease by eating marmot meat or through flea bites when handling infected animals. Mongols have always hunted marmots, but from the thirteenth century onward, they did so more systematically and on a larger scale, leading to increased exposure to marmot-borne diseases. Hunters also targeted marmot predators, setting the stage for more contacts with potentially infected animals. Because furs were precious, hunters chased the marmots' predators—wolves, foxes, polecats, and Pallas's cats—which themselves could become disease transmitters. Other marmot predators such as snow leopards, hawks, and falcons were in high demand at Mongol courts, where they were used in imperial hunts and where they made contact with more humans. Moreover, the methodical culling of marmot predators led to the proliferation of marmots and other plague-bearing rodents in mountains, steppes, and cultivated fields.

These exposures ensured that plague circulated in the steppe and northern forests throughout the thirteenth and early fourteenth century. However, as long as burrowing rodents and humans for the most part lived separately, the risk of a major human outbreak was limited because transmission required repeated close contact. The risk became serious, however, when *Y. pestis* reached animals like mice, gerbils, and rats that live alongside sedentary human populations. As new scholarship has demonstrated, when domestic rodents and humans eat the same food, the chance of plague transmission explodes. This is why stagnant and dense populations were historically more imperiled than were nomads. But undesired sharing between people and domestic rodents was common during siege warfare, which put Mongols in proximity to possible sources of infection.[13]

When the plague broke out in earnest in the fourteenth century, contemporaries distinguished it from other major infectious diseases of the time, such as smallpox, cholera, and dysentery. According to various descriptions in Arabic, Latin, and Chinese sources, most people believed that plague was the result of miasma, polluted air, and that it could be airborne or caused by person-to-person contact. Both were true causes of plague contagion, alongside transmission by flea bites. One form of plague, the bubonic variety, was transmitted by flea bites and exposure to the bodily fluids of infected animals. Bubonic plague attacks the lymphatic system; it is an extremely painful condition involving a range of symptoms, from influenza-like fever and chills to explosive pustules, gangrene, and organ failure. According to modern studies, bubonic plague killed about 60 percent of people who contracted it during the peak of the Black Death, between 1346 and 1353. Pneumonic plague, which occurs when *Y. pestis* penetrates the lungs, is even more dangerous. Researchers estimate that about 90 percent of those infected died. (A third form of plague—septicemic plague, which attacks the blood—is also highly lethal, but it was and remains much less common than the other forms.) Although contemporaries could not have known about the flea-borne transmission responsible for the bubonic form, they recognized that the disease was extremely contagious and that it spread fast indoors. They also understood that even a victim's belongings could transmit infection. And they grasped that the Black Death was everywhere the same phenomenon—a disease that covered the world.[14]

By the time the Mediterranean region faced the Black Death, the Mongols knew it well. They had likely experienced the disease in China, while besieging Kaifeng in 1232, and Chinese sources mention devastating epidemics in Yuan territory in 1307–1313, 1331, and 1344–1345. The Mongols learned to respond to contagious disease, developing sanitation practices including quarantines. Recurrent outbreaks of plague and other diseases also inspired new shamanic rituals of protection. This was a common side effect of empire-building, which exposed people to foreign conditions with which their bodies had not learned to cope, often resulting in high susceptibility to contagion. The Mongols fought plague while building an empire in China and Central Asia, just as the Romans faced plague and malaria, the Ottomans were beset with plague and cholera, and the British vaccinated against smallpox in India.[15]

As for the people of the Horde, they were living with plague some years before the siege of Caffa. Contemporaries speculated that the Black Death emerged from the "land of darkness," the fur reservoir that lay north of the Ordaid territories and was a natural focus of *Y. pestis*. The disease likely appeared in the region of Lake Issyk Kul, a major trade station on the border between the Ordaids and the Chagatayids, where a 1338–1339 epidemic decimated a Nestorian community. Records do not establish definitively that the outbreak was plague, but that is the most probable culprit. No one knows the exact routes by which the Black Death made its way to Europe, but we do know that plague circulated all along the northern road and struck its major stations one after another.

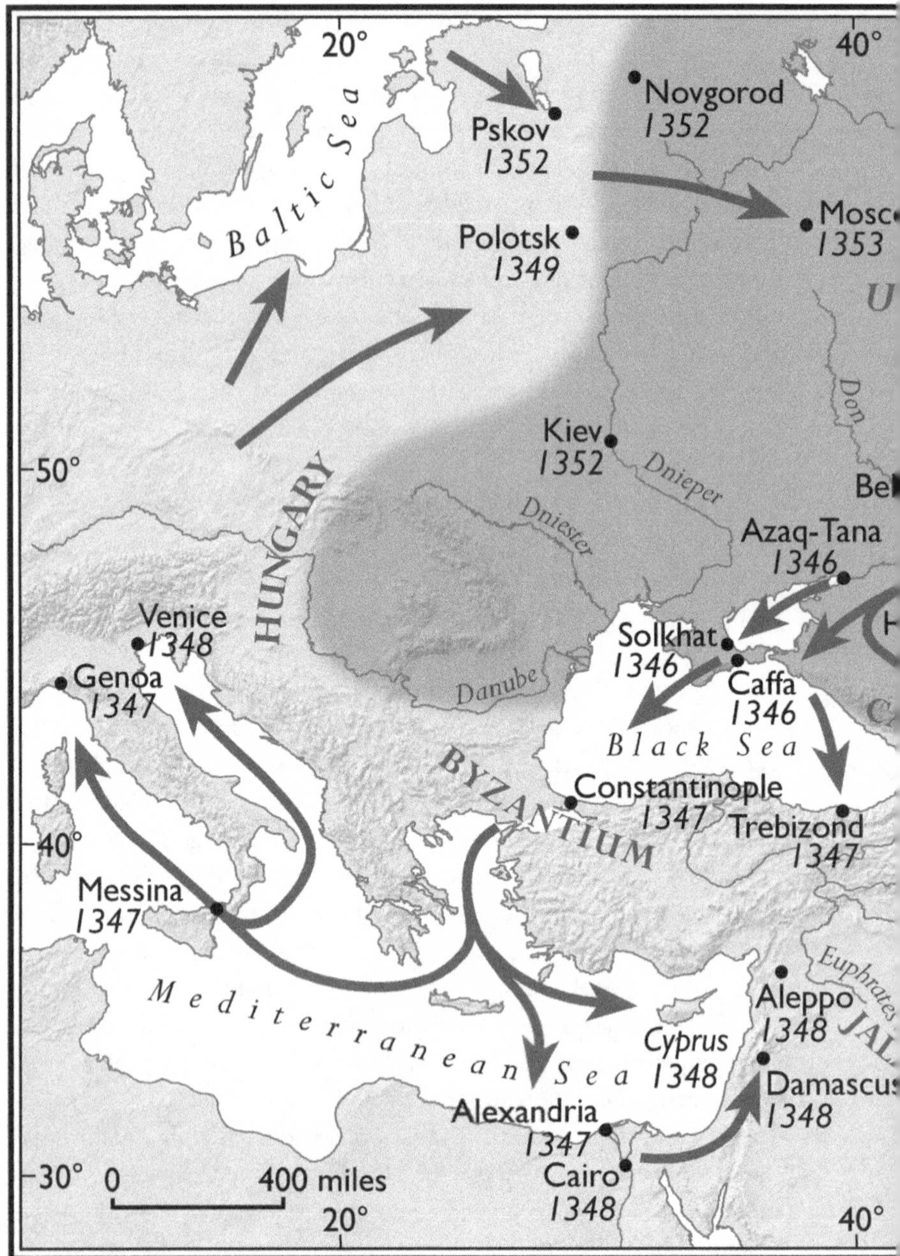

20°
40°
Baltic Sea
Novgorod
1352
Pskov
1352
Polotsk
1349
1353
Don
Kiev
1352
Dnieper
50°
HUNGARY
Dniester
Azaq-Tana
1346
Venice
1348
Genoa
1347
Solkhat
1346
Caffa
1346
Danube
Black Sea
BYZANTIUM
Constantinople
1347
Trebizond
1347
40°
Messina
1347
Euphrates
Aleppo
1348
Mediterranean Sea
Cyprus
1348
Damascus
1348
Alexandria
1347
Cairo
1348
30°
0
400 miles
20°
40°

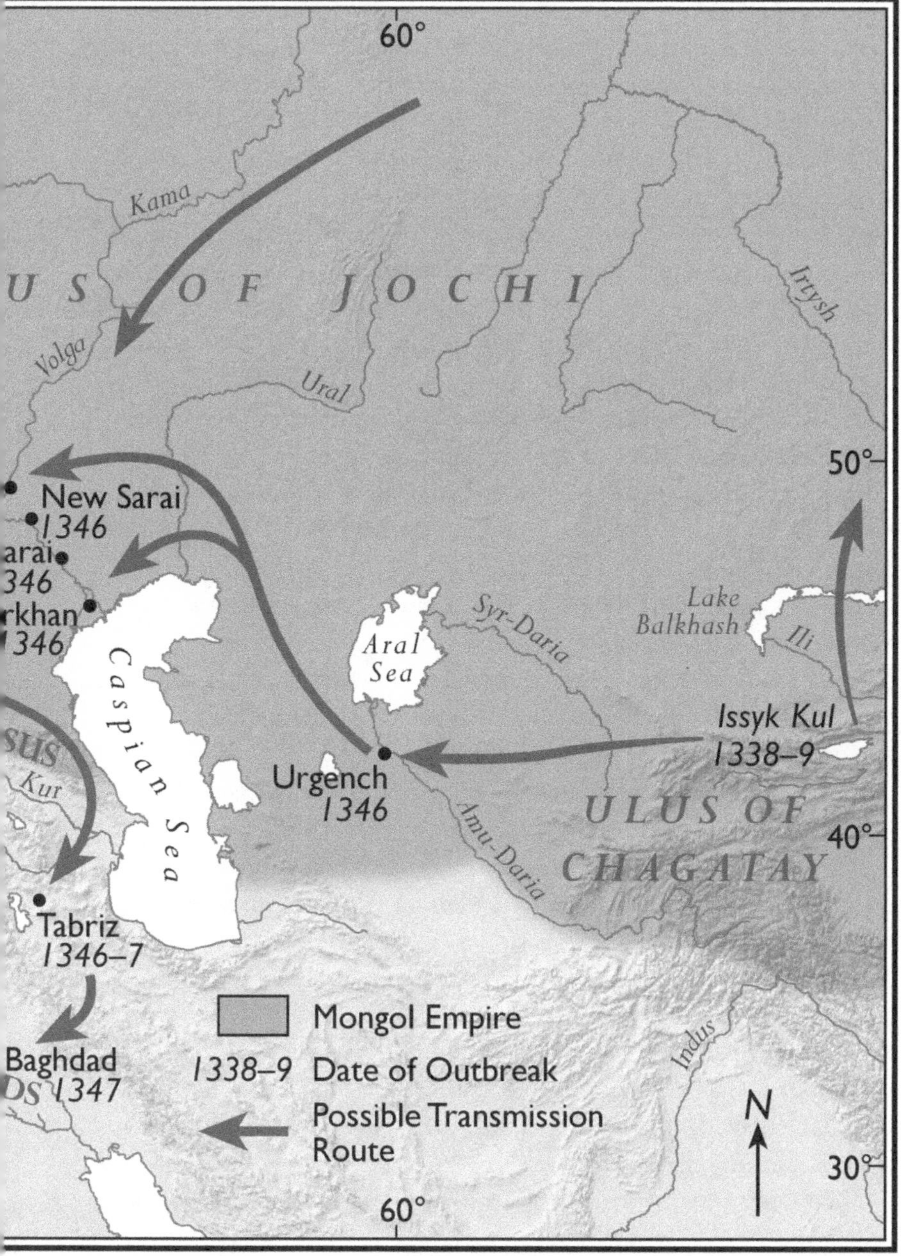

Possible transmission routes of the Black Death across central Eurasia.

In spring and summer 1346, plague was reported in Urgench, Sarai, Azaq, and most other Jochid cities. In fall it was in Solkhat, the inland capital of Crimea, before it broke out in the ranks of Janibek's army at the foot of Caffa, the endpoint of the northern road.[16]

While grain was the main vector of contamination in the southwestern portion of the road, furs were the more likely source in the northeastern portion. Several Russian towns, including the fur hub of Novgorod, were hit by the Black Death between 1349 and 1353. Although incidence waned after 1353, there are reports of outbreaks in 1364, 1374, and 1396 as well. The people of the Horde continued to live with plague until the fifteenth century.[17]

The impact of the Black Death was both widespread and deep. Above all, it was a demographic disaster—to date, the largest in Afro-Eurasian history. Scholars estimate that more than a third of Europe's population died. In the Mediterranean region, the mortality rate was even higher, around 40 percent. The Middle East may have suffered even greater depopulation than Europe. The Muslim scholar Al-'Aynī was told that there were up to twenty thousand deaths per day at the height of the plague in Cairo, a city whose population before the outbreak was about half a million. Traveling across Syria and Palestine in 1348, Ibn Battuta reported that plague killed between 1,000 and 2,000 people a day in the most populous cities like Damascus, which was home to approximately 80,000 people before the plague struck.[18]

The plague was most devastating in densely populated areas, but clearly it did not spare farmers or herders. A Russian source reported that the plague killed "Tatars" and others everywhere in the Horde. What is more, Sarai and the steppe cities of the Jochids were quite urban, although not as concentrated as European cities. The sources give no figures, yet the Horde must have suffered a significant decline in urban, rural, and nomadic populations during the Black Death. As regions were depopulated, cultivated land, orchards, and herds were left unattended, harming the economy.

Urban decline was particularly striking in the north of the Horde. Bulgar was a case in point. Situated on the east bank of the lower Volga, 600 miles upstream from New Sarai, Bulgar had been settled since at least the seventh century and was among the Horde's most important economic hubs. But when the fur road became the plague road, the city and surrounding region quickly deteriorated. Disease and the economic downturn combined to kill off a city that was likely already struggling somewhat from the competition with New Sarai. Bulgar's crowded necropolis provides a glimpse of what the people there experienced. Archaeologists have excavated some three hundred graves, more than half of them containing the remains of babies and young children. Women, too, died young: the burials show a peak of mortality at fifteen to twenty years old, probably due to childbearing.[19]

The Jochid political system proved resilient for a time. In the early 1350s, while plague killed Grand Prince Simeon and many other Russian elites, Janibek and his close entourage outlived the epidemic and soon were able to conquer Tabriz.[20] But as a globalized power, the Horde would go on to suffer more serious consequences. The economic shock of the pandemic hit hard in Europe, the Middle East, and Central and East Asia, and the effects would come back on the Horde like a boomerang. The volume of long-distance commerce shrank, as roads were cut off and gaps formed in trade routes, making travel increasingly difficult and dangerous. In the 1350s parts of the northern road collapsed. The Horde was an extraordinarily adaptive regime, but this time the changes it experienced were overwhelming. The Horde was tied to a world that had begun to unravel and could not help suffering as a result.[21]

When Powerful We Can Invade, When Weak We Can Retreat

The winds buffeting the Horde included not just the pandemic but also the disintegration of the wider Mongol Empire. The 1350s were the beginning of the end for the Yuan, the Mongol dynasty that ruled China.

Starting in 1352, China simultaneously suffered a decade of epidemics and a series of natural disasters, including major flooding of the Yellow River. The public held the Mongols responsible for failing to adequately address their needs, which were exacerbated by political instability within the Yuan regime. People also blamed the government for mismanaging agrarian resources, a consequential problem in light of the floods. Popular revolts spread first along the eastern coast, then to the north of the Yellow River, and finally to the south of the Yangzi. The revolts, led by Han Chinese, coalesced into the movement of the Red Turbans, which became the most tenacious uprising the Mongols had faced since the time of Chinggis Khan.[22]

The Red Turbans and other rebellious factions struggled for more than fifteen years, but they steadily gained ground until they could push the Yuan out of their Chinese territories. In 1368 Great Khan Toghon Temür abandoned Khanbalik, his winter capital, to the rebels and retreated northward to what today is called Inner Mongolia. The following year, the Red Turbans captured the Yuan summer capital of Shangdu, which was already half-destroyed, and further expanded their control. The movement had become a fledgling regime; its leaders claimed the name Ming, the Bright. It was a title suitable to the rebels' ambition and was a clear warning to the Mongols: a new dynasty was being born from the ashes of the Yuan.[23]

The rise of the Ming was undoubtedly alarming for the Mongols, particularly those of the Yuan. But the Yuan Mongols did not consider the great khan's retreat the end of their regime. The Yuan may have abandoned China, but the Mongols believed they had taken the mandate of Tengri with them, and they continued to control territories north and west of the Ming. The Yuan kept its name, and its leaders maintained that they were the rightful rulers of China; they never recognized Ming sovereignty. The Yuan also remained a powerful threat on the Ming's borders after their withdrawal from China, a threat the Ming took seriously.[24]

In retrospect, the withdrawal from China looks like an ejection, but the Mongols understood their retreat as a strategic one—a scheme to refocus the Yuan's resources and efforts and ultimately restore what had been lost. Abandoning nonvital territories and evacuating to protected areas constituted an old maneuver, used by generations of Mongols and other steppe dwellers when they needed to regroup and face a dangerous adversary. The tenth-century *Tangshu,* a history of the Chinese Tang dynasty, features a Türk officer advising his khan not to build cities, because the nomads' strength lay in their mobility: "When powerful we can invade," the officer advises, "when weak we can retreat."[25] Just as tactical withdrawal was a hallmark of Mongol battlefield operations, regimes, too, would withdraw in times of turmoil. It was a risky strategy, though, demanding discipline, endurance, and faith in Tengri's blessing.

In the case of the Yuan, withdrawal came with two major costs, both of which the Jochids felt. First, the loss of China dramatically reduced the sphere of the Mongol exchange. For more than a century, the Horde had shared measurement standards with the rest of the Mongol territories. Coins and calendars could be converted across the Mongol realms. The various uluses used Mongol language and script (as well as local languages) and recognized the same *gerege*—safe-conduct documents, also known as (*paiza*). Each Mongol regime relied on similar institutions, including the yam, quriltai, keshig, and schemes of religious tolerance, albeit that each had been adapted to local circumstances. After 1368, none of these standards applied to China; it had dropped out of the Mongol world system. We do not possess evidence on how the Jochids perceived the Toluid turmoil, yet we do know that the Jochids stopped issuing gerege after 1370.[26]

A second major cost of withdrawal lay in the opportunity it presented to the Mongols' competitors. The gradual collapse of the Yuan in China signaled to subjects across the Mongol Empire that it was time to realize their own ambitions. Warlike groups emerged within the hordes, some loosely organized and short-lived, others more durable. These groups did not necessarily seek to overthrow the Mongol system but rather to obtain a share of its benefits. Thus groups outside the golden lineage began to act with increasing autonomy and to claim resources distributed through the tümen. Alongside the Ming, then, a constellation of new powers took shape from China to Hungary. As we will see, something similar happened in the Horde, as it split into three sectors, two of them ruled by non-Jochid begs—although it must be stressed that these begs, unlike the Ming, wished to preserve the authority of a wavering Mongol regime, not to undermine and replace that authority.

Indeed, the breakup of the uluses preceded the downfall of the Yuan, which speaks to the fundamentally political nature of the problems facing the Mongol Empire in the mid-fourteenth century. As much pressure as the pandemic and its economic fallout created, neither could be blamed for the collapse of the Ilkhanids. Nor was the pandemic primarily responsible for the schism in the ulus of Chagatay, which in 1347 broke into eastern and western polities. The eastern half bordered the Yuan and later the Ming in the east and the Syr-Daria in the west, covering a huge territory that Persian and Turkic speakers called Moghulistan,

Illustration of a *gerege* (c. 1360s), a tablet guaranteeing its carrier safe passage through Mongol territories and access to *yam* facilities. This tablet is the last known gerege produced in the Horde and contains an Uighur inscription and a *taotie* mask. The mask is a Chinese representation of the face of a monstrous animal with powers said to ward off evil.

"Mongol country."[27] The other half, extending westward from the Syr-Daria, was centered on Transoxiana. Both portions were ruled by Chinggisids, but the prestige of the golden lineage remained especially high in the western area, where the nomads claimed the name of Chagatay, which they denied those in the eastern area.

The ongoing embrace of the Chinggisid legacy, even as the uluses broke down, should give us pause. Was the second half of the fourteenth century marked by the dissolution of the Mongol Empire, or by its revision and adaptation to new conditions? Some regions, like China, did break away, but in others, new leaders arose with the goal of taking part in the Mongol system, not of destroying it. One of the regions where the Mongol system was embraced by leaders outside the golden lineage was the Horde. As the Horde fragmented and fell under the control of qarachu begs, its component parts continued to associate themselves with the prestige of the Jochid line. Not only that, but the Horde's leaders ruled their territories much as Batu, Berke, and the others had. Mongol institutions were designed for flexibility, and they showed it by surviving deep struggles within the Horde.

Anarchy

The conquest of Tabriz in winter 1356–1357 marked the culmination of Jochid expansion. For a century, Jochid rulers had dreamed of possessing Tabriz. Janibek finally realized that ambition, but he did not have much time to enjoy the accomplishment. On his way back from battle, he fell ill and died in the Sarai area in July 1357. When Birdibek, who was still stationed in Tabriz, heard the news of his father's death, he gathered his troops and prepared to leave the city at once. While Tabriz may have beckoned Birdibek's ancestors, the greater prize—the Jochid throne—still lay in the lower Volga. Birdibek appointed a governor to supervise the Tabriz area and set off for the heartland of the Horde.

Local powers in Tabriz took advantage of the conquerors' unexpected departure. As soon as the Horde's warriors left, various would-be sovereigns arose, including Birdibek's governor. The city and surrounding Azerbaijan region quickly fell to the Jalayirids—non-Chinggisid Mongols who claimed the Ilkhanid legacy. Deeply rooted in Iraq, the Jalayirids already controlled Baghdad. Even the Shirvan shah, who had watched the Derbent-Shirvan pass for the Horde, submitted to the Jalayirids. Like most of the Caucasians, the Shirvan shah sided with the strong, for no one expected to see the Jochid troops back any time soon.[28]

In the Horde the khan's succession was monopolizing everyone's attention. Rumors held that Janibek had been killed: Muslim sources claimed that his begs strangled him, while the Russians insisted the khan had been killed on Birdibek's orders.[29] No one knew for sure, yet all seemed convinced that foul play was involved. Birdibek ultimately took the throne with the support of several powerful begs and his grandmother Taidula, who had been Özbek's chief wife and remained a leading political figure after his death, just as Bayalun had in her own time.

Insecure in his new position, Birdibek purged his potential competitors. He targeted every male descendant of Özbek for elimination, regardless of age and position within the family. The purge was extraordinarily violent even by what had become Jochid standards; Birdibek ordered the murder of his twelve brothers and his own son.[30] In response, most of the begs and Jochid princes refused to support Birdibek. In 1358, while Birdibek was still on the throne, at least three others claimed his office. Soon there would be many more aspirants, as Birdibek's tenure at the pinnacle of Jochid power proved brief. He died in 1359, probably by another's hand, but the exact circumstances are not clear. Evidence suggests that Taidula knew the cause and precise date of Birdibek's death but kept them secret.

In just two years or so on the throne, Birdibek did more damage to Jochid politics than the plague had. Birdibek eliminated everyone in his generation with a strong right to the throne and ensured that no such person existed in the next. He horrified his own people, and the court genealogists held him responsible for the political turmoil that started under his rule. They considered Birdibek the last Batuid khan, for those who took the throne after him mostly came from secondary Jochid lines.[31]

After Birdibek's death, new khans came and went, but Taidula was the most important figure in the court. Her authority had grown since she became Özbek's wife, and after twenty years at the center of government, she knew how to play Jochid politics. She demonstrated her acumen when she helped put Janibek and then Birdibek on the throne. Taidula had one of the largest incomes in the Horde, and her network of trade partners extended into the cities of Crimea, the Volga, and the Don. While most Jochid leaders adopted Islam, Taidula publicly embraced Christianity and used her position to cultivate ties with the Orthodox clergy, the Venetians, and the pope.[32] But she would be the last representative of the house of Özbek, the most glorious family of the golden lineage since the time of Batu. In 1360 Taidula, too, was murdered. The sources do not indicate by whom or under what circumstances, but her assassination must have been connected to her involvement in the political struggles of the period. Soon after Taidula's death, no fewer than six khans claimed to rule, all at once. Each minted coins mentioning New Sarai. None of the would-be khans had popular support, and none of them would last.[33]

The extinction of the Batuid line led to the unravelling of Jochid society. For a hundred and fifty years, the Horde's hierarchical organization had been based on the bonds of each Jochid lineage with the main branch of the Batuids. With the Batuids gone, the hierarchy was decapitated. Nor were the Ordaids prepared to fill the void the Batuids left behind. The Ordaids relied on the Batuids to keep their own throne, and after Taidula's death, their dominant position in the Horde's eastern wing was undermined by princes from secondary lines, who took over in 1361. The sudden collapse of both the Batuids and the Ordaids created an unprecedented power vacuum and a rush to fill it. Frictions between self-proclaimed khans turned into a blood feud that lasted almost two decades, a period that contemporaries recorded as *bulqaq:* anarchy.[34]

The Jochids were paying the price for more than half a century of increasingly authoritarian control. Since Toqto'a's enthronement, each transfer of power had led to a political purge. Not only that, but the Horde's deliberative political institutions had been sidelined. Perhaps most importantly, in 1342 Janibek had turned the quriltai into a mere rubber stamp. Janibek was not the consensual candidate, but he was the only person eligible, because he, too, had his brothers killed before he was elected. He also packed the ceremonies with his supporters, further ensuring that there would be no debate.[35] With no one to oppose Janibek, the assembly had no need to dramatize the tension among competitors and perform the old rituals of agreement. The deritualization of Jochid politics was both a feature of authoritarianism and a sign that it had metastasized.

Some of the consequences were arguably beneficial. Succession no longer involved extended interregnums, which bred uncertainty among the peoples of the Horde and the merchants who traded with them. But the harms of the might-makes-right approach were far greater than were the advantages. As soon as the Jochids began resolving political disagreement through killing rather than negotiation, there was no end to the violence. Having murdered his opponents, a new khan might hold onto power, but that only meant that internecine warfare was in abeyance. The last bout of killing lingered in the collective consciousness until the next succession came, at which point repressed anger rose to the surface. Every political assassination provoked retaliation; there was no other way, because in the steppe world, revenge was a moral duty transmitted from one generation to the next. In the fourteenth century, moral necessity became collective self-destruction.

The great irony is that authoritarianism did not yield authority. In the Mongol world, fratricide could not go on producing effective politics, which was based on consensus rather than coercion. A khan who had to coerce his ulus could never muster the unity necessary to collect his far-flung commanders and lead them in conquest, nor could he rely on the loyalty of distant and independent-minded officials. Such a khan could neither expand his tax base nor obtain revenues from the people he nominally ruled, because he could not count on the backing of tax collectors and other administrators. And without revenues, the khan could not uphold the imperatives of sharing and circulation—his sacred obligation and the foundation of the political order.

In the late 1350s, rather than continue to struggle against an authoritarian khan, two powerful clusters of hordes broke away. The western cluster was known as the right wing. It was led by a beg named Mamai, with his headquarters in Crimea. The eastern begs and hordes, the left wing, gathered under Tengiz-Buqa, a beg from the lower Syr-Daria. The Jochid khan—whomever he was at any given moment—ruled only the center, around Sarai and New Sarai. Both cities were depleted by the bulqaq, the plague, and ecological disaster, including repeated droughts. Along with cities such as Bulgar and Azaq, Sarai and New Sarai were drained of workers, craftsmen, and merchants. New Sarai was one of the first Jochid settlements to show signs of decline, and by the 1370s cemeteries had replaced Sarai's populated districts, turning the place into a necropolis.[36] The decline and de-urbanization of the main lower valleys was in many respects a consequence of political decentralization during the bulqaq: as the court lost control, and wealth and military power moved outward to the left and right wings, the khan's shift men, postmen, and steppe patrols, who for generations had supervised the movement of people and goods, loosened their grip. In doing so, they allowed more settlers and herders to leave the lower valleys. Some of the migrants went west, to the northern shores of the Azov, in Mamai's wing. Others went east and formed a new horde that stretched along the lower Syr-Daria toward Sighnaq, the political center of Tengiz-Buqa's wing.[37] In winter groups of herders continued to come to the lower Volga, but in summer they avoided the area of the declining cities and preferred grazing along the Don.

The abandonment of steppe settlements, like the retreat of the Yuan, might be seen as a strategic withdrawal. When the settlements became too hazardous, herders and sedentary people alike moved on, knowing that, in times of crisis, it made sense to rid themselves of that which was not essential. And that is what the cities had become. The plague made density dangerous, and the reduction in trade negated the economic attractions of settled cities. Cities therefore ceased to be useful tools of domination. On top of this, the many would-be khans of the bulqaq turned Sarai and New Sarai into war zones—despite their decreasing strategic and economic importance, both cities remained important to the Horde's pretenders, as Sarai and New Sarai were closely connected to the legacies of Batu and Özbek. A final inducement to leave the cities was climate change, which marred the herding grounds around the steppe cities. At the end of the thirteenth century, a global cooling trend known as the Little Ice Age began. Effects across the Northern Hemisphere were varied, but in the Horde, the Little Ice Age resulted in more frequent periods of *dzud*—sudden changes in weather that caused famines and significant losses of livestock. Generations of herders tolerated the changing conditions, but amid the plague and the bulqaq, the reasons to stay were few.[38]

Responding to all these pressures, nomadic elites adapted their seasonal rounds and looked elsewhere for prosperity. This was not chaos; it was the Mongol way: decentralize, split, and scatter. Much as the hordes of Orda and Batu thrived separately, much as Chinggis sought to control rivalry by granting his sons separate territories, and much as eldest sons were sent off to raise their families far from their fathers, the people of the Horde moved on from the regime's geographic and political center when staying was no longer wise. Withdrawal had always been an effective way to avoid the civil wars that could result from political struggle, and this time withdrawal would help to limit the spread of plague as well.

Thus the cities that the competing khans fought over were in large part ghost towns. No matter; the khans could not hold them. In the

1360s some khans occupied Sarai's throne for only a few weeks. These self-proclaimed khans lacked the authority to mobilize the tümens and so could rely on few horsemen. It would fall to other leaders to find a new modus vivendi for the Horde—a functional politics that would keep the people working toward the collective good that the ulus of Jochi had once known. With the golden lineage in disarray, these leaders were the qarachu begs.

The Begs Take Over

In the 1360s and 1370s, most of the qarachu begs still trusted the Mongol world order. They believed the Horde needed a strong khan and centralized power. The powerful begs who operated in all three of the Horde's domains fought over the leadership—not to install themselves, for they were not Jochids and therefore lacked rightful claims. Rather, they supported various claimants who could call on the prestige of the golden lineage. But none of these coalitions of Jochids and begs was able to rally all three of the major hordes, or, apparently, the minor ones scattered around the Horde. The khans supported by the begs of the western and eastern territories lacked control of the ancestral center and the prestige that came with it, while the khans supported by the begs of the lower Volga could not gather enough warriors to assert their domination. In addition, the khans of the lower Volga lacked capable administrators. The last khan who governed with a full keshig was Janibek. Under Birdibek, the hereditary keshig fragmented, and most of the shift men left the lower Volga to escape the political purges and support other throne contenders. As the bulqaq went on, the Jochids needed the qarachu begs more than ever, because only they could compensate for the disintegration of the keshig.

An exception to begs' support for restoration of the Jochid khan came from northern Khwarezm, where the end of the Batuids led not to a scramble to support the next khan but rather to secession, as the Qonggirad seized Urgench and claimed autonomy. The Qonggirad had long been in charge of the region, but on behalf of the khan. That had been the situation under Özbek, who had made the transformative decision to grant his in-law Qutluq-Temür administrative authority in the Horde's Khwarezmian territory. The same structure held when Qutluq-Temür was succeeded in the 1340s by Amīr Nanguday, another Jochid in-law. Like Qutluq-Temür, Nanguday was far more powerful than earlier qarachu begs, but he was still allied with the khan.[39]

Nanguday was killed during the political purges of 1361–1362, at the beginning of the bulqaq. His daughter and sons took over and formed what became known as the Sufi-Qonggirad, a new dynasty that claimed independence from the Horde. Their authority stemmed in part from their connections with the golden lineage; in part from their military power, as they controlled the nomadic warriors of northern Khwarezm; and finally from their status as pious Muslims and patrons of Islamic institutions. In particular, Nanguday's family was closely aligned with Sufism; late sources suggest that Nanguday was a disciple of Sayyid Atā, an influential Sufi shaykh. Sufism was a bridge to urban and nomadic Khwarezmians alike. Sufis were active among the nomads, and local nomadic elites had family ties with Sufi leaders. Urban Khwarezmians, meanwhile, were predominantly Muslim and held the Sufi saints and their followers in high esteem.[40]

Assertions of independence are, of course, not the same as independence in reality. To become truly independent, the Sufi-Qonggirad needed to establish commercial ties of their own with key trading partners in Central Asia, Iran, and India. Urgench, long a major trade hub, offered advantages in this respect. The Sufi-Qonggirad needed only to keep business flowing there and, instead of sending tax collections to the Jochids, save the returns for themselves. To this end, in 1362–1363, they ordered new silver coins minted without the mention of the khan's name and, soon after, started to mint gold coins as well.[41] In 1366–1367, they expanded their reach, collecting taxes from Khiva and Kath, the capitals of Chagatayid southern Khwarezm. In Mongol eyes, the qarachu Sufi-Qonggirad had no rights to claim imperial taxes, but the Chagatayids were too weak to maintain control over their ancestral territory.[42]

While the Sufi-Qonggirad took no part in the scramble for the Jochid throne, and while their actions earned Mongol scorn, it is notable that even they in many ways sought to replicate strategies of Mongol rule. Their template for governance was the Mongol one, prioritizing customs receipts, a centralized currency regime, and vassalage. Though the Sufi-Qonggirad regime was dominated by Muslims, it did not adopt a model akin to that of the Mamluks or other Middle Eastern sultanates. And the Sufi-Qonggirad did not forswear Mongol styles of political legitimation. Islamic leadership and the golden lineage were both critical to their ruling mandate, just as they were for Berke and his successors.

Likewise, the leaders of the left and right wings were committed to Mongol patterns of rule, but, unlike the Sufi-Qonggirad, these begs were partisans of the status quo ante: they wanted to reunite the Horde under a single khan. Perhaps the most influential of these begs was Mamai, a military commander of Kiyad descent who had married Birdibek's daughter Tulunbek. Like the Qonggirad, the Kiyad were among the Mongol families that provided Jochid in-laws and the Horde's ruling begs. Deeply involved in the Horde's internal politics and its foreign policy, Mamai became Birdibek's beglerbeg. Mamai led the western begs—the right wing. At least nine hordes answered to him. His huge territory including the northern Black Sea, Crimea, and the northern Caucasus. Crimea, in particular, produced substantial income for Mamai, remaining one of the richest regions in the Horde despite ongoing tensions between the Genoese and the Horde's chiefs.[43]

After Birdibek's death, Mamai associated himself with several would-be khans, but none was able to hold onto power. This was not a problem for Mamai, who was, at least in the west, the power behind the throne, regardless of who occupied it. For instance, ʿAbdallāh, who was said to be Özbek's son, served as Mamai's puppet khan.[44] Tulunbek was a critical partner of Mamai. After ʿAbdallāh died in 1370, Tulunbek took the throne for a few years, ensuring that Mamai would retain de facto authority. Only when Tulunbek and Mamai agreed that there was a sufficiently pliable Jochid candidate for the throne did she step aside.[45] This was another new direction in the political culture of the Horde: now a qarachu beg and Jochid princess could rule together and promote their own khan.

Mamai joined the competition for the Volga Valley, helping to turn it into the anarchic frontier between the eastern and western begs. The two camps repeatedly captured and lost Sarai and New Sarai, so that neither Mamai nor the others were able fully to control the central territory and benefit from the prestige of holding the lands of Batu and Özbek. Still, the fact that a qarachu beg could even dream of ruling the old capitals was a testament to how much had changed. Mamai did not see it that way, though, or he did not say so if he did. He claimed to embody the continuity of the Horde and its institutions, his wife Tulunbek providing him a connection to the legacy he could not obtain by force.

While Mamai and assorted begs fought over who would occupy the seat of power, the Horde's western neighbors and vassals took advantage of the disorder. The subjects of the sedentary fringe understood the opportunity the bulqaq offered: this was a chance to gain freedom of action and force the Mongols to make territorial and political concessions. With this in mind, Russians and Lithuanians began to test Mamai. Each power followed its own strategy in order to renegotiate its bonds with the Horde, a strategy contoured by their respective relationships with the Jochids.

For the Lithuanians, that relationship had begun in the 1320s, under Özbek. With the Horde throwing its support behind Moscow in the north of the Russian principalities, the southern principalities—including Kiev, Smolensk, Galicia, and Volynia—receded farther from the center of political attention, increasing their vulnerability to outsiders who hoped to win them away from the Jochids. For a time, Nogay and his forces stood as an obstacle to ambitious foreigners, protecting the southern Russian princes against incursions. After Nogay's death, however, the Jochids loosened their grip on the Horde's southwestern border, allowing competitors to expand over the region.

Among the most capable of these competitors were the Lithuanians, who took Kiev in the early 1320s. In 1324 Özbek acknowledged the new political reality and signed a treaty with the Lithuanian ruler. The Lithuanians saw this as a step toward further conquest; Özbek, by contrast, saw a new vassal, one that could replace the Russians on the southwestern border. As long as the territory was administered by people loyal to the Horde, it did not matter if they were Russians or Lithuanians; they would be left in peace. So the Lithuanians accepted their position. They avoided conflicts with the Jochids, handled diplomatic contacts between the Horde and the Germans and Polish, followed the Horde's commercial policies, and collected and paid the tribute. A pattern then emerged between the Lithuanians and Jochids. In 1340 the Lithuanians occupied Volynia and Galicia, becoming the Horde's new vassals there, too.

Algirdas, the Lithuanian ruler after 1345, aimed to continue the trend, expanding his wealth and influence by extending his vassalage within the Horde. Doing so would entail both fighting the Horde and allying with it—that is, he would have to violently upset the status quo by displacing another vassal, and he would have to obtain Mamai's blessing for having done so. Around 1362 Algirdas's army set out to take control of areas under the relatively weak government in Moscow. The Lithuanians marched along the lower Dnieper, achieving the submission of the principalities of Chernigov and Pereslavl. In the fall the Lithuanians crossed the Dnieper and attacked the region of Podolia, a trade hub on the Dniester southwest of Kiev.[46] The Podolian river ports would give the Lithuanians Black Sea access and an opportunity to oversee and tax traffic on the river. Not only that, but the area also had rich agricultural resources. But Podolia, a tribute-paying region of the Horde, was protected by Jochid warriors stationed near the Syniukha River. The Lithuanians would have to fight not Russians but Mongols. That is precisely what Algirdas's forces did, and they emerged victorious. Although this was not quite the triumph the Lithuanians would later claim, the balance of power had clearly shifted in the region.

Mamai might have committed a larger force to crush the Lithuanians, but he had more urgent battles to fight in the lower Volga. Besides, Mamai regarded the Lithuanians as a useful balancing agent against Moscow. Again, as long as the Lithuanians kept sending the tribute, the Jochids would tolerate them. We do not know if Mamai officially confirmed Algirdas's authority over Podolia, but sources show that the Lithuanians continued to send Podolia's *Tributum Thartharorum,* the "Tartar tribute," to the Jochid khans until the fifteenth century.[47]

As for the Russians in the northern principalities, they had their own internal issues, which colored relations with the Jochids. In particular, Tver remained on cold terms with Moscow. Initially Dmitrii Ivanovich, the kniaz of Moscow, benefited from Mamai's support; around 1363, Mamai confirmed Dmitrii as grand prince. But by 1370 Mamai had grown frustrated with Dmitrii's poor performance in delivering the tribute, so Mamai stripped the throne from Dmitrii and gave it to Mikhail Alexandrovich, the kniaz of Tver. Dmitrii, however, did not intend to let Mikhail rule in his place. Dmitrii gathered his army and forbade the prince of Tver from entering the city of Vladimir and occupying the seat of the grand prince. Dmitrii also regained Mamai's patronage, sending the beg gifts, visiting him at his horde, and ultimately retaining the throne of Vladimir. But while Dmitrii had won this round, he could not rest easy. It was clear that Mamai could be fickle and might again retract his support.

That is exactly what happened a few years later, around 1374–1375, after the leaders of a group of Russian cities refused to obey Mamai's envoys and had them killed—the envoys had probably demanded tax payments and compensation for deferred tributes. Mamai retaliated, but his warriors were repulsed. According to the Russian chronicles, the Jochid forces were considerably weakened by the plague, which was roaring in the steppe at the time and was cutting down Mamai's troops. Capitalizing on the Horde's plague-stricken position, the Russians doubled down on their rebellion, claiming that Mamai was demanding unconscionable tributes. Mamai held Grand Prince Dmitrii responsible for the uprising. Fearing that, this time, diplomacy would not be enough, Dmitrii decided to face Mamai and strike first.[48] In 1378, while Mamai was busy gathering his warriors for a campaign against Moscow, Dmitrii led his army directly to Mamai's camp. When the two armies met on the Vozha River, the grand prince defeated Mamai, marking the first time since the conquest in the late 1230s that the Russians defeated the Mongols in a large-scale battle. In August 1380, Mamai and the Russians met again, this time at Kulikovo, a field along the Don located deep in Mamai's lands. The Jochid army was crushed again, solidifying Dmitrii's place in Russian history as Dmitrii Donskoi—Dmitrii of the Don. To this day, Dmitrii Donskoi is venerated as a saint of the Russian Orthodox Church.[49]

Yet, while Dmitrii's victories over Mamai were clear, they were hardly decisive in ending the "Tatar yoke." In fact the Russian advantage was short-lived, and by the middle of the 1380s, the Russians would again be paying tribute to Mongol rulers. Dmitrii's heroic stature in modern Russia reflects less the importance of his contributions—his triumphs came at a low ebb of Jochid power, and even then he was unable to bring about independence from the Mongols—than the political project of Russian nationalist historiography, based on the sixteenth-century elaboration of the Tatar yoke idea by the Muscovite Church. Dmitrii's defiance has made him a symbol of Russian self-determination and enlightened Christian nationhood, against the depredations of Muslim, Pagan, and foreign influence. The irony is that the nation celebrated by Russian nationalists, the church, and citizens in general, is the nation associated with the house of Moscow, whose rise was enabled by Mongols. Following the Daniilovich dynasty, it was a family of Moscow boyars, the Romanovs, who became rich and powerful enough to consolidate and reign over the modern Russian nation-state beloved of the Russian nationalist imagination. Yet that nation, envisioned in opposition to the Tatar yoke, might never have existed had the Jochids not disrupted the Kievan system and favored the house of Moscow, elevating it to the heights of Russian power.[50]

Disintegration

The demise of the Ilkhanids was supposed to be the Horde's crowning achievement—the realization of its moral right to vengeance and an opportunity to solidify the supremacy of the northern road. But leadership of the most important Eurasian trade corridor hardly mattered when the Black Death made large-scale trade unfeasible. And it turned out that the decline of the Ilkhanids cost the Jochids more than they gained from it. The fragmentation of the Ilkhanids meant that, instead of a strong challenger who played by the rules, the Jochids had to deal with a constellation of smaller, unreliable neighbors. Indeed, throughout the Mongol Empire, the dominated were rising up. The collapse of Ilkhanid regime, and its replacement by the former regime's regional factions, showed that Mongol power was not permanent. Elites who had benefited from the Mongol system—whether the Ilkhanid emirs, the Qonggirad, or the Lithuanians—could assert themselves and take over. Even a popular uprising like the Red Turbans could displace Mongol rule.

At the end of the fourteenth century, the Horde was more intact than the other Mongol states, yet the shift in the relative power of the khan and begs was in many ways similar to developments among the Ilkhanids and ulus Chagatay. Even if the tradition of Chinggis Khan remained prestigious across Eurasia, Eurasia was out of Chinggisid control. The leaders of this new world embraced Chinggis's prestige and the methods, but they did not descend from the golden lineage. This was true of Mamai and the Sufi-Qonggirad, and it would be true of one of the great historical figures to emerge from the Mongol disintegration: Temür, alias Tamerlane. As we will see in the next chapter, Temür's rise to power would soon illustrate the opportunities the post-crisis world offered to non-Chinggisid elites claiming the mantle of Mongol-style rule.[51]

That the Mongol style survived the Mongol Empire is a fact of history that deserves to be taken seriously. No one knew what shape the Mongol-centered world would take after the empire's disintegration, yet that shape would turn out to be strongly influenced by the flexible systems that Chinggis Khan invented and his heirs adapted. This was all in keeping with the nomadic conception of power. The Mongol regime was built to withstand change, for change was both inevitable and beyond the control of mere human beings. After all, *sülde,* the vital force that created empires, was Tengri's to bestow. Tengri had blessed the golden lineage, but others could be blessed as well. Perhaps the truest marker of the genius of Mongol rule, then, was that when Tengri gave sülde to others, they still turned to Chinggis's ideas and his legacy for strength.

8

Younger Brothers

The combined crises of the bulqaq, the Black Death, and the dissolution of the Yuan and Ilkhanids tested the Horde mightily. But the ulus of Jochi survived, thanks to its flexibility. When the security and prosperity of the people could be maintained only by devolving power from the khan to the begs, then devolution is what happened. The rise of leading qarachu begs, like Mamai, was a revision in service of continuity. The inhabitants of positions of power were changing, but the overall structure of nomadic rule remained.

The end of the fourteenth century and beginning of the fifteenth would see a related dynamic. A new khan, Toqtamish, would rise and reunify the Horde. But he kept control only as long as the begs allowed. Toqtamish was a new kind of Jochid leader in that he was of neither the Batuid nor the Ordaid lineage. But Toqtamish was very much a leader in the style of his Jochid predecessors in that he was committed to conquest, advancing trade through financial reform, and maximizing the Horde's diplomatic gains. Toqtamish would make and break alliances as necessary, which is how he managed to partner with Tamerlane, then fight a protracted war with him, then ally once more.

In the wake of Toqtamish, however, the Horde definitively splintered into several regimes. Yet each of these looked back to Toqtamish and the Jochid khans as their founders. In one sense, the fifteenth century was the end of the Horde, for the Jochid central authority collapsed, never to be restored. But in another sense, the era brought about merely a reorganization of the authority formerly invested in the khan and his keshig. For decades after Birdibek, power in the Horde had been slowly flowing outward from the lower Volga. This trend continued in the fifteenth century, as the people of the Horde found creative ways to serve their needs while the world changed around them. The breakup of the Horde was, it turned out, the best way to preserve the Horde—if not the specific regime, then the kind of regime it had been. The Horde's successor states imagined themselves as continuous with the traditions of Chinggis and Jochi. These states would carry Mongol traditions forward for hundreds of years, dominating the western steppe and Central Asia into the nineteenth century.

Piecing the Horde Back Together

Since its earliest days, the Horde maintained two principal factions, which largely worked in harmony: the White Horde of Batu and the Blue Horde of Orda. The dominance of these hordes ended in 1359–1360, with the deaths of the Batuid khan Birdibek and the Ordaid khan. Birdibek was followed by a series of squabbling pretenders, none of whom was able to establish a solid claim to the throne. The Blue Horde, by contrast, quickly established new leadership in the person of Qara-Nogay. Qara-Nogay's election was announced in front of the people in the Ordaid capital of Sighnaq, and the news spread from there to the cities of the Syr-Daria River, along the Aral Sea, and on to the nomadic camps. The new khan must have been something of a shock: for the first time, the left-hand wing was not ruled by a descendant of Orda. Qara-Nogay's lineage traced instead to one of Orda's brothers—Toqa Temür, Jochi's youngest son.

Qara-Nogay's rule did not last long but, importantly, he was succeeded on the throne by members of his family, crystallizing their lineage as the Blue Horde's ruling family. Perhaps the most powerful of this new line of leaders was Qara-Nogay's cousin Urus, who became khan of the Blue Horde around 1368. Urus was a khan in the mold of Özbek: Urus coupled expansionist intentions—he sought to extend his control to Sarai—with

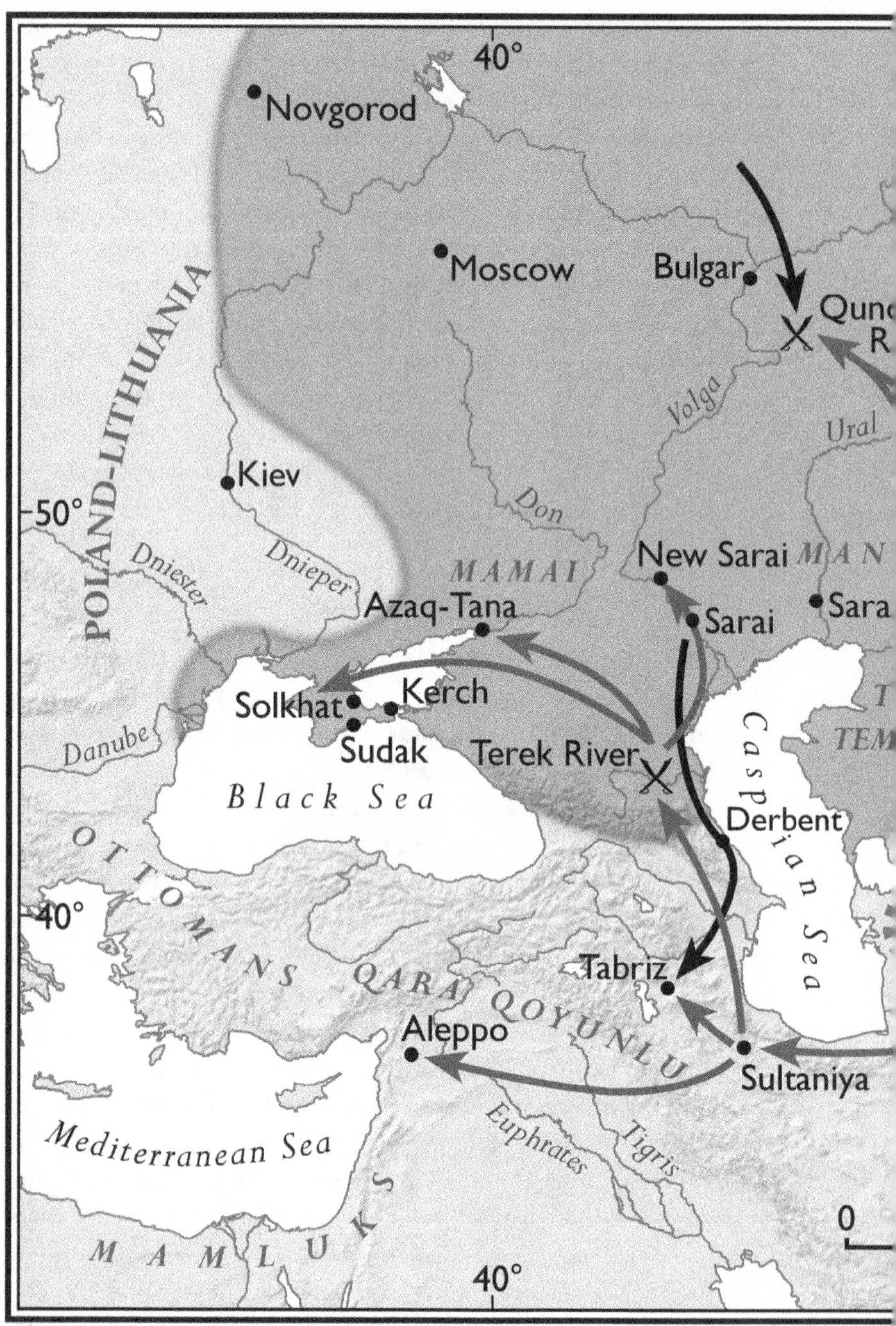
40°
Novgorod
Moscow
Bulgar
POLAND-LITHUANIA
Volga
Ural
Kiev
50°
Don
Dniester
Dnieper
MAMAI
New Sarai
Azaq-Tana
Sarai
Solkhat
Kerch
Sudak
Danube
Terek River
Black Sea
Caspian Sea
Derbent
OTTOMANS
40°
QARA QOYUNLU
Tabriz
Aleppo
Sultaniya
Euphrates
Tigris
Mediterranean Sea
MAMLUKS
0
40°

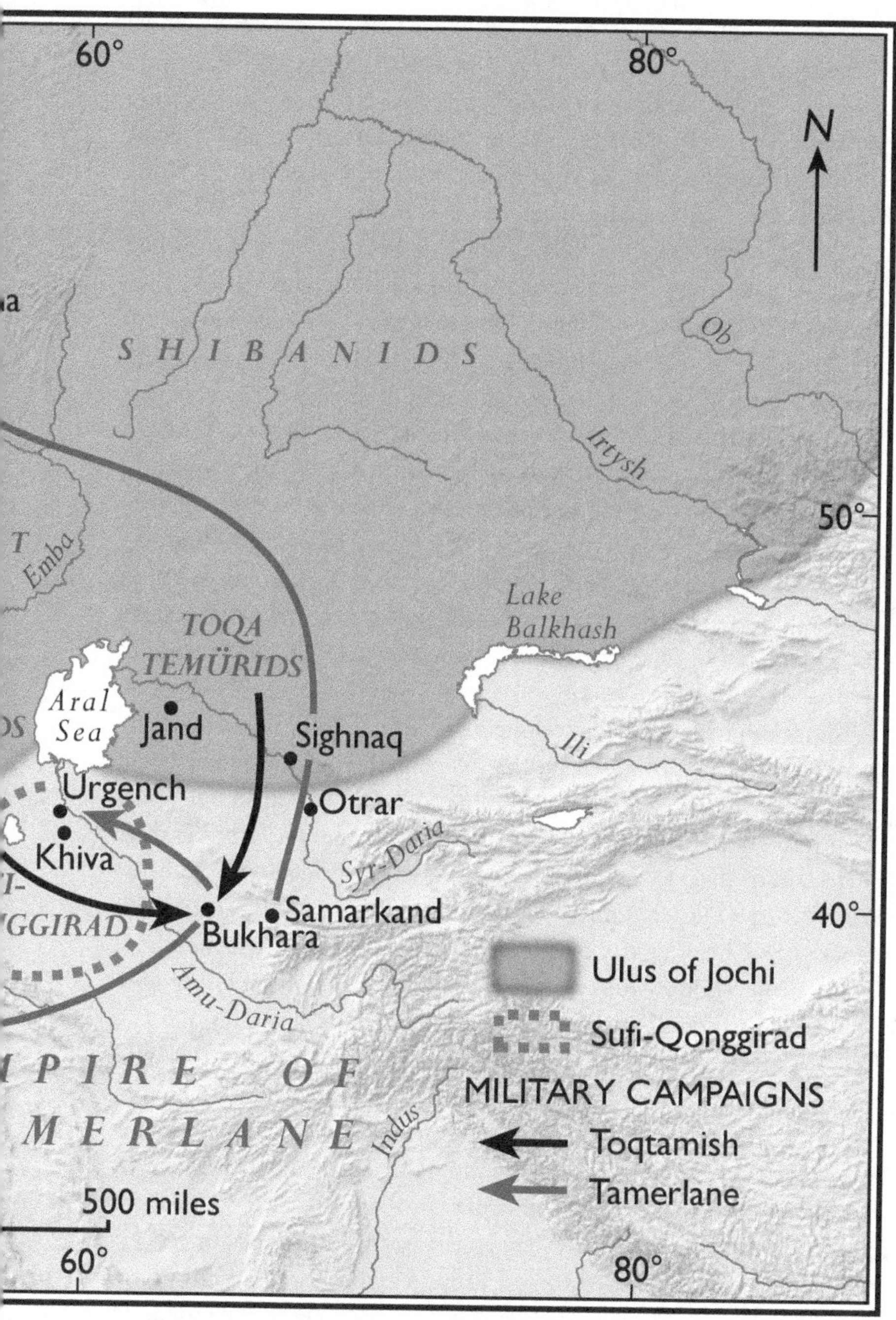

The Horde, c. 1380–1390, showing the major campaigns of Toqtamish and Tamerlane, as well as the new territory of Poland-Lithuania, taken from the Horde in the west.

authoritarian instincts. He demanded unconditional support from the descendants of Toqa Temür and their followers, and any defiance could be met with harsh punishment.[1] Urus's violent ways earned himself consequential enemies. In particular, Urus's murder of Toy Khoja, a fellow Toqa Temürid chieftain and rival for the khanship, resulted in a blood feud that eventually brought an end to Urus's reign.

The agent of revenge was Toqtamish, Toy Khoja's son. Not only had Urus murdered Toqtamish's father, but the khan had also vitiated Toqtamish's family's rights by forcing their *els,* their hereditary peoples, to join Urus's horde. Els were subjugated peoples gifted to various chieftains as a result of conquests; to strip a family of its els was an extremely harsh punishment, the imposition of a kind of social death and a means of disempowering a whole princely lineage. But even though Toqtamish was deprived of his natural base of support, he found ways to enhance his strength and popularity. He was a descendent of Jochi through his father and was a Qonggirad through his mother; Toqtamish was thus well positioned to call on the assistance of wealthy and influential people. The Qonggirad of northern Khwarezm had many warriors to place at his disposal.[2]

Toqtamish had no keshig to inherit, so instead he built his own. He spent the early 1370s wandering the steppe gathering young horsemen without ties. As long as they were willing to fight, Toqtamish welcomed them into his warband. The warriors set out to plunder Urus's camps, herders, and villages, and as they gained booty they attracted more followers.[3] But while Toqtamish's independence and guerilla tactics unnerved Urus, his warriors could not by themselves threaten the khan. Urus's army was known to be one of the best of the times. It had conducted successful military operations in the lower Volga and taken Sarai. Urus even held Sarai long enough to mint coins there. Toqtamish would need further backing to contend with the khan, so he turned to a powerful neighbor. Around 1375 Toqtamish allied with an emir who was known to his contemporaries as Temür al-Lank, Temür the Lame. In the West he is usually called Tamerlane.

Like Mamai, the powerful beg in the west, Tamerlane started his career as an officer in the Mongol Empire and married a Chinggisid princess. Also like Mamai, Tamerlane took advantage of the bulqaq to become a regional leader, gaining command of the western Chagatayids, who were centered on wealthy Transoxiana. When Toqtamish's envoys

Rulers of India's Mughal Dynasty, with Tamerlane at center (India, c. 1707–1712). The Central Asian conqueror and other leaders of the late Mongol Empire were revered by succeeding dynasties, which sought legitimacy by emphasizing connections to Chinggis Khan and his descendants. (Pictures from History / Bridgeman Images)

reached Tamerlane, he was busy campaigning against the eastern Chagatayids, deep in their territory beyond the Syr-Daria River. Tamerlane's war position made alliance with Toqtamish a good choice. Tamerlane's forces were committed in the east, leaving his northern flank relatively open to the expansionist Urus. Sighnaq, Urus's capital, was just over the old Chagatayid-Jochid border, heightening the potential threat. But with Toqtamish's help, Tamerlane's remaining uncommitted troops could stiffen the border. Recognizing that each had something to offer the other, Tamerlane and Toqtamish joined forces. Tamerlane provided men, horses, and weapons. More importantly, he agreed to let Toqtamish occupy territory around Otrar, a possession of Tamerlane's. Sitting only a few miles south of Sighnaq, Otrar was strategically located for a defense against Urus. By the same token, Otrar was an ideal mustering point and location from which to launch attacks.[4]

As Toqtamish gained strength, he received more recruits from among the Shirin, Barin, Arghun, and Qipchaq peoples attached to Urus. These groups were the hereditary peoples of Toqtamish's father—the els assigned to him by right, who had been coerced into joining Urus's horde. Complaining of oppression by the khan and his sons, those remaining in Urus's horde were prepared to break off and join Toqtamish, so he and his commanders worked out a plan to siphon the els away during Urus's migration to the summer pastures. Urus's guards would be preoccupied during the mass migration, allowing Toqtamish to lead his peoples away from Urus's horde. The plan worked, but, unsurprisingly, it was not long before Urus realized that large numbers of his herders had disappeared. The khan gathered his fastest warriors and pursued the escapees. Urus and his men fell on Toqtamish's camp in the middle of the night, but they were outnumbered and Toqtamish's warriors were determined to defend themselves. Urus was killed during the fighting; locals later reported that Toqtamish's twelve-year-old son Jalāl al-Dīn delivered the death blow. In the aftermath, Toqtamish eliminated Urus's sons one after the other. Finally, around 1378, Toqtamish announced total victory. From Sighnaq, the center of the Blue Horde—not from the lower Volga, the center of the White Horde and the traditional seat of Jochid power—Toqtamish declared himself khan of ulus Jochi.[5]

Toqtamish never assembled the Jochids or organized a quriltai to confirm his office. Nonetheless, he won respect across the Horde and the steppe at large. Word spread that Toqtamish had *farr,* a Persian concept similar to sülde—the divine favor that made strong leaders and strong states. Toqtamish's territory grew quickly, as Jochid begs fell in behind him. Tired of the Horde's infighting, they pushed for union and gave their approval of a khan who seemed to have Tengri and Allah on his side. By the close of 1378, Toqtamish controlled most of the cities on the middle and lower Syr-Daria, an important region for camel, cattle, and horse breeding as well as trade, because the transcontinental road crossing the region was still partially active. In 1379 the Sufi-Qonggirad regime allied with and subordinated themselves to Toqtamish, and in the following year he mastered the entire southeastern frontier of the Horde.[6]

The new khan's next move would be northward, into the Volga Valley and Sarai. Toqtamish convinced the Shibanids, descendants of Jochi's fifth son, to support his conquest of the lower Volga. The Shibanids were the powerful chiefs of Ibir-Sibir, a vast region in western Siberia, and allies of the Qonggirad. With Shibanid support, Toqtamish was able to capture Sarai in a matter of months. Thereafter, in late 1380, Toqtamish targeted the western hordes, under Mamai's direct leadership. The Shibanids were happy to join this campaign as well. They did not trust Mamai, who had rejected their claim to the Batuid throne.[7]

To eliminate Mamai, Toqtamish followed a sophisticated plan based on parallel military and political operations. The military project was relatively simple, as Mamai's forces had been decimated by the plague and by the prince of Moscow in September 1380. Taking advantage of the situation, Toqtamish sent warriors into Mamai's camp in October. The attack took place on the banks of the Kalka River, where the Mongols had smashed the Russians and the Qipchaqs more than a century and a half earlier. Mamai's camp was destroyed, but he managed to escape to his stronghold in Crimea.[8]

While Mamai was licking his wounds, Toqtamish isolated him politically by inviting the support of the western begs. They had backed Mamai previously but had nothing to lose by changing sides: they would be allowed to keep their positions as councilors, tax collectors, ambassadors, and city governors. Not only that, but by joining Toqtamish the begs would hasten an end to civil war, which harmed everyone. The benefit for Toqtamish was twofold because the defection of the begs would undermine Mamai while providing Toqtamish a turnkey administration in the west, with skilled secretaries, accountants, guards, minters, and judges who knew the region.

One of the first to accept the deal was the beg of the Crimean city of Solkhat, whom the khan immediately delegated to conclude an agreement with the Genoese consul of Caffa. In 1375 Mamai had wrested from the Genoese eighteen locations surrounding Sudak, but now Toqtamish and his Solkhat beg offered to restore the territory to the Genoese. The Genoese were eager to negotiate, as the agrarian lands around Sudak were critical to their trade operations. During Janibek's siege in the 1340s, the Caffans had gone hungry for weeks; they learned that fortifying their harbors was meaningless as long as they could not control their agricultural countryside. In exchange for generous land grants, Toqtamish asked the Genoese for their loyalty, and they provided it. In late 1380 or early 1381, the fugitive Mamai came to Caffa seeking shelter, but loyalty meant refusing to harbor the khan's enemies, so the Genoese seized Mamai and kept him hostage. After the beg of Solkhat signed a written treaty swearing to uphold the khan's agreement with the Genoese, the Genoese fulfilled their loyalty obligation by killing Mamai on the spot.[9]

In fact, the Genoese got much more than land for their loyalty. They also received rights to travel freely across the Horde's territories; to retrieve slaves, cattle, and horses taken from them; and to be reimbursed for losses due to war and robbery. Finally, the Genoese asked the khan to mint new silver coins of better quality, a request that was soon satisfied as part of monetary reforms enacted by Toqtamish. This agreement was the first of three the Genoese were to seal with Toqtamish. All of them were written in Mongol script, continuing the tradition of Chinggis, and certified with the large square seal of the khan, embossed in gold. The agreements were translated into Latin and Genoese by experienced interpreters who also knew Qipchaq, Persian, and Slavic—all the main languages of the Horde.[10]

Toqtamish's concessions to the Genoese may seem extravagant, yet, for the khan, the deal was worth making. Mamai's head was a precious trophy because it erased the key power competitor within the Horde. And, more immediately, eliminating Mamai pacified southern Crimea, allowing Toqtamish to focus on the rebellious Russian princes: they had fought Mamai and won, and now they were Toqtamish's problem. In August 1382 Toqtamish successfully besieged Moscow and partially burnt it—a show of strength that reminded Dmitrii Donskoi that he was still the Horde's vassal. Dmitrii begged for mercy, and Toqtamish forgave him on the conditions that he deliver the tribute and that his eldest son visit the khan's horde as a hostage.

Toqtamish was a canny strategist. He allowed his enemies to tear each other apart before delivering the final blow—for example, taking advantage of Mamai's defeat by Moscow before turning around and attacking Moscow in order to assert his own authority. Toqtamish also exercised patience, first handling Urus, then Mamai, then Dmitrii. Though Toqtamish was an easterner who had grown up disconnected from western politics, he quickly grasped that Crimea was the key to power in the west, so he courted the Genoese. And he knew how to peel the western begs away from Mamai. The rewards were considerable:

Urus and Mamai were eliminated, the Genoese were loyal, and the Russians were paying tribute again.[11]

The consolidation of power under Toqtamish was a creative response to the collapse of the Ordaids and Batuids, enabling the Horde to escape a deeper crisis of the kind that befell the Ilkhanids after the death of Abū Saʿīd. The creativity lay in the unprecedented nature of Toqtamish's ascent: the Toqa Temürids had never steered the Horde before. It was not inevitable that secondary Jochid lines would emerge to take control, or that one would take the lead without war against the others. Yet, at some point in the 1370s, the Jochids collectively acknowledged the primacy of two lineages, the Shibanids and Toqa Temürids. Only members of these two lines had the pedigree and popular support to claim Batu's throne, and the Toqa Temürids were clearly first among equals.[12]

There are several reasons why the Toqa Temürids emerged as the primary lineage. First, they benefited from the fact that Toqa Temür had been Jochi's youngest son. In the steppe inheritance system, the youngest was the "hearth keeper," who watched over his parents' belongings until those belongings were his to inherit. Analogizing from the family to the state was a constant among the Mongols, and by this logic the Toqa Temürids were the keepers of Jochi's ulus, gifted with the ability to protect and unify the family members.[13]

A second Toqa Temürid advantage lay in the charismatic leader who solidified their lineage. Toqtamish's history made him a sympathetic figure; others wanted to rally around him and see his moral rights vindicated. His military successes also elevated his stature, helping him to win over the Shibanids and motivating them to withdraw from the competition for succession.

A third and final source of the Toqa Temürids' advantage was their beneficial alliances. In general, the Muslim Toqa Temürids and Shibanids both enjoyed good relations with Islamic clergy and elites, earning them friends in Khwarezm, Crimea, the Caucasus, Siberia, and the Volga region. But the Toqa Temürids also allied with the Qonggirad, making them considerably stronger militarily. And Qonggirad support probably helped to mollify the Shibanids. The Qonggirad were well positioned to mediate between the two Jochid houses, for the Qonggirad had marriage partnerships with both. With the Shibanids in Toqtamish's camp, he could be consensus candidate for Batu's throne, enjoying support from across the Jochid houses and the begs—of course, with exception of certain power rivals, such as Mamai.

This, then, was the solution to the long political crisis that followed Birdibek's death: a profound change in the hierarchy of Jochid lineages. Since Qonichi, no ruler from the Blue Horde had directed ulus Jochi. Now it was not just easterners but also Toqa Temürids in charge. After Toqtamish took power, his name was praised every Friday during the Muslim prayer service and appeared on every silver coin produced in the Horde.[14]

Defection

In 1385 Toqtamish made his first diplomatic overture to the Mamluk sultan al-Zāhir Barqūq. The Mongol envoys brought Barqūq slaves, hawks, and seven types of cotton textiles. It had been ten years since the Horde and the sultanate last had diplomatic contact, and the khan wanted to revive the alliance. In the past the Jochids and Mamluks had joined against the Ilkhanids; now, the Horde faced a new enemy with designs on the Ilkhanid territories. Tamerlane, Toqtamish's erstwhile partner, was on the Horde's Caucasian doorstep, having launched military operations into Azerbaijan. By the time Toqtamish approached the sultan, Tamerlane had already conquered Tabriz and other locations. Northern Khwarezm was another friction point, as the Jochid-Qonggirad alliance there disrupted Tamerlane's planned conquest of the region.[15]

The imminent danger to the Horde was that of a blockade, strangling the Jochids as Hülegü once had. By 1385 Transcaucasian passage was critical to the Horde's exchange with the Mediterranean world, because in that year, the Genoese rebelled once more, waging war on Solkhat and preventing access to the sea route via Crimea. But traders did not have to rely on Crimea if instead they could exploit the Derbent-Shirvan pass, the overland connection from the Horde to Syria, Anatolia, and Egypt. However, access to the pass was no certainty, because Tamerlane's forces stood on the south side of the pass, with the potential to block the Jochids' land route just as the Genoese blocked the harbors.[16]

The Mamluks were similarly concerned about the effects of an embargo, as importing slave warriors remained crucial to their military capabilities. Barqūq, himself a former slave, acquired some 5,000 slave warriors of his own during his sixteen years as sultan. His numerous emirs purchased slaves by hundreds. But the situations in Crimea and the Caucasus endangered the slave trade on two fronts. Exports from Caffa, the Mamluks' largest supplier of slaves, had ground to a halt, and Tabriz, the second-largest supplier, was in the hands of Tamerlane. Given Tamerlane's ambitions to expand across the Middle East and establish leadership over Muslims, the Mamluks could not trust him to make decisions in their interests. Tamerlane was Barqūq's main competitor, threatening the sultanate economically and politically.[17]

Toqtamish's plan was to multiply military fronts by launching simultaneous attacks from the northern Caucasus, eastern Anatolia, and Syria, trapping Tamerlane's army between the Jochid and Mamluk forces. The Mamluk sources do not confirm that Barqūq promised to support the strategy, but we do know that he was prepared to take actions against Tamerlane. The same sources record that Barqūq allied with the Turkmen confederation of the Qara Qoyunlu against Tamerlane and sent forces against Tamerlane in Aleppo in 1387. As for Toqtamish, in winter 1385–1386, he led his warriors against Derbent, pushed through the Caucasian pass, and plundered Tabriz. Tamerlane replied with a counterattack and fought Toqtamish to a stalemate, possibly involving the negotiation of a ceasefire. But even with a truce in effect, Tamerlane continued to pursue his conquest of Azerbaijan.[18]

During the winter of 1387–1388, Toqtamish resumed the fight, challenging Tamerlane on their other common border in Transoxiana. The khan gathered forces from northern Khwarezm and the middle Syr-Daria, crossed the Amu-Daria, and laid siege to Bukhara. Tamerlane sent troops to reinforce the city, but as they approached, the Jochids lifted the siege and went on to plunder the surrounding region. In 1389 Toqtamish's and Tamerlane's troops clashed on the banks of the Syr-Daria, probably several times. The forces were well-matched, and the war season ended with another stalemate.[19]

Tamerlane needed help to break the impasse, and he got it from within the Horde itself. His chief collaborator was a beg named Edigü, leader of the powerful Manghit clan. The Manghit were among the secondary Mongol groups that made large gains during the succession crisis of the 1360s and 1370s. When Toqtamish took the throne, Manghit territory stretched from the Ural River to the Emba and included the important city of Saraijuq. The Manghit benefited from their location on the frontier between Batu's and Orda's territories, where the Manghit welcomed nomadic families from both sides seeking peace and protection amid the infighting of the bulqaq. By the time Toqtamish and Tamerlane were at war, Edigü was said to have 200,000 horsemen. That number is likely an exaggeration, but it reveals how strong the Manghit were perceived to be. Edigü was not only a powerful ally, he was also a motivated one. He resented Toqtamish for favoring the Qonggirad and the western begs, who monopolized the Horde's most lucrative positions to the detriment of the eastern Manghit. Working with Tamerlane offered Edigü an opportunity to undermine Toqtamish; Edigü visited Tamerlane in secret and proposed a new war plan.[20]

With Edigü's guidance, Tamerlane carefully prepared his next move. In January 1391 he launched a large-scale campaign, and after an exhausting five-month chase, his troops met Toqtamish's in a major battle at the confluence of the Qundurcha and Volga rivers. Unexpectedly lacking the support of the Manghit warriors, the Jochid army was smashed. Tamerlane ordered the torching of the khan's camp, captured women and children as spoils, and confiscated Toqtamish's gold, jewelry, herds, tents, and carts. But that was all. Tamerlane had no intention of conquering the Horde; he took his substantial booty and headed back to his headquarters in Samarkand.[21]

The war, however, was far from over. Toqtamish withdrew northward, to the middle Volga region, where he reorganized his headquarters. He must have moved quickly because by 1393 he had recovered enough authority and military strength to go dunning his vassals for tribute payments. In particular, Toqtamish reminded the Polish-Lithuanian king Vladislav Jagiello to send tax receipts and to "let the merchants circulate on the roads" for the benefit of the "great ulus."[22] (Jagiello had inherited the throne of Lithuania from his father and in 1385 was invited to take the Polish throne as well. He ruled alongside Vytautas, his cousin, who was grand duke of Lithuania.) The exchange between the Horde and Poland-Lithuania had grown more important, given that Tamerlane controlled the Caucasian door and the Genoese hindered the Crimean one.[23]

By 1394 Toqtamish had regained enough power to campaign in the Caucasus again. He sent his ambassadors to the Mamluk sultan and the Ottoman sultan Bayezid. Together they discussed the terms of a joint attack on Tamerlane. No known joint attack occurred, but both the Mamluks and Ottomans stationed forces to fight Tamerlane in advance of Toqtamish's own attack, in winter 1394–1395. The khan's troops entered the Derbent-Shirvan pass and in early spring 1395 met Tamerlane's army on the Terek River, north of Derbent. Toqtamish lost the battle and fled northward with Tamerlane's horsemen on his heels. According to the Mamluk ambassador to the khan's court, Toqtamish was defeated because of the defection of one of his main commanders. A beg named Aktau, who had his own political dispute with Toqtamish, suddenly left the battlefield with his thousands of warriors.[24]

Once again Toqtamish had lost the support of a key beg, giving Tamerlane the edge he needed. But this time the results were far worse. Rather than simply plunder Toqtamish's camp, Tamerlane also scattered the khan's army and his peoples and spent the whole summer and following winter raiding the Jochid hordes and cities. New Sarai, Hajji Tarkhan, and Azaq, including the Venetian district of Tana, suffered so badly that contemporary observers thought they would never recover. It was clear to all the major players in the west that the geopolitical situation had changed. The Mamluk ambassador hurried to escape the region, heading for Caffa where he expected to find a ship to leave for Egypt. But the Genoese saw no reason to do favors for the ally of the defeated Toqtamish. Indeed, the Genoese had already sent Tamerlane messengers carrying gifts of precious furs in hopes that he would spare their city. The Genoese extracted 50,000 dirhams from the ambassador in exchange for safe passage, and when Tamerlane's troops devastated Crimea in August 1395, they left Caffa untouched.[25]

Exploiting Toqtamish's retreat, Edigü the Manghit extended their realm westward. Around 1397 Edigü allied with Temür Qutluq, a Toqa Temürid and his sister's son, and installed him on the Jochid throne. Edigü became beglerbeg and commanded the army. From the banks of the Dnieper, probably near Kremenchuk in modern-day Ukraine, Edigü subdued the western begs. He took the Crimean cities and villages and brought the Genoese rebels to heel.[26]

Toqtamish, his warriors, and their families withdrew to southern Russia and Lithuania, where Vytautas, the Lithuanian ruler, offered them herding grounds. Together with Vytautas, Toqtamish planned to reconquer the Horde. Their combined army made several successful operations in the lower Dniester and in Crimea, and in 1399 they crossed the Dnieper to negotiate with Edigü. But Edigü refused and sent a small but determined force into battle on the banks of the Vorskla, a tributary of the Dnieper. Despite being outnumbered, the beg's army inflicted a humiliating defeat on Toqtamish, his men, and his Lithuanian and Polish troops.[27]

Ever tenacious and resourceful, Toqtamish went back to old friends in an effort to restore himself to the throne. He joined with the Shibanids and created an embryonic power in Ibir-Sibir, in southwestern Siberia. In 1405 Toqtamish sent an embassy to Tamerlane seeking to ally against Edigü. Despite years of fighting with Toqtamish, Tamerlane apparently agreed to restore the alliance the two had built some twenty-five years earlier, because at this point the Manghit were much more dangerous than the former khan. Yet there would be no redemption for Toqtamish. Both he and Tamerlane died that year.[28]

After Toqtamish

It is commonly said that Tamerlane destroyed the Horde, but this view is wrong for two reasons. First, the fall of Toqtamish was primarily a result of internal competition from the Manghit. Second, the Horde was not destroyed. It survived even the turmoil of the late fourteenth and early fifteenth centuries.

On the first point, even Persian sources, which all favor Tamerlane, emphasize that Toqtamish lost the war because he was unable to keep the nomadic elite on his side. The results included the damaging defection of 1391 and the ruinous defection of 1395. The khan had shown himself to be a capable leader on the battlefield and in foreign affairs, playing the game of diplomacy with all the enthusiasm and ability of esteemed predecessors like Berke and Möngke-Temür. Where Toqtamish faltered was in the realm of internal politics. He privileged the western begs in order to win them away from Mamai, a decision that made sense in the late 1370s and early 1380s. But Toqtamish failed to adjust in light of the Manghit's growing power, making an enemy of Edigü. What brought down Toqtamish, then, was not an inability to stand up to Tamerlane but rather his attempt to rule the Horde without the consent of the Manghit.[29]

On the second point—the claim that the Horde was destroyed—it is simply not the case that Toqtamish took the Horde with him into defeat. The material world of the Horde recovered relatively quickly; ruined places were rebuilt, and the centers of transcontinental trade were largely restored. In fact, the only significant city that was permanently abandoned after the war was New Sarai, but its downfall had begun with Birdibek's death, well before Tamerlane's campaign in the lower Volga. The recovery of the western steppe was obvious to fifteenth-century travelers, merchants, and diplomats, who wrote lively accounts of the wealth and activity of the region. There was regular exchange between Moscow and the Volga Valley, and Kazan emerged as a hub of the fur trade. Hajji Tarkhan, half-destroyed by Tamerlane, rose from the ashes to become a powerhouse in the salt trade by the 1430s. Astrakhan, as Hajji Tarkhan came to be known, continued to develop over the centuries and is today one of the major population centers of southern Russia.[30]

The settlements near the mouth of the Don also survived Tamerlane's onslaught. Tana continued to operate as a trade harbor; according to Josafa Barbaro, a Venetian merchant based in Tana, there were hundreds of thousands of nomads living in the lower Volga in the 1430s:

> As soon as the horde is lodged, incontinently they unlade their baggage, leaving large ways between their lodgings. If it be in the winter the beasts are so many that they make wonderful moor and if it be in summer spreading much dust. . . . In this army are many artisans, as clothiers, smiths, armourers, and of all other crafts and things that they need. And if someone demanded whether they go like the Gypsies or not, I answered, no. For [their places of residence], saving that they are not walled, seemed very great and faire cities.[31]

Yet, if it is wrong to claim that the Horde ended with Toqtamish's 1395 defeat at the Terek River, it is true that much changed in the wake of Toqtamish's wars with Tamerlane and the Manghit. In the late fourteenth century, the Kiyad and the Qonggirad had been the most powerful Mongol clans in the Horde, but with the rise of Tamerlane and the Manghit, they were evicted from the political scene. Tamerlane conducted a total of five campaigns in Khwarezm against the Qonggirad, sapping their military strength, draining their treasury, and eventually extinguishing their leadership class. Qonggirad survivors integrated into other clans according to the familiar social process of the steppe. Indeed, the descendants of Tamerlane and the Manghit absorbed many Qonggirad. They would never return to power.[32]

Another area of change was the Horde's political system, on which Toqtamish left a deep mark. Most importantly, he created new institutions. The keshig took on a new shape as the ordo-bazaar. It was still a huge mobile administration that accompanied the people and their herds and governed the regime. But the heads of the administration were now the khan's hereditary peoples; the governing council, taking the place of the keshig elders, comprised four qarachu begs, one each from the Shirin, Barin, Arghun, and Qipchaqs. This governing council had remarkable new powers: its decisions could supersede even those of the quriltai. In effect, a council of qarachu begs had become sovereign. They could depose the khan when it suited them, so that suddenly the keshig-equivalent (the ordo-bazaar) was permanent, while the khan was replaceable.[33]

Toqtamish also introduced change by redirecting tarkhan privileges away from the clergy. The purpose of the status was unchanged: it was still used to win the loyalty of influential people by giving them benefits that ensured their investment in the regime. But tarkhan status was no longer primarily for faith leaders. Toqtamish was the first khan to dispense tarkhan privileges mainly to local elites. Toqtamish's generosity recalled that of Batu and Ögödei. To appease the Manghit, Toqtamish gave Edigü tax immunity and vast herding grounds east of the Volga, which only further enriched an entrenched enemy. To conciliate the Genoese, Toqtamish gave them lands in southern Crimea and much more, and, in return for military help, he granted Vytautas all the southern lands inhabited by the Ruthenians, Eastern Slavic peoples. In these cases, Toqtamish was not simply granting land-use rights: he was giving away sovereignty over the land. The Polish-Lithuanian rulers would rely on the khan's land grant in the course of their competition with Moscow over the Ruthenian lands. The Russians claimed the territory was theirs, yet the Polish-Lithuanians could point to the khans' land donation.[34]

Despite the failure of the Vorskla battle, the alliance between Toqtamish, Jagiello, and Vytautas shaped a "loyal brotherhood and eternal friendship," as Polish-Lithuanian and post-Jochid rulers put it in the letters and treaties they would regularly exchange in the sixteenth century. Under Vytautas's rule, thousands of Muslim nomads that belonged to Toqtamish's hereditary peoples settled in Lithuania. The French diplomat Guillebert de Lannoy, visiting the region in the early fifteenth century, saw "Tatars" in and around the city of Trakai. These became the Lithuanian Tatars, the Lipka community, whose descendants still live today in Europe.[35] The alliance with Poland-Lithuania was also critical to maintenance of the economic exchange with Europe. The nomads exported animals to Persia and parts of Europe along the via de Polonia, the land road tracing the northern littoral of the Black Sea through Poland and Moldavia. Indeed, after 1453, the connection with Poland-Lithuania became the Horde's key trade artery, for in that year the Ottomans conquered Constantinople, establishing control over the straits and over the connections between the Black Sea and the Mediterranean world.

The natives of the western steppe remembered Toqtamish as a unifying figure. In particular, he was seen as bringing together the Blue and White hordes. Until recently historians looking back on the history of the Jochids regarded the Blue and White hordes as having been thoroughly separate regimes until Toqtamish brought them together. This view was inaccurate; other leaders had also commanded the whole ulus of Jochi. But it is true that Toqtamish overcame generations of accrued animosity in knitting the Horde back together. For this reason, it is not hard to see why many in the western steppe considered Toqtamish a founding figure.

Perhaps Toqtamish's most important legacy is that he left power while still living. In the thirteenth century, the khan remained on the throne until he died, after which there might be a lengthy interregnum followed by a quriltai, which established a successor on the basis of the consensus-driven governing traditions established by Chinggis Khan. Throughout the fourteenth century, too, the khan died on the throne, but his death would be followed by acrimonious disputes and political purges instead of an election based on negotiation. By the end of the fourteenth century, however, the khan could experience political death while still breathing air and even dreaming of a return to the throne. This was a true novelty of Toqtamish's reign, one that solidified the shift in the balance of power from the khan to the begs. Under the previous, lineage-focused approach, the office of the khan was identical with the person who occupied it, and only when unoccupied could the throne be legitimately taken by another. Begs could help seat a khan, but they couldn't unseat one without instigating a blood feud. Now, with legitimacy determined primarily by begs rather than lineage, a khan could be removed from power and the throne transferred to another, theoretically without violence.

In fact Toqtamish was removed violently, but it is critical to keep in mind that, after the battle of the Vorskla River, Edigü felt no urgent need to kill Toqtamish. The khan's political death was enough, as the throne did not need to be physically vacant in order for a succession to occur. This proved to be the durable solution to the problem of political purges. From Toqtamish's time onward, the Jochids avoided fratricide. By acknowledging the principle of their leader's symbolic death, they enabled constructive institutional innovations. The Toqa Temürids and the Shibanids would remain the principal ruling houses in Central and Western Asia until the nineteenth century, in no small part because they avoided hollowing out their lineages as the Batuids had.

A New Generation

Toqtamish dueled with Tamerlane, but the winning party was the Manghit. Edigü's influence grew and spread across the majority of the Jochid hordes. His prestige was based in part on his status as beglerbeg, a role that he earned through demonstrated command skill; in part on his proximity to the Toqa Temürids; and in part on his appeal as a devout Muslim. Edigü's wife made the pilgrimage to Mecca in 1416 with a retinue of 300, and Edigü surrounded himself with Sufis throughout his life. His career as a major politician lasted three decades.

Edigü left an enduring legacy. Peoples tracing themselves to him carried the ways of the Jochids forward in time, forming a key link between the Horde and the states that came after it. It is due to the cultural and political transmission effected by Edigü and other leading begs that, in important respects, the Horde never truly fell, even if its name was eventually erased from maps. One of the vehicles for the endurance of Jochid political and social life was Edigü's horde, which, after his death in 1419, became known as the Nogay horde. Historians do not know how to explain the connection between the names Manghit and Nogay. We don't know what ties the Manghit to Nogay, the first Jochid beglerbeg and one of the transformative figures in the Horde's history. Yet the equation of the Manghit and the Nogay horde is clear in the fifteenth-century sources.[36]

The zenith of the Manghit-Nogay horde came in the late fifteenth century and the first half of the sixteenth. The horde's authority was strongest north and east of the Caspian, including in the northern Khwarezm region. Edigü's descendants inherited the title and position of beglerbeg and had substantial impact on the nomadic powers that took shape in the lower river valleys and the areas of the Jochid cities between the 1430s and the 1460s. Edigü's heirs took part in the leadership of a new generation of hordes: more numerous than their predecessors, more autonomous, and even more mobile.[37] The hordes included the trans-Volga horde (sometimes known as the Great Horde), and the hordes of Kazan, Astrakhan, Qasimov, Siberia, Crimea, and Khiva. Later these hordes were known as Tatar khanates. The hordes were led by khans in association with qarachu elites bearing the titles of beg, emir, and *mirza*. Collectively the hordes counted themselves members of the same *ulugh ulus*—great ulus. Their people considered Batu, Özbek, Janibek, Toqtamish, and other prestigious Jochids their founders. All of the post-Jochid hordes were primarily Muslim.

One of these hordes, that of the Uzbeks, emerged from the Shibanids, with the support of the Manghit-Nogay. The first leader was the Shibanid Abū al-Khayr, who founded his own ulus in the former lands of the Blue Horde and was elected its khan in 1429. Edigü's grandson Waqqas Bey was a major backer of Abū al-Khayr and became the khan's beglerbeg. Waqqas Bey and Abū al-Khayr shared a key objective, as both sought to restore northern Khwarezm to the Jochids. They worked together to take the region back from the descendants of Tamerlane.[38] With the assistance of the Manghit, Abū al-Khayr occupied northern Khwarezm in 1430. In 1446 he conquered the cities of the lower and middle Syr-Daria and made Sighnaq his winter capital.

Abū al-Khayr was not the only one building a regime in the region, and his Uzbeks faced considerable competition and flux. In 1457, after

Abū al Khayr was defeated by the Mongol Oyirad, another rising force, the Manghit abandoned him. Thousands of Abū al-Khayr's former supporters, including Manghit, moved eastward to join two Toqa Temürids, Kiray and Janibek, who were establishing themselves in the Chu Valley. Kiray and Janibek later conquered the Qipchaq steppe and, in the early sixteenth century, their peoples became known as Qazaqs, a name that endures among the modern Kazakhs.[39] The abandonment of Abū al-Khayr left the Shibanid-Uzbek ulus in a precarious position, but the ulus did finally consolidate in 1500 under Abū al-Khayr's grandson, Muhammad Shībānī. Thus, by the early sixteenth century, the two chief lineages of the late Horde—the Shibanids and the Toqa Temürids—had founded two enduring peoples under new names. From the Shibanids arose the Uzbeks in northern Khwarezm and Transoxiana and from the Toqa Temürids arose the Qazaqs in the Chu Valley and Qipchaq steppe.

As for the Manghit-Nogay, they continued to flourish as an independent force, playing a power-balancing role reminiscent of the Horde's over the centuries. The Manghit-Nogay had a powerful army and were therefore valuable allies, but they husbanded their allegiances carefully, ensuring that partnerships would not undercut their own autonomy. Like the Horde under Möngke-Temür, Özbek, and Toqtamish, the Manghit-Nogay were canny diplomats. The Manghit-Nogay had abandoned Abū al-Khayr in the 1450s, but in the early sixteenth century the Manghit-Nogay agreed to ally with Muhammad Shībānī and support him as khan, while warning that their support would last only as long as Muhammad Shībānī allowed them "full freedom in affairs of state." As one of the strongest political and military forces in the Volga-Ural and Crimean regions, the Manghit-Nogay were sovereigns and kingmakers, not vassals. They operated an independent foreign policy and interacted closely with both the Russians and the Ottomans before splitting into the Great and Little Nogay Hordes, the former associated with Moscow and the latter with the Ottomans. The Manghit-Nogay, in their various guises, continued to be influential powers north and east of the Caspian into the eighteenth century, before they were absorbed by the expanding Russian Empire.[40]

The descendants of all the post-Jochid groups—including the Uzbeks, Qazaqs, and Manghit-Nogay—never stopped telling the stories of their forebears, influencing the cultures of Eastern Europe and West and Central Asia unto this day.

In a seventeenth-century tale from the *Chinggis Nāme,* the natives of the Volga-Ural steppe reformulated the biography of Chinggis Khan to better reflect the politics of their own communities. According to the tale, Chinggis's elder brothers threatened his life and forced him into hiding. Ten begs decided to search for him and to invite him to be their ruler. After a long ride, they finally found Chinggis, and, overcome with joy, celebrated by releasing their horses. To bring the khan home to his people, the begs built a cart for him to sit on and hitched themselves to the cart as if they were the horses. One beg, who was crippled and could not pull, sat next to Chinggis and drove the rest.[41]

The allegory of the begs illustrates the principle of nomadic government that emerged in the fifteenth century. Now it was the begs who chose their ruler, and his power came from exclusively from human exertion rather than supernatural power. The khan's authority came not from the favor Allah or Tengri showed his lineage but from the begs' support, which the khan maintained through the old Mongol ways: distribution of gifts and regular opportunities to accrue booty. If the khan failed to keep the begs on his side, they could depose him without fear of divine punishment. The story is one of shared governance, with the khan as the chief but unable to navigate the ship—or cart—of state by himself. As Mária Ivanics has shown, the cart driver in the story refers to the beglerbeg, a position that did not exist in Chinggis's time yet was written into the legend in light of later political developments. The cart, Ivanics argues, refers to the steppe peoples themselves.[42]

Historians commonly describe the fifteenth century as the period when the Jochid central power declined and fragmented. This is accurate as far as it goes. The problems that arise are interpretive. What does it mean when a central authority breaks down? The fifteenth century certainly looks like the end of something—both the Jochid and the wider Mongol order. Yet we need not see the downfall of a lineage as a kind of failure; in the steppe world, the Jochids and the Mongols were leaders in a long line of them, intersecting with other lines, all of them participating in the social vitality and political ingenuity of nomadic

20°
40°
60°
60°
Baltic Sea
Novgorod
HORDE OF KAZAN
Kazan
MUSCOVY
Moscow
Qasimov
HORDE OF QASIMOV
POLAND-LITHUANIA
Volga
Ural
Kiev
MANGHIT-NOGAY
TRANS-VOLGA HORDE
Saraijuq
Sarai
HORDE OF ASTRAKHAN
Hajji Tarkhan
Danube
HORDE OF CRIMEA
Black Sea
Aral Sea
Syr-Daria
Caspian Sea
OTTOMAN EMPIRE
Derbent
Tiflis
Urgench
Khiva
Amu-Daria
Baku
Tabriz
40°
AQ-QOYUNLU
Mediterranean Sea
Euphrates
Tigris
Baghdad
QAZAQS Nomadic or Semi-Nomadic Power
MING Sedentary Power
0
250
500
The Gulf
Nile
20°
40°
60°

The transformation of the Horde into several hordes and so-called khanates in the fifteenth century, including the Qazaqs, Uzbeks, and Manghit-Nogay.

peoples. The dissolution of Jochid power did not mean the nomadic world was falling apart; it was just one of many ways that the nomads responded to the absence of the larger protecting framework of the Mongol Empire. Jochi's ulus had to transform so as to solve its crisis and enable a return to security and prosperity. Dissolution was an organic mutation, analogous in some ways to what the economist Joseph Schumpeter called "creative destruction." Pekka Hämäläinen describes a similar process in his analysis of the Lakota people of North America, whom he calls "shapeshifters with a palpable capacity to adapt to changing conditions around them and yet remain Lakotas." The ulus of Jochi followed a related historical course.[43]

After the Horde dissolved, the nomads continued to sustain themselves through expansion and ethnic incorporation. Various nomadic groups had always joined the Mongols and broken away, and the Mongols themselves had constantly evolved culturally and socially in the course of assimilating others. The nomadic successors of the Horde also continued to develop new forms of hierarchy and decision making by adapting the models they inherited, just as Chinggis, Batu, Berke, Özbek, and Toqtamish had. It is true that the fifteenth century saw the end of something important: Mongol domination. But the steppe tradition outlived the conquerors who called upon it. The commercial infrastructure of the Mongol exchange also outlasted its creators, a patrimony that preserved trade between east and west and enabled the continuing dissemination of ideas and narratives across Eurasia. Nomadic concepts of rule and social and economic organization predated and survived both the Mongol and Jochid regimes, their durability resulting from the appreciation for change built into those concepts. For a time it was the Mongol Empire and its components—the Yuan, the Ilkhanids, the Horde, the ulus of Chagatay—that stewarded nomadic ways of life and governance. These political entities disappeared, but nomadic life and governance continued.

An ethos and culture built on movement must be flexible. It must adapt to the novel conditions the earth offers. The migration round means constant change: every few days a new scene, new terrain. Another river to cross. Another encounter with people different from oneself, with their own sense of what the world is and what their place is within that world. Nomads know this, and their empires embodied that knowledge.

Epilogue

THE HORDE'S MIRROR

Since his enthronement in 1462, Grand Prince Ivan of Moscow had not paid the tribute to the Horde. By the late 1470s, Ahmad Khan was ready to punish him for his neglect. Ahmad led the Volga horde, the symbolic center of the Jochid realms but no longer the focal point where the various hordes met for collective gatherings. Ahmad had a clear ambition to change this situation—to reunify ulus Jochi and to revive the imperial policy of previous khans, as demonstrated by his energetic diplomacy: Ahmad allied with Venice and the Lithuanians against the Ottomans, who were threatening Jochid positions in Crimea and the lower Danube.[1] But internal conflicts were keeping Ahmad from accomplishing his objectives. In 1478 Crimea fell into the hands of Mengli Giray, another Jochid khan, who was backed by the Ottomans. And Ivan was working to unify the lands north of the Oka River in order to strengthen Moscow's position. Ahmad needed to act quickly, lest his aspiration go unfulfilled. In 1479 he sent his tax collectors to Moscow to take what belonged to him, including arrears, but the grand prince refused to obey.[2] It would take a war to bring Ivan back into line. The lines of allegiance were drawn: Moscow and Crimea against Ahmad and Poland-Lithuania.[3]

In spring 1480 Ahmad and his warriors made camp on the banks of the Ugra River, about 150 miles south of Moscow, to await reinforcements promised by Kazimierz, the king of Poland-Lithuania. A Russian army arrayed on the other side of the river. The two sides waited for months; then, in November, Ahmad's forces departed. Ahmad Khan had learned that the princes of southwestern Russia had rebelled against Kazimierz and, led by Mengli Giray, were heading toward Sarai. Fearful of being trapped between Ivan's army and the southwestern princes, and recognizing that the approaching winter would subject his troops to shortages of food and clothing, Ahmad chose to withdraw. Yet, as was so often the case when Mongols retreated, there was a strategy at work. Ahmad believed he had in fact accomplished what he needed to: that he had so intimidated Ivan that the grand prince would pay the tribute and beg for peace. And Ivan was indeed worried. He wrote to his ally Mengli Giray in 1481, "Ahmad Khan came against me, but all-merciful God wanted to save us from him and did so."[4]

In Russian scholarship the "Stand on the Ugra River" is often presented as the event that ended the Tatar yoke in the Russian principalities. Yet, interestingly, in 1480 no Russian source claimed to be freed from the Tatar yoke. In the fifteenth century, the Grand Duchy of Moscow did not reject the political legacy of the Mongols. Quite the opposite: Moscow was an expanding state that looked to the Horde as a source of its legitimacy and its power. It would be another three-quarters of a century before the Stand on the Ugra River was perceived as a significant date in Muscovite history. Only in distant hindsight, after much political change in Russia, did Russians come to see the stand as the moment when their nation at last turned back the Mongols' supposedly damaging and ideologically suspect form of rule. Later historians even understood the stand as the end of the Horde.[5]

Next to the Ugra River event, historians have pointed to other dates that signified the end of the Horde: 1502, when Mengli Giray defeated Ahmad's son and successor in battle, and 1552–1556 when Ivan IV annexed Kazan and Astrakhan and thereby asserted a tenuous control over the Volga Valley.[6] The 1502 battle, however, was a contest among Jochids for control of the area around Sarai, which the nomads knew as *Takht eli,* the region of the throne and a sacred place.[7] A fight among Jochids, by itself, could hardly signify the end of the Horde. As for Ivan IV's

The 1480 stand on the Ugra river, from *Litsevoi Letopisnii Svod,* the *Illustrated Chronicle of Ivan the Terrible* (c. 1567). Russian nationalist historiography understands this event as the end of the Horde's domination in West Asia (the "Tatar yoke"), yet contemporaries neither perceived the standoff as a victory for Grand Prince Ivan of Moscow nor viewed the period of Mongol rule as a time of oppression. (National Library, St. Petersburg, Russia / Sputnik Bridgeman Images)

precarious conquests of Kazan and Astrakhan in the 1550s, by that time, ulus Jochi had already left the lower Volga. The expansionist Jochid hordes of the sixteenth century may have recognized the sülde of the lower Volga, but they had moved to different terrain.

Whatever date we choose to mark the end of the Horde, its lingering influence was clear even among the Muscovites. As Thomas Allsen puts it, "The Moscovite embrace of the Mongol legacy . . . was fraught with contradiction." On the one hand, Russians learned to disdain the Tatar yoke. On the other hand, Russian rulers never hesitated to call upon the Horde as its predecessor under the rubric of *translatio imperii*—the idea that the legitimacy of one empire may be passed to the next. Much as German kings saw their Holy Roman Empire as a successor to Rome and Byzantium, the Muscovites claimed to inherit the Horde's imperial right of conquest. Thus it was only when Ivan IV conquered the Volga Valley that he began to call himself an emperor. Specifically, he took the title of tsar, which Russians had hitherto used to describe and address the Horde's khans. Indeed, to further Moscow's claim as successor of the Jochid empire, Ivan IV always asked European rulers to include among his titles "tsar of Kazan and Astrakhan."[8] In the burgeoning Russian Empire, the Horde lived on as an important political force.

Fifteenth- and sixteenth-century Muscovite leaders respected the political legitimacy of individual Jochids and sought them out as governing partners. Around 1452 Ivan IV's grandfather granted lands on the left bank of the Oka River to Prince Qasim, a Toqa Temürid. The site became known as Qasimov City, the capital of a khanate created by the Russians. Ivan IV also sustained the Khanate of Qasim, which he used to interfere in the politics of the "Tatars." In 1575, when Ivan IV suddenly decided to abdicate the grand princely throne, he assigned Simeon Bekbulatovich, the khan of Qasimov and the great grandson of Ahmad Khan, as his successor. Ivan had no intention of leaving power permanently and retook the throne a year later. But it is not by coincidence that he chose a Jochid as the throne's caretaker. Simeon's status still embodied ruling legitimacy some two hundred years after Toqtamish had established the authority of the Toqa Temürid lineage. Ivan was acting like the begs who sat a khan on the throne and dismissed him when needed. After Ivan retook the throne, Simeon became kniaz of Tver and Torzhok for almost a decade.[9]

The Russian experience was mirrored across formerly Mongol-dominated lands. The political practices and concepts developed by Chinggis Khan and his descendants supplied the symbolic and institutional framework of the state in early-modern Iran, China, and Central Asia, along with Russia. Expansionist regimes such as the Ming, Safavids, Polish-Lithuanians, and Ottomans saw the Mongols as their imperial model.[10] But this legacy was eventually lost in transmission because of the anti-nomadic policies and ideologies that marked the Eurasian imperialism of the seventeenth through twentieth centuries. Latter-day empires understood agriculture and industry as superior to nomadism, economically and morally, and asserted that only from sedentary and urban circumstances could cherished notions of political consensus and religious freedom emerge. In the historical imagination fostered by liberalism, nationalism, and humanism—cast in Christian and Islamic terms—consensus-building and toleration were the exclusive province of the "civilized" and the "modern," leaving the Mongols mere pirates of the land. That Mongol rulers developed unique, effective, and humane approaches to political negotiation and social integration became unthinkable.

These qualities of Mongol rule were most obvious in the Horde, the region of the Mongol Empire that interacted most intensively with the future imperial powers. Why did these powers look longingly to Athens, Rome, Constantinople, and Baghdad while ignoring the Horde? The answer is implicit in the framing of the question: it was city life that nurtured empire and cultivated the virtues of imperial citizenship. Density brought people together, enabling the sparks of creativity that in turn produced progress and greatness. Never mind that the Mongols enabled, maintained, and grew the most extensive exchange in people, goods, and ideas in the premodern world.

If the Horde was forgotten, it was also because the Jochids left few obvious architectural and lexical markers of their imprint on the world. There was so much to learn from and admire in the ruins and the endurance of the great cities, whereas the Horde imparted to posterity scant signifiers of its dominance and grandeur. The Horde's cities, though significant for purposes of governance and economic growth, were more ephemeral than those of the Mediterranean and Africa. Lacking fortifications and built more of earth than of stone, Jochid cities left only meager ruins at which to marvel. Some Jochid sites did prove durable, but they were absorbed into Russia, their past overwritten. And there were no court chronicles to magnify the reign of the Jochid khans, which helps explain why the Horde has been less studied and celebrated than the Yuan and the Ilkhanids. The Toluids ensured a copious record of their deeds, inspiring centuries of subsequent research in China and the Middle East. With a bit of digging, though, the Jochids' legacy also becomes palpable—in the lands they once governed and in the wider world they touched. Even today, sites all over Russia, Eastern Europe, and Central Europe bear names that connect them to the Horde. And numerous Mongol words entered the Russian language in the thirteenth and fourteenth centuries and are still used: *dengi* (money), *tamozhnik* (customs officer), *tovar* (commodities), *bumaga* (paper). And, of course, "horde" exists in many languages.[11]

With this book, I wanted at first to challenge the typical "Manifest Destiny" narrative of the westward Mongol campaigns initially. It seemed impossibly simplistic that the Mongols were motivated by an unalloyed desire for conquest. In fact, Chinggis Khan had no grand design to conquer the world. Furthermore, it was never his goal to attack and loot cities but rather to submit the steppe nomads. The presumed rapine of Mongol conquest also had to be contested, because the available evidence shows that Chinggis was not a mass murderer. Instead, he assimilated dominated people into his Mongols. What mattered to Chinggis was to subjugate the Felt-Walled Tents, the nomadic peoples of East Asia. The strongest resistance Chinggis faced came not from cities and sedentary areas but from inside the regime he built in the steppe. This was the drama that shaped Chinggis, his people, and his descendants. The conquests of China, Iran, and Russia were side effects of an nomad-on-nomad war in which sedentary neighbors had interfered.

From these side effects emerge fascinating and novel interpretations of history. For one thing, nomadism is not necessarily resistant to state-building; in the case of the Jochids, the opposite is true: nomads built a complex and durable empire precisely in order to accomplish the goals inherent in their political theory. The Mongols wanted a regime that—analogous with their own communities and kinship groups—could absorb and harmonize everything social. But in the process of growing, they found themselves butting up against resistant populations. Rejecting the Mongols' all-embracing attitude toward religion, the military, work, and family, rebels arose against conscription and the Mongol labor and taxation regimes. This is a historical constant: every state-making project has its twin, the population that resists state power.[12] During the early Mongol Empire a number of Felt-Walled Tents refused incorporation in Chinggis's imperial matrix; their defiance triggered the conquest of West Asia and then Eastern Europe, provoking more resistance. Thus did settled people become antistatist rebels.

Importantly, that state was an equestrian one, constantly in motion. The Mongols defied the assertion that "an empire cannot be ruled on horseback," an old piece of advice given to Chinese conquerors and found in the *Shiji,* a monumental history composed in the late second and early first centuries BCE. The conception of nomads as warriors and settlers as administrators was widespread in Islamic political theory too. The fourteenth-century Arab historiographer Ibn Khaldun—a contemporary of Toqtamish and Tamerlane and one of the most cited medieval scholars—developed a philosophy of the history of dynastic states in which nomads became rulers, settled, and thereby lost their *'asabiyya:* their sense of solidarity or "group feeling." "The rulers of a state, once they have become sedentary, always imitate in their ways of living those of the state to which they have succeeded and whose condition they have seen and generally adopted," Ibn Khaldun wrote.[13] In other words, nomads could conquer, but their distinctiveness would soon dissolve as the conquerors took on the character of their settled subjects.

The Mongol trajectory, however, does not fit Ibn Khaldun's theory. The Mongols did not settle and did not become like their subjects; on the contrary, they absorbed foreign cultures into their own. The Mongols' power was mostly based on their ability to synthesize diversity. For the Jochids in particular, cultural change was not a one-way phenomenon. They did not become Slavs or Islamic-style rulers, even as they adopted Slavic peoples and Islamic principles. Nor did Jochid subjects necessarily become indistinguishable from Mongols, even though the Horde profoundly changed the peoples it dominated. The Jochids reinvented themselves without losing themselves. If we take Ibn Khaldun literally, then he was surely wrong—the dichotomy between nomadic and settled peoples does not exist. But there is merit in his sense of power as something mutable. Both ruler and ruled are changed by their relationship, or else the ruler does not last long.

One might defend the literal version of Ibn Khaldun on the grounds that, after their encounter with settled people, the Jochids did build cities, albeit less dense cities than those found in Egypt and Central Asia. This is true, of course, but Jochid city-building was not a form of sedentarization. Even as the Jochids built cities, powerful nomadic leaders still migrated seasonally. City-building reflected less cultural change than geopolitical strategy. The Jochids were not adopting a sedentary lifestyle but rather were using their cities to impose their laws on settled subjects and neighbors.[14] One lesson, then, is that pastoralism is not a primitive stage on the path to modernization. Pastoralism is a different choice, one that enabled the Jochids to fashion a unique imperial entity that mimicked no sedentary model. It is not by chance that the Jochid style of rule outlived the Horde in much of its former territory. The Manghit-Nogays, Tatars, Uzbeks, Qazaqs, and other heirs of the Horde kept nomadism alive, practicing its approaches to consensus, lineage, hierarchical sharing, and mobility not because these peoples were hidebound traditionalists or ignorant of the ways of settled peoples but because these approaches were proven to work.

One of the benefits of focusing on the Horde is the opportunity to emphasize its distinctiveness within the Mongol Empire. The Horde shared many common features with the other Chinggisid domains but showed significant differences too. These differences were among the sources of the Horde's endurance and of its special impact on the non-Mongol world.

What contributed first to the distinctiveness of the Horde was the location and ecology of the Jochid territories. The homeland of the Horde lay at the intersection of Asia, the Middle East, and Europe. The Jochids were a bridge between the Mongol Empire and the western frontier of the Eurasian steppe. From their unique position, the Jochids attracted exchange and allegiance with Hungarians, Bulgarians, Byzantines, Italians, Germans, Russians, Mamluks, and Greeks and later Ottomans, Poles, and Lithuanians. Other Mongol regimes were also trade-oriented, but not to the same extent as the Horde.

The Horde also was the most northerly of the Mongol uluses, which had dramatic effects on its development. As a northern power, the Horde dominated the fur trade; other Mongols took part, receiving and shipping furs in their territories, yet only the Jochids were able to extract wealth from fur production itself. But northerliness also came with constraints, and these too contoured the development of the Horde. The economies of northern societies under Jochid domination were less driven by human labor than those of the southern societies controlled by the Toluids, mainly because the north was less populous. In China and Iran, large labor forces were devoted to agriculture, while the economics of the Horde derived more from trade and capital.[15] Governance strategies in the north were correspondingly unique. The Horde could not simply tax its subjects; they were too few and their baseline productivity too minimal. Instead, the Horde invested in its subjects by means of land grants, legal protections, and urbanization projects, thereby enhancing the production of tradable commodities such as livestock, fur, salt, fish, wax, silver, and other nonagricultural goods.[16] For the Jochids, tribute was a transaction, with investments yielding productivity yielding tax revenue, enabling further investments. It is not clear that other Mongol regimes had a similarly transactional approach to tribute, although more study is needed in order to understand the breadth of Mongol tribute dynamics.

Most importantly, the Jochids developed distinctive technologies of governance. While the Toluids preferred direct rule, the Jochids ruled indirectly. As Pekka Hämäläinen notes, comparing Mongols to Comanches, the Jochids were able "to control resources without controlling societies and possess power without possessing space."[17] The Jochids' relation to the eastern Slavic peoples is a case in point. The khan administered his Russian principalities through local princes who interacted with his officers and his court only as needed. Thus there was no permanent Mongol administrative presence among the Russian population, and the political subordination of the principalities was relatively invisible on a day-to-day basis. This system nonetheless enabled political interaction when valuable and kept economic avenues open. Princes, clergy, officials, messengers, and merchants could easily travel back and forth between the principalities and the hordes for purposes of politics and trade.[18]

The relationship between the Jochids and their sedentary subjects is key to understanding the longevity of the Horde as compared to the Yuan and the Ilkhanids. Jochids and settlers typically were physically separate, but they were not alien to each other. They had frequent contacts during the seasonal rounds, when the hordes approached northern cities such as Bulgar and traversed the settlements along the river valleys. And though the Jochids and their subjects saw the world differently, they found ways to communicate, for instance through religious figures welcomed into the khans' courts and by preserving good relations with the boyars. The Horde headed off possible resentment among sedentary outsiders by providing them opportunities in Jochid settlements and at home. Artisans and traders from all over found work in Sarai and New Sarai, while monks, priests, and lay elites in the principalities owed their financial success to the khan's protection.

Finally, what was perhaps most distinctive about the Horde was the Jochids' ability to reconcile Islamic and Mongol ways of rule. The Horde used Mongol institutions such as tarkhan exemptions to uphold the administrative structures of khan and keshig while also investing in Islamic cultural and religious institutions. The impact on Islam itself was considerable, as the Jochids brought together diverse Muslim heritages within a single society. The Horde linked together Seljuq, Abbasid, Volga Bulgar, and Khwarezmian Islamic practices, fostering a sense of unity among otherwise-disparate peoples. It is due in part to the Horde that Sufism became such a powerful force in Central Asia. Yet the Islamization of the Horde after Berke did not blunt the advance of Christianity in the Jochid territories, and Buddhists continued to hold an important place among the Jochid elites and herders. And the same Mongols who adopted Islam, Christianity, and Buddhism continued to perform steppe rituals, to honor the ancestors, and to uphold Chinggis, his descendants, and Tengri.

Through its singular adaptiveness and assimilative capacities, the Horde changed the world. The Horde shaped the politics of Russia and of Central Asia and firmly anchored Islam in the Caucasus and Eastern Europe. The Horde brought steppe peoples to Mamluk Egypt and Franciscans to Crimea and the lower Volga. The Mongol exchange, of which the Jochids were the key agents, knit together east and west. And all of this was achieved through processes of evolution that made the

Horde at once unique and recognizably Mongol. There was as much a Jochid way of empire as there was a Roman way, an Ottoman way, and a British way. When we think about the legacy of empires, we of course recognize the cosmopolitan effects of the Mediterranean, European, and Ottoman powers that made the world smaller through practices of tolerance, coercion, exploitation, protection, investment, and conquest. These empires are credited with driving global history. But nomads drove global history, too, and none more so than the people of the Horde.

Glossary

ak orda	White Horde, western wing of the Horde
anda	alliance of sworn brotherhood
aqa	elder brothers, senior members of a lineage
basqaq	civil commander in charge of a sedentary population, tasked especially with tax collection (syn. daruga, darughachi)
beg	nomadic leader
beglerbeg	eldest or highest-ranking beg; supreme commander
bitigchi	imperial secretaries
bo'ol	free men, warriors
boyar	nobleman, landowner (Slavic)
bulqaq	anarchy, crisis; referring specifically to the period (1360s and 1370s) following the collapse of the senior Jochid lineages
darughachi, daruga	civil officer in charge of a sedentary population, tasked especially with tax collection (syn. basqaq)
dhimmi	legally protected non-Muslim under Muslim rule (Arabic)
Etügen	the Earth (deity)
ger	felt tent (also known as yurt)
gerege	passports, documents guaranteeing safe conduct (also known as paiza)
güregen	imperial husband
ini	younger brothers, junior members of a lineage
inju	personal property, dowry, or premortem inheritance
kebte'ül	night guard and member of the keshig

keshig	personal guard or administrator, man in permanent service to khan; pl. keshigten
khan	ruler
khatun	wives and daughters of the khan
kök orda	Blue Horde, eastern wing of the Horde
kniaz	Russian prince; pl. kniazia
kumis	fermented mare's milk (also known as airag)
kuda anda	alliance through marriage
kupchir	property tax paid in food, drink, clothing, and animals
lestvitsa	principle of princely succession (Russian)
minggan	military unit of a thousand warriors
morin yam	relay postal service on horseback
narin yam	secret communication system, faster than other yam services
nuntug	homeland, site for retirement and burial
oboq	named groups whose members claimed a single, often legendary, ancestry
ochigin	youngest son, "hearth-keeper"
ongon	felt effigies, sometimes carried as talismans
ordo	defined space surrounding khan's palace-tent, protected by keshigten, often housing the central administration of the khan's domain
ordo geren	khan's tents
ortaq	licensed merchant
qarachu	non-Chinggisid nomadic elite who served the golden lineage (late evolution of bo'ol status)
qoruq	burial grounds
qubi	share of conquered people, goods, and territory
quda	marriage partner
quriltai	great assembly
sarai	palace, city
sharil	Buddhist relic
sülde	vital force binding people together; ruler's charisma
tamga	lineage mark (on animals, coins, or seals)

tammachi	garrison troops stationed along borders and in newly settled colonies
tangsuq	unusual and highly prized gifts
tarkhan	status exempting protected classes (e.g., high clergy, craftsmen, certain military men) from taxes and conscription
Tengri	the Sky, Heavens (deity)
tergen yam	relay supply system for heavy loads
tümen	military decimal system; contingent of ten thousand men
Ulugh Kul	"Great Center," the khan's private domain
ulus	people; political community
uruq	lineage
voivode	high-ranking military, and later civil, office (Slavic)
yam	relay stations for messages and supplies (also known as örtöö)
yarlik	imperial order
yasa	code of conduct derived from Chinggis Khan's teachings; imperial regulations
yeke Mongghol ulus	the Mongol Empire

Notes

INTRODUCTION

1. See John A. Boyle, *The Mongol World Empire* (London: Variorum Reprints, 1977). On historiographical development of the concept of the Mongol world empire, see Timothy May, *The Mongol Conquests in World History* (London: Reaktion, 2012), 7–23. Janet Abu-Lughod offers important insights into the meaning of a world system when she explains that "no world system is *global* in the sense that all parts articulate evenly with one another." What makes a world system is the interdependence of various geographically distinct subsystems. Janet L. Abu-Lughod, *Before European Hegemony: The World System A.D. 1250–1350* (New York: Oxford University Press, 1989), 32 (emphasis original).

2. Pamela Kyle Crossley, *Hammer and Anvil: Nomad Rulers at the Forge of the Modern World* (Lanham, MD: Rowman and Littlefield, 2019), 149–155; Jane Burbank and Frederick Cooper, *Empires in World History: Power and Politics of Difference* (Princeton: Princeton University Press, 2010), 104–115.

3. May, *The Mongol Conquests,* 22.

4. See Crossley, *Hammer and Anvil,* xvii–xxiii; May, *The Mongol Conquests,* 8.

5. See Thomas T. Allsen, *Mongol Imperialism: The Policies of the Grand Qan Möngke in China, Russia, and the Islamic Lands, 1251–1259* (Berkeley: University of California Press, 1987); Thomas T. Allsen, *Commodity and Exchange in the Mongol Empire: A Cultural History of Islamic Textiles* (New York: Cambridge University Press, 1997); Thomas T. Allsen, *Culture and Conquest in Mongol Eurasia* (New York: Cambridge University Press, 2001); Thomas T. Allsen, *The Royal Hunt in Eurasian History* (Philadelphia: University of Pennsylvania Press, 2006); Thomas T. Allsen, *The Steppe and the Sea: Pearls in the Mongol Empire* (Philadelphia: University of Pennsylvania Press, 2019).

6. See especially May, *The Mongol Conquests;* Michal Biran, "The Mongol Empire and Inter-Civilizational Exchange," in *The Cambridge World History,* vol. 5: *Expanding Webs of Exchange and Conflict,* ed. B. Z. Kedar and M. E. Wiesner-Hanks

(Cambridge: Cambridge University Press, 2015), 534–558; Hodong Kim, "The Unity of the Mongol Empire and Continental Exchange over Eurasia," *Journal of Central Eurasian Studies* 1 (2009): 15–42.

7. See, for instance, methodological reflections in Eugenio Menegon, "Telescope and Microscope: A Micro-Historical Approach to Global China in the Eighteenth Century," *Modern Asian Studies* 54, no. 4 (2020): 1315–1344.

8. Karl Wittfogel and Fêng Chia-shêng, *History of Chinese Society: Liao (907–1125)* (Philadelphia: American Philosophical Association, 1949), 508.

9. Lhamsuren Munkh-Erdene, "Where Did the Mongol Empire Come From? Medieval Mongol Ideas of People, State and Empire," *Inner Asia* 13, no. 2 (2011): 211–237, 211. On the evolution of the Mongol ulus into *yeke Mongghol ulus* (the Mongol Empire or Great State), see Timothy Brook, *Great State: China and the World* (London: Profile Books, 2019), 7–9.

10. Ron Sela, *Ritual and Authority in Central Asia: The Khan's Inauguration Ceremony,* Papers on Inner Asia no. 37 (Bloomington: Indiana University Research Institute for Inner Asian Studies, 2003).

11. See also Pekka Hämäläinen, *The Comanche Empire* (New Haven: Yale University Press, 2008), who titles his conclusion, "The Shape of Power."

12. Russian historians based in the United States, such as George Vernadsky, were able to use terms other than "Tatar yoke." The notion of a Mongol or Tatar yoke finds its way into more recent English-language scholarship, e.g., Charles J. Halperin, *The Tatar Yoke* (Columbus, OH: Slavica, 1986); and Leo de Hartog, *Russia and the Mongol Yoke: The History of the Russian Principalities and the Golden Horde, 1221–1502* (London: British Academic Press, 1996).

13. Devin DeWeese, *Islamization and Native Religion in the Golden Horde: Baba Tükles and Conversion to Islam in Historical and Epic Tradition* (University Park: Pennsylvania State University Press, 1994).

14. See Charles J. Halperin, *Russia and the Golden Horde: The Mongol Impact on Medieval Russian History* (Bloomington: Indiana University Press, 1985); Halperin, *The Tatar Yoke;* Hartog, *Russia and the Mongol Yoke;* Donald Ostrowski, *Muscovy and the Mongols: Cross-Cultural Influences on the Steppe Frontier, 1304–1589* (Cambridge: Cambridge University Press, 1998).

15. Janet Martin, for example, notes Russian economic development under Mongol sovereignty, although she does not seek to explain the phenomenon. Janet Martin, "North-Eastern Russia and the Golden Horde (1246–1359)," in *The Cambridge History of Russia,* vol. 1, ed. Maureen Perrie (Cambridge: Cambridge University Press, 2006), 132.

16. See Michael Khodarkovsky, *Russia's Steppe Frontier: The Making of a Colonial Empire, 1500–1800* (Bloomington: Indiana University Press, 2002).

17. *Barbaro i Kontarini o Rossii: k istorii italo-russkikh sviazei v XV v.,* ed. and trans. E. Ch. Skrzhinskaia (Leningrad: Nauka, 1971), 148.

18. The oldest written steppe epic, Ötemish Hājjī's *Chinggis nāme,* dates to the mid-sixteenth century. There are several editions, including Utemish Khadzhi [Ötemish Hājjī], *Chingiz-name,* ed. and trans. V. P. Iudin, Iu. G. Baranova, and M. Kh. Abuseitova (Almaty: Gilim, 1992); and *Kara tavarikh,* trans. I. M. Mirgaleev and E. G. Sayfetdinova (Kazan: Sh. Marjani Institute of History of the Tatarstan Academy of Sciences, 2017).

19. We can be confident that court chronicles from the Horde were not merely lost, because there is no mention of their existence in later works patronized by the leaders of the Horde's successor regimes, such as the Uzbek and Khivan khans. If such court literature had existed, it would have been referenced in these subsequent sources.

20. See Utemish Khadzhi, *Chingiz-name;* DeWeese, *Islamization and Native Religion;* Mária Ivanics and Mirkasym A. Usmanov, *Das Buch der Dschingis-Legende. Däftär-i Čingiz-nāmä* (Szeged: Department of Altaic Studies, University of Szeged, 2002).

1 ⁜ THE RESILIENCE OF THE FELT-WALLED TENTS

1. On Qiu Chuji, see Igor de Rachewiltz and Terry Russell, "Ch'iu Ch'u-chi," in *In the Service of the Khan: Eminent Personalities of the Early Mongol-Yüan Period (1200–1300),* ed. Igor de Rachewiltz, Chan Hok-lam, Hsiao Ch'i-ch'ing, and Peter W. Geier, 208–223 (Wiesbaden: Harrassowitz, 1993).

2. The report of Qiu Chuji's journey to the West was written by his disciple Li Zhichang and published in 1228 under the title *Qiu Chang Chun Xi You Ji (Travels to the West of Qiu Chang Chun).* English translations include Emil Bretschneider, "Si Yu Ki (Ch'ang Ch'un, 1221–24)," in *Mediaeval Researches from Eastern Asiatic Sources,* 2 vols. (London: Trübner, 1888), vol. 1: 35–108; and *The Travels of an Alchemist; the Journey of the Taoist, Ch'ang-ch'un, from China to the Hindukush at the Summons of Chingiz Khan, Recorded by His Disciple, Li Chih-ch'ang,* trans. Arthur Waley (London: Routledge, 1931). Quotations from Bretschneider, "Si Yu Ki," 86.

3. On the expression "Felt-Walled Tents," see *Secret History,* § 202. Unless otherwise specified, quotations from the *Secret History* are from *The Secret History of the Mongols: A Mongolian Epic Chronicle of the Thirteenth Century,* trans. Igor de Rachewiltz (Leiden: Brill, 2004). See also Christopher Atwood, "How the Mongols Got a Word for Tribe—and What It Means," *Studia Historica Mongolica* 10 (2010): 63–89. On the Mongol terms *irgen* (people) and *aimag* or *aimagiin xolboo* (tribe or tribes), see Christopher Atwood, "The Administrative Origins of Mongolia's 'Tribal' Vocabulary," *Eurasia: Statum et Legem* 1, no. 4 (2015): 7–45, esp. 17–25, 38. Atwood argues that, rather than a social group, "oboq" seems to designate the name inherited from

an ancestor, but scholars commonly translate oboq as clan based on ancestry. See also Françoise Aubin, "Mongolie," *Encyclopedia Universalis* (1978), vol. 11, 243; Christopher Atwood, "Mongol Tribe," in *Encyclopedia of Mongolia and the Mongol Empire* (New York: Facts on File, 2004), 389–391; Paul Buell and Judith Kolbas, "The Ethos of State and Society in the Early Mongol Empire: Chinggis Khan to Güyük," *Journal of the Royal Asiatic Society* 26 (2016): 43–56.

4. On Mongol effigies, see Isabelle Charleux, "From Ongon to Icon: Legitimization, Glorification and Divinization of Power in Some Examples of Mongol Portraits," in *Representing Power in Ancient Inner Asia: Legitimacy, Transmission and the Sacred,* ed. Isabelle Charleux, Grégory Delaplace, Roberte Hamayon, and Scott Pearce, 209–261 (Bellingham, WA: Center for East Asian Studies, Western Washington University, 2010). On Tengri, see Mahmūd al-Kāshgarī, *Dīwān lughāt al-Turk,* ed. Kilisli Rifat Bey (Istanbul, 1333–1335 [1915–1917]), vol. 3, 278–279; English translation: *Dīwān lughāt al-Turk,* trans. Robert Dankoff and James Kelly (Duxbury, MA: Tekin, 1982–1985), vol. 2, 342–343; and Gerhard Doerfer, *Türkische und mongolische Elemente im Neupersischen* (Wiesbaden: F. Steiner, 1965), vol. 2, 577–585; V. F. Büchner [G. Doerfer], "Täñri," *Encyclopaedia of Islam* (Leiden: Brill, 2000), vol. 10: 186–188. On sülde see Charleux, "From Ongon to Icon," 217; and Tatyana Skrynnikova, "*Sülde*—The Basic Idea of the Chinggis-Khan Cult," *Acta Orientalia Hungaricae Academiae Scientiarum* 46, no. 1 (1992–1993): 51–60.

5. On the social structure of the early Mongols, see Tatyana Skrynnikova, "Relations of Domination and Submission: Political Practice in the Mongol Empire of Chinggis Khan," in *Imperial Statecraft: Political Forms and Techniques of Governance in Inner Asia, Sixth-Twentieth Centuries,* ed. David Sneath, 85–115 (Bellingham, WA: Center for East Asian Studies, Western Washington University, 2006); and Atwood, "Mongol Tribe," 390–391.

6. Skrynnikova, "Relations of Domination and Submission," 93–96. Some earlier sources describe bo'ol as slaves, but bo'ol were not economically dependent. On Mongol genealogies see Rashīd al-Dīn, *(Fazlullah's-Jami'u't-tawarikh) Compendium of Chronicles: A History of the Mongols,* trans. Wheeler Thackston (Cambridge, MA: Dept. of Near Eastern Languages and Civilizations, Harvard University, 1998–1999), 79–82; Christopher Atwood, "Six Pre-Chinggisid Genealogies in the Mongol Empire," *Archivum Eurasiae Medii Aevi* 19 (2012): 5–58. On Mongol exogamy, see Jennifer Holmgren, "Observations on Marriage and Inheritance Practices in Early Mongol and Yuan Society, with Particular Reference to the Levirate," *Journal of Asian History* 20, no. 2 (1986): 127–192, 136.

7. See Peter Golden, "The Türk Imperial Tradition in the Pre-Chinggisid Era," in *Imperial Statecraft: Political Forms and Techniques of Governance in Inner Asia, Sixth-Twentieth Centuries,* ed. David Sneath, 23–61 (Bellingham, WA: Center for East Asian Studies, Western Washington University, 2006). On the Kereit, see İsenbike Togan, *Flexibility and Limitation in Steppe Formations: The Kerait Khanate and Chinggis Khan* (Leiden: Brill, 1998).

8. On the childhood and early adulthood of Chinggis Khan, see Paul Ratchnevsky, *Genghis Khan: His Life and Legacy,* trans. Thomas Nivison Haining (Oxford: Blackwell, 1991), 19–31; Michal Biran, *Chinggis Khan* (Oxford: Oneworld, 2007), esp. 32–40.

9. Larry V. Clark, "The Theme of Revenge in the Secret History of the Mongols," in *Aspects of Altaic Civilization II,* ed. Larry Clark and Paul Draghi, 33–57 (Bloomington: Indiana University Asian Studies Research Institute, 1978); Roberte Hamayon, "Mérite de l'offenseur vengeur, plaisir du rival vainqueur," in *La vengeance: Études d'ethnologie, d'histoire et de philosophie,* ed. Raymond Verdier (Paris: Cujas, 1980), vol. 2, 116.

10. On the marriage agreement between Yesügei Ba'atur and Dei Sechen, Börte's father, see *Secret History,* § 61–66; on the joint Mongol and Kereit military operations against the Merkit to rescue Börte, see *Secret History,* § 104–113.

11. Golden, "The Türk Imperial Tradition," 42–44. Bilge Kagan's quotation is from the Kül Tigin inscription (S4) to (S8), parentheses in original translation, from T. Tekin, *A Grammar of Orkhon Turkic* (Bloomington: Indiana University Press, 1968), 261–262. The Mongols could not decipher old Turkic, but they had access to Chinese translations. See Juvaynī, *Genghis Khan: The History of the World Conqueror,* trans. J. A. Boyle (Seattle: University of Washington Press, 1997), 54–55; *Secret History,* § 186–187.

12. *Secret History,* § 186; Rashīd al-Dīn, *Compendium of Chronicles,* 348; Nicola Di Cosmo, "Why Qara Qorum? Climate and Geography in the Early Mongol Empire," *Archivum Eurasiae Medii Aevi* 21 (2014–2015): 67–78.

13. Paul Buell, "Early Mongol Expansion in Western Siberia and Turkestan (1207–1219): A Reconstruction," *Central Asiatic Journal* 36, no. 1/2 (1992): 1–32, 2, 4. See also Paul Buell, "Sübötei Ba'atur (1176–1248)," in *In the Service of the Khan: Eminent Personalities of the Early Mongol-Yüan Period (1200–1300),* ed. Igor de Rachewiltz, Chan Hok-lam, Hsiao Ch'i-ch'ing, and Peter W. Geier (Wiesbaden: Harrassowitz, 1993), 14–15.

14. The nine tails were and still are the symbol of Mongol unity and, by extension, of the Mongol nation. *Secret History,* § 202; Rashīd al-Dīn, *Compendium of Chronicles,* 89–909. See also Igor de Rachewiltz, "The Title Činggis Qan / Qayan Reconsidered," in *Gedanke und Wirkung. Festschrift zum 90. Geburstag von Nikolaus Poppe,* ed. Walther Heissig and Klaus Sagaster (Wiesbaden: O. Harrassowitz, 1989), 281–298; Biran, *Chinggis Khan,* 39; Golden, "The Türk Imperial Tradition," 40–42.

15. Florence Hodous, "The *Quriltai* as a Legal Institution in the Mongol Empire," *Central Asiatic Journal* 56 (2012–2013): 87–102; Ron Sela, *Ritual and Authority in Central Asia: The Khan's Inauguration Ceremony* (Bloomington: Indiana University Research Institute for Inner Asian Studies, 2003); Christopher Atwood, "Chinggis Khan," in *Encyclopedia of Mongolia and the Mongol Empire* (New York: Facts on File, 2004), 98–99; Lhamsuren Munkh-Erdene, "Where Did the Mongol Empire

Come From? Medieval Mongol Ideas of People, State and Empire," *Inner Asia* 13, no. 2 (2011): 211–237. The 1206 quriltai was the second enthronement of Temüjin. Twenty years earlier, a small group of followers had elected him khan. *Secret History*, § 120–126.

16. Skrynnikova, "Relations of Domination and Submission," 85–104.

17. *Secret History*, § 154; Skrynnikova, "Relations of Domination and Submission," 92–93, quoting Rashīd al-Dīn's *Compendium of Chronicles.*

18. Although the decimal system assured the largest units could comprise 10,000 men, in practice units usually contained between 6,000 and 8,000 warriors, and sometimes fewer. See Thomas T. Allsen, "Mongol Census Taking in Rus', 1245–1275," *Harvard Ukrainian Studies* 5, no. 1 (1981): 32–53, 52; Timothy May, *The Mongol Art of War: Chinggis Khan and the Mongol Military System* (Yardley, PA: Westholme, 2007), 27–41; Buell and Kolbas, "The Ethos of State and Society in the Early Mongol Empire," 54; and Bryan Miller, "Xiongnu 'Kings' and the Political Order of the Steppe Empire," *Journal of the Economic and Social History of the Orient* 57 (2014): 1–43. Miller shows that the Xiongnu were the first to engineer a decimal system for growing and organizing a nomadic empire. There is little written evidence as to how the decimal system functioned among the Xiongnu in regard to spoils redistribution, but it was used for conscription and perhaps also for census-taking.

19. *Secret History*, § 213, quoted and translated in Buell and Kolbas, "The Ethos of State and Society in the Early Mongol Empire," 55.

20. Skrynnikova, "Relations of Domination and Submission," 85–87; Munkh-Erdene, "Where Did the Mongol Empire Come From?" esp. 211–219. The keshig had its origin in both old Turkic military institutions and in the Liao-Khitan *ordo*, imperial camps housing Liao administrators and guards. The original meaning of keshig is "rotations," or "shifts." See Christopher Atwood, "Keshig," in *Encyclopedia of Mongolia and the Mongol Empire* (New York: Facts on File, 2004), 297–298; Peter Andrews, *Felt Tents and Pavilions: The Nomadic Tradition and Its Interaction with Princely Tentage*, 2 vols. (London: Melisende, 1999), vol. 1, 281, 312, 324–325; May, *The Mongol Art of War*, 32–36; Buell and Kolbas, "The Ethos of State and Society in the Early Mongol Empire," 54.

21. See Buell, "Söbötei Ba'atur," 13–26.

22. According to Hodous, "The principle function of a *quriltai* seems to have been in formally granting to a new person or to new decisions." Hodous, "The *Quriltai* as a Legal Institution in the Mongol Empire," 91.

23. Buell, "Early Mongol Expansion," 5–7; Rachewiltz, *The Secret History of the Mongols*, 734–735 and 1045–1050 (Appendix 1); Thomas Allsen, "Prelude to the Western Campaigns: Mongol Military Operations in the Volga-Ural Region, 1217–1237," *Archivum Eurasiae Medii Aevi* 3 (1983), 9.

24. In the contemporary sources, there is confusion between the campaigns of 1207–1208 and 1217–1219. Both were directed to the north and northwest and were led by Jochi, Sübötei, and Jebe. See Buell, "Early Mongol Expansion," 6–8, esp. note 13; *Secret History*, § 198–200; Christopher Atwood, "Jochi and the Early Western Campaigns," in *How Mongolia Matters: War, Law, and Society*, ed. Morris Rossabi (Leiden: Brill, 2017), 39–40, 55 (Appendix).

25. *Secret History*, § 198.

26. *Secret History*, § 195, 209. The *Secret History* indicates that Sübötei and Jebe were appointed as commanders at the quriltai 1206, but this is most likely a mistake.

27. Michal Biran, *The Empire of the Qara Khitai in Eurasian History: Between China and the Islamic World* (Cambridge: Cambridge University Press, 2005), 76.

28. Biran, *Qara Khitai*, 78–80, 146–153.

29. The Muslim historiography was dominated by the official versions of Juvaynī, *The History of the World Conqueror*, trans. John Andrew Boyle (Manchester: Manchester University Press, 1958), 63–74; and Rashīd al-Dīn, *Compendium of Chronicles*, 228–231. See Biran, *Qara Khitai*, 80–86, 180–191, 194–196.

30. Biran, *Qara Khitai*, 82–83, 195–196. The Muslim sources are Juvaynī, *The History of the World Conqueror*, 65–68, 70–73; and Rashīd al-Dīn, *Compendium of Chronicles*, 230–231. Chinese sources are listed in Buell, "Sübötei Ba'atur," 18.

31. Buell, "Early Mongol Expansion," 10–12; Atwood, "Jochi and the Early Western Campaigns," 38–45.

32. See Peter Golden, "Imperial Ideology and the Sources of Political Unity amongst the Pre-Činggisid Nomads of Western Eurasia," *Archivum Eurasiae Medii Aevi* 2 (1982): 37–76; Peter Golden, "Cumanica I: The Qipčaqs in Georgia," *Archivum Eurasiae Medii Aevi* 4 (1984): 45–87; Peter Golden, "Cumanica II: The Ölberli (Ölperli): The Fortunes and Misfortunes of an Inner Asian Nomadic Clan," *Archivum Eurasiae Medii Aevi* 6 [1985 (1987)]: 5–29. For a reflection on self-governing peoples fleeing the oppression of state-making projects, see James C. Scott, *The Art of Not Being Governed: An Anarchist History of Upland Southeast Asia* (New Haven: Yale University Press, 2009), esp. ix–xviii; Allsen, "Prelude to the Western Campaigns," 6–8.

33. Allsen, "Prelude to the Western Campaigns," 9; Atwood, "Jochi and the Early Western Campaigns," 43–44.

34. On the iron wagons, see Buell, "Sübötei Ba'atur," 15; Andrews, *Felt Tents and Pavilions*, vol. 1, 317; and Atwood, "Jochi and the Early Western Campaigns," 38 n9. On the Battle of Chem River, see Buell, "Early Mongol Expansion," 10; Buell, "Sübötei Ba'atur," 15–16; Atwood "Jochi and the Early Western Campaigns," 38–45. See also Rashīd al-Dīn, *Compendium of Chronicles*, 53, 227.

35. Biran, *Chinggis Khan*, 48–49.

36. *Secret History,* § 249; Biran, *Chinggis Khan,* 49; Rashīd al-Dīn, *Compendium of Chronicles,* 203, 204, 289–290.

37. Jūzjānī, *Tabakāt-i-Nāsirī: A General History of the Muhammadan Dynasties of Asia, Including Hindūstān, from A.H. 194 [810 a.d.], to A.H. 658 [1260 a.d.], and the Irruption of the Infidel Mughals into Islam,* 2 vols. (Calcutta: Asiatic Society of Bengal, 1881–1897), vol. 2, 960–965; *Secret History,* § 250–253; Rashīd al-Dīn, *Compendium of Chronicles,* 213–226; Biran, *Chinggis Khan,* 50–52.

38. Vasilij V. Bartol'd [W. Barthold], *Turkestan Down to the Mongol Invasion,* 2nd ed. (Oxford: Oxford University Press, 1928), 393–395; Biran, *Chinggis Khan,* 51–52.

39. Jūzjānī, *Tabakāt-i-Nāsirī,* 270–272, 963–966; Bartol'd, *Turkestan Down to the Mongol Invasion,* 393–396; and Ratchnevsky, *Genghis Khan: His Life and Legacy,* 120; Juvaynī, *The History of the World Conqueror,* 77–81. Buell, "Early Mongol Expansion," esp. 14–16; and Buell, "Sübötei Ba'atur," 16–17, put the battle of the Quylï River in 1209–1210. However, Atwood, "Jochi and the Early Western Campaigns," 45–50, convincingly shows that the battle occurred in 1219, according to available sources. This river may have been located in west-central Kazakhstan.

40. Ibn al-Athīr, *The Chronicle of Ibn al-Athīr for the Crusading Period from al-Kāmil fī'l-ta'rīkh,* Part 3: *The Years 589–629/1193–1231: The Ayyūbids after Saladin and the Mongol Menace,* trans. D. S. Richards (Aldershot, UK: Ashgate, 2008), 204–205. See also Biran, *Qara Khitai,* 75–80.

41. Aubin, "Mongolie," 244; May, *The Mongol Art of War,* 3, 103–104.

42. Biran, *Qara Khitai,* 70–74, 77–80.

43. Ibn al-Athīr, *The Chronicle,* 205; Juvaynī, *The History of the World Conqueror,* 77–81. For an overview of divergent sources regarding the Otrar episode, see Bartol'd, *Turkestan Down to the Mongol Invasion,* 397–399. On the possible co-occurrence with the Quylï River battle, see Atwood, "Jochi and the Early Western Campaigns," 48–49.

44. Ibn al-Athīr, *The Chronicle,* 205–206.

45. Ibn al-Athīr, *The Chronicle,* 206; Bartol'd, *Turkestan Down to the Mongol Invasion,* 399.

46. Atwood, "Jochi and the Early Western Campaigns," 51. On the key role of scouts in Mongol warfare, see Andrews, *Felt Tents and Pavilions,* vol. 2, 1296. There were originally three tümen in the Westward. The third, led by Toquchar, was recalled for disobeying an order from Chinggis Khan: May, *The Mongol Art of War,* 95–96.

47. Ibn al-Athīr, *The Chronicle,* 210; Juvaynī, *The History of the World Conqueror,* 142–149; *K'art'lis c'xovreba: A History of Georgia,* trans. and with commentary by Stephen Jones (Tbilisi: Artanuji, 2014), 321; *Vardan Arewelts'i's Compilation of*

History, trans. R. Bedrosian (Long Branch, NJ: Sources of the Armenian Tradition, 2007), 84.

48. Rashīd al-Dīn, *Compendium of Chronicles,* 242–243, 359; Juvaynī, *The History of the World Conqueror,* 83, 86–90; Bartol'd, *Turkestan Down to the Mongol Invasion,* 415–416; Allsen, "Prelude to the Western Campaigns," 11–12; Buell, "Early Mongol Expansion," 26–27.

49. Ibn al-Athīr, *The Chronicle,* 210. There are also reasons to doubt the veracity of this anecdote. See Bartol'd, *Turkestan Down to the Mongol Invasion,* 72, 420–421.

50. Jūzjānī, *Tabakāt-i-Nāsirī,* 976; Ibn al-Athīr, *The Chronicle,* 207–210; Juvaynī, *The History of the World Conqueror,* 97–109, 115–123; Rashīd al-Dīn, *Compendium of Chronicles,* 245–249.

51. Rashīd al-Dīn, *Compendium of Chronicles,* 253–255; Juvaynī, *The History of the World Conqueror,* 81–86; Thomas Allsen, "Ever Closer Encounters: The Appropriation of Culture and the Apportionment of Peoples in the Mongol Empire," *Journal of Early Modern History* 1, no. 1 (1997): 2–23, 4.

52. Ibn al-Athīr, *The Chronicle,* 203.

53. Ibn al-Athīr, *The Chronicle,* 211, 215–216; Rashīd al-Dīn, *Compendium of Chronicles,* 249–252.

54. Atwood, "Jochi and the Early Western Campaigns," 50–54; Juvaynī, *The History of the World Conqueror,* 123–128; Rashīd al-Dīn, *Compendium of Chronicles,* 254–255; Ibn al-Athīr, *The Chronicle,* 214, 227–228.

55. Ibn al-Athīr, *The Chronicle,* 205; Biran, *Qara Khitai,* 86–87.

56. Ibn al-Athīr, *The Chronicle,* 228–229, 305–307; Juvaynī, *The History of the World Conqueror,* 133–138; Bartol'd, *Turkestan Down to the Mongol Invasion,* 437–446. In August 1231, while hiding in a Kurdish village, Jalāl al-Dīn was finally murdered by an anonymous aggressor. John A. Boyle, "Jalāl al-Dīn," *Encyclopaedia of Islam,* vol. 2 (Leiden: Brill, 1991), 392–393.

57. Thomas Allsen, "Sharing Out the Empire: Apportioned Lands under the Mongols," in *Nomads in the Sedentary World,* ed. Anatoly M. Khazanov and André Wink, 172–190 (Richmond, UK: Curzon, 2001); *Secret History,* § 260; Rashīd al-Dīn, *Compendium of Chronicles,* 253–254; Atwood, "Jochi and the Early Western Campaigns," 50–54.

2 INTO THE WEST

1. Jennifer Holmgren, "Observations on Marriage and Inheritance Practices in Early Mongol and Yuan Society, with Particular Reference to the Levirate," *Journal of Asian History* 20, no. 2 (1986): 127–192, 146–151; Christopher Atwood, "Family," in *Encyclopedia of Mongolia and the Mongol Empire* (New York: Facts on File, 2004), 173–174.

2. ʿAlāʾ al-Dīn ʿAtā Malik Juvaynī, *Genghis Khan: The History of the World Conqueror,* ed. and trans. John Andrew Boyle (1958; Seattle: University of Washington Press, 1997), 42–43; Thomas Allsen, "Sharing out the Empire: Apportioned Lands under the Mongols," in *Nomads in the Sedentary World,* ed. Anatoly M. Khazanov and André Wink (Richmond, UK: Curzon, 2001), 172–173, 184.

3. Christopher Atwood, "Jochi and the Early Western Campaigns," in *How Mongolia Matters: War, Law, and Society,* ed. Morris Rossabi (Leiden: Brill, 2017), 35–38; *Muʿizz al-ansāb. Proslavliaiushchee genealogii,* ed. A. K. Muminov, trans. Sh. Kh. Vokhidov (Almaty: Daik-Press, 2006), 38–40; Juvaynī, *Genghis Khan: The History of the World Conqueror,* 42; Allsen, "Sharing out the Empire," 172–190; Peter Jackson, "From Ulus to Khanate: The Making of the Mongol States, c. 1220–c. 1290," in *The Mongol Empire and Its Legacy,* ed. Reuven Amitai-Preiss and David O. Morgan (Leiden: Brill, 1999), 12–38.

4. Rashīd al-Dīn, *Rashiduddin Fazlullah's-Jamiʿu't-tawarikh. Compendium of Chronicles: A History of the Mongols,* trans. Wheeler Thackston (Cambridge, MA: Dept. of Near Eastern Languages and Civilizations, Harvard University, 1998–1999), 281; Thomas Allsen, "Ever Closer Encounters: The Appropriation of Culture and the Apportionment of Peoples in the Mongol Empire," *Journal of Early Modern History* 1, no. 1 (1997): 2–23, 4; Peter Jackson, *The Mongols and the West: 1221–1410* (New York: Pearson / Longman, 2005), 42.

5. Sometimes-conflicting details of Jochi's keshig appear in *The Secret History of the Mongols: A Mongolian Epic Chronicle of the Thirteenth Century,* trans. Igor de Rachewiltz (Leiden: Brill, 2004), § 202; Rashīd al-Dīn, *Compendium of Chronicles,* 93, 97, 102, 279; *Muʿizz al-ansāb,* 39–40.

6. Grigor of Akancʿ, *History of the Nation of the Archers (The Mongols),* trans. Robert P. Blake and Richard N. Frye (Cambridge, MA: Harvard-Yenching Institute, 1954), 297, 299. See also Peter Andrews, *Felt Tents and Pavilions: The Nomadic Tradition and Its Interaction with Princely Tentage,* 2 vols. (London: Melisende, 1999), vol. 2, 1294.

7. *Kirakos Gandzaketsʿi's History of the Armenians,* trans. Robert Bedrosian (New York: Sources of the Armenian Tradition, 1986), 165–166; *The Hundred Years' Chronicle, Kʿartʿlis cʿxovreba: A History of Georgia,* trans. Stephen Jones (Tbilisi: Artanuji, 2014), 321; Mamuka Tsurtsumia, "Couched Lance and Mounted Shock Combat in the East: The Georgian Experience," *Journal of Medieval Military History* 12 (2014): 81–108.

8. *Kirakos Gandzaketsʿi's History of the Armenians,* 166; Ibn al-Athīr, *The Chronicle of Ibn al-Athīr for the Crusading Period from al-Kāmil fīʾl-taʾrīkh,* part 3: *The Years 589–629 / 1193–1231: The Ayyūbids after Saladin and the Mongol Menace,* trans. D. S. Richards (Aldershot, UK: Ashgate, 2008), 214–216; Peter Jackson, "The Testimony of the Russian 'Archbishop' Peter Concerning the Mongols (1244 / 1255): Precious Intelligence or Timely Disinformation?" *Journal of the Royal Asiatic Society* 26,

nos. 1–2 (2016): 65–77, 73n46, 74. There is confusion in the sources concerning the Westward's 1221 and 1222 Caucasus campaigns. See especially Grigor of Akanc', *History of the Nation of the Archers*, chapters 3 and 4; and Rashīd al-Dīn, *Compendium of Chronicles*, 110.

9. Some historians believe the Mongols entered the Darial Pass, but this would have been a huge diversion and makes no sense given that they eventually attacked Derbent. See, for instance, David Nicolle and Viktor Shpakovs'kyi, *Kalka River 1223: Ghengis Khan's Mongols Invade Russia*, illus. Viktor Korol'kov (Oxford: Osprey, 2001), 50–52.

10. *The Hundred Years' Chronicle*, 321–322.

11. Ibn al-Athīr, *The Chronicle*, 221–222.

12. Ibn al-Athīr, *The Chronicle*, 221–222; *Kirakos Gandzakets'i's History of the Armenians*, 167; Rashīd al-Dīn, *Compendium of Chronicles*, 110, 259–260; *The Hundred Years' Chronicle*, 321–322. The sources provide a confused description of the Mongol crossing of the Greater Caucasus, which historians have attempted to reconstruct: Nicolle and Shpakovs'kyi, *Kalka River 1223*, 50–52; Carl Fredrik Sverdrup, *The Mongol Conquests: The Military Operations of Genghis Khan and Sübe'etei* (Solilhull, UK: Helion, 2017), 199–202; Thomas Allsen, "The Mongols and North Caucasia," *Archivum Eurasiae Medii Aevii* 7 (1991): 11–17.

13. Ibn al-Athīr, *The Chronicle*, 222. Richards uses "race" to translate the word *jins*. I have substituted "stock," which I believe is a more accurate translation.

14. Ibn al-Athīr, *The Chronicle*, 223.

15. *The Chronicle of Novgorod, 1016–1471*, trans. Robert Michell and Nevill Forbes (London: Offices of the Society, 1914), 64–65. See also Nicolle and Shpakovs'kyi, *Kalka River 1223*, 22.

16. Nicolle and Shpakovs'kyi, *Kalka River 1223*, 58, 60.

17. *The Chronicle of Novgorod*, 65.

18. The Mongol commander is called Gemya-Beg in the *Chronicle of Novgorod*, 65. Stephen Pow has convincingly identified Gemya-Beg as Jebe. According to Pow, "The silence and ambiguity surrounding Jebe's fate in pro-Mongol sources of the thirteenth century can perhaps be explained by a taboo surrounding the disgraceful circumstances of his capture and execution." Stephen Pow, "The Last Campaign and Death of Jebe Noyan," *Journal of the Royal Asiatic Society* 27, no. 1 (2017): 31–51, 31.

19. Ibn al-Athīr, *The Chronicle*, 223; *The Chronicle of Novgorod*, 65–66. Nicolle and Shpakovs'kyi, *Kalka River 1223*, 92; Iskander Izmaylov, "Pokhodi v vostochnuiu Evropu," in *Istoriia Tatar s drevneishikh vremen*, vol. 3: *Ulus Dzhuchi (Zolotaia Orda) XIII–seredina XV v.*, ed. Rafael Khakimov and Mirkasim Usmanov (Kazan: Institut Istorii im. Sh. Mardjani, 2009), 135–137.

20. Ibn al-Athīr, *The Chronicle,* 224; *The Chronicle of Novgorod,* 66–67.

21. Ibn al-Athīr, *The Chronicle,* 224.

22. The chronology in the sources is unclear. See Thomas Allsen, "Prelude to the Western Campaigns: Mongol Military Operations in the Volga-Ural Region, 1217–1237," *Archivum Eurasiae Medii Aevi* 3 (1983), 10–11.

23. See Paul Buell, "Sübötei Ba'atur (1176–1248)," in *In the Service of the Khan: Eminent Personalities of the Early Mongol-Yüan Period (1200–1300),* ed. Igor de Rachewiltz, Chan Hok-lam, Hsiao Ch'i-ch'ing, and Peter W. Geier (Wiesbaden: Harrassowitz, 1993), 19; Ibn al-Athīr, *The Chronicle,* 224; *The Chronicle of Novgorod,* 66–67.

24. Allsen, "Prelude to the Western Campaigns," 13. Pro-Toluid sources suggest that Jochi was not doing his duty—a possibly false accusation. See Atwood, "Jochi and the Early Western Campaigns"; Rashīd al-Dīn, *Compendium of Chronicles,* 360.

25. *Secret History,* § 265–268; Paul Ratchnevsky, *Genghis Khan: His Life and Legacy,* trans. Thomas Nivison Haining (Oxford: Blackwell, 1991), 140–144; Michal Biran, *Chinggis Khan* (Oxford: Oneworld, 2007), 61–62.

26. *Secret History,* § 269–270.

27. Juvaynī, *Genghis Khan: The History of the World Conqueror,* 553. Allsen, "Prelude to the Western Campaigns," 17, labels Bashman's tactics "guerilla warfare."

28. *Hei ta Shi-lu* quoted and translated by Allsen, "Prelude to the Western Campaigns," 18; Juvaynī, *Genghis Khan: The History of the World Conqueror,* 268–270. See also Rashīd al-Dīn, *Compendium of Chronicles,* 324; Buell, "Sübötei Ba'atur," 22–25.

29. Allsen, "Prelude to the Western Campaigns," 18–19; Paul Pelliot, "A propos des Coumans," *Journal Asiatique,* ser. 11, vol. 15, no. 2 (1920): 125–185, 166.

30. Allsen, "Prelude to the Western Campaigns," 15–16; Izmaylov, "Pokhodi v vostochnuiu Evropu," 137–141, 143–146. *The Chronicle of Novgorod,* 81, claims the Mongols slaughtered all the Bulgars they encountered during the campaign, but we know this is not true, as there are records of captives integrating into the Mongol Empire.

31. Allsen, "Prelude to the Western Campaigns," 21; Buell, "Sübötei Ba'atur," 19–20; Donald Ostrowski, "The 'tamma' and the Dual-Administrative Structure of the Mongol Empire," *Bulletin of the School of Oriental and African Studies* 61, no. 2 (1998): 262–277; Timothy May, *The Mongol Art of War: Chinggis Khan and the Mongol Military System* (Yardley, PA: Westholme, 2007), 36–38; Christopher Atwood, "Tammachi," in *Encyclopedia of Mongolia and the Mongol Empire,* 527.

32. Dimitri Korobeinikov, "A Broken Mirror: The Kipçak World in the Thirteenth Century," in *The Other Europe in the Middle Ages: Avars, Bulgars, Khazars, and Cumans,* ed. Florin Curta and Roman Kovalev, 379–412 (Leiden: Brill, 2008).

33. Izmaylov, "Pokhodi v vostochnuiu Evropu," 148, *The Chronicle of Novgorod,* 81. Friar Julian quotation from S. A. Anninsky, "Izvestiia vengerskikh missionerov XIII–XIV vv. o tatarakh v Vostochnoi Evrope," *Istoricheskii arkhiv* 3 (1940), 86–87.

Next to Friar Julian's report, the main sources on the Mongol invasion of the Rus are the Chronicles of Novgorod and Galicia-Volhynia, which are more reliable and less biased than the other Russian chronicles. See also Alexander Majorov, "The Conquest of Russian Lands in 1237–1240," in *The Golden Horde in World History,* ed. Rafael Khakimov, Vadim Trepavlov, and Marie Favereau (Kazan: Institut Istorii im. Sh. Mardjani, 2017), 86–110.

34. Rashīd al-Dīn, *Compendium of Chronicles,* 325, 327.

35. Izmaylov, "Pokhodi v vostochnuiu Evropu," 152–153; Majorov, "The Conquest of Russian Lands in 1237–1240," 87.

36. *The Chronicle of Novgorod,* 81–84; Rashīd al-Dīn, *Compendium of Chronicles,* 53, 148, 280–281, 327; Izmaylov, "Pokhodi v vostochnuiu Evropu," 149–152; Majorov, "The Conquest of Russian Lands in 1237–1240," 88–91.

37. *Galitsko-Volynskaia letopis' (The Chronicle of Galycia-Volhynia)* (St. Petersburg: Aleteyia, 2005), 108–109; *Letopis' po ipatskomu spisku (Hypathian Chronicle)* (St. Petersburg: Arkheograficheskaia komissiia, 1871), 522–523; Majorov, "The Conquest of Russian Lands in 1237–1240," 93–98, 100–104. See also Izmaylov, "Pokhodi v vostochnuiu Evropu," 158–160.

38. Izmaylov, "Pokhodi v vostochnuiu Evropu," 141–143.

39. The Mongols applied the same strategy in Hungary in 1241–1242. Master Roger in Anonymous and Master Roger, *Magistri Rogerii epistula miserabile carmen super destruction Regni Hungariae par tartaror facta. Epistle to the Sorrowful Lament upon the Destruction of the Kingdom of Hungary by the Tatars,* ed. János M. Bak and Martyn Rady (Budapest: Central European University Press, 2010), 210–213.

40. Izmaylov, "Pokhodi v vostochnuiu Evropu," 144, 148.

41. Izmaylov, "Pokhodi v vostochnuiu Evropu," 153–154.

42. Majorov, "The Conquest of Russian Lands in 1237–1240," 91–92; Izmaylov, "Pokhodi v vostochnuiu Evropu," 149. On Xili Gambu, see Ruth Dunnell, "Xili Gambu and the Myth of Shatuo Descent: Genealogical Anxiety and Family History in Yuan China," *Archivum Eurasiae Medii Aevi* 21 (2014–2015), 83–102.

43. Buell, "Sübötei Ba'atur," 23. Ismaylov rejects the claim that weather conditions severely affected the Mongol invasion, at least with respect to Novgorod: Izmaylov, "Pokhodi v vostochnuiu Evropu," 153–154.

44. Master Roger, *Magistri Rogerii epistula,* 160–161; Ulf Büntgen and Nicola Di Cosmo, "Climatic and Environmental Aspects of the Mongol Withdrawal from Hungary in 1242 CE," *Scientific Reports* 6 (2016), article no. 25606. The richest contemporary sources on the Mongol invasion of Hungary are Master Roger's and Archdeacon Thomas of Split, *Historia Salonitanorum atque Spalatinorum pontificum. History of the Bishops of Salona and Split,* ed. Damir Karbic, Mirjana Matijevic Sokol, and James Ross Sweeney (Budapest: Central European University Press, 2006). For additional primary sources, see Gian Andri Bezzola, *Die Mongolen in abendländischer*

Sicht, 1220–1270: ein Beitrag zur Frage der Völkerbegegnungen (Bern: Francke, 1974), 66–109.

45. Master Roger, *Magistri Rogerii epistula,* 136–141.

46. Hansgerd Göckenjan, "Pokhod na zapad i zavoevanie Vostochnoi Evropy," in *Istoriia Tatar s drevneishikh vremen,* vol. 3: *Ulus Dzhuchi (Zolotaya Orda) XIII–seredina XV v.,* ed. Rafael Khakimov and Mirkasim Usmanov (Kazan: Institut Istorii im. Sh. Mardjani, 2009), 163.

47. Master Roger, *Magistri Rogerii epistula,* 156–159, 160n1; Thomas of Split, *Historia Salonitanorum atque Spalatinorum pontificum,* 254–259.

48. Master Roger, *Magistri Rogerii epistula,* 168–169.

49. Master Roger, *Magistri Rogerii epistula,* 170–175.

50. Master Roger, *Magistri Rogerii epistula,* xlv–xlvii, 136–141, 146–149, 172–177; István Vásáry, "The Jochid Realm, the Western Steppes, and Eastern Europe," in *The Cambridge History of Inner Asia: The Chinggisid Age,* ed. Nicola Di Cosmo, Allen Frank, and Peter Golden (Cambridge: Cambridge University Press, 2009), 70–72.

51. Master Roger, *Magistri Rogerii epistula,* 180–185; Thomas of Split, *Historia Salonitanorum atque Spalatinorum pontificum,* 260–271. Thomas's account notes that, although the Mongols were able to bypass the bridge, they used seven war engines to destroy the Hungarian guards and take the bridge anyway.

52. Master Roger, *Magistri Rogerii epistula,* 184–185; Jackson, *The Mongols and the West,* 64.

53. Master Roger, *Magistri Rogerii epistula,* 190–193, 206–209, 214–219.

54. Denis Sinor, "John of Plano Carpini's Return from the Mongols," *Journal of the Royal Asiatic Society* 89, no. 3–4 (1957): 193–206. For the Latin text, see *Storia dei Mongoli,* ed. P. Daffinà, C. Leonardi, M. C. Lungarotti, E. Menestò, and L. Petech (Spoleto: Centro italiano di studi sull'alto Medioevo, 1989), 117. Carpini's source was Russian; see *The Nikonian Chronicle,* ed. and trans. Serge A. Zenkovsky and Betty J. Zenkovsky, 5 vols. (Princeton, NJ: Kingston Press, 1984–1989), vol. 2, 321: "But he [Batu] retreated when he learned of the death of the Great Khan." In contrast, Rashīd al-Dīn, *Compendium of Chronicles,* 328, 330, notes that other leaders (Güyük and Möngke) were recalled to Mongolia in the fall of 1240, a year before Ögödei's death, which suggests that there may have been other reasons for Batu and Sübötei's precipitous withdrawal.

55. Büntgen and Di Cosmo, "Climatic and Environmental Aspects," 4; Master Roger, *Magistri Rogerii epistula,* 210–211.

56. Göckenjan, "Pokhod na zapad," 164; Master Roger, *Magistri Rogerii epistula,* 218–221. Sübötei's biographers also erased Jochi's role as a leader in the Merkit campaign. On the Toluid attempts to undercut the legitimacy and accomplishments of the Jochids, see Atwood, "Jochi and the Early Western Campaigns."

57. Allsen, "Prelude to the Western Campaigns," 22.

58. Büntgen and Di Cosmo, "Climatic and Environmental Aspects," 5.

59. Andrews, *Felt Tents and Pavilions,* vol. 2, 1291; Ibn al-Athīr, *The Chronicle,* 216; John of Plano Carpini in *The Mongol Mission: Narratives and Letters of the Franciscan Missionaries in Mongolia and China in the Thirteenth and Fourteenth Centuries,* ed. Christopher Dawson (London: Sheed and Ward, 1955), 13–14.

3 NEW HORDES

1. Utemish Khadzhi (Ötemish Hājjī), *Chingiz-name,* trans. and ed. V. P. Iudin, Iu. G. Baranova, and M. Kh. Abuseitova (Almaty: Gilim, 1992), 92–93, 121–122; Thomas Allsen, "Princes of the Left Hand: The Ulus of Orda in the Thirteenth and Fourteenth Centuries," *Archivum Eurasiae Medii Aevi* 5 (1985–1987), 12n25.

2. Juvaynī, *The History of the World Conqueror,* trans. John Andrew Boyle (Manchester: Manchester University Press, 1958), 266–267; Rashīd al-Dīn, *Rashiduddin Fazlullah's-Jami'u't-tawarikh: Compendium of Chronicles: A History of the Mongols,* trans. Wheeler Thackston (Cambridge, MA: Dept. of Near Eastern Languages and Civilizations, Harvard University, 1998–1999), 347–348; Allsen, "Princes of the Left Hand," 8–9; *Mu'izz al-ansāb. Proslavliaiushchee genealogii,* ed. A. K. Muminov, trans. Sh. Kh. Vokhidov (Almaty, 2006), 39; Rashīd al-Dīn, *Compendium of Chronicles,* 348–351; Allsen, "Princes of the Left Hand," 10.

3. Juvaynī, *The History of the World Conqueror,* 42.

4. Allsen, "Princes of the Left Hand," 15n39; C. de Bridia, *The Tartar Relation* (1237), §23, 27, in Thomas Tanase, ed., *Dans l'empire mongol* (Toulouse: Anacharsis, 2014), 179–181; George D. Painter, "The Tartar Relation," in *The Vinland Map and the Tartar Relation,* ed. R. A. Skelton, T. E. Marston, and G. D. Painter, new ed. (New Haven: Yale University Press, 1995), 32, 36, 76–77, 80–81.

5. Juvaynī, *The History of the World Conqueror,* 249, 255; Rashīd al-Dīn, *Compendium of Chronicles,* 348, 391–392, Allsen, "Princes of the Left Hand," 14.

6. Rashīd al-Dīn, *Compendium of Chronicles,* 312, 393.

7. Juvaynī, *The History of the World Conqueror,* 248–255; John of Plano Carpini in *The Mongol Mission: Narratives and Letters of the Franciscan Missionaries in Mongolia and China in the Thirteenth and Fourteenth Centuries,* ed. Christopher Dawson (London: Sheed and Ward, 1955), 62; Rashīd al-Dīn, *Compendium of Chronicles,* 393; Allsen, "Princes of the Left Hand," 14; Christopher Atwood, "*Ulus* Emirs, *Keshig* Elders, Signatures, and Marriage Partners: The Evolution of a Classic Mongol Institution," in *Imperial Statecraft: Political Forms and Techniques of Governance in Inner Asia, Sixth–Twentieth Centuries,* ed. David Sneath (Bellingham, WA: Center for East Asian Studies, Western Washington University, 2007), 160. For the anthropology of consensus rituals, a common practice across

societies, see, e.g., John Rich, "Consensus Rituals and the Origins of the Principate," in *Il princeps romano: autocrate o magistrato?* ed. J-L. Ferrary and J. Scheid, 101–138 (Pavia: IUSS Press, 2015).

8. See Juvaynī, *Genghis Khan: The History of the World Conqueror,* 40.

9. Atwood, "*Ulus* Emirs," 160–161.

10. Jennifer Holmgren, "Observations on Marriage and Inheritance Practices in Early Mongol and Yuan Society, with Particular Reference to the Levirate," *Journal of Asian History* 20, no. 2 (1986): 127–192, 138, quoting the *Yuan shi.* See also Atwood, "*Ulus* Emirs," 161.

11. Rashīd al-Dīn, *Compendium of Chronicles,* 348.

12. On the old Turkic term *keshig,* see Atwood, "*Ulus* Emirs," 143n1.

13. Atwood, "*Ulus* Emirs," 143–147; Marco Polo, *The Book of Ser Marco Polo, the Venetian: Concerning the Kingdoms and Marvels of the East,* trans. and ed. Sir Henry Yule (London: J. Murray, 1921), vol. 1, book 2, 379; Louis Bazin, *Les systèmes chronologiques dans le monde turc ancien* (Paris: Editions du CNRS, 1991), 385–412; Veronika Kapišovská, "Expressing Time in Mongolian from Nomadic Tradition to Urban Life," *Mongolica Pragensia: Ethnolinguistics and Sociolinguistics in Synchrony and Diachrony* (2004): 63–89; and Brian Baumann, *Divine Knowledge: Buddhist Mathematics According to the Anonymous Manual of Mongolian Astrology and Divination* (Leiden: Brill, 2008), 60–97.

14. Peter Andrews, *Felt Tents and Pavilions: The Nomadic Tradition and Its Interaction with Princely Tentage,* 2 vols. (London: Melisende, 1999), vol. 1, 275–287, 292–294, 324–327, 395–396; William of Rubruck in *The Mongol Mission: Narratives and Letters of the Franciscan Missionaries in Mongolia and China in the Thirteenth and Fourteenth Centuries,* ed. Christopher Dawson (London: Sheed and Ward, 1955), 129. For an overview of the sources, see Christopher Atwood, "Imperial Itinerance and Mobile Pastoralism: The State and Mobility in Medieval Inner Asia," *Inner Asia* 17, no. 2 (2015): 293–349, 295.

15. Atwood, "*Ulus* Emirs," 151–152; Andrews, *Felt Tents and Pavilions,* vol. 1, 520, quoting Plano Carpini in Dawson, *The Mongol Mission,* 60.

16. Rashīd al-Dīn, *Compendium of Chronicles,* 279; Atwood, "*Ulus* Emirs," 147–150.

17. Atwood, "*Ulus* Emirs," 160–161.

18. Rashīd al-Dīn, *Compendium of Chronicles,* 117; Tatiana Skrynnikova, "Relations of Domination and Submission: Political Practice in the Mongol Empire of Chinggis Khan," in *Imperial Statecraft: Political Forms and Techniques of Governance in Inner Asia, Sixth-twentieth Centuries,* ed. David Sneath (Bellingham, WA: Center for East Asian Studies, Western Washington University, 2007), 105–115.

19. *The Secret History of the Mongols: A Mongolian Epic Chronicle of the Thirteenth Century,* trans. Igor de Rachewiltz (Leiden: Brill, 2004), § 224; Atwood, "*Ulus* Emirs," 151.

20. Plano Carpini in Dawson, *The Mongol Mission,* 39–40.

21. Christopher Atwood, "Quriltai," in *Encyclopedia of Mongolia and the Mongol Empire* (New York: Facts On File, 2004), 462; Marco Polo, *The Book of Ser Marco Polo,* vol. 1, book 2, 376–380; Bazin, *Les systèmes chronologiques,* 395; Baumann, *Divine Knowledge,* 84–85.

22. Plano Carpini in Dawson, *The Mongol Mission,* 60–66; Atwood, "Quriltai," 462.

23. Plano Carpini and Rubruck in Dawson, *The Mongol Mission,* 41–42, 52, 91, 116, 210.

24. Nicola Di Cosmo, "Why Qara Qorum? Climate and Geography in the Early Mongol Empire," *Archivum Eurasiae Medii Aevi* 21 (2014–2015): 67–78, 76; Maria Fernandez-Gimenez, "The Role of Mongolian Nomadic Pastoralists' Ecological Knowledge in Rangeland Management," *Ecological Applications* 10, no. 5 (2000): 1318–1326.

25. See Atwood, "Imperial Itinerance," esp. 333–334.

26. Rashīd al-Dīn, *Compendium of Chronicles,* 328–329; Atwood, "Imperial Itinerance," 312–314; John Masson Smith Jr., "Dietary Decadence and Dynastic Decline in the Mongol Empire," *Journal of Asian History* 34, no. 1 (2000): 35–52; Di Cosmo, "Why Qara Qorum?" 73.

27. Rubruck in Dawson, *The Mongol Mission,* 210; Atwood, "Imperial Itinerance," 295–296, 327.

28. Rubruck in Dawson, *The Mongol Mission,* 129, 184.

29. Atwood, "Imperial Itinerance," 295.

30. Sandrine Ruhlmann, *Inviting Happiness: Food Sharing in Post-Communist Mongolia,* trans. Nora Scott (Brill: Leiden, 2019), 49, 54, 193–195; Grégory Delaplace, "The Place of the Dead: Power, Subjectivity and Funerary Topography in North-Western Mongolia," in *States of Mind: Power, Places and the Subject in Inner Asia,* ed. David Sneath (Bellingham, WA: Center for East Asian Studies, Western Washington University), 54–55.

31. Rubruck in Dawson, *The Mongol Mission,* 99.

32. Plano Carpini in Dawson, *The Mongol Mission,* 28.

33. Ringhingiin Indra, "Mongolian Dairy Products," in *Mongolia Today: Science, Culture, Environment and Development,* ed. Dendeviin Badarch, Raymond A. Zilinskas, and Peter J. Balint (Richmond, UK: Routledge, 2003; repr. London: Routledge, 2015), 80; E. Neuzil and G. Devaux, "Le Koumys, hier et aujourd'hui," *Bulletin de la Société de Pharmacie de Bordeaux* 138 (1999), 99; Sandra Olsen, "Early Horse Domestication on the Eurasian Steppe," in *Documenting Domestication: New Genetic and Archaeological Paradigms,* ed. M. A. Zeder, D. G. Bradley, E. Emshwiller, and B. D. Smith (Berkeley: University of California Press, 2006), 264.

34. Rubruck in Dawson, *The Mongol Mission,* 202. Dawson's translation erroneously indicates 105 carts, while the original specifies 500. Guillaume de Rubrouck, *Voyage*

dans l'empire mongol, trans. Claude Kappler and René Kappler (Paris: Editions Payot, 1985), 222; Indra, "Mongolian Dairy Products," 73, 80.

35. J. S. Toomre, "Koumiss in Mongol Culture: Past and Present," in *Milk and Milk Products from Medieval to Modern Times,* ed. Patricia Lysaght, 130–139 (Edinburgh: Canongate Academic, 1994); Olsen, "Early Horse Domestication," 264–265.

36. Indra, "Mongolian Dairy Products," 80–81; Neuzil and Devaux, "Le Koumys, hier et aujourd'hui," 100–105.

37. Juvaynī, *Genghis Khan: The History of the World Conqueror,* 267; see also Jūzjānī, *Tabakāt-i-Nāsirī: A General History of the Muhammadan Dynasties of Asia, Including Hindūstān, from A.H. 194 [810 a.d.], to A.H. 658 [1260 a.d.], and the Irruption of the Infidel Mughals into Islam,* trans. H. G. Raverty, 2 vols. (Calcutta: Asiatic Society of Bengal, 1881–1897; repr. New Delhi: Oriental Books Reprint Corporation, 1970), vol. 2, 176.

38. Rashīd al-Dīn, *Compendium of Chronicles,* 338–339.

39. Rashīd al-Dīn, *Compendium of Chronicles,* 338.

40. Marie Favereau "The Mongol Peace and Global Medieval Eurasia," *Comparativ* 28, no. 4 (2018): 54–57. On the modern Mongol understanding of happiness, see Ruhlmann, *Inviting Happiness.*

41. Rubruck in Dawson, *The Mongol Mission,* 135.

42. Thomas Allsen, "Spiritual Geography and Political Legitimacy in the Eastern Steppe," in *Ideology and the Formation of Early States,* ed. H. J. M. Claessen and G. J. Osten (Leiden: Brill, 1996), 117–118, 120–121, 124, 129; Tatiana Skrynnikova, "Mongolian Nomadic Society of the Empire Period," in *Alternatives of Social Evolution,* ed. N. N. Kradin, A. V. Korotayev, et al. (Vladivostok: Far Eastern Division of the Russian Academy of Sciences, 2000), 298–299; Rashīd al-Dīn, *Compendium of Chronicles,* 83–84. The location of Chinggis's "grave" was purposely hidden and remains a matter of controversy. Burqan Qaldun must not be confused with Ejen-Khoro, in the region of Ordos in Inner Mongolia, where, according to a fifteenth-century tradition, the relics of Chinggis Khan are preserved.

43. According to the seventeenth-century source Abū'l-Ghāzī, *Shajarat-i Turk,* Batu founded the city of Saraijuq: *Histoire des Mongols et des Tatares par Aboul-Ghâzi Béhâdour Khân,* trans. and ed. Petr I. Desmaisons (St. Petersburg, 1871–1874; reprint Amsterdam: Philo Press, 1970), 181. Bartold, *Sochineniia,* iv, 395, translated into English by J. M. Rogers, "The Burial Rites of the Turks and Mongols," *Central Asiatic Journal* 14, no. 2–3 (1970): 195–227, 221–222; John A. Boyle, "The Thirteenth-Century Mongols' Conception of the After Life: The Evidence of Their Funerary Practices," *Mongolian Studies* 1 (1974): 5–14, 8; Devin DeWeese, *Islamization and Native Religion in the Golden Horde: Baba Tükles and Conversion to Islam in Historical and Epic Tradition* (University Park: Penn State University Press, 1994), 193–199; Vadim Trepavlov, *Istorija Nogajskoj Ordy* (Vostochnaia literatura,

RAN: Moscow, 2001), 589; Jūzjānī, *Tabakāt-i-Nāsirī: A General History of the Muhammadan Dynasties of Asia,* vol. 2, 1173. See also John A. Boyle, "A Form of Horse Sacrifice amongst the 13th and 14th-Century Mongols," *Central Asiatic Journal* 10, no. 3–4 (1965): 145–150, 145.

44. Plano Carpini in Dawson, *The Mongol Mission,* 13–14; Friar C. de Bridia, *Tartar Relation* §47 in *Dans l'empire mongol,* 190; *The Vinland Map,* 94–95.

45. Juvaynī, *Genghis Khan: The History of the World Conqueror,* 267. The word *sarāy* has a Persian origin but was commonly used by Turkic speakers. It was not a common term for Mongolian speakers and East Asian people in general. According to both written sources and archaeology, the site was new. Today it is known as Selitrennoe Gorodishche. Like Great Khan Ögödei, Batu probably had several seasonal palaces along his horde's migration route, but Sarai was the most important or at least was seen as such by contemporary witnesses.

46. Rubruck in Dawson, *The Mongol Mission,* 207, 210.

47. Allsen, "Spiritual Geography," 121; Isabelle Charleux, "The Khan's City: Kökeqota and the Role of a Capital City in Mongolian State Formation," in *Imperial Statecraft: Political Forms and Techniques of Governance in Inner Asia, Sixth-Twentieth Centuries,* ed. David Sneath (Bellingham, WA: Center for East Asian Studies, Western Washington University, 2007), 178–179; Di Cosmo, "Why Qara Qorum?" 69–70; Francis Woodman Cleaves, "The Sino-Mongolian Inscription of 1346," *Harvard Journal of Asiatic Studies* 15, no. 1–2 (1952), 25, 69; Francis Woodman Cleaves, "The Sino-Mongolian Inscription of 1362 in Memory of Prince Hindu," *Harvard Journal of Asiatic Studies* 12, no. 1–2 (1949), 1–133, 13; Rashīd al-Dīn, *Compendium of Chronicles,* 328–329; Plano Carpini and Rubruck in Dawson, *The Mongol Mission,* 59, 183–184; *Mongolian-German Karakorum Expedition,* vol. 1: *Excavations in the Craftsman Quarter at the Main Road,* ed. Jan Bemmann, Ulambayar Erdemebat, and Ernst Pohl (Wiesbaden: Reichert, 2010).

48. Plano Carpini and Rubruck in Dawson, *The Mongol Mission,* 40, 129, 133, 156, 209–210; Charleux, "The Khan's City," 185–186. After five weeks marching with Batu's horde, Rubruck's companion cried of exhaustion.

49. Plano Carpini in Dawson, *The Mongol Mission,* 56–57.

50. Rubruck in Dawson, *The Mongol Mission,* 95, 102–104; Andrews, *Felt Tents and Pavilions,* vol. 1, xli, 224, 256–263.

51. Rubruck in Dawson, *The Mongol Mission,* 94–95.

52. Rubruck in Dawson, *The Mongol Mission,* 108.

53. Plano Carpini in Dawson, *The Mongol Mission,* 52; Marco Polo, *The Book of Ser Marco Polo,* vol. 1, book 1, 262; Andrews, *Felt Tents and Pavilions,* vol. 2, 1297.

54. Andrews, *Felt Tents and Pavilions,* vol. 1, esp. xxxiv–xxxv; on the village as a "microcosmos," see Claude Levi-Strauss, *Tristes Tropiques* (Paris: Plon, 1955), 229–284.

55. Rashīd al-Dīn, *Compendium of Chronicles,* 160; Andrews, *Felt Tents and Pavilions,* vol. 1, 519–530, esp. 523; Plano Carpini and Rubruck in Dawson, *The Mongol Mission,* 56, 126.

56. Plano Carpini and Rubruck in Dawson, *The Mongol Mission,* 18, 95, 103–104; Andrews, *Felt Tents and Pavilions,* vol. 1, 387. See also *Mengda beilu,* a Chinese source composed in 1221, which describes a Mongol camp in East Asia, a useful point of comparison: *Men-da bey-lu: Polnoe opisanie Mongolo-Tatar, Faksimile ksilografa,* trans. and ed. N. Ts. Munkuev (Moscow: Nauka, 1975), 79–80.

57. Plano Carpini and Rubruck in Dawson, *The Mongol Mission,* 17–18, 95, 117.

58. Plano Carpini and Rubruck in Dawson, *The Mongol Mission,* 14–15, 117. Camps included yam-houses, which were made available to envoys.

59. Plano Carpini in Dawson, *The Mongol Mission,* 14–18, 61; Peter Jackson, "The Testimony of the Russian 'Archbishop' Peter Concerning the Mongols (1244/5): Precious Intelligence or Timely Disinformation?" *Journal of the Royal Asiatic Society* 26, no. 1–2 (2016): 65–77.

60. Andrews, *Felt Tents and Pavilions,* vol. 1, 227; Plano Carpini and Rubruck in Dawson, *The Mongol Mission,* 57, 61–65, 94–95.

61. Anatoly M. Khazanov, *Nomads and the Outside World* (Cambridge: Cambridge University Press, 1984), 44–53; Andrews, *Felt Tents and Pavilions,* vol. 2, 1291–1294; Atwood, "Imperial Itinerance," 298–299; Plano Carpini in Dawson, *The Mongol Mission,* 55–56. Andrews suggests that Volgograd was the northern limit of Batu's route, but archaeological evidence places the limit 200 miles north of Volgograd, in the vicinity of Ukek, which is also where Rubruck marked the northern bound. Rubruck in Dawson, *The Mongol Mission,* 114–115, 126.

62. Atwood, "Imperial Itinerance," 302–303; Rubruck in Dawson, *The Mongol Mission,* 94–95, 129. These numbers are based on my calculations. See also William Rockhill, *The Journey of William of Rubruck to the Eastern Parts of the World,* 1253–55 (London: printed for the Hakluyt Society, 1900), 127n1; and Andrews, *Felt Tents and Pavilions,* vol. 2, 1296–1297, which suggests a maximum speed of twelve miles per day, based on the recorded speed of oxen drawing heavy loads in Australia today. Historians calculate that Ögödei's horde covered almost the same total annual distance in the area of Qaraqorum. Charleux, "The Khan's City," 187, based on Shiraishi Noriyuki, "Seasonal Migrations of the Mongol Emperors and the Peri-Urban Area of Kharakhorum," *International Journal of Asian Studies* 1, no. 1 (2004): 105–119. For a comparison of the early khans' routes, see Atwood, "Imperial Itinerance," 293–349.

63. Plano Carpini and Rubruck in Dawson, *The Mongol Mission,* 55, 114, 124, 209.

64. Plano Carpini and Rubruck in Dawson, *The Mongol Mission,* 35–36, 126; Andrews, *Felt Tents and Pavilions,* vol. 2, 1297.

65. Plano Carpini in Dawson, *The Mongol Mission,* 55, 59–60.

66. Plano Carpini in Dawson, *The Mongol Mission,* 60; *Secret History,* § 279–281, 297; Juvaynī, *Genghis Khan: The History of the World Conqueror,* 33; Allsen, "Princes of the Left Hand," 12–13. For more on the yam, see Gerhard Doerfer, *Türkische und mongolische Elemente im Neupersischen* (Wiesbaden: F. Steiner, 1963–1975), [vol. 4] 110–118, nr. 1812; Didier Gazagnadou, *The Diffusion of a Postal Relay System in Premodern Eurasia,* trans. L. Byrne (Paris: Editions Kimé, 2016), 47–63, translation of Gazagnadou, *La Poste à relais. La diffusion d'une technique de pouvoir à travers l'Eurasie. Chine, Islam, Europe* (Paris: Kimé, 1994); Adam Silverstein, *Postal Systems in the Pre-Modern Islamic World* (Cambridge: Cambridge University Press, 2007), reviewed by Thomas Allsen, "Imperial Posts, West, East and North: A Review Article," *Archivum Eurasiae Medii Aevi* 17 (2010), 241–242; Márton Vér, "The Origins of the Postal System of the Mongol Empire," *Archivum Eurasiae Medii Aevi* 22 (2016), esp. 235–239; Márton Vér, "The Postal System of the Mongol Empire in Northeastern Turkestan" (Ph.D. diss., University of Szeged, 2016); Márton Vér, *Old Uyghur Documents Concerning the Postal System of the Mongol Empire* (Turnhout, Belgium: Brepols, 2019).

67. Michael Weiers, "Mongolische Reisbegleitschreiben aus Čaγatai," *Zentralasiatische Studien* 1 (1967): 7–54; Vér, "The Postal System of the Mongol Empire," 53–58; Dai Matsui, "Unification of Weight and Measures by the Mongol Empire as Seen in the Uigur and Mongol Documents," in *Turfan Revisited: The First Century of Research into the Arts and Cultures of the Silk Road,* ed. Desmond Durkin-Meisterernst et al., 197–202 (Berlin: Reimer, 2004).

68. Peter Olbricht established this typology in *Das Postwesen in China unter der Mongolenherrschaft im 13. und 14. Jahrhundert* (Wiesbaden: O. Harrassowitz, 1954), 45–101; Rashīd al-Dīn, *Compendium of Chronicles,* 328–329.

69. Plano Carpini in Dawson, *The Mongol Mission,* 58.

70. *The Chronicle of Novgorod, 1016–1471,* trans. Robert Michell and Nevill Forbes (London: Offices of the Society, 1914), 95–96; *The Nikonian Chronicle,* ed. and trans. Serge A. Zenkovsky and Betty J. Zenkovsky, 5 vols. (Princeton, NJ: Kingston Press, 1984–1989), vol. 3, 34–35.

71. Plano Carpini in Dawson, *The Mongol Mission,* 65.

72. *The Chronicle of Novgorod,* 95–97; Thomas Allsen, "Mongol Census Taking in Rus', 1245–1275," *Harvard Ukrainian Studies* 5, no. 1 (1981): 32–53, 43.

73. Paul Buell and Judith Kolbas, "The Ethos of State and Society in the Early Mongol Empire: Chinggis Khan to Güyük," *Journal of the Royal Asiatic Society* 26 (2016): 43–56, 58; Allsen, "Mongol Census Taking," 34.

74. Allsen, "Mongol Census Taking," 37; Plano Carpini and Rubruck in Dawson, *The Mongol Mission,* 37–38, 212.

75. Plano Carpini in Dawson, *The Mongol Mission,* 38–39; Marie-Félicité Brosset, *Histoire de la Géorgie depuis l'Antiquité jusqu'au XIXe siècle* (St. Petersburg, 1849–1858), vol. 1, 551.

76. The new gold coinage of Ögödei is dated 630 H./1232–1233 CE. The first known Qaraqorum silver coinage is dated 635 H./1237–1238 CE. Buell and Kolbas, "The Ethos of State and Society in the Early Mongol Empire," 57–58, 60.

77. Plano Carpini in Dawson, *The Mongol Mission,* 41; *Vardan Arewelts'i's Compilation of History,* trans. R. Bedrosian (Long Branch, NJ: Sources of the Armenian Tradition, 2007), 88; Judith Kolbas, *The Mongols in Iran: Chingiz Khan to Uljaytu, 1220–1309* (London: Routledge, 2006), 124–128, 134; Buell and Kolbas, "The Ethos of State and Society in the Early Mongol Empire," 57–58, 63.

78. Juvaynī, *Genghis Khan: The History of the World Conqueror,* 21, 517–521, 525; Allsen, "Mongol Census Taking," 39. For an extensive description of the census led by Arghun and Batu in a contemporary source, see Brosset, *Histoire de la Géorgie,* vol. 1, 550–552.

79. Juvaynī, *Genghis Khan: The History of the World Conqueror,* 268; Allsen, "Mongol Census Taking," 41–42.

80. Allsen, "Mongol Census Taking," 44, 51.

81. Allsen, "Mongol Census Taking," 49, notes that it was a nomad custom to express the size of their community in terms of the number of tents. In a sedentary context, the Mongols probably counted houses rather than households. See also Thomas T. Allsen, "Ever Closer Encounters: The Appropriation of Culture and the Apportionment of Peoples in the Mongol Empire," *Journal of Early Modern History* 1, no. 1 (1997): 2–23, 4.

82. Brosset, *Histoire de la Géorgie,* vol. 1, 552; Christopher Atwood, "Validation by Holiness or Sovereignty: Religious Toleration as Political Theology in the Mongol World Empire of the Thirteenth Century," *International History Review* 26, no. 2 (2004): 237–256; Marie Favereau, "Tarkhan: A Nomad Institution in an Islamic Context," *Revue des mondes musulmans et de la Méditerranée* 143 (2018): 181–205.

83. Martin Dimnik, "The Rus' Principalities (1125–1246)," in *The Cambridge History of Russia,* vol. 1: *From Early Rus' to 1689,* ed. Maureen Perrie (Cambridge: Cambridge University Press, 2006), 98–126; V. L. Ianin, "Medieval Novgorod," in *The Cambridge History of Russia,* vol. 1, 188–200.

4 THE GREAT MUTATION

1. Ibn ʿAbd al-Zāhir, *al-Rawd al-zāhir fi sīrat al-malik al-Zāhir* (al-Riyād, 1976), 215–216, translated in Fatima Sadeque, *Baybars I of Egypt* (Dacca: Oxford University Press, 1956), 354–355. A later and more complete version of the Mamuk envoys' report appears in Ibn Abī al-Fadā'il, "al-Nahj al-sadīd wa-l-durr al-farīd fīmā baʿd Tārīkh Ibn al-ʿAmīd," in *Histoire des sultans Mamlouks,* trans. and ed. Edgard Blochet, *Patrologia Orientalis* 12 (1916): 456–462. See also Marie Favereau, *La Horde*

d'or et le sultanat mamelouk. Naissance d'une alliance (Cairo: Institut française d'archéologie orientale, 2018), 19–40.

2. Sources disagree on the location and timing of Batu's death. According to *Mu'izz al-ansāb. Proslavliaiushchee genealogii,* ed. A. K. Muminov, trans. Sh. Kh. Vokhidov (Almaty, 2006), 40, Sartaq ruled for a few months from 650 H. / 1252–1253 CE to 651 H. / 1253–1254 CE, indicating that Batu must have died before this time. And Rashīd al-Dīn claims Batu died in Sarai at the age of forty-eight. *Rashiduddin Fazlullah's-Jami'u't-tawarikh. Compendium of Chronicles: A History of the Mongols,* trans. Wheeler Thackston (Cambridge, MA: Dept. of Near Eastern Languages and Civilizations, Harvard University, 1998–1999), 361. But these accounts must be mistaken, as Rubruck saw Batu at the end of 1254. William of Rubruck in *The Mongol Mission: Narratives and Letters of the Franciscan Missionaries in Mongolia and China in the Thirteenth and Fourteenth Centuries,* ed. Christopher Dawson (London: Sheed and Ward, 1955), 125–129.

3. Rashīd al-Dīn, *Compendium of Chronicles,* 361; Juvaynī, *The History of the World Conqueror,* trans. John Andrew Boyle (Manchester: Manchester University Press, 1958), 268; Rubruck in Dawson, *The Mongol Mission,* 124; Utemish Khadzhi (Ötemish Hājjī), *Chingiz-name,* trans. and ed. V. P. Iudin, Iu. G. Baranova, and M. Kh. Abuseitova (Almaty: Gilim, 1992), 96.

4. Rashīd al-Dīn, *Compendium of Chronicles,* 283; Reuven Amitai-Preiss, *Mongols and Mamluks: The Mamluk-Īlkhānid War 1260–1281* (Cambridge: Cambridge University Press, 1995), 11–12, 15.

5. Amitai-Preiss, *Mongols and Mamluks,* 11–12, 15–16.

6. See Peter Jackson, "The Dissolution of the Mongol Empire," *Central Asiatic Journal* 22, no. 3–4 (1978): 186–244, 221.

7. According to Peter Jackson, "The Dissolution of the Mongol Empire," 209, Chinggis Khan himself granted Azerbaijan and the Caucasus territory of Arran and to the Jochids. But Thomas Allsen, drawing on the *Yuan Shi,* demonstrates that it was in fact Möngke who granted these lands to Berke. Thomas T. Allsen, *Mongol Imperialism: The Policies of the Grand Qan Möngke in China, Russia, and the Islamic Lands, 1251–1259* (Berkeley: University of California Press, 1987), 58. See also al-Qāshānī, *Tārīkh-i Uljāītū Sultān,* ed. Mahīn Hambalī (Tehran, 1969), 146.

8. Rashīd al-Dīn, *Compendium of Chronicles,* 361; Allsen, *Mongol Imperialism,* 61–63, 104; Thomas Allsen, "Princes of the Left Hand: The Ulus of Orda in the Thirteenth and Fourteenth Centuries," *Archivum Eurasiae Medii Aevi* 5 (1985–1987), 16–17.

9. Amitai-Preiss, *Mongols and Mamluks,* 21–22, 26–35.

10. Denise Aigle, *The Mongol Empire between Myth and Reality: Studies in Anthropological History* (Leiden: Brill, 2014), 199–218; Bernard Lewis, *Islam: From the Prophet Muhammad to the Capture of Constantinople,* 2 vols. (1974; New York: Oxford University Press, 1987), vol. 1, 84–85.

11. Amitai-Preiss, *Mongols and Mamluks,* 34–45.

12. Allsen, *Mongol Imperialism,* 218–219; Allsen, "Princes of the Left Hand," 17–18; Jackson, "The Dissolution of the Mongol Empire," 227–230.

13. Allsen, "Prelude to the Western Campaigns: Mongol Military Operations in the Volga-Ural Region, 1217–1237," *Archivum Eurasiae Medii Aevi* 3 (1983), 16; Jean Aubin, "L'ethnogenèse des Qaraunas," *Turcica* 1 (1969): 65–94; Jackson, "The Dissolution of the Mongol Empire," 239–244; al-Harawī, *Tārīkh Nāma-i Harāt,* ed. Gulām Riḍā Tabātabā'ī Majd (Tehran, 2004), 260–276. On Berke's coinage, see Dzmitry Huletski and James Farr, *Coins of the Golden Horde: Period of the Great Mongols (1224–1266)* (self pub., 2016).

14. *Mu'izz al-ansāb,* 43. Rashīd al-Dīn, *Compendium of Chronicles,* 362; Jackson, "The Dissolution of the Mongol Empire," 222–223, 226–227, 232–233; Peter Jackson, *The Mongols and the Islamic World: From Conquest to Conversion* (New Haven: Yale University Press, 2017), 141–144.

15. Rashīd al-Dīn, *Compendium of Chronicles,* 111; Michael Hope, *Power, Politics, and Tradition in the Mongol Empire and the Īlkhānate of Iran* (Oxford: Oxford University Press, 2016), 96–97.

16. Jackson, "The Dissolution of the Mongol Empire," 233–234; Allsen, *Mongol Imperialism,* 54–63, 203–207, 218–220; Amitai-Preiss, *Mongols and Mamluks,* 78–80; Favereau, *La Horde d'or et le sultanat mamelouk,* 69–90; Marco Polo, *The Book of Ser Marco Polo, the Venetian: Concerning the Kingdoms and Marvels of the East,* trans. and ed. Sir Henry Yule (London: J. Murray, 1921), vol. 2, book 4, 494–495; Rashīd al-Dīn, *Compendium of Chronicles,* 362, 511–512; Virgil Ciocîltan, *The Mongols and the Black Sea Trade in the Thirteenth and Fourteenth Centuries* (Leiden: Brill, 2012), 47–49, 61–68; Judith Kolbas, *The Mongols in Iran: Chingiz Khan to Uljaytu, 1220–1309* (London: Routledge, 2006), 151–170.

17. Michal Biran, *Qaidu and the Rise of the Independent Mongol State in Central Asia* (Richmond, UK: Curzon, 1997), 21–22. It is difficult to know when Hülegü stopped sending the Jochids their share. This might have been just before or after Berke launched his attack in the Caucasus. According to Kolbas, the payouts ended after the military conflict began (*The Mongols in Iran,* 164). Further complicating the timeline, Wassāf, a fourteenth-century administrator and historian of the Ilkhanids, saw the expulsion of the ortaqs as the main cause of the conflict between Berke and Hülegü: Vladimir Tizengauzen, trans., *Sbornik materialov, otnosiashchikhsia k istorii Zolotoi Ordy,* vol. 2: *Izvlecheniia iz persidskikh sochinenii* (Moscow: Izd. Akademii nauk SSSR, 1941), 80–82. However, the expulsion of the ortaqs was more likely a consequence of the conflict, as various sources place it shortly after Berke's first operations in the Caucasus.

18. Marco Polo, *The Book of Ser Marco Polo,* vol. 2, book 4, 495–496; Rashīd al-Dīn, *Compendium of Chronicles,* 511–512. According to Jackson, "The Dissolution of the Mongol Empire," 234, Hülegu responded, attacking Berke in Jumādā II

661/April–May 1263. But Rashīd al-Dīn recorded that on 11 Jumādā II 661, Hülegü was in Tabriz and Berke in the lower Volga, so no such altercation is possible.

19. Ibn ʿAbd al-Zāhir, *al-Rawd,* 171; al-Nuwayrī, *Nihāyat al-arab fī funūn al-adab,* ed. Muhammad ʿAbd al-Hādī Shuʿayrī, vol. 30 (Cairo, 1990), 87; David Ayalon, "The Great Yāsa of Chingiz Khān: A Re-examination (Part B)," *Studia islamica* 34 (1971), 172.

20. Jackson, "The Dissolution of the Mongol Empire," 216–219; Peter Jackson, "World-Conquest and Local Accommodation: Threat and Blandishment in Mongol Diplomacy," in *History and Historiography of Post-Mongol Central Asia and the Middle East: Studies in Honour of John E. Woods,* ed. J. Pfeiffer and Sh. A. Quinn (Wiesbaden: Harrassowitz, 2006), 17; Peter Jackson, "The Testimony of the Russian 'Archbishop' Peter Concerning the Mongols (1244/5): Precious Intelligence or Timely Disinformation?" *Journal of the Royal Asiatic Society* 26, no. 1–2 (2016), 65–77, 76; Allsen, *Mongol Imperialism,* 49, 74, 177; Amitai-Preiss, *Mongols and Mamluks,* 157–159. See also Charles Melville, "Anatolia under the Mongols," in *The Cambridge History of Turkey,* vol. 1: *Byzantium to Turkey 1071–1453,* ed. Kate Fleet (Cambridge: Cambridge University Press, 2009), 53–57.

21. Claude Cahen "Kaykāʾūs," *Encyclopedia of Islam,* 2nd ed., 12 vols. (Leiden: Brill, 1978), vol. 4, 813–814.

22. Claude Cahen, *Pre-Ottoman Turkey: A General Survey of the Material and Spiritual Culture and History, c. 1071–1330* (New York: Taplinger, 1968), 277–279, 283; Melville, "Anatolia under the Mongols," 57–60; Jean Richard, "Byzance et les Mongols," *Byzantinische Forschungen* 25 (1999): 83–100; Amitai-Preiss, *Mongols and Mamluks,* 158–159; Georges Pachymérès, *Relations historiques,* ed. Albert Failler, trans. Laurent Vitalien, 5 vols. (Paris: Belles Lettres, 1984), vol. 1, 184–185, 188–189, 234–235.

23. Ibn ʿAbd al-Zāhir, *al-Rawd,* 125. Depending on the sources, Berke was either the brother-in-law or son-in-law of the Seljuq sultan. See Favereau, *La Horde d'or et le sultanat mamelouk,* 79.

24. Franz Dölger, *Regesten der Kaiserurkunden des oströmischen Reiches von 565–1453,* vol. 3: years 1204–1282 (Munich: Beck, 1932), 40, nbs 1902–1903–1904; Reuven Amitai, "Diplomacy and the Slave Trade in the Eastern Mediterranean: A Re-examination of the Mamluk-Byzantine-Genoese Triangle in the Late Thirteenth Century in Light of the Existing Early Correspondence," *Oriente Moderno* 88, no. 2 (2008), 363–364; Sergei Karpov, "Grecs et Latins à Trébizonde (xiiie–xve siècle): Collaboration économique, rapports politiques," in *État et colonisation au Moyen Âge et à la Renaissance,* ed. M. Balard, 413–424 (Lyon: La Manufacture, 1989); Richard, "Byzance et les Mongols," 96n34.

25. Pachymérès, *Relations historiques,* vol. 1, 234–239, 242–243. On the delayed embassy, see Ibn ʿAbd al-Zāhir, *al-Rawd,* 173–174, 202–203; Dölger, *Regesten,* 44–45 (nb. 1919),

46 (nb. 1930), 47 (nb. 1933), 49 (nbs. 1937–1938); Amitai, "Diplomacy and the Slave Trade," 359–360.

26. Pachymérès, *Relations historiques*, vol. 1, 300–313; *Die Seltschukengeschichte des Ibn Bībī*, trans. Herbert W. Duda (Copenhagen: Munksgaard, 1959), 285.

27. Rubruck in Dawson, *The Mongol Mission*, 93.

28. Roman K. Kovalev, "The Infrastructure of the Northern Part of the 'Fur Road' between the Middle Volga and the East during the Middle Ages," *Archivum Eurasiae Medii Aevi* 11 (2000–2001), 35.

29. Al-Mas'ūdī, quoted in Kovalev, "The Infrastructure," 27.

30. For an overview of the fur trade before and after the Mongol conquests, see Janet Martin, *Treasure of the Land of Darkness: The Fur Trade and Its Significance for Medieval Russia* (Cambridge: Cambridge University Press, 1986).

31. Ibn al-Athīr quoted in Janet Martin, "The Land of Darkness and the Golden Horde: The Fur Trade under the Mongols XIII–XIVth Centuries," *Cahiers du Monde russe et soviétique* 19, no. 4 (1978): 404.

32. Kovalev, "The Infrastructure," 25–64; Martin, "The Land of Darkness," 401–421.

33. Rubruck in Dawson, *The Mongol Mission*, 90.

34. Rashīd al-Dīn, *Compendium of Chronicles*, 512. Historians disagree over Hülegü's status and title at the end of his life. See Thomas T. Allsen, "Changing Forms of Legitimation in Mongol Iran," in *Rulers from the Steppe: State Formation on the Eurasian Periphery*, ed. G. Seaman and D. Marks (Los Angeles: Ethnographics Press, University of Southern California, 1991), 226–227; Reuven Amitai-Preiss, "Evidence for the Early Use of the Title *il-khan* among the Mongols," *Journal of the Royal Asiatic Society* 1, no. 3 (1991): 353–362; Reuven Amitai-Preiss, *Mongols and Mamluks*, 13–15; Kolbas, *The Mongols in Iran*, 193–234.

35. Rubruck in Dawson, *The Mongol Mission to Asia*, 124; Abū'l-Ghāzī, *Histoire des Mongols*, 181; Devin DeWeese, *Islamization and Native Religion in the Golden Horde: Baba Tükles and Conversion to Islam in Historical and Epic Tradition* (University Park: Penn State University Press, 1994), 83–87; István Vásáry, "'History and Legend' in Berke Khan's Conversion to Islam," in *Aspects of Altaic Civilization III*, ed. Denis Sinor, 230–252 (Bloomington: Indiana University, 1990); Favereau, *La Horde d'or et le sultanat mamelouk*, 27–39.

36. The text of Berke's letter is summarized and recorded in Arabic sources, esp. Ibn 'Abd al-Zāhir, *al-Rawd*, 171; al-Nuwayrī, *Nihāyat al-arab*, vol. 30, 87. See also Ayalon, "The Great Yāsa of Chingiz Khān," 167–169; Marie Favereau, "The first letter of Khan Berke to Sultan Baybars, according to the Mamluk sources (661 / 1263)" (in Russian), *Zolotoordynskaia Tsivilizatsia* 4 (2011): 101–113.

37. Baybars al-Dawādār, *Zubdat al-fikra, fī tārīkh al-hijra*, ed. D. S. Richards (Berlin: Das arabische Buch, 1998), 82–83.

38. Amitai-Preiss, *Mongols and Mamluks,* 30–31; Aigle, *The Mongol Empire between Myth and Reality,* 5–6, 73–74; Ibn 'Abd al-Zāhir, al-Rawd, 215, 217; al-Nuwayrī, Nihāyat al-arab, vol. 27, 358–359; DeWeese, *Islamization and Native Religion in the Golden Horde,* 84.

39. *Mu'izz al-ansāb,* 41; Ibn 'Abd al-Zāhir, *al-Rawd,* 216; Ibn Abī al-Fadā'il, "al-Nahj," 459–460. Some scholars, such as Joseph Fletcher, have argued that political fratricide was a Mongol practice. Joseph Fletcher, "Turco-Mongolian Monarchic Tradition in the Ottoman Empire," *Harvard Ukrainian Studies* 3–4 (1979–1980): 236–251. But others have demonstrated that this view is incorrect; see Marie Favereau and Liesbeth Geevers, "The Golden Horde, the Spanish Habsburg Monarchy, and the Construction of Ruling Dynasties," in *Prince, Pen and Sword: Eurasian Perspectives,* ed. Maaike van Berkel and Jeroen Duindam (Leiden: Brill, 2018), 458–470.

5 THE MONGOL EXCHANGE

1. Rashīd al-Dīn, *Rashiduddin Fazlullah's-Jami'u't-tawarikh. Compendium of Chronicles: A History of the Mongols,* trans. Wheeler Thackston (Cambridge, MA: Dept. of Near Eastern Languages and Civilizations, Harvard University, 1998–1999), 279, 348–351; *Mu'izz al-ansāb. Proslavliaiushchee genealogii,* ed. A. K. Muminov, trans. Sh. Kh. Vokhidov (Almaty, 2006), 39–40; Thomas Allsen, "Princes of the Left Hand: The Ulus of Orda in the Thirteenth and Fourteenth Centuries," *Archivum Eurasiae Medii Aevi* 5 (1985–1987), 10, 34–35.

2. Marco Polo, *The Book of Ser Marco Polo, the Venetian: Concerning the Kingdoms and Marvels of the East,* trans. and ed. Sir Henry Yule (London: J. Murray, 1921), vol. 2, book 4, 479; John of Plano Carpini in *The Mongol Mission: Narratives and Letters of the Franciscan Missionaries in Mongolia and China in the Thirteenth and Fourteenth Centuries,* ed. Christopher Dawson (London: Sheed and Ward, 1955), 12; Walther Heissig, *The Religions of Mongolia,* trans. Geoffrey Samuel (Berkeley: University of California Press, 1980), 101–110.

3. Marco Polo, *The Book of Ser Marco Polo,* vol. 2, book 4, 479; Plano Carpini in Dawson, *The Mongol Mission,* 59–60; Allsen, "Princes of the Left Hand," 12–13, 27–28.

4. Marco Polo, *The Book of Ser Marco Polo,* vol. 2, book 4, 479–481, 484–486.

5. Plano Carpini in Dawson, *The Mongol Mission,* 30; William of Rubruck in *The Mongol Mission: Narratives and Letters of the Franciscan Missionaries in Mongolia and China in the Thirteenth and Fourteenth Centuries,* ed. Christopher Dawson (London: Sheed and Ward, 1955), 170–171. See also Allsen, "Princes of the Left Hand," 13–14, 29, 33–34. Modern Samoyeds live in the Lower Ob area, whereas medieval Samoyeds dwelled in the Sayan Mountains.

6. Marco Polo, *The Book of Ser Marco Polo,* vol. 2, book 4, 479; Rashīd al-Dīn, *Compendium of Chronicles,* 348. See also Allsen, "Princes of the Left Hand," 19.

7. Rashīd al-Dīn, *Compendium of Chronicles,* 435; Vladimir Belyaev and Sergey Sidorovich, "Juchid Coin with Chinese Legend," *Archivum Eurasiae Erasiae Medii Aevi* 20 (2013): 5–22; Yihao Qiu, "Independent Ruler, Indefinable Role: Understanding the History of the Golden Horde from the Perspectives of the Yuan Dynasty," *Revue des mondes musulmans et de la Méditerranée* 143 (2018), 41–42; Utemish Khadzhi, *Chingiz-name,* trans. and ed. V. P. Iudin, Iu. G. Baranova, and M. Kh. Abuseitova (Almaty, 1992), 101 [45 a]. Kölüg (meaning "best" and "strong pack horse") had been a name or title of the Turkic Khaghan. I am grateful to Ilnur Mirgaleev for sharing this information.

8. Nurettin Ağat, *Altınordu (Cuçi oğulları) Paraları Kataloğu 1250–1502. Ek olarak şecere ve tarih düzeltmeleri* (Istanbul, 1976), 54–55; István Vásáry, "The Jochid Realm: The Western Steppe and Eastern Europe," in *The Cambridge History of Inner Asia: The Chinggisid Age,* ed. Nicola Di Cosmo, Allen Frank, and Peter Golden (Cambridge: Cambridge University Press, 2009), 76–77; Pavel Petrov, "Jochid Money and Monetary Policy in the 13th–15th Centuries," in *The Golden Horde in World History,* ed. Rafael Khakimov, Vadim Trepavlov, and Marie Favereau, 614–629 (Kazan: Sh. Marjani Institute of the History of the Tatarstan Academy of Sciences, 2017), 619–620.

9. Petrov, "Jochid Money and Monetary Policy," 620–621.

10. Rashīd al-Dīn, *Compendium of Chronicles,* 520; Michal Biran, *Qaidu and the Rise of the Independent Mongol State in Central Asia* (Richmond, UK: Curzon, 1997), 23–25.

11. Transoxiana, literally "beyond the Oxus River," was the historical name for the region stretching between the Amu-Daria (Oxus) and Syr-Daria rivers.

12. Rashīd al-Dīn, *Compendium of Chronicles,* 521–522; Biran, *Qaidu,* 26–29; Hodong Kim, "The Unity of the Mongol Empire and Continental Exchange over Eurasia," *Journal of Central Eurasian Studies* 1 (2009): 15–42, 26.

13. Rashīd al-Dīn, *Compendium of Chronicles,* 535; Biran, *Qaidu,* 30–33.

14. It is not entirely clear in the sources whether the rebellious princes sent Nomuqan first to Qaidu or directly to Möngke-Temür. On Qaidu's politics, see Biran, *Qaidu,* 27–28, 37–67; Kim, "The Unity of the Mongol Empire," 20–26; Yihao Qiu, "An Episode of the Conflict between Qaidu and Yuan in Mamluk Arabic Chronicles," in *Mongol Warfare between Steppe and Sown,* ed. Francesca Fiaschetti and Konstantin Golev (Leiden: Brill, forthcoming).

15. Biran, *Qaidu,* 63–65.

16. Thomas Allsen, "Mongol Census Taking in Rus', 1245–1275," *Harvard Ukrainian Studies* 5, no. 1 (1981): 32–53, 46–47.

17. On the development of tarkhan status in the Horde, see Marie Favereau, "Tarkhan: A Nomad Institution in an Islamic Context," *Revue des mondes musulmans et de la Méditerranée* 143 (2018): 181–205.

18. Alexandr Zimin, "Iarlyki tatarskikh khanov russkim mitropolitam," in *Pamiatniki russkovo prava,* vol. 3: *Pamiatniki prava perioda obrazovaniia russkovo tsentralizovannovo gosudarstva, XIV–XV vv.,* ed. Lev V. Cherepnin (Moscow, 1955), 467–468.

19. On Mongol religious toleration, see Christopher Atwood, "Validation by Holiness or Sovereignty: Religious Toleration as Political Theology in the Mongol World Empire of the Thirteenth Century," *International History Review* 26, no. 2 (2004): 237–256.

20. V. L. Ianin, "Medieval Novgorod," in *The Cambridge History of Russia,* vol. 1: *From Early Rus' to 1689,* ed. Maureen Perrie (Cambridge: Cambridge University Press, 2006), 196.

21. At some point between 1266 and 1272, Möngke-Temür ordered the Novgorodians to allow German traders safe passage. The Russian version of Möngke-Temür's order appears in *Gramoty Velikovo Novgoroda i Pskova,* ed. Sigizmund N. Valk (Moscow/Leningrad, 1949), 57; Ianin, "Medieval Novgorod," 199.

22. Rashīd al-Dīn, *Compendium of Chronicles,* 519.

23. Reuven Amitai-Preiss, *Mongols and Mamluks: The Mamluk-Ilkhanid War, 1260–1281* (Cambridge: Cambridge University Press, 1995), 89–90; Anne Broadbridge, *Kingship and Ideology in the Islamic and Mongol Worlds* (Cambridge: Cambridge University Press, 2008), 59–61. Around 1271–1272, Möngke-Temür wrote to the Mamluk sultan to encourage him to fight Abaqa and possibly to ally with Qaidu, but no concrete plan was ever established.

24. The exact date of the foundation of the Genoese settlement in Caffa is unknown. It is mentioned for the first time in 1281: Gheorghe Bratianu, *Actes des notaires génois de Péra et de Caffa de la fin du XIIIe siècle (1281–1290)* (Bucharest: Académie Roumaine, 1927), 74. However, the sources refer to an established Genoese trading post, so the settlement must have been built a few years earlier. Virgil Ciocîltan, *The Mongols and the Black Sea Trade in the Thirteenth and Fourteenth Centuries* (Leiden: Brill, 2012), 152–157.

25. Victor Spinei, "La genèse des villes du Sud-Est de la Moldavie et les rapports commerciaux des XIIIe–XIVe siècles," *Balkan Studies* 35, no. 2 (1994): 197–269, 248.

26. Spinei, "La genèse des villes du Sud-Est de la Moldavie," 222, 228–229.

27. Spinei, "La genèse des villes du Sud-Est de la Moldavie," 210, 221, 244–245, 253, 256; Ernest Oberländer-Târnoveanu "Numismatical Contributions to the History of South-Eastern Europe at the End of the 13th Century," *Revue roumaine d'Histoire* 26, no. 3 (1987): 245–258.

28. Spinei, "La genèse des villes du Sud-Est de la Moldavie," 204–206, 234–236.

29. On the Genoese trading posts on the Black Sea, see Spinei, "La genèse des villes du Sud-Est de la Moldavie," 212–215. For the text of the Treaty of Nymphaeum,

see Camillo Manfroni, "Le relazioni fra Genova l'impero bizantino e i Turchi," *Atti della societa ligure di storia patria* 28 (1896): 791–809.

30. Spinei, "La genèse des villes du Sud-Est de la Moldavie," 219, 232–234; Sergei Karpov, "The Grain Trade in the Southern Black Sea Region: The Thirteenth to the Fifteenth Century," *Mediterranean Historical Review* 8, no. 1 (1993): 55–73.

31. See Marco Polo, *The Book of Ser Marco Polo,* vol. 2, book 4, 479–486; Ibn Fadl Allāh al-ʿUmarī, *Das mongolische Weltreich: Al-'Umarī's Darstellung der mongolischen Reiche in seinem Werk Masālik al-absār fi mamālik al-amsār,* ed. and trans. Klaus Lech (Wiesbaden: Harrassowitz, 1968), 75–77, 80 (in Arabic), 142–143, 145 (in German). See also Allsen, "Princes of the Left Hand," 30; and Janet Martin, "The Land of Darkness and the Golden Horde: The Fur Trade under the Mongols XIII–XIVth Centuries," *Cahiers du Monde russe et soviétique* 19, no. 4 (1978): 401–421.

32. Marie Favereau, "The Mongol Peace and Global Medieval Eurasia," *Comparativ* 28, no. 4 (2018): 49–70, 66–67. See also Thomas Allsen, "Mongolian Princes and Their Merchant Partners, 1200–1260," *Asia Major,* 2, no. 2 (1989): 83–126; Elizabeth Endicott-West, "Merchant Associations in Yüan China: The Ortogh," *Asia Major* 2, no. 2 (1989): 127–153.

33. Marco Polo, *The Book of Ser Marco Polo,* vol. 2, book 4, 479–481; Biran, *Qaidu,* 64–66. The precise date and cause of Möngke-Temür's death remain unknown. Rashīd al-Dīn claimed that the khan died in 681 AH / 1282–1283 (*Compendium of Chronicles,* 362) and, as far as I know, the first coins bearing the name of Töde-Möngke date to 682 AH. Roza Sagdeeva, *Serebrianie monety khanov Zolotoi Ordy* (Moscow, 2005), 11–12.

34. Rashīd al-Dīn, *Compendium of Chronicles,* 438; Biran, *Qaidu,* 64–65; Allsen, "Princes of the Left Hand," 21.

35. Rashīd al-Dīn, *Compendium of Chronicles,* 349.

36. On Nogay's origins, see *Muʿizz al-ansāb,* 43. On diplomatic exchange between Nogay and Baybars, see Broadbridge, *Kingship and Ideology,* 59–60.

37. Rashīd al-Dīn, *Compendium of Chronicles,* 365–366. On the peace between Nogay and the Ilkhanids, see also Broadbridge, *Kingship and Ideology,* 60.

38. *Moskovskii letopisnii svod kontsa XV veka. (Polnoe sobranie russkikh letopisei),* vol. 25 (Moscow, Leningrad: Izdatel'stvo Akademii Nauk SSSR, 1949), 153–154.

39. Georges Pachymérès, *Relations historiques,* ed. Albert Failler, trans. Laurent Vitalien, 5 vols. (Paris: Belles Lettres, 1984), vol. 1, 302, 448; Thomas Tanase, "Le 'khan' Nogaï et la géopolitique de la mer Noire en 1287 à travers un document missionnaire: la lettre de Ladislas, custode de Gazarie," *Annuario Istituto Romeno di Cultura e Ricerca Umanistica* 6, no. 7 (2004–2005), 277.

40. Tanase, "Le 'khan' Nogaï," 287–288; Peter Jackson, *The Mongols and the West, 1221–1410* (Harlow, UK: Pearson-Longman, 2005), 204–205.

41. For more on the rise of Nogay, see Nikolai Veselovskii, *Khan iz temnikov Zolotoi Ordy. Nogai i evo vremia* (Petrograd, 1922); Ciocîltan, *The Mongols and the Black Sea,* 248–264; Tanase, "Le 'khan' Nogaï," 272–277.

42. Rashīd al-Dīn, *Compendium of Chronicles,* 362–363; Baybars al-Dawādār, *Zubdat al-fikra fī ta'rīkh al-hijra,* in *Sbornik materialov, otnosiashchikhsia k istorii Zolotoi Ordy,* vol. 1: *Izvlecheniia iz sochinenii arabskikh,* ed. Vladimir Tizengauzen [Tiesenhausen] (St. Petersburg: Izdano na izhdivenie grafa S.G. Stroganova, 1884), 83–84 (in Arabic), 106 (Russian transl.); Jackson, *The Mongols and the West,* 205.

43. Kim, "The Unity of the Mongol Empire," 26; Rashīd al-Dīn, *Compendium of Chronicles,* on Nogay offering a *sharil:* 567; on Jochids' attack through Derbent: 573.

44. Girolamo Golubovich, *Biblioteca bio-bibliografica della Terra Santa e dell' Oriente Francescano,* vol. 2: *Addenda al sec. XIII e Fonti pel sec. XIV, con tre carte geografiche dell' Oriente Francescano de' sec. XIII–XIV* (Florence: Collegio di s. Bonaventura, 1913), nb. 14, 262; Tanase, "Le 'khan' Nogaï," 292–294.

45. Tanase, "Le 'khan' Nogaï," 269–270, 274, 290–298.

46. Rashīd al-Dīn, *Compendium of Chronicles,* 363.

47. For Russian sources on "Tudan's raid," see *Lavrent'evskaia letopis'* (*Polnoe sobranie russkikh letopisei,* vol. 1), (Leningrad: Izdatel'stvo Akademii Nauk SSSR, 1926–1927), col. 527; *Simeonovskaia letopis'* (*Polnoe sobranie russkikh letopisei,* vol. 18), (St. Petersburg: Tipografiia M.A. Aleksandrova, 1913), 82; *Vladimirskii letopisets. Novgorodskaia vtoraia (Arkhivskaia) letopis'* (*Polnoe sobranie russkikh letopisei,* vol. 30), (Moscow: Rukopisnye pamiatniki Drevnei Rusi, 2009), 98. See also Donald Ostrowski, *Muscovy and the Mongols: Cross-Cultural Influences on the Steppe Frontier* (Cambridge: Cambridge University Press, 1998), 150–151.

48. The exact position of Salji'üdai is unclear. Toqto'a called him "his officer," and Rashīd al-Dīn describes Salji'üdai as an *amīr,* military commander, in service to the Jochid khan. Rashīd al-Dīn, *Compendium of Chronicles,* 364, 381–382; *Mu'izz al-ansāb,* 41. See also Tatyana Skrynnikova, "Relations of Domination and Submission: Political Practice in the Mongol Empire of Chinggis Khan," in *Imperial Statecraft: Political Forms and Techniques of Governance in Inner Asia, Sixth–Twentieth Centuries,* ed. David Sneath (Bellingham, WA: Center for East Asian Studies, Western Washington University, 2007), 111–112; Christopher Atwood, "Titles, Appanages, Marriages, and Officials: A Comparison of Political Forms in the Zünghar and Thirteenth-Century Mongol Empires," in *Imperial Statecraft: Political Forms and Techniques of Governance in Inner Asia, Sixth-Twentieth Centuries Centuries,* ed. David Sneath (Bellingham, WA: Center for East Asian Studies, Western Washington University, 2007), 226; and Ishayahu Landa, "From Mongolia to Khwārazm: The Qonggirad Migrations in the Jochid *Ulus* (13th–15th c.)," *Revue des mondes musulmans et de la Méditerranée* 143 (2018), 217.

49. Petrov, "Jochid Money and Monetary Policy," 622; Oberländer-Târnoveanu, "Numismatical Contributions," 245–258; István Vásáry, *Cumans and Tatars: Oriental Military in the Pre-Ottoman Balkans, 1185–1365* (Cambridge: Cambridge University Press, 2005), 90–91; Aleksandar Uzelac, "Echoes of the Conflict between Tokhta and Nogai in the Christian World," *Zolotoordynskoe obozrenie* 5, no. 3 (2017), 510. The sources also refer to Cheke as "Jöge."

50. Rashīd al-Dīn, *Compendium of Chronicles,* 365; Ciocîltan, *The Mongols and the Black Sea,* 161–162.

51. Rashīd al-Dīn, *Compendium of Chronicles,* 365.

52. Pachymérès, *Relations historiques,* vol. 1 part 3, 289–290; see also Uzelac, "Echoes of the Conflict," 512; Rashīd al-Dīn, *Compendium of Chronicles,* 365; Ciocîltan, *The Mongols and the Black Sea,* 253.

53. Marco Polo, *The Travels of Marco Polo,* 314; Rashīd al-Dīn, *Compendium of Chronicles,* 364–366. On Polo's rendering of the Jochid civil war, see Uzelac, "Echoes of the Conflict," 515–516.

54. Vásáry, *Cumans and Tatars,* 71–98; Ciocîltan, *The Mongols and the Black Sea,* 259–279.

55. Christopher Atwood, "*Ulus* Emirs, *Keshig* Elders, Signatures, and Marriage Partners: The Evolution of a Classic Mongol Institution," in *Imperial Statecraft: Political Forms and Techniques of Governance in Inner Asia, Sixth-Twentieth Centuries,* ed. David Sneath (Bellingham, WA: Center for East Asian Studies, Western Washington University, 2007), 160–161.

56. Rashīd al-Dīn, *Compendium of Chronicles,* 364. On qarachu, including Salji'üdai, see Skrynnikova, "Relations of Domination and Submission," 100–101, 104–115, 110–111.

57. On Nogay's rule, see Devin DeWeese, *Islamization and Native Religion in the Golden Horde: Baba Tükles and Conversion to Islam in Historical and Epic Tradition* (University Park: Penn State University Press, 1994), 88–89.

6 THE NORTHERN ROAD

1. Francesco Balducci Pegolotti, *La pratica della mercatura,* ed. Allen Evans (Cambridge, MA: Medieval Academy of America, 1936; reprint 1970), 21–23.

2. See Sir Henry Yule, *Cathay and the Way Thither: A Collection of Medieval Notices of China,* 4 vols. (London: printed for the Hakluyt Society, 1913–1916), vol. 3, 49; Hodong Kim, "The Unity of the Mongol Empire and Continental Exchange over Eurasia," *Journal of Central Eurasian Studies* 1 (2009): 15–42, 27–28; Marie Favereau, "The Mongol Peace and Global Medieval Eurasia," *Comparativ* 28, no. 4 (2018): 49–70, 63–66.

3. Marco Polo, *The Book of Ser Marco Polo, the Venetian: Concerning the Kingdoms and Marvels of the East,* trans. and ed. Sir Henry Yule (London: J. Murray, 1921), vol. 2, book 4, 480–484.

4. Rashīd al-Dīn, *Rashiduddin Fazlullah's-Jami'u't-tawarikh. Compendium of Chronicles: A History of the Mongols,* trans. Wheeler Thackston (Cambridge, MA: Dept. of Near Eastern Languages and Civilizations, Harvard University, 1998–1999), 349; *Muʿizz al-ansāb. Proslavliaiushchee genealogii,* ed. A. K. Muminov, trans. Sh. Kh. Vokhidov (Almaty, 2006), 39. See also Thomas Allsen, "Princes of the Left Hand: The Ulus of Orda in the Thirteenth and Fourteenth Centuries," *Archivum Eurasiae Medii Aevi* 5 (1985–1987), 18–19.

5. Rashīd al-Dīn, *Compendium of Chronicles,* 349–350. Allsen, "Princes of the Left Hand," 23–24. Michal Biran, *Qaidu and the Rise of the Independent Mongol State in Central Asia* (Richmond: Curzon, 1997), 65–66, 69–74.

6. Antoine Mostaert and Francis W. Cleaves, *Les lettres de 1289 et 1305 des ilkhan Arghun et Öljeitu à Philippe le Bel* (Cambridge, MA: Harvard-Yenching Institute, Harvard University Press, 1962), 55–56 (Mongolian text), 56–57 (French translation). See also Peter Jackson, "World Conquest and Local Accommodation: Threat and Blandishment in Mongol Diplomacy," in *History and Historiography of Post-Mongol Central Asia and the Middle East: Studies in Honour of John E. Woods,* ed. Judith Pfeiffer and Sholeh Quinn (Wiesbaden: Harrassowitz, 2006), 15–16.

7. Allsen, "Princes of the Left Hand," 22–25. Biran, *Qaidu,* 64–66; Yingsheng Liu, "War and Peace between the Yuan Dynasty and the Chaghadaid Khanate (1312–1323)," in *Mongols, Turks, and Others: Eurasian Nomads and the Sedentary World,* ed. Reuven Amitai and Michal Biran (Leiden: Brill, 2005), 340–342.

8. Rashīd al-Dīn, *Compendium of Chronicles,* 583, 649, 654; Kim, "The Unity of the Mongol Empire," 26–27; Anne Broadbridge, *Kingship and Ideology in the Islamic and Mongol Worlds* (Cambridge: Cambridge University Press, 2008), 87–93, 95, 131; Marie Favereau, "The Mamluk Sultanate and the Golden Horde: Tension and Interaction during the Mongol Peace," in *The Mamluk Sultanate from the Perspective of Regional and World History: Economic, Social and Cultural Development in an Era of Increasing International Interaction and Competition,* ed. Reuven Amitai and Stephan Conermann (Bonn: V&R Unipress, 2019), 355–356; John A. Boyle, "Dynastic and Political History of the Il-Khans," in *The Cambridge History of Iran,* vol. 5: *The Saljuq and Mongol Periods,* ed. John A. Boyle (Cambridge: Cambridge University Press, 1968), 392–393.

9. Vincenzo Promis, "Continuazione della Cronaca di Jacopo da Varagine dal 1297 al 1332," *Atti della societa' ligure di storia patria* 10 (1874), 500–501; al-Nuwayrī, *Nihāyat al-Arab fī funūn al-adab,* in Vladimir Tizengauzen [Tiesenhausen], ed., *Sbornik materialov, otnosiashchikhsia k istorii Zolotoi Ordy,* vol. 1: *Izvlecheniia iz sochinenii arabskikh* (St. Petersburg: Izdano na izhdivenie grafa S.G. Stroganova, 1884), 140 (in Arabic), 162 (in Russian transl.); Virgil Ciocîltan, *The Mongols and*

the Black Sea Trade in the Thirteenth and Fourteenth Centuries (Leiden: Brill, 2012), 163–173; Nicola Di Cosmo, "Mongols and Merchants on the Black Sea Frontier in the Thirteenth and Fourteenth Centuries: Convergences and Conflicts," in *Mongols, Turks and Others: Eurasian Nomads and the Sedentary World,* ed. Reuven Amitai and Michal Biran (Leiden: Brill, 2005), 412–413; Girolamo Golubovich, *Biblioteca bio-bibliografica della Terra Santa e dell' Oriente Francescano,* vol. 3: *1300–1330* (Florence: Collegio di s. Bonaventura, 1919), 173–174.

10. Pavel Petrov, "Jochid Money and Monetary Policy in the 13th–15th Centuries," in *The Golden Horde in World History,* ed. Rafael Khakimov, Vadim Trepavlov, and Marie Favereau (Kazan: Sh. Marjani Institute of the History of the Tatarstan Academy of Sciences, 2017), 621.

11. Petrov, "Jochid Money and Monetary Policy," 623.

12. See Andrei Ponomarev, *Evoliutsiia denezhnykh sistem Prichernomor'ia i Balkan v XIII–XV vv.* (Moscow, 2011), 167–178. Pavel Petrov, Ia. V. Studitskii, and P. V. Serdiukov, "Provodilas' li Toktoi Obshchevosudarstvennaia reforma 710 g.kh. Kubanskii klad vremeni Uzbek-Khana," in *Trudy Mezhdunarodnykh numizmaticheskikh konferencii. Monety i denezhnoe obrashchenie v mongol'skikh gosudarstvakh XIII–XV vekov* (Moscow, 2005), 142–147, 205. Petrov, "Jochid Money and Monetary Policy," 622–624.

13. Petrov, "Jochid Money and Monetary Policy," 622.

14. See Petrov, Studitskii, and Serdiukov, "Provodilas' li Toktoi Obshchevosudarstvennaia reforma," 145–147.

15. There is some confusion in the sources between Toqto'a's last embassy to the Mamluks and Özbek's first. Doris Behrens-Abouseif, *Practising Diplomacy in the Mamluk Sultanate: Gifts and Material Culture in the Medieval Islamic World* (London: I. B. Tauris, 2014), 64–65. Depending on the sources, Toqto'a died either in a shipwreck or by poisoning while he was aboard ship: *Muʿizz al-ansāb,* 41; Devin DeWeese, *Islamization and Native Religion in the Golden Horde: Baba Tükles and Conversion to Islam in Historical and Epic Tradition* (University Park: Penn State University Press, 1994), 108.

16. DeWeese, *Islamization,* 118–119 and more generally, for sources narrating Özbek's rise to power, see 106–22; Ibn Battuta, *Voyages,* vol. 2: *De la Mecque aux steppes russes et à l'Inde,* trans. and ed. C. Defrémery, B. R. Sanguinetti, and S. Yerasimos (Paris: Éditions Anthropos, 1982), 230n60.

17. German Fedorov-Davydov, *Obshchestvennii stroi Zolotoi Ordy* (Moscow: Izdatel'stvo Moskovskovo universiteta, 1973), 103–107; DeWeese, *Islamization,* 106–122.

18. DeWeese, *Islamization,* 93–94, 120.

19. DeWeese, *Islamization,* 107–115; Thomas Tanase, "A Christian Khan of the Golden Horde? 'Coktoganus' and the Geopolitics of the Golden Horde at the Time of Its Islamisation," *Revue des mondes musulmans et de la Méditerranée,*143 (2018), 58–60.

Abū Bakr al-Qutbī al-Ahrī, *Ta'rīkh-i Shaykh Uways. History of Shaikh Uwais: An Important Source for the History of Adharbaijān in the Fourteenth Century,* trans. and ed. J. B. van Loon ('s-Gravenhage: Uitgeverij Excelsior, 1954), 49.

20. In the Ilkhanid territory, the *beglerbeg* was one of the *keshig* elders, but the same may not have been true in the Horde. On the status of *beglerbeg* among the Ilkhanids, see Christopher Atwood, "*Ulus* Emirs, *Keshig* Elders, Signatures, and Marriage Partners: The Evolution of a Classic Mongol Institution," in *Imperial Statecraft: Political Forms and Techniques of Governance in Inner Asia, Sixth-Twentieth Centuries,* ed. David Sneath (Bellingham, WA: Center for East Asian Studies, Western Washington University, 2007), 156–157, 163–164.

21. Ibn Battuta, *Voyages,* vol. 2, 225, 263, 269; Iurii Seleznev, *E'lita Zolotoi Ordy: Nauchno-spravochnoe izdanie* (Kazan, 2009), 92–93; Atwood, "*Ulus* Emirs, *Keshig* Elders," 160–163. Nothing is known about Qutluq-Temür's father beyond his name, Najm al-Dawla al-Dīn, and his Islamic faith. Qutluq-Temür's mother was Özbek's maternal aunt.

22. According to Mirkhwand, a Persian historian of the fifteenth century, Qutluq-Temür died in 736 H. / 1335–1336: Fedorov-Davydov, *Obshchestvennii stroi Zolotoi Ordy,* 90.

23. Petrov, "Jochid Money and Monetary Policy," 624. On the proliferation of uluses within the Horde, see Arkadiy Grigor'ev and Ol'ga Frolova, "Geograficheskoe opisanie Zolotoi Ordy v Entsiklopedii al-Kalkashandi," in *Tiurkologicheskii sbornik 2001* (Moscow: Vostochnaia literatura, 2002).

24. Ibn Battuta, *Voyages,* vol. 2, 231 ; Eugène Jacquet, "Le livre de l'Estat du grand Caan, extrait d'un manuscrit de la Bibliothèque du Roi," *Journal Asiatique* 6 (1830), 59–60; Yule, *Cathay and the Way Thither,* vol. 4, 89–90; Fedorov-Davydov, *Obshchestvennii stroi Zolotoi Ordy,* 89–93, 100–107. Information on Özbek's reforms comes almost exclusively from the Arabic sources.

25. Allsen, "The Princes of the Left Hand," 25–26; Kanat Uskenbay, "Left Wing of the Ulus of Jochi in the 13th–the Beginning of the 15th Centuries," in *The Golden Horde in World History,* ed. Rafael Khakimov, Vadim Trepavlov, and Marie Favereau (Kazan: Sh. Marjani Institute of the History of the Tatarstan Academy of Sciences, 2017), 207.

26. See Uskenbay, "Left Wing of the Ulus of Jochi," 209. Fourteenth-century cemeteries along the Syr-Daria show an increasing number of burials mixing steppe and Islamic traditions.

27. Allsen, "Princes of the Left Hand," 25–26.

28. On the name "Black Tatar," see Ciocîltan, *The Mongols and the Black Sea,* 276; on the Bulgarian conquest of Nogay's former dominions, see 266–269.

29. A al-Nuwayrī, *Nihāyat al-Arab,* ed. Tizengauzen, 141 (in Arabic), 162–163 (Russian transl.); Ibn Abī al-Fadā'il, *al-Nahj al-sadīd wa-l-durr al-farīd fīmā ba'd Tārīkh Ibn al-'Amīd,* Vladimir Tizengauzen [Tiesenhausen] ed., *Sbornik materialov,*

otnosiashchikhsia k istorii Zolotoi Ordy, vol. 1: *Izvlecheniia iz sochinenii arabskikh* (St. Petersburg: Izdano na izhdivenie grafa S.G. Stroganova, 1884), 185–186 (in Arabic), 196–198 (Russian transl.); al-ʿUmarī, *Masālik al-absār fī mamālik al-amsār,* Vladimir Tizengauzen [Tiesenhausen] ed., *Sbornik materialov, otnosiashchikhsia k istorii Zolotoi Ordy,* vol. 1: *Izvlecheniia iz sochinenii arabskikh* (St. Petersburg: Izdano na izhdivenie grafa S.G. Stroganova, 1884), 214 (in Arabic), 235–236 (Russian transl.); Ciocîltan, *The Mongols and the Black Sea,* 264–267, 269–270.

30. Ciocîltan, *The Mongols and the Black Sea,* 269, 271, 276; István Vásáry, *Cumans and Tatars: Oriental Military in the Pre-Ottoman Balkans, 1185–1365* (Cambridge: Cambridge University Press, 2005), 122–133, 149–155.

31. Janet Martin, *Medieval Russia: 980–1584,* 2nd ed. (Cambridge: Cambridge University Press, 2007), 178.

32. Favereau, "The Mamluk Sultanate and the Golden Horde," 359–360. The Jochids also married their daughters to Armenian rulers, who like Russian elites were seen as kin of a lower caste.

33. Martin, *Medieval Russia,* 174.

34. Martin, *Medieval Russia,* 186.

35. Martin, *Medieval Russia,* 193–194.

36. *The Chronicle of Novgorod, 1016–1471,* trans. Robert Michell and Nevill Forbes (London: Offices of the Society, 1914), 119–121. See also Anton A. Gorskii, *Moskva i Orda,* 2nd ed. (Moscow: Nauka, 2005), 42–59.

37. John Fennell, "The Tver' Uprising of 1327: A Study of the Sources," *Jahrbücher für Geschichte Osteuropas* 15 (1967): 161–179; Donald Ostrowski, *Muscovy and the Mongols: Cross-Cultural Influences on the Steppe Frontier* (Cambridge: Cambridge University Press, 1998), 151–153, incl. n37.

38. Martin, *Medieval Russia,* 196.

39. Martin, *Medieval Russia,* 217.

40. Martin, *Medieval Russia,* 198–199, 202–206. The Novgorodians so opposed Moscow's rule that they did not even acknowledge the enthronement of Ivan II, Ivan Kalita's son, who ruled from 1353 to 1359.

41. Al-Ahrī, *Taʾrīkh-i Shaykh Uways,* 52–53, 58–59.

42. Liu, "War and Peace between the Yuan Dynasty and the Chaghadaid Khanate (1312–1323)," 346.

43. Promis, "Continuazione della Cronaca di Jacopo da Varagine," 500–501; Ciocîltan, *The Mongols and the Black Sea,* 178n141.

44. DeWeese, *Islamization,* 97–100; Tanase, "A Christian Khan of the Golden Horde?" 53. On Özbek's Black Sea policies, see Ciocîltan, *The Mongols and the Black Sea,* 173–199.

45. Favereau, "The Mamluk Sultanate and the Golden Horde," 357–361; Broadbridge, *Kingship and Ideology,* 132n142.

46. Reuven Amitai, "Resolution of the Mamluk-Mongol War," in *Mongols, Turks and Others: Eurasian Nomads and the Sedentary World,* ed. Reuven Amitai and Michal Biran (Leiden: Brill, 2005), 359, 366–369; Broadbridge, *Kingship and Ideology,* 101–114, 134–136; Benjamin Kedar, "Segurano-Sakrān Salvaygo: un mercante Genovese al servizio die Sultani Mamalucchi, c. 1303–1322," in *Fatti e idée di storia economica nei secoli XII–XX. Studi dedicati a Franco Borlandi* (Bologna: Il Mulino, 1976), reprinted in Benjamin Kedar, *The Franks in the Levant, 11th to 14th Centuries* (Aldershot, UK: Variorum, 1993).

47. Victor Spinei, "La genèse des villes du Sud-Est de la Moldavie et les rapports commerciaux des XIIIe–XIVe siècles," *Balkan Studies* 35, no. 2 (1994): 197–269, 246. Pegolotti, *La pratica della mercatura,* 42.

48. Spinei, "La genèse des villes du Sud-Est de la Moldavie," 224; Sergei Karpov, "The Grain Trade in the Southern Black Sea Region: The Thirteenth to the Fifteenth Century," *Mediterranean Historical Review* 8, no. 1 (1993): 55–73, 61–62, 63–64.

49. Ciocîltan, *The Mongols and the Black Sea Trade,* 133–134.

50. Louis de Mas-Latrie, "Privilèges commerciaux accordés à la république de Venise par les princes de Crimée et les empereurs mongols du Kiptchak," *Bibliothèque de l'école des chartes* 29 (1868), 583–584; Di Cosmo, "Mongols and Merchants," 411.

51. Mas-Latrie, "Privilèges commerciaux," 580–595; A. P. Grigor'ev and V. P. Grigor'ev, *Kollektsiia zolotoordynskikh dokumentov XIV veka iz Venetsii* (St. Petersburg, 2002), 5–33; István Vásáry, "Immunity Charters of the Golden Horde Granted to the Italian Towns Caffa and Tana," in Vásáry, *Turks, Tatars and Russians in the 13th–16th Centuries* (Aldershot, UK: Ashgate, 2007), ch. 12, 1–13; Marie Favereau, "Convention constitutive. L'approche historique des contrats: le cas des Vénitiens et de la Horde d'Or," in *Dictionnaire des conventions,* ed. Philippe Batifoulier et al. (Villeneuve d'Ascq: Presses universitaires du Septentrion, 2016), 82–87. For the original documents, see State Archives of Venice, *Libri Pactorum:* Liber Albus, ff. 249, 250, 251; III, ff. 225, 236, 247; V, f. 160; *Commemoriali:* VI, ff. 80–81.

52. German A. Fedorov-Davydov, *The Culture of the Golden Horde Cities,* trans. H. Bartlett Wells (Oxford: B. A. R., 1984), 19–22.

53. Ibn Battuta, *Voyages,* vol. 2, 257–258. See also Fedorov-Davydov, *The Culture of the Golden Horde Cities,* 16. There were some 75,000 inhabitants according to an Arabic source: Vladimir Tizengauzen [Tiesenhausen] ed., *Sbornik materialov, otnosiashchikhsia k istorii Zolotoi Ordy,* vol. 1: *Izvlecheniia iz sochinenii arabskikh* (St. Petersburg: Izdano na izhdivenie grafa S.G. Stroganova, 1884), 550. This number sounded reliable to archeologists: Vadim Egorov, *Istoricheskaia geografiia Zolotoi Ordy v XIII–XIV vv.* (Moscow, 1985), 115.

54. Ibn Battuta, *Voyages,* vol. 2, 257; Fedorov-Davydov, *The Culture of the Golden Horde Cities,* 19.

55. Fedorov-Davydov, *The Culture of the Golden Horde Cities,* 8, 17–19, 25. See also Emma Zilivinskaya and Dmitry Vasilyev, "Cities of the Golden Horde," in *The Golden Horde in World History,* ed. Rafael Khakimov, Vadim Trepavlov, and Marie Favereau (Kazan: Sh. Marjani Institute of the History of the Tatarstan Academy of Sciences, 2017), 630–660.

56. Ibn Battuta, *Voyages,* vol. 2, 263.

57. DeWeese, *Islamization,* 94–100; Roman Hautala, "Comparing the Islamisation of the Jochid and Hülegüid *Uluses:* Muslim and Christian Perspectives," *Revue des mondes musulmans et de la Méditerranée* 143 (2018), 73–76; Tanase, "A Christian Khan of the Golden Horde?" 52–53; Peter Jackson, *The Mongols and the Islamic World: From Conquest to Conversion* (New Haven: Yale University Press, 2017), 354–355; Lyuba Grinberg, "From Mongol Prince to Russian Saint," *Kritika: Explorations in Russian and Eurasian History* 12, no. 3 (2011): 647–673.

58. Fedorov-Davydov, *The Culture of the Golden Horde Cities,* 16, 31–32; Grinberg, "From Mongol Prince to Russian Saint," 669–670.

59. Walther Heissig, *The Religions of Mongolia,* trans. Geoffrey Samuel (Berkeley: University of California Press, 1980), 102.

60. Grinberg, "From Mongol Prince to Russian Saint," 658.

61. Grinberg, "From Mongol Prince to Russian Saint," esp. 656; S. B. Veselovskii, "Iz istorii drevnerusskovo zemlevladeniia," *Istoricheskie Zapiski* 18 (1946): 56–91.

62. Grinberg, "From Mongol Prince to Russian Saint," 659, 665.

63. See V. L. Ianin, "Medieval Novgorod," in *The Cambridge History of Russia,* vol. 1: *From Early Rus' to 1689,* ed. Maureen Perrie (Cambridge: Cambridge University Press, 2006), 200, 208–209; Grinberg, "From Mongol Prince to Russian Saint," 653n20. Private land ownership might have emerged in Russia between the tenth and twelfth centuries, but sources for the period are scant.

64. Charles Melville, "The End of the Ilkhanate and After: Observations on the Collapse of the Mongol World Empire," in *The Mongols' Middle East: Continuity and Transformation in Ilkhanid Iran,* ed. Bruno de Nicola and Charles Melville (Leiden: Brill, 2016), 309–335; Broadbridge, *Kingship and Ideology,* 138–147. According to al-Maqrīzī, *Kitāb al-sulūk li-maʿrifat duwal al-mulūk,* I / 2, ed. Muhammad Mustafā Ziyāda (Cairo, 1936), 772–774, Abū Saʿīd and his "six children" died from plague, but this is not confirmed by any reliable contemporary source.

65. Melville, "The End of the Ilkhanate and After," 324.

66. al-Ahrī, *Taʾrīkh-i Shaykh Uways,* 72–76; Utemish Khadzhi, *Chingiz-name,* trans. and ed. V. P. Iudin, Iu. G. Baranova, and M. Kh. Abuseitova (Almaty, 1992), 107–108; Abū'l-Ghāzī Bahādūr Khān, *Histoire des Mongols et des Tatares par Aboul-Ghâzi*

Béhâdour Khân, trans. and ed. Petr I. Desmaisons (St. Petersburg, 1871–1874; repr. Amsterdam: Philo Press, 1970), 184–185. See also DeWeese, *Islamization,* 95n57.

67. Broadbridge, *Kingship and Ideology,* 161–162; al-Ahrī, *Taʾrīkh-i Shaykh Uways,* 77; Roza Sagdeeva, *Serebrianie monety khanov Zolotoi Ordy* (Moscow, 2005), 29, nb. 264.

68. See Zilivinskaia and Vasilyev, "Cities of the Golden Horde," 644; and Emma Zilivinskaia, "Caravanserais in the Golden Horde," *Silk Road* 15 (2017): 13–31.

7 WITHDRAWAL

1. Sergei Karpov, "Génois et Byzantins face à la crise de Tana de 1343 d'après les documents d'archives inédits," *Byzantinische Forschungen* 22 (1996): 33–51; Sergei Karpov, "Black Sea and the Crisis of the Mid XIVth Century: An Underestimated Turning Point," *Thesaurismata* 27 (1997): 65–77; Sergei Karpov, "Venezia e Genova: rivalità e collaborazione a Trebisonda e Tana, secoli XIII–XV," in *Genova, Venezia, il Levante nei secoli XII–XIV,* ed. G. Ortalli and D. Puncuh, 257–272 (Venice: Istituto veneto di scienze, lettere ed arti, 2001), 270–272.

2. See Hannah Barker, "Laying the Corpses to Rest: Grain, Embargoes, and *Yersinia pestis* in the Black Sea, 1346–1348," *Speculum* 96, no. 1 (2021).

3. Louis de Mas-Latrie, "Privilèges commerciaux accordés à la république de Venise par les princes de Crimée et les empereurs mongols du Kiptchak," *Bibliothèque de l'école des Chartes XXIX* 6th series, no. 4 (1868), 587–589; Virgil Ciocîltan, *The Mongols and the Black Sea Trade in the Thirteenth and Fourteenth Centuries* (Leiden: Brill, 2012), 214–216; Nicola Di Cosmo, "Black Sea Emporia and the Mongol Empire: A Reassessment of the Pax Mongolica," *Journal of the Economic and Social History of the Orient* 53, no. 1–2 (2010): 83–108, 97–98.

4. Barker, "Laying the Corpses to Rest."

5. Gabriele de' Mussis, "Historia de Morbo," in *The Black Death,* ed. and trans. Rosemary Horrox (Manchester: Manchester University Press, 1994), 19; A. G. Tononi, "La Peste dell'anno 1348," *Giornale Ligustico de Archeologia, Storia e Letteratura* 11 (1884), 144–145; Di Cosmo, "Black Sea Emporia and the Mongol Empire," 97–98; Gilles li Muisis, "Recueil des Chroniques de Flandres," in *The Black Death,* ed. and trans. Rosemary Horrox (Manchester: Manchester University Press, 1994), 46. Timothy May, *The Mongol Conquests in World History* (London: Reaktion Books, 2012), 199–210; Timothy Brook, *Great State: China and the World* (London: Profile Books, 2019), 53–56.

6. Barker, "Laying the Corpses to Rest."

7. Mussis, "Historia de Morbo," 16–20.

8. Barker, "Laying the Corpses to Rest"; Mark Wheelis, "Biological Warfare at the 1346 Siege of Caffa," *Emerging Infectious Diseases* 8, no. 9 (2002): 971–975.

9. Abū Bakr al-Qutbī al-Ahrī, *Ta'rīkh-i Shaykh Uways. History of Shaikh Uwais: An Important Source for the History of Adharbaijān in the Fourteenth Century,* trans. and ed. J. B. van Loon ('s-Gravenhage: Mouton, 1954), 59; Charles Melville, "The End of the Ilkhanate and After: Observations on the Collapse of the Mongol World Empire," in *The Mongols' Middle East: Continuity and Transformation in Ilkhanid Iran,* ed. Bruno De Nicola and Charles Melville (Leiden: Brill, 2016), 319.

10. On transmission of plague from animals to humans, see Susan D. Jones, Bakyt Atshabar, Boris V. Schmid, Marlene Zuk, Anna Amramina, and Nils Chr. Stenseth, "Living with Plague: Lessons from the Soviet Union's Antiplague System," *Proceedings of the National Academy of Sciences* 116, no. 19 (2019): 9155–9163. See also Maria Spyrou, Rezeda Tukhbatova, Chuan-Chao Wang, et al., "Analysis of 3800-Year-Old *Yersinia pestis* Genomes Suggests Bronze Age Origin for Bubonic Plague," *Nature Communications* 9, no. 1 (2018): article no. 2234, 1–10; Monica Green, "Editor's Introduction to *Pandemic Disease in the Medieval World: Rethinking the Black Death,*" *Medieval Globe* 1, no. 1–2 (2014): 9–26.

11. Monica Green, "Editor's Introduction," 13; Barker, "Laying the Corpses to Rest." On the possible origins of the Black Death within the territory of the Mongol Empire, see Robert Hymes, "Epilogue: A Hypothesis on the East Asian Beginnings of the *Yersinia pestis* Polytomy," *Medieval Globe* 1 (2014): 285–308; Philip Slavin, "Death by the Lake: Mortality Crisis in Early Fourteenth-Century Central Asia, " *Journal of Interdisciplinary History* 50, no. 1 (2019): 59–90, 61.

12. Hymes, "Epilogue," 289–291.

13. Barker, "Laying the Corpses to Rest."

14. May, *The Mongol Conquests,* 199–200; Brook, *Great State,* 60–61. On the emergence of "a single uniform disease structure," see Peter Jackson, *The Mongols and the Islamic World: From Conquest to Conversion* (New Haven: Yale University Press, 2017), 405–408.

15. Brook, *Great State,* 59, 63–67, 70–71; Hymes, "Epilogue," 285–308; Uli Schamiloglu, "Preliminary Remarks on the Role of Disease in the History of the Golden Horde," *Central Asian Survey* 12, no. 4 (1993): 447–457; Nükhet Varlık, "New Science and Old Sources: Why the Ottoman Experience of Plague Matters," *Medieval Globe* 1 (2014): 193–227; John of Plano Carpini and William Rubruck in *The Mongol Mission: Narratives and Letters of the Franciscan Missionaries in Mongolia and China in the Thirteenth and Fourteenth Centuries,* ed. Christopher Dawson (London: Sheed and Ward, 1955), 12, 105–106.

16. The Muslim writer Ibn al-Wardī reported the plague outbreak in Solkhat: Jackson, *The Mongols and the Islamic World,* 407. For research and debate surrounding routes of plague transmission, see Monica Green, "Taking 'Pandemic' Seriously: Making the Black Death Global," *Medieval Globe* 1 (2014): 27–61; Yujun Cui, Chang Yu, Yanfeng Yan, et al., "Historical Variations in Mutation Rate in an Epidemic

Pathogen, *Yersinia pestis*," *Proceedings of the National Academy of Science* 110, no. 2 (2013): 577–582; Hymes, "Epilogue," 285–308.

17. Schamiloglu, "Preliminary Remarks," 449–450; Lawrence N. Langer, "The Black Death in Russia: Its Effects upon Urban Labor," *Russian History* 2, no. 1 (1975): 53–67.

18. al-ʿAynī, *ʿIqd al-Jumān*, in Vladimir Tizengauzen, ed., *Sbornik materialov, otnosiashchikhsia k istorii Zolotoi Ordy*, vol. 1: *Izvlecheniia iz sochinenii arabskikh* (St. Petersburg: Izdano na izhdivenie grafa S. G. Stroganova, 1884), 497–498, 529; Green, "Taking 'Pandemic' Seriously," 30–31.

19. The Bulgar necropolis, known as "Ust'-Jerusalem necropolis," was excavated between 1996 and 2003. The site dates from the second half of the fourteenth and the first half of the fifteenth centuries. S. Vasiliev, S. Boruckaia, I. Gazimzianov, "Paleodemograficheskie pokazateli Ust'-Ierusalimskovo mogil'nika (g.Bolgar)," in *Drevnost' i srednevekov'e Volgo-Kam'ia. Materialy tret'ikh Khalikovskikh chtenii* (Kazan, 2004), 38–40; Maria Spyrou, Rezeda Tukhvatova, Michal Feldman, et al., "Historical *Y. pestis* Genomes Reveal the European Black Death as the Source of Ancient and Modern Plague Pandemics," *Cell Host and Microbe* 19, no. 6 (2016): 874–881.

20. *Troitskaia letopis'. Rekonstruktsiia teksta*, ed. Mikhail D. Priselkov (St. Petersburg: Nauka, 2002), 368; Janet Martin, *Medieval Russia, 980–1584*, 2nd ed. (Cambridge: Cambridge University Press, 2007), 199.

21. See Janet Abu-Lughod, *Before European Hegemony: The World System A.D. 1250–1350* (Oxford: Oxford University Press, 1989), 37, on the necessarily multicausal explanations of the decline of eastern powers. Abu-Lughod argues that world hegemony was already shifting westward during the time of the Black Death, but I do not find this convincing.

22. Brook, *Great State*, 73–76.

23. David Robinson, *Empire's Twilight: Northeast Asia under the Mongols* (Cambridge, MA: Harvard University Press, 2009), 285–286. Khanbalik was located within the boundaries of what is now Beijing.

24. Robinson, *Empire's Twilight*, 367–368. On the Ming as successors of the Mongols, see Yihao Qiu, "Mirroring Timurid Central Asia in Maps: Some Remarks on Knowledge of Central Asia in Ming Geographical Documents," *Acta Orientalia Academiae Scientiarum Hungaricae* (2021); Hidehiro Okada, "China as a Successor State to the Mongol Empire," in *The Mongol Empire and Its Legacy*, ed. Reuven Amitai-Preiss and David Morgan (Leiden: Brill, 1999), 260–272.

25. Quotation from the *Tangshu (Book of Tang)*, cited by Sechin Jagchid, "The Kitans and Their Cities," *Central Asiatic Journal* 25, no. 1–2 (1981), 71. See also Isabelle Charleux, "The Khan's City: Kökeqota and the Role of a Capital City in Mongolian State Formation," in *Imperial Statecraft: Political Forms and Techniques of Governance in Inner Asia, Sixth–Twentieth Centuries*, ed. David Sneath (Bellingham, WA: Center for East Asian Studies, Western Washington University, 2007), 175n1.

26. The last known gerege from the Horde dates back to the rule of ʿAbdallāh Khan. There are no sources available on direct relations between the Horde and the Yuan after 1368.

27. Beatrice F. Manz, "The Empire of Tamerlane as an Adaptation of the Mongol Empire: An Answer to David Morgan, 'The Empire of Tamerlane: An Unsuccessful Re-Run of the Mongol State?'" *Journal of the Royal Asiatic Society* 26, no. 1–2 (2016): 281–291, 285–286. On the terms "Moghulistan" and "Moghul Khanate," which are more accurate than "Eastern Chaghatai Khanate," see Hodong Kim, "The Early History of the Moghul Nomads: The Legacy of the Chaghatai Khanate," in *The Mongol Empire and Its Legacy*, ed. Reuven Amitai-Preiss and David Morgan (Leiden: Brill, 1999), 290n1.

28. al-Ahrī, *Taʾrīkh-i Shaykh Uways*, 76–79; Anne Broadbridge, *Kingship and Ideology in the Islamic and Mongol Worlds* (Cambridge: Cambridge University Press, 2008), 162–167.

29. For Russian sources on Janibek's violent death, which are all late sources, see *Letopisnii sbornik, imenuemii Patriarshei ili Nikonovskoi letopis'iu* (Nikonian Chronicle). *Polnoe sobranie russkikh letopisei*, vol. 10 (Moscow: Iazyki russkoi kul'tury, 2000), 229; *Letopisnii Sbornik, imenuemii Tverskoi letopis'iu. Polnoe sobranie russkikh letopisei*, vol. 15 (St. Petersburg, 1863), col. 66; *Letopisi belorussko-litovskie. Polnoe sobranie russkikh letopisei*, vol. 35 (Moscow: Nauka, 1980), 47. For Islamic sources, see al-Ahrī, *Taʾrīkh-i Shaykh Uways*, 78–79; Muʿīn al-Dīn Natanzī, *Muntakhab al-tavārīkh-i Muʿīnī* (Iskandar Anonymous), in Vladimir Tizengauzen, *Sbornik materialov, otnosiashchikhsia k istorii Zolotoi Ordy*, vol. 2: *Izvlecheniia iz persidskikh sochinenii*, ed. Aleksandr Romaskevitch and Semen Volin (Moscow: Izdatel'stvo Akademii Nauk SSSR, 1941), 128–129; Hāfiz-ī Abrū, *Dhayl-i jāmiʿ al-tawārīkh-i Rashīdī. Dopolnenie k sobraniiu istorii Rashida*, trans. and ed. E. R. Talyshkhanov (Kazan, 2011), 194–195; Abū'l-Ghāzī Bahādūr Khān, *Histoire des Mongols et des Tatares par Aboul-Ghâzi Béhâdour Khân*, trans. and ed. P. I. Desmaisons (St. Petersburg, 1871–1874; repr. Amsterdam: Philo Press, 1970), 185.

30. See the Nikonian Chronicle: *Letopisnii sbornik, imenuemii Patriarshei ili Nikonovskoi letopis'iu*, 229; and the Trinity Chronicle: *Troitskaia letopis'. Rekonstruktsiia teksta*, ed. Mikhail D. Priselkov (St. Petersburg: Nauka, 2002), 376. According to Ötemish Hājjī, Birdibek killed not only his brothers but other relatives as well: Utemish Khadzhi (Ötemish Hājjī), *Chingiz-name*, trans. and ed. V. P. Iudin, Iu. G. Baranova, and M. Kh. Abuseitova (Almaty: Gilim, 1992), 108.

31. István Vásáry, "The Beginnings of Coinage in the Blue Horde," *Acta Orientalia Academiae Scientiarum Hungaricae* 62, no. 4 (2009), 373; Abū'l-Ghāzī Bahādur Khān, *Histoire des Mongols et des Tatares par Aboul-Ghâzi Béhâdour Khân*, ed. and trans. P. I. Desmaisons (St. Petersburg, 1871–1874; repr. St Leonards: Ad Orientum, 1970), 186; Iurii Seleznev, *E'lita Zolotoi Ordy: Nauchno-spravochnoe izdanie* (Kazan: Izdatel'stvo "Fen" Akademii Nauk Respubliki Tatarstan, 2009), 110. Historians

disagree over whether Birdibek's successor Qulpa (or Qulna) was a descendant of Özbek. After Qulpa, Taidula supported Khidr and Nawrūz, who were not Batuids: Ötemish Hājjī, *Chingiz-name*, 112–113.

32. On Taidula, see Marie Favereau and Liesbeth Geevers, "The Golden Horde, the Spanish Habsburg Monarchy, and the Construction of Ruling Dynasties," in *Prince, Pen, and Sword: Eurasian Perspectives*, ed. Maaike van Berkel and Jeroen Duindam (Leiden: Brill, 2018), 469–470.

33. István Vásáry, "The Jochid Realm: The Western Steppe and Eastern Europe," in *The Cambridge History of Inner Asia: The Chinggisid Age*, ed. Nicola Di Cosmo, Allen Frank, and Peter Golden (Cambridge: Cambridge University Press, 2009), 80.

34. See Vásáry, "The Beginnings of Coinage in the Blue Horde," 373.

35. al-Ahrī, *Ta'rīkh-i Shaykh Uways*, 76.

36. German Fedorov-Davydov, *The Culture of the Golden Horde Cities* (Oxford: British Archaeological Reports, 1984), 15, 20–21, 26.

37. Fedorov-Davydov, *The Culture of the Golden Horde Cities*, 10; German Fedorov-Davydov, *Obshchestvennii stroi Zolotoi Ordy* (Moscow: Izdatel'stvo Moskovskovo universiteta, 1973), 147–148.

38. Uli Schamiloglu, "Climate Change in Central Eurasia and the Golden Horde," in *The Golden Horde in World History*, ed. Rafael Khakimov, Vadim Trepavlov, and Marie Favereau (Kazan: Institut Istorii im. Sh. Mardjani, 2017), 665.

39. Ishayahu Landa, "From Mongolia to Khwārazm: The Qonggirad Migrations in the Jochid *Ulus* (13th–15th c.)," *Revue des mondes musulmans et de la Méditerranée* 143 (2018), 218. Some scholars have claimed that Nanguday and Qutluq-Temür were relatives, but there is no clear evidence of this.

40. Yuri Bregel, *Shir Muhammad Mirab Munis and Muhammad Riza Mirab Agahi, Firdaws al-Iqbāl: History of Khorezm* (Leiden: Brill, 1999), 89; Landa, "From Mongolia to Khwārazm," 215–231; Devin DeWeese, "A Khwārazmian Saint in the Golden Horde: Közlük Ata (Gözlī Ata) and the Social Vectors of Islamisation," *Revue des mondes musulmans et de la Méditerranée* 143 (2018): 107–132.

41. Interestingly, the Sufi-Qonggirad did not stamp their own names on their coins: see Petrov, "Jochid Money," 626. These anonymous coins might have been minted by wealthy Khwarezmian families, a result of the decentralization of control characteristic of the Jochid fragmentation.

42. Landa, "From Mongolia to Khwārazm," 219–222; and Michal Biran, "The Mongols in Central Asia from Chinggis Khan's Invasion to the Rise of Temür: The Ögödeid and Chaghadaid Realms," 58–60, both in *The Cambridge History of Inner Asia: The Chinggisid Age*, ed. Nicola Di Cosmo, Allen Frank, and Peter Golden (Cambridge: Cambridge University Press, 2009).

43. Ibn Khaldūn, *Kitāb al-'Ibar,* in *Sbornik materialov, otnosiashchikhsia k istorii Zolotoi Ordy,* vol. 1: *Izvlecheniia iz sochinenii arabskikh,* ed. Vladimir Tizengauzen (St. Petersburg: Izdano na izhdivenie grafa S. G. Stroganova, 1884), 373, 389; Roman Pochekaev, *Mamai. Istoriia "antigeroia" v istorii* (St. Petersburg: Evrazia, 2010), 16–29; Ilnur Mirgaleev, "The Time of Troubles in the 1360s and 1370s," in *The Golden Horde in World History,* ed. Rafael Khakimov, Vadim Trepavlov, and Marie Favereau (Kazan: Institut Istorii im. Sh. Mardjani, 2017), 689–692; Seleznev, *E'lita,* 119–124.

44. Seleznev, *E'lita,* 24–25.

45. Ibn Khaldūn, *Kitāb al-'Ibar,* 373, 389.

46. Dariusz Kołodziejczyk, *The Crimean Khanate and Poland-Lithuania: International Diplomacy on the European Periphery (15th–18th Century), a Study of Peace Treaties Followed by Annotated Documents* (Leiden: Brill, 2011), 5; Stefan Maria Kuczyński, *Sine Wody* (Warsaw: Nakł. uczniów, 1935), 55–57.

47. Feliks Shabul'do, "Chy buv jarlyk Mamaja na ukrajins'ki zemli? (Do postanovky problemy)," *Zapysky Naukovoho tovarystva imeni Shevchenka* 243 (2002): 301–317; Kołodziejczyk, *The Crimean Khanate,* 5n4.

48. On relations between Moscow and the Horde during the rule of the Grand Prince Dmitri Ivanovich, see Anton Gorskii, *Moskva i Orda* (Moscow: Nauka, 2005, 2000), 80–118; Martin, *Medieval Russia,* 228–238.

49. Vásáry, "The Jochid Realm," 81; Gorskii, *Moskva i Orda,* 99–100.

50. Donald Ostrowski, *Muscovy and the Mongols: Cross-Cultural Influences on the Steppe Frontier,* 1304–1589 (Cambridge: Cambridge University Press, 1998), 244–248.

51. Christopher Atwood, "*Ulus* Emirs, *Keshig* Elders, Signatures, and Marriage Partners: The Evolution of a Classic Mongol Institution," in *Imperial Statecraft: Political Forms and Techniques of Governance in Inner Asia, Sixth–Twentieth Centuries,* ed. David Sneath (Bellingham, WA: Center for East Asian Studies, Western Washington University, 2007), 163–165; Thomas Allsen, "Eurasia after the Mongols," in *The Cambridge World History,* ed. Jerry Bentley, Sanjay Subrahmanyam, and Merry Wiesner-Hanks (Cambridge: Cambridge University Press, 2016), 159–165.

8 ⊱ YOUNGER BROTHERS

1. István Vásáry, "The Beginnings of Coinage in the Blue Horde," *Acta Orientalia Academiae Scientiarum Hungaricae* 62, no. 4 (2009): 382–383.

2. Devin DeWeese, "Toktamish," in *Encyclopaedia of Islam,* 2nd ed., vol. 10 (Leiden: Brill, 2000), 560–561; Ilnur Mirgaleev, "Succession to the Throne in the Golden Horde: Replacement of the Batuids by the Tuqai-Timurids," *Zolotoordynskoe obozrenie/Golden Horde Review* 5, no. 2 (2017): 347–348.

3. Joo-Yup Lee, "The Political Vagabondage of the Chinggisid and Timurid Contenders to the Throne and Others in Post-Mongol Central Asia and the Qipchaq Steppe: A Comprehensive Study of Qazaqlïq, or the Qazaq Way of Life," *Central Asiatic Journal* 60, no. 1–2 (2017): 59–95, 64; and Joo-Yup Lee, *Qazaqlïq, or Ambitious Brigandage, and the Formation of the Qazaqs: State and Identity in Post-Mongol Central Eurasia* (Leiden: Brill, 2016), 97–103.

4. DeWeese, "Toktamish," 561.

5. Ötemish Hājjī, *Chingiz-name,* ed. and tr. Veniamin P. Iudin (Alma-Ata: Gilim, 1992), fol. 54b–57b; DeWeese, "Toktamish," 561–562.

6. On Toqtamish's farr, see Ötemish Hājjī, *Chingiz-name,* 54b; Jean Aubin, "Comment Tamerlan prenait les villes," *Studia Islamica* 19 (1963): 87–89.

7. Ötemish Hājjī, *Chingiz-name,* 58a–59a.

8. Virgil Ciocîltan, *The Mongols and the Black Sea Trade in the Thirteenth and Fourteenth Centuries* (Leiden: Brill, 2012), 225; Roman Pochekaev, *Mamay: Istoriia 'antigeroia' v istorii* (St. Petersburg: Evraziya, 2010), 92–96.

9. Ciocîltan, *The Mongols and the Black Sea Trade,* 226–231.

10. Enrico Basso, "Il 'bellum de Sorcati,' ed i trattati del 1380–87 tra Genova e l'Orda d'Oro," *Studi Genuensi* 8, new series (1990): 11–26; Ciocîltan, *The Mongols and the Black Sea Trade,* 235–236; Pavel Petrov, "Jochid Money and Monetary Policy in the 13th–15th Centuries," in *The Golden Horde in World History,* ed. M. Favereau, R. Hautala, R. Khakimov, I. M. Mirgaleev, and V. V. Trepavlov (Kazan: Sh. Marjani Institute of History of the Tatarstan Academy of Sciences, 2017), 626–627. We know of at least four treaties concluded between the Jochids and the Genoese: the treaties of November 27, 1380 (signed by an unidentified Jochid figure, Konak Beg); February 24, 1381; July 28, 1383; and August 12, 1387: S. de Sacy, "Pièces diplomatiques tirées de la république de Gênes," *Notices et extraits des manuscrits de la bibliothèque du Roi* 9 (Paris, 1827), 52–58.

11. Ciocîltan, *The Mongols and the Black Sea Trade,* 233–234.

12. The Shibanids briefly accessed the Jochid throne in the 1360s: Ötemish Hājjī, *Chingiz-name,* fol. 53a–54a. Theirs was, however, a very short reign: Vásáry, "The Beginnings of Coinage," 373. Historians have numerous theories as to why the Shibanids and Toqa Temürids dominated the other lineages. See Ilnur Mirgaleev "'Shuab-i pandzhgana' Rashid ad-dina: perspektivy izucheniia," *Zolotoordynskoe obozrenie / Golden Horde Review* 1 (2013): 57–64; Mirgaleev, "Succession to the Throne," 344–351; Marie Favereau and Liesbeth Geevers, "The Golden Horde, the Spanish Habsburg Monarchy, and the Construction of Ruling Dynasties," in *Prince, Pen and Sword: Eurasian Perspectives,* ed. Maaike van Berkel and Jeroen Duindam (Leiden: Brill, 2018), 470–477.

13. Genealogical sources record that Toqa Temür was the youngest of Jochi's sons, numbering more than a dozen, or that he was at least considered the youngest by

his contemporaries, possibly due to this mother's rank: Mirgaleev, "Succession to the Throne," 344–346.

14. Vásáry, "The Beginnings of Coinage," 372, 377–383.

15. Anne Broadbridge, *Kingship and Ideology in the Islamic and Mongol Worlds* (Cambridge: Cambridge University Press, 2008), 171–173.

16. S. Bocharov and A. Sitdikov, "The Solkhat's War and Its Reflection in the Fortification of Caffa," *Classica et Christiana* 9, no. 2 (2014): 413–426.

17. Julien Loiseau, *Les Mamelouks (XIIIe–XVIe siècle). Une expérience du pouvoir dans l'islam médiéval* (Paris: Seuil, 2014), 64, 69; Marie Favereau, "The Golden Horde and the Mamluks," in *The Golden Horde in World History,* ed. M. Favereau, R. Hautala, R. Khakimov, I. M. Mirgaleev, and V. V. Trepavlov (Kazan: Sh. Marjani Institute of History of the Tatarstan Academy of Sciences, 2017), 340–343.

18. Broadbridge, *Kingship and Ideology,* 172–173.

19. On the chronology of Toqtamish's military conflicts with Tamerlane, see Ilnur Mirgaleev, "Bitvy Toktamish-khana s Aksak Timurom," in *Voennoe delo Zolotoi Ordy: problemy i perspektivy izucheniia. Materialy kruglovo stola, pro. v ramkakh Mezhdunarodnovo Zolotoordynskovo Foruma, Kazan', 29–30 marta 2011 g.,* ed. I. Mirgaleev (Kazan: Institut Istorii im. Sh. Mardzhani A.N.R.T., 2011), 170–182; on the sources, see Ilnur Mirgaleev, *Politicheskaia istoriia Zolotoi Ordy perioda pravleniia Toktamysh-khana* (Kazan: Alma-Lit, 2003).

20. Vadim Trepavlov, *The Formation and Early History of the Manghït Yurt* (Bloomington: Indiana University, Research Institute for Inner Asian Studies, 2001), 12–15; Ibn al-Furāt, "Ta'rīkh al-duwal wa-l-mulūk," in *Sbornik materialov, otnosiashchikhsia k istorii Zolotoi Ordy,* vol. 1: *Izvlecheniia iz sochinenii arabskikh,* ed. V. G. Tizengauzen (St. Petersburg: Izdano na izhdivenie grafa S. G. Stroganova, 1884), 356–357.

21. F. B. Charmoy, "Expédition de Timour-i Lènk ou Tamerlan contre Toqtamiche, khân de l'ouloûs de Djoûtchy en 793 de l'hégire ou 1391 de notre ère," *Mémoires de l'Académie Impériale des sciences de St Pétersbourg,* 6th series, 3 (1836): 89–505; Mirgaleev, "Bitvy Toktamish-khana," 170–182.

22. The vassalage agreement between Toqtamish and Jagiello was reached either in 1382 or around 1386. See Dariusz Kołodziejczyk, *The Crimean Khanate and Poland-Lithuania: International Diplomacy on the European Periphery (15th–18th Century), a Study of Peace Treaties Followed by Annotated Documents* (Leiden: Brill, 2011), 6n7; for Toqtamish's letter to Jagiello, see l. 20–21. An edited version of the agreement appears in I. Berezin, *Khanskie Iarlyki, iarlyk khana Zolotoi Ordy Tokhtamysha k pol'skomu koroliu Jagailu 1392–1393* (Kazan: N. Kokovin, 1850).

23. *Barbaro i Kontarini o Rossii: k istorii italo-russkikh sviazei v XV v.,* ed. and trans. E. Ch. Skrzhinskaia (Leningrad: Nauka, 1971), 125.

24. Broadbridge, *Kingship and Ideology,* 185–186; Charmoy, "Expédition de Timour-i Lènk," 118; Iurii Seleznev, *E'lita Zolotoi Ordy: Nauchno-spravochnoe izdanie* (Kazan: Izdatel'stvo "Fen" Akademii Nauk Respubliki Tatarstan, 2009), 30; Ilnur Mirgaleev, "Bitvy Toktamish-khana s Aksak Timurom," in *Voennoe delo Zolotoi Ordy: problemy i perspektivy izucheniia. Materialy kruglovo stola, pro. v ramkakh Mezhdunarodnovo Zolotoordynskovo Foruma, Kazan', 29–30 marta 2011 g.,* ed. Ilnur Mirgaleev (Kazan: Institut Istorii im. Sh. Mardzhani A.N.R.T, 2011), 170–182.

25. Ibn al-Furāt, *"Ta'rīkh al-duwal,"* 356–357; Michele Bernardini, "Tamerlano, i Genovesi e il favoloso Axalla," in *Europa e Islam tra i secoli XIV e XVI,* 2 vols., ed. Michele Bernardini, Clara Borrelli, et al. (Naples: Istituto universitario orientale, 2002), vol. 1, 394.

26. Marie Favereau, "Tarkhan: A Nomad Institution in an Islamic Context," *Revue des mondes musulmans et de la Méditerranée* 143 (2018): 186–187.

27. Kołodziejczyk, *The Crimean Khanate,* 7–8; DeWeese, "Toktamish," 563.

28. Depending on the sources, Toqtamish was killed in battle by a rival khan, by Edigü's son, or by Edigü himself: DeWeese, "Toktamish," 563; Devin DeWeese, *Islamization and Native Religion in the Golden Horde: Baba Tükles and Conversion to Islam in Historical and Epic Tradition* (University Park: Pennsylvania State University Press, 1994), 338.

29. Ciocîltan, *The Mongols and the Black Sea Trade,* 230.

30. The site of New Sarai shows archaeological evidence of Tamerlane's destruction, but the site of Sarai does not: German A. Fedorov-Davydov, *The Culture of the Golden Horde Cities,* trans. H. Bartlett Wells (Oxford: B.A.R, 1984), 26. On the salt trade and Astrakhan in the 1430s, see Skrzhinskaia, *Barbaro,* 132.

31. Josafa Barbaro, *Travels to Tana and Persia,* trans. W. Thomas and S. A. Roy, ed. Lord Stanley of Alderley (London: Printed for the Hakluyt Society, 1873), 18; original Italian quoted in Skrzhinskaia, *Barbaro,* 123–124.

32. Mirgaleev, "Succession to the Throne," 347–348; Trepavlov, *The Formation,* 21–22; Ishayahu Landa, "From Mongolia to Khwārazm: The Qonggirad Migrations in the Jochid *Ulus* (13th–15th c.)," *Revue des mondes musulmans et de la Méditerranée* 143 (2018): 219, 224–225.

33. Pero Tafur, *Andanças é viajes de Pero Tafur por diversas partes del mundo avidos: 1435–1439,* ed. Marcos Jiménez de la Espada (Madrid: Imprenta de Miguel Ginesta, 1874), 166–167; Uli Schamiloglu, "The Qaraçi Beys of the Later Golden Horde: Notes on the Organisation of the Mongol World Empire," *Archivum Eurasiae Medii Aevi* 4 (1984): 283–297; Christopher Atwood, "*Ulus* Emirs, *Keshig* Elders, Signatures, and Marriage Partners: The Evolution of a Classic Mongol Institution," in *Imperial Statecraft: Political Forms and Techniques of Governance in Inner Asia, Sixth–Twentieth Centuries,* ed. David Sneath (Bellingham: Western Washington University, Mongolia and Inner Asia Studies Unit, 2006), 141–173, 158.

34. Trepavlov, *The Formation,* 15, 47; Kołodziejczyk, *The Crimean Khanate,* 7–8.

35. Kołodziejczyk, *The Crimean Khanate,* 9. The expression of friendship appears in doc. 7 on page 554 and doc. 10 on page 584. On Lipka Tatars, see M. Połczyński, "Seljuks on the Baltic: Polish-Lithuanian Muslim Pilgrims in the Court of Ottoman Sultan Süleyman I," *Journal of Early Modern History* 19, no. 5 (2015): 409–437.

36. DeWeese, *Islamization,* 340–341, 343; Trepavlov, *The Formation,* 2–3.

37. Edigü was said to have around twenty sons. Vadim Trepavlov, *Istoriia Nogaiskoi Ordy* (Moscow: Vostochnaia literatura, 2001), 85–97; Trepavlov, *The Formation,* 20, 24–32.

38. DeWeese, *Islamization,* 344–347; Trepavlov, *Istoriia,* 97–100. Toqtamish's people are often called "Uzbek" in Persian sources.

39. Yuri Bregel, "Uzbeks, Qazaqs and Turkmens," in *The Cambridge History of Inner Asia: The Chinggisid Age,* ed. Nicola Di Cosmo, Allen Frank, and Peter Golden (Cambridge: Cambridge University Press, 2009) 223–225; Joo-Yup Lee, *Qazaqlïq,* 102–109; Joo-Yup Lee, "The Political Vagabondage," 80–84.

40. Kamāl al-Dīn 'Alī Bīnā'ī, "Shaybani Nama," in *Materialy po istorii Kazakhskikh khanstv XV-XVII vv. Izvlecheniia iz persidskikh i tiurkskikh sochinenii,* trans S. G. Ibragimov and K. A. Pishchulina (Alma Ata: Nauka, 1969), 104; Trepavlov, *The Formation,* 38; DeWeese, *Islamization,* 348–352; Joo-Yup Lee, *Qazaqlïq,* 109–120; Joo-Yup Lee, "The Political Vagabondage," 84–87.

41. Mária Ivanics and M. A. Usmanov, *Das Buch der Dschingis-Legende (Däftär-i Čingiz-nāmä)* (Szeged: Department of Altaic Studies, University of Szeged, 2002), 52–53 (folio 19r.); Mária Ivanics, "Der Sippenbaum im Buch der Dschingis-Legende," in *Man and Nature in the Altaic World,* ed. Kellner-Heinkele Barbara, Boykova Elena, and Heuer Brigitte, Proceedings of the 49th Permanent International Altaistic Conference, Berlin, July 30–August 4, 2006 (Berlin: Klaus Schwarz Verlag, 2012), 179–191.

42. I am grateful to Mária Ivanics for bringing this allegory to my attention at a conference in Leiden in 2016. For related discussions, see Beatrice Manz Forbes, "The Clans of the Crimean Khanate 1466–1532," *Harvard Ukrainian Studies* 2, no. 3 (1978): 282–309; Trepavlov, *Istoriia,* 87–88; Trepavlov, *The Formation,* 22.

43. See, generally, Joseph Schumpeter, *Capitalism, Socialism, and Democracy* (New York: Harper and Row, 1942); Pekka Hämäläinen, *Lakota America* (New Haven: Yale University Press, 2019), 9.

EPILOGUE

1. Allen Frank, "The Western Steppe: Volga-Ural Region, Siberia and the Crimea," in *The Cambridge History of Inner Asia: The Chinggisid Age,* ed. Nicola Di Cosmo, Allen Frank, and Peter Golden (Cambridge: Cambridge University Press, 2009),

253; Ilia Zaitsev, "Pis'mo khana Bol'shoi ordy Akhmada turetskomu sultanu Mekhmedu II Fatikhu 881 goda khidzhry," *Vostochnii Arkhiv* 2–3 (1999): 4–15.

2. On the 1479 episode, which may be apocryphal, see Edward L. Keenan, "The *Jarlyk* of Axmed-Xan to Ivan III: A New Reading," *International Journal of Slavic Linguistics and Poetics* 12 (1969): 31–47, 33–46.

3. Michael Khodarkovsky, *Russia's Steppe Frontier* (Bloomington: Indiana University Press, 2002), 78.

4. Khodarkovsky, *Russia's Steppe Frontier,* 80.

5. On the Russian and Soviet historiography of the Horde, the Stand on the Ugra River, and the Tatar yoke, see Charles Halperin, "Soviet Historiography on Russia and the Mongols," *Russian Review* 41, no. 3 (1982): 306–322; Charles Halperin, "The Tatar Yoke and Tatar Oppression," *Russia Mediaevalis* 5, no. 1 (1984): 20–39; Charles Halperin, "Omissions of National Memory: Russian Historiography on the Golden Horde as Politics of Inclusion and Exclusion," *Ab Imperio* 3 (2004): 131–44; Donald Ostrowski, *Muscovy and the Mongols: Cross-Cultural Influences on the Steppe Frontier, 1304–1589* (Cambridge: Cambridge University Press, 1998), 135–248.

6. On the battle between Mengli Giray and Ahmad Khan's son and successor, see Leslie Collins, "On the Alleged 'Destruction' of the Great Horde in 1502," in *Manzikert to Lepanto: The Byzantine World and the Turks, 1071–1571,* ed. A. Bryer and M. Ursinus (Amsterdam: A. M. Hakkert, 1991), 361–399.

7. See Vadim Trepavlov, "The Takht Eli Khanate: The State System at the Twilight of the Golden Horde," *Revue des mondes musulmans et de la Méditerranée* 143 (2018): 235–247.

8. Thomas Allsen, "Technologies of Governance in the Mongolian Empire: A Geographic Overview," in *Imperial Statecraft: Political Forms and Techniques of Governance in Inner Asia, Sixth–Twentieth Centuries,* ed. David Sneath (Bellingham, WA: Center for East Asian Studies, Western Washington University, 2007), 164.

9. On various possible interpretations of Simeon's enthronement, see Charles Halperin, "Ivan IV and Chinggis Khan," *Jahrbücher für Geschichte Osteuropas* 51, no. 4 (2003): 481–497.

10. David M. Robinson, "The Ming Court and the Legacy of the Yuan Mongols," in *Culture, Courtiers, and Competition: The Ming Court (1368–1644),* ed. David M. Robinson (Cambridge, MA: Harvard University Asia Center, 2008), 366–369.

11. Some of these words, like *bumaga,* have a Turkic origin but entered Russian during the Mongol period. Donald Ostrowski, "The Mongol Origins of Muscovite Political Institutions," *Slavic Review* 49, no. 4 (1990): 534.

12. James Scott, *The Art of Not Being Governed: An Anarchist History of Upland Southeast Asia* (New Haven: Yale University Press, 2009), esp. 326.

13. Ibn Khaldun, *An Arab Philosophy of History: Selections from the Prolegomena of Ibn Khaldun of Tunis,* trans. Charles Issawi (London: J. Murray, 1950), 309.

14. Nicola Di Cosmo, "Ancient Inner Asian Nomads: Their Economic Basis and Its Significance in Chinese History," *Journal of Asian Studies* 53, no. 4 (1994): 1092–1126.

15. Christopher Atwood, "The Political Economy of the Mongol Empire: Placing Cultural Exchange in Its Economic Context" (lecture, "The Mongols and Global History" conference, Villa I Tatti, Florence, December 10–11, 2018).

16. Allsen, "Technologies of Governance," 129.

17. Pekka Hämäläinen, "Dark Matters of History: Uncovering Nomadic Empires" (lecture, Institute for History at Leiden University, December 6, 2019).

18. Ostrowski, *Muscovy and the Mongols,* 36–63.

Acknowledgments

A book is always a collective work, and this one is born from several encounters that decisively changed my vision of the Mongol Empire. The book began when Pekka Hämäläinen invited me to take part in his five-year project on nomadic empires in world history. I have been fortunate to work with him and am grateful for his generous feedback, frank advice, and unwavering support. His scholarship has been an endless source of inspiration, and the Rothermere American Institute at Oxford, the project's academic home, offered a provocative and lively space for discussion that never failed to stimulate me. I would like to thank as well the other members and associates of the project: Julien Cooper, Mandy Izadi, Bryan Miller, Maya Petrovich, and Irina Shingiray. Very special thanks go to Briony Truscott, the project administrator, for her help and patience. Also at Oxford, Veera Supinen worked with me on the manuscript at various stages, improving it greatly. This book would not exist without her sharp insight and warm encouragement. My debt to her is huge.

I owe an enormous intellectual debt to a number of scholars with whom I've shared inspiring conversations and debates: Ilya Afanasyev, Reuven Amitai, Andrey E. Astafiev, Chris Atwood, James Belich, Maaike van Berkel, Romain Bertrand, Michal Biran, Jonathan Brack, Elio Brancaforte, Anne Broadbridge, Isabelle Charleux, Erica Charters, Nicola Di Cosmo, John Darwin, Jeroen Duindam, François-Xavier Fauvelle, Liesbeth Geevers, Jos Gommans, Monica Green, Marek Jankowiak, Anatoly Khazanov, Dariusz Kołodziejczyk, Julien Loiseau, Beatrice Forbes Manz, David Morgan, Sergei Panteleev, Andrew C. S. Peacock, Pavel N. Petrov, Evgeniy Pigarev, Michael Połczyński,

Jonathan Shepard, Naomi Standen, Luke Treadwell, Vadim Trepavlov, and István Vásáry. In addition, the generous anonymous colleagues who read my manuscript for the press saved me from many omissions and mistakes. Any that remain are mine exclusively.

I have presented parts of this book at many seminars and conferences, including at the Centre d'Études Mongoles et Sibériennes in Paris; the Forum on the Golden Horde organized by the Tatarstan Academy of Sciences in Kazan; the Empires to be Remembered conference in Vienna; a conference organized by the Mangystau State Historical and Cultural Reserve, Aktau, Kazakhstan; and The Mongols and Global History conference at Villa I Tatti, Harvard University, in Florence. I wish to thank the conveners and participants for their comments and advice. I wish also to extend my gratitude to the Oxford History Department and the University of Paris Nanterre, especially my current research laboratory, the MéMo, for their support. The research informing this book received funding from the European Research Council under the European Union's Seventh Framework Programme (FP7/2007-2013) / ERC grant agreement no. 615040.

Several friends and colleagues helped me complete the research for this book during the long closure of archives, libraries, and museums accompanying the COVID-19 pandemic. My thanks to Gabrielle van den Berg, Zvezdana Dode, Francesca Fiaschetti, Konstantin Golev, Andrey Maslovsky, Ilnur Mirgaleev, Leonard Nedashkovsky, Yihao Qiu, Sandrine Ruhlmann, Anastasia Tepliakova, and Márton Vér. In addition, I owe special thanks to Debora Fajnwaks for her solid support and astute counsel.

I am grateful to the institutions that house the objects depicted in the book's illustrations, including the Azov Historical, Archaeological, and Paleontological Museum-Reserve; the State Hermitage Museum in St. Petersburg; the Chester Beatty Library, Dublin; the Metropolitan Museum of Art in New York; the Berlin Staatsbibliothek; the Bibliothèque nationale in Paris; and the University of Edinburgh.

Several people guided me in transforming the manuscript into a book. I would like to express my deep gratitude to Chris Rogers, who believed in my project, supported me all the way, and was always immensely helpful. With great professionalism and sharp determination, Kathleen McDermott at Harvard University Press shepherded the book from idea to reality. I am grateful to Simon Waxman for editing the text with his masterful sense of prose and infallible eye for detail. It was also a great pleasure to work with Anne McGuire, who provided invaluable help. The maps were created by Alexander Kent from Canterbury Christ Church University, and Mara Nakama drew the illustrations. I owe both of them a debt of gratitude for their efficiency and superb work.

My greatest debt is to my family and especially to Julien Doumenjou, who sustained my project by doing everything I could not do while I was writing. Without him nothing would have been possible. Finally, I would like to dedicate this book to the memory of my grandmother Georgette Balbarie, who left us while I was writing the last pages.

Index

Note: Page numbers in *italics* refer to maps and illustrations.